A History of Modern La

Concise History of the Modern World

Covering the major regions of the world, each history in this series provides a vigorous interpretation of its region's past in the modern age. Informed by the latest scholarship, but assuming no prior knowledge, each author presents developments within a clear analytic framework. Unusually, the histories acknowledge the limitations of their own generalizations. Authors are encouraged to balance perspectives from the broad historical landscape with discussion of particular features of the past that may or may not conform to the larger impression. The aim is to provide a lively explanation of the transformations of the modern period and the interplay between long-term change and "defining moments" of history.

Published

A History of Modern Africa: 1800 to the Present
Richard Reid

A History of Modern Latin America: 1800 to the Present
Teresa A. Meade

Forthcoming

A History of Modern East Asia
Charles Armstrong

Chosen Nation: A History of the American People since 1886
Maurice Isserman

Europe since 1815
Albert Lindemann

A History of Russia since 1700
Rex Wade

A History of Modern Latin America

1800 to the Present

Teresa A. Meade

WILEY-BLACKWELL

A John Wiley & Sons, Ltd., Publication

This edition first published 2010
© 2010 Teresa A. Meade

Blackwell Publishing was acquired by John Wiley & Sons in February 2007. Blackwell's
publishing program has been merged with Wiley's global Scientific, Technical, and Medical
business to form Wiley-Blackwell.

Registered Office
John Wiley & Sons Ltd, The Atrium, Southern Gate, Chichester, West Sussex, PO19 8SQ,
United Kingdom

Editorial Offices
350 Main Street, Malden, MA 02148-5020, USA
9600 Garsington Road, Oxford, OX4 2DQ, UK
The Atrium, Southern Gate, Chichester, West Sussex, PO19 8SQ, UK

For details of our global editorial offices, for customer services, and for information about how to
apply for permission to reuse the copyright material in this book please see our website at
www.wiley.com/wiley-blackwell.

Library of Congress Cataloging-in-Publication Data

Meade, Teresa A.
    A history of modern Latin America : 1800 to the present / Teresa A. Meade.
       p. cm. — (Concise history of the modern world)
    Includes bibliographical references and index.
    ISBN 978-1-4051-2050-0 (hardcover : alk. paper) — ISBN 978-1-4051-2051-7
(pbk. : alk. paper)   1. Latin America—History.   I. Title.
    F1410.M433 2010
    980—dc22
                                                                    2009027967

Set in 10/13pt Photina by Graphicraft Limited, Hong Kong
Printed in Singapore by Ho Printing Singapore Pte Ltd

01   2010

Contents

List of Figures

List of Maps

Preface

This book covers well over 200 years of Latin American history. It begins with a brief summary of European colonialism, laying the groundwork for the succeeding chapters on the history of the independent nation-states that make up modern Latin America. Presenting such a history is not easy: Latin America is immense and diverse; events that have a huge impact on one nation or region (such as the US war with Mexico in the 1840s), may affect others only tangentially, or not at all. Moreover, textbooks of this sort inevitably experience a crucial conflict. The text should present a broad, general interpretation that makes sense of many disparate details and events, yet it is impossible to explore fully each and every event undergirding the big picture. Another inevitable tension is chronology (time) versus topics, as well as time versus place (country or region). Since historical events build on and grow out of whatever comes before and lead into and influence that which comes after, it is very difficult to extract a happening from its context, especially given the many cultural, social, economic, and political contexts surrounding every historical moment.

Historians must always grapple with this dilemma of presentation: the author can stick to certain themes and relay a general analysis fitted roughly into a chronology or, alternatively, can relate the history of one country, or group of countries, one at a time. The country-by-country approach is often more precise, but difficult to use in the standard history class, while covering many nations in one full sweep can become confusing. Ultimately it really doesn't matter which approach is used if the end product is stripped of the fascinating stories and the lives of people who contribute to the overall narrative.

This book presents Latin American history as seen through the prism of social class, gender, race, and ethnicity. Specific historical events and trends – such as the slave revolt in Haiti, the patriarchal rules governing marriage in Brazil, construction of the Panama Canal, or the Mexican Revolution – are explained according to this interpretive approach. The seemingly unconnected events in the histories of Latin American societies come together in a narrative that is more than the sum of its parts; rather the parts, selected for their explanatory value, help us understand the whole. Thus I present examples of what transpired in a single nation at a specific time as representative of a wider phenomenon and to serve as a window into the ideas, conflicts, social movements, cultural trends, and ascribed meanings that have made an appearance on Latin America's historical landscape. The resulting interpretation derives from a process of sifting and sorting through an immense amount of material; choices have been made as to what to include and, often with terrible regret, what to leave out.

Readers who seek a general level of analysis and broad historical narrative will find it here. The book refers to and describes major issues and events, drawing on many valuable texts, monographs, document sets, journalistic and fictional accounts of Latin America's rich history. At the same time, it was often necessary to allow one event to serve as the archetypical illustration of important trends. For example, a discussion of Argentina's labor movement is used to reflect the struggle between workers and owners that unfolded under specific conditions but also took place in many countries. Labor in other areas is then covered in broad strokes, with the assumption that readers and instructors will draw on other examples to fill out the narrative. I settled on this approach after more than 20 years of college teaching, mainly in a small liberal arts institution, where it soon became apparent that students are better able to grasp the big picture when given smaller, concrete incidents to exemplify the story on which the broader interpretation is based. Relying solely on "big theories" and moving from country to country and event to event makes students' eyes glaze over and note-taking turn to doodling. Blame could be placed on poor training in geography, the ethnocentrism of US society, the internet, or what have you, but the truth remains that we often develop our understanding of history by building out from a specific example or single historical event. Similarly, the generalities of history often become clear when we focus on a concrete example, or a few examples, to illustrate the point.

Finally, history is based on original sources. The particular interpretation historians have drawn from those sources, even the conflicting conclusions they derive after looking at the same or similar documents, is the heart and soul of the enterprise. Interspersed throughout this narrative are first-hand accounts, documents, and excerpts from fiction, displayed in boxes. These boxes have two purposes. On the one hand, they can serve as the basis of discussion in a class; on the other, they demonstrate the kinds of materials historians draw on to construct a narrative, thereby allowing the reader of the text to critically judge the author's interpretation. Although I am well aware that readers sometimes skip over this additional material, seeing it as irrelevant to the text, I am hopeful that instructors and students will pause to examine an original document, a quirky historical fact, and a literary comment, in the course of reading the broader narrative. The use of primary sources allows the reader and the student of history to take up the analytical process for her or himself. A Further Reading section at the end lists books chapter by chapter for ease of reference.

In addition to documents and first-hand accounts, I have also chosen to weave in historical, and also sometimes fictional, asides, from various authors, including the Uruguayan Eduardo Galeano. Galeano compiled a three-volume "based on fact" fictional interpretation of major events in the history of the Americas from the pre-Columbian period to the late twentieth century. He did this, he anthropomorphized, because "Poor History had stopped breathing: betrayed in academic texts, lied about in classrooms, drowned in dates, they had imprisoned her in museums and buried her, with floral wreaths, beneath statuary bronze and monumental marble."[1] As a historian and teacher, I naturally beg to differ a bit with his conclusion, since those of us who teach and write strive to present history as a lively narrative, not dull facts drowned in dates. However, Galeano is right when he exhorts us to rescue history from hero worship and to question the sources, since neither they, nor the facts they present, "speak for themselves." In his trilogy *Memory of Fire*, Galeano freely and provocatively writes the history of the Americas. Drawing on documents, he creates a fanciful narrative of the past, which at points misses the mark and at others nails it precisely.

In the end, we are all interpreters of history, trying to make sense of our own past and our place within the era in which we are living; and for that we rely on books and the explanations contained within them. Although this *History of Modern Latin America* is a very small contribution to that daunting enterprise, I hope readers will find the events and people who comprise the narrative of Latin America's past interesting, the explanation of that history understandable and enlightening, and the interpretation challenging. History should be nothing less.

Acknowledgments

In the course of writing this book, I have been assisted by many colleagues whom I am happy to acknowledge. Christopher Wheeler, now at Oxford University Press, first talked to me about this project over a drink at the American Historian Association conference where we discussed our mutual admiration for the work of Eric Hobsbawm. I have never met Mr. Hobsbawm, but I want to thank him for his many inspiring and profound insights, as well as Christopher and Tessa Harvey at Blackwell for the conversation that pulled me into this book. Many thanks to Peter Coveney, my editor at Wiley-Blackwell, who saw the book through to completion, and to his assistants Deirdre Ilkson and Galen Smith, who competently and cheerfully answered my millions of queries along the way. My special thanks to Caroline Richards for copyediting.

Colleagues and friends in Latin America and the United States have assisted with comments, corrections, and encouragement. I especially want to thank Cecilia Belej, Susan Besse, Avi Chomsky, Alejandra Vassallo, Barbara Weinstein, Ann Zulawski, and the anonymous readers for their insights, clarifications, and advice. Over the years I have accumulated a debt to my students at Union College who worked as research assistants, proofreaders, typists, contributors, and critics: Nancy Borowick, Heather Cunningham, Colin Foard, Kelvin Martinez, Stacy Paull, Jazmin Puicon, and Jessica Simpson. I especially want to thank Jane Earley for her assistance with this book, the Union College Faculty Development Grant for research and travel funds, and the librarians of Schaefer Library for help tracking down sources.

Alison Raphael applied her copyediting wizardry to the first draft and improved the prose. Working with Alison, whom I have known since the mid-1970s when we met researching our dissertations in Rio de Janeiro, was a special treat. My sister, Martha Meade, read the entire manuscript from start to finish, offered comments based on her years of teaching high school history and caught a number of errors. My family, Darren, Claire, and Andor Skotnes, provided expertise with computers, photographs, and technical and editorial advice. Andor, especially, I can never thank enough.

It is impossible to acknowledge all the people who contributed to this book, mainly because the process of writing a textbook draws on the resources of an entire profession. My debt is primarily to the many scholars who have explored, analyzed, photographed, mapped, and charted the history of Latin America. Compiling a narrative from mountains of books, articles, web pages, and news articles was both an inspiring and a humbling experience. The scholarship on Latin America is truly impressive; whatever errors and inadequacies remain in this text are my own.

About the cover image

The painting on the cover is *Cánto a la Naturaleza* (*Song to Nature*) by Paula Nicho Cumes, an indigenous Kaqchikel Maya Indian from San Juan Comalapa. One of the foremost Maya female artists in Guatemala today, Nicho Cumes' work is noted for original and unusual themes, reflective of an authentic, self-taught, style.

For more about Paula Nicho Cumes and other Maya artists, see the web site http://www.artemaya.com/.

1 | Introduction to the Land and Its People

Latin America is a vast, geographically and culturally diverse region stretching from the southern border of the United States to Puerto Toro at the tip of Chile, the southernmost town of the planet. Encompassing over 8 million square miles, the 20 countries that make up Latin America are home to an estimated 550 million people who converse in at least five European-based languages and six or more main indigenous languages, plus African Creole and hundreds of smaller language groups.

Historians disagree over the origin of the name "Latin America." Some contend that geographers in the sixteenth century gave the name "Latin America" to the new lands colonized by Spain and Portugal in reference to the Latin-based languages imposed on indigenous people and imported African slaves in the newly acquired territories. More recently, others have argued that the name originated in France in the 1860s under the reign of Napoleon III, as a result of that country's short-lived attempt to fold all the Latin-language-derived countries of the Americas into a neocolonial empire. Although other European powers (Britain, Holland, and Denmark) colonized parts of the Americas, the term "Latin America" generally refers to those territories in which the main spoken language is Spanish or Portuguese: Mexico, most of Central and South America, and the Caribbean islands of Cuba, Puerto Rico, and the Dominican Republic. The former French possessions of Haiti and other islands of the Caribbean, French Guiana on the South American continent, and even Quebec in Canada, could be included in a broadened definition of Latin America. However, this book defines Latin America as the region that fell under Spanish and Portuguese domination beginning in the late fifteenth and into the mid-sixteenth centuries. The definition also encompasses other Caribbean and South American countries such as Haiti and Jamaica among others, since events in those areas are important to our historical narrative. This definition follows the practice of scholars in recent years, who have generally defined Latin America and the Caribbean as a socially and economically interrelated entity, no matter what language or culture predominates.

Geography

Latin America boasts some of the largest cities in the world, including four of the top 20: Mexico City, São Paulo (Brazil), Bogotá (Colombia) and Lima (Peru). When defined by greater metropolitan area – the city plus outskirts – Buenos Aires (Argentina) and Rio de Janeiro (Brazil) join the list of the world's megacities, the term for a metropolis of more than 10 million people. Population figures, however, are controversial since most of these gigantic urban centers include, in addition to the housed and settled population, transitory masses of destitute migrants living in makeshift dwellings or in the open air. It is hard for census takers and demographers to obtain an accurate count under those circumstances.

Not only does Latin America have some of the largest population centers in the world, but its countryside, jungles, mountains, and coastlines are major geographical and topographical landmarks (see Map 1.1). The 2-million-square-mile Amazon Basin is the largest rainforest in the world. Spanning the far north of Brazil, stretching into Bolivia, Peru, Ecuador, Colombia, French Guiana, Guyana, Suriname, and Venezuela, it is home for approximately 15 percent of all living species on the planet. South and to the east of the Amazon Basin in the Brazilian state of Mato Grosso lays the Pantanal, the world's largest wetlands. Other superlatives include the highest mountain range of the Americas (the Andes) that stretches nearly the entire length of the continent; second in the world to the Himalayas of Asia in height, the Andes are much longer, geologically younger, and very seismically active. The Andean peak Aconcagua in Chile is the highest mountain in the Americas, which at 22,834 ft. exceeds Dinali (Mt. McKinley) in Alaska by over 2,000 ft. The Atacama Desert, spanning Argentina, Bolivia, and Chile, is the driest place on earth and the largest depository of sodium nitrates on the planet. Elsewhere in the Andean region is Lake Titicaca, the most elevated navigable body of water in the world. This huge lake forms the boundary between Peru and Bolivia, and the Bolivian city of La Paz is the world's highest-altitude capital city. Angel Falls in Venezuela is the highest waterfall in the world; at 3,212 ft. it is almost 20 times higher than Niagara Falls. Angel Falls connects through tributaries to the world's largest river (in volume), the Amazon. In its 25,000 miles of navigable water, this mighty "River Sea," as the Amazon River is called, contains 16 percent of the world's river water and 20 percent of the fresh water on Earth.

People

The sheer diversity of the population of Latin America and the Caribbean has made the region extremely interesting culturally, but has also affected the level of economic and political equality. Latin America is exceedingly diverse, a place where the interaction, cross-fertilization, mutation, interpenetration, and reinvention of cultures from Europe, Asia, Africa, and indigenous America has produced a lively and rich set of traditions in music, art, literature, religion, sport, dance, and political and economic

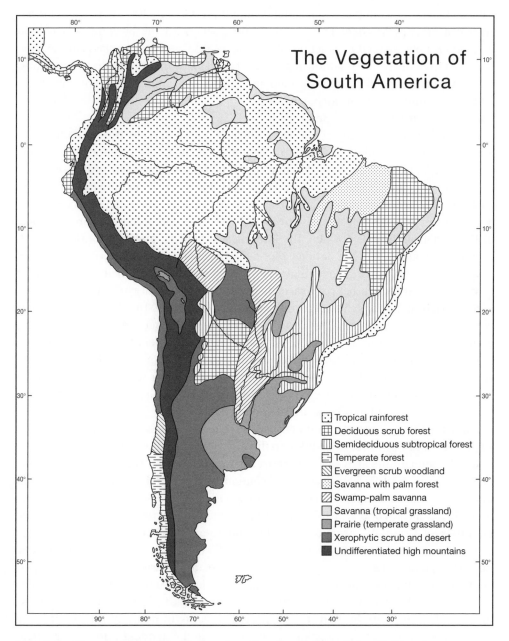

The Vegetation of South America

Tropical rainforest
Deciduous scrub forest
Semideciduous subtropical forest
Temperate forest
Evergreen scrub woodland
Savanna with palm forest
Swamp-palm savanna
Savanna (tropical grassland)
Prairie (temperate grassland)
Xerophytic scrub and desert
Undifferentiated high mountains

Map 1.1 The vegetation of South America. (Courtesy Cathryn L. Lombardi and John V. Lombardi, *Latin American History: A Teaching Atlas*, ca. 1983. By permission of The University of Wisconsin Press.)

trends. Bolivia, for example, elected an indigenous president in 2005 who was a former coca leaf farmer. President Evo Morales won easily with the backing of poor and indigenous Bolivians but has met hostility from wealthy and middle-class citizens who benefited from the country's natural gas exports and follow more "Western" traditions. Thus ethnic and racial strife has accompanied synthesis and cultural enrichment as cultures continue to confront each other more than 500 years past the original fifteenth-century encounter. (See Map 1.2.)

In Bolivia and Peru people who trace their ethnicity back to the pre-Columbian era constitute the majority, while in Colombia, Ecuador, El Salvador, Guatemala, Honduras, Mexico, Nicaragua, Panama, Paraguay, and Venezuela people of mixed European and indigenous ancestry, known as mestizos, constitute the majority. Africans were imported as slaves from the sixteenth until the mid-nineteenth centuries, and their descendants still comprise over half of the population in many areas. People in the Caribbean islands of Cuba, the Dominican Republic, and Puerto Rico, as well as in many South American nations, especially Brazil, are descendants of a mixture of Africans and Europeans, called mulattos or Afro-descendant, a more appropriate term that refers to heritage rather than race. Blacks are in the majority in Haiti and in many of the Caribbean nations that were in the hands of the British, Dutch, French, or other colonial powers. Everywhere in Latin America there is evidence of racial mixture, giving rise to the term *casta*, which the Spaniards used to denote any person whose ancestors were from all three major ethnic groups: indigenous, European, and African. Although this has a pejorative connotation in some regions, the creation of such a term suggests that racial mixture in Latin America is so extensive as to make it often awkward, and imprecise, to list each combination.

Large numbers of Europeans immigrated to Latin America in the late nineteenth and early twentieth centuries. In addition to the majority who came from Spain, Portugal, and Italy, immigrants arrived from France, Germany, Poland, Russia, and the Middle Eastern countries of Turkey, Syria, and Lebanon; a large number of Eastern European and German Jews sought refuge in Latin America both before and in the years immediately after World War II. Many European migrants settled in the Southern Cone countries of Uruguay, Argentina, Chile, and the southernmost region of Brazil. Japanese also immigrated to Brazil, especially to São Paulo, where they were resettled on coffee plantations and eventually moved into urban areas to form the largest community of Japanese outside Japan. In addition, Japanese moved in large numbers to Peru, while Koreans and Chinese migrated to every part of Latin America. Chinese and East Indians were brought as indentured servants to many of the countries of the Caribbean region beginning in the nineteenth and extending into the twentieth century.

Because race in Latin America was from the earliest days of the arrival of Europeans identified along a continuum from indigenous and black at one end and white Europeans at the other, any discussion of racial categories has been very complicated. By contrast, the US largely enforced a system of bipolar identity inherited from British colonialism, which then solidified in the late nineteenth century after the Civil War. Nonetheless, race everywhere is socially constructed – for example, it is estimated

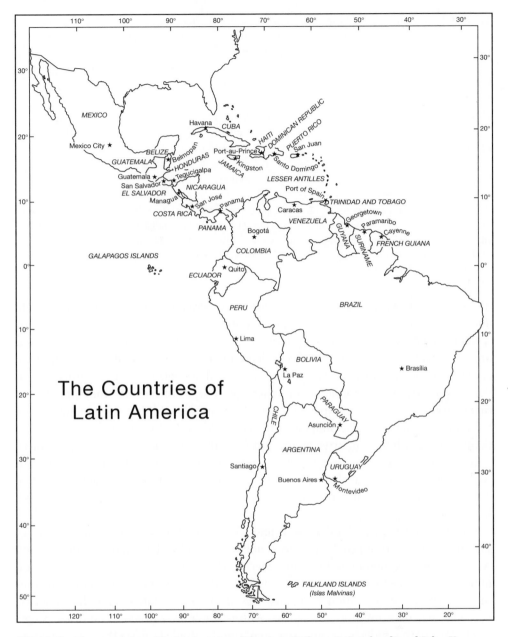

Map 1.2   The countries of Latin America. (Courtesy Cathryn L. Lombardi and John V. Lombardi, *Latin American History: A Teaching Atlas*, ca. 1983. By permission of The University of Wisconsin Press.)

Table 1.1   Racial origins of the population of Latin Americans

Identified as	Number	Percent of total
White	217 million	33.3
Mestizo	165.3 million	31.3
Mulatto	90.3 million	17.3
Indigenous	60.8 million	11.6
Black	24.8 million	4.7
Asian	1.4 million	0.3
Other/Unknown	6.2 million	1.2

(Venezuela no longer tabulates ethnic/racial categories; however, its population is 26,749,000. Applying to this the country's 1998 ratios [mestizo 67%, white 21%, black 10%, indigenous 2%] the yields for the entire region would change slightly: Population 549,552,000; white 33.7%, mestizo 33.3%, mulatto 16.4%, Amerindian or native peoples 11.2%, 5.7%, black 5%, Asian 0.3%, other/unknown 1.1%).
Source: World Factbook, 2007.

that nearly half of those who identify in the US as African American have some white ancestors – and in Latin America race is a conflicted category. Many Latin Americans who identify as white, and are seen as white because of their social status, education, and physical features, might not be considered white in the US and vice versa. There are any number of stories of black South American diplomats who were outraged when they encountered discrimination in Washington DC, not because they objected to racial profiling, but because they considered themselves white. It is estimated that of a total population of 522.8 million in the countries of Latin America, a third define themselves as white; a quarter as mestizo (mixed white and Indian); 17 percent as mulatto/Afro-descendant (mixed white and African); about 12 percent as Indian (with Peru and Bolivia as the only countries with a majority Indian population); five percent as black; less than one percent as Asian; and the remaining as other/unknown (see Table 1.1).

While exact figures are hard to determine, we can draw several conclusions, the most salient of which is that people who are wholly or partially of indigenous, African, and Asian ancestry predominate in Latin America. Certainly no discrimination against a minority should be tolerated anywhere, but in Latin America it bears remembering that the history of discrimination is against the *majority* population, not the minority. Secondly, whereas indigenous people constitute a minority in most countries, people of whole or partial indigenous ancestry comprise the single largest ethnic/racial group in Latin America as a whole.

Economies

Nature has graced Latin America with stunning natural landmarks, but the gains achieved through human interaction are not all positive since huge numbers of its people are impoverished, while a small group in each country is extremely wealthy. The World Bank calculates that most of the population lacks basic services such as water, sanitation, access to health care and vaccinations, education, and protection from crime. Nearly 25 percent of Latin Americans live on less than US$2.00 a day. Although Bolivia, Colombia, Paraguay, and Chile rank as the countries with the greatest inequality, the sheer numbers of poor in Brazil and in Mexico pose some of the greatest challenges to those nations' resources. According to United Nations development reports, lack of access to basic infrastructure serves as a major impediment to anti-poverty initiatives throughout the region.

Historians argue over the source of Latin America's inequality, some tracing it back to the days of European conquest over large indigenous populations and centuries of exploitation of imported African slaves. Others note that Latin American leaders have failed to promote the type of policies for the efficient exploitation of the continent's vast natural resources that would be required to raise the standard of living of the majority of its people. Another group points to the need to improve Latin America's commercial relations with the rest of the world, or to build ties among themselves, as through the North American Free Trade Agreement (NAFTA), which links Canada, the US, and Mexico; the Central American Free Trade Agreement (CAFTA); MERCOSUR (called MERCOSUL in English), which includes Argentina, Brazil, Paraguay, Uruguay, and Venezuela; and the Andean Community of Nations (CAN), encompassing Bolivia, Colombia, Ecuador, Peru, and Venezuela. A few nations, especially Chile and Brazil, have pursued bilateral trade agreements with the US, the European Union, and nations in Asia. Similar initiatives by the Peruvian and Panamanian governments to enter into trade pacts with the US have met with stiff opposition from their local labor unions and farmers.

The debates these agreements have generated do not focus on trade per se, but on the long-term impact of entering into compacts with larger, more developed, and technologically more advanced nations. Critics charge that Mexico has benefited little from NAFTA; in fact, NAFTA has resulted in a flood of agricultural commodities into the Mexican market from the US and Canada, where they are produced far more efficiently and cheaply. As a result, Mexican farmers have been driven off the land and into urban squalor, or across the border to the US, in order to survive. Critics of free trade pacts argue that the free flow of capital the agreements nominally protect has proved beneficial only to the rich nations, and perhaps to the wealthy classes of emerging economies. They argue that the pacts have accelerated income inequalities both within Latin America and outside it, in relation to the rest of the world. Contained within the trade debate is the larger issue of neoliberalism, sometimes called the "Washington Consensus," referring to the push from the United States to keep markets in developing nations open and available for investment and trade agreements favorable to the US. The real impact of foreign investment, and disagreements among and between Latin American governments over the impact of earlier liberal and recent neoliberal policies, is a topic that weaves through this text.

Although critics point to the detrimental impact of free trade deals on agricultural production, especially in Mexico, the fact is that most people throughout Latin

America live in cities. By 1960 the majority of the population was involved in non-agricultural production; that is, in the service sector, manufacturing, private and public bureaucracies, and the informal sector. The common assumption is that people making a living in the informal sector – selling what they can on the street, engaged in casual and day labor, or peddling "illegal" wares and services – are very poor. That may be true, with the exception of certain illegal activities such as prostitution, trading in contraband, etc., in which case it is hard to make any overriding assumptions. Yet some entrepreneurs selling homemade crafts, foodstuffs and other objects in local markets earn a very good living – comparable to, or even better than, those employed in manufacturing and the formal economy. The national economy, however, may suffer because of the difficulty of collecting taxes on informal-sector earnings.

A sizeable middle class has emerged in most of the continent's large cities, concentrated in growing domestic and transnational manufacturing sectors, financial and commercial institutions, government bureaucracies and service sectors, and traditional professional occupations. Probably owing to the precariousness of its position, the middle class has not been a consistently strong voice in the political arena. By the late twentieth century, however, this previously timid group had become a more sustained and consistent actor in many emerging democracies.

Politics

The Latin American political landscape has been as diverse as its geography and culture. Since the end of Spanish and Portuguese colonialism in the nineteenth century, the region has been host to monarchies, local strongman (*caudillo*) rule, populist regimes, participatory democracy of parliamentary, socialist, and capitalist varieties, military and civilian dictatorships, and bureaucratic one-party states, to name a few. The US has played a strong role, especially during the twentieth century. The lament of Mexico's autarchic leader, Porfirio Díaz, could be said to be applicable to the continent as a whole: "So far from God, so close to the United States." British historian Eric Hobsbawm once remarked wryly that Latin America's proximity to the US has had the effect of it being "less inclined than any other part of the globe to believe that the USA is liked because 'it does a lot of good round the world.'"[1]

Latin America's history is replete with conflict resulting from the unequal distribution of resources among and between nations, classes, racial and ethnic groups, and individuals. In the nineteenth century Brazil, Argentina, and Uruguay went to war against Paraguay from 1864 to 1870 in the War of the Triple Alliance. This devastating conflict wiped out half of Paraguay's population and over 80 percent of its men. The most extensive war, the Mexican Revolution of 1910–21, resulted in the death of an estimated one million people both on and off the battlefield, of a population of 15 million. Other twentieth-century conflicts considered highly costly in terms of human life were the War of the Chaco between Bolivia and Paraguay (1932–5), in which an estimated 150,000 people died, and the civil conflict in Guatemala (1978–96), in which at least 200,000 Guatemalan Indians and mestizos were killed at the direction of a series of brutal military regimes. The country whose history has been most associated with violence is Colombia. From 1948 to 1966 an estimated 200,000–500,000 Colombians (the number varies widely) died in a war between political parties and factions that is known as *La Violencia.*

One erroneous stereotype, however, depicts Latin America as *exceptionally* violent, as a place of war, unstable governments, and social strife. In actuality, probably fewer Latin Americans have died as participants in wars and revolutions than is the case in other continents. This is due in large part to the relatively small role Latin American nations played in history's major international conflagrations, including World Wars I and II and Japan's war against China (1937–9). Unfortunately, the number of casualties throughout the world has been tremendous: the 20–30 million who died in the Taiping Rebellion in China (1850–64), the massacre of an estimated 1.6 million Armenians in 1915–16, the World War II Holocaust, the Cambodians left to die in the "killing fields" of Pol Pot (1968–87), or the 1994 Rwanda Genocide in which anywhere from 600,000 to one million Tutsis and their Hutu sympathizers were killed in 100 days. The fact that Latin Americans have not historically killed each other in rebellions nor carried out mass slaughters in any greater number than peoples in other parts of the world (and probably fewer) draws into question the cultural stereotyping to which the region has been subjected.

In recent times, progressive and moderate leaders elected to office in many countries of Latin America have attempted to find solutions to the longstanding problems of widespread poverty, malnutrition, lack of education, human rights abuses, and inequality. This political phenomenon, labeled the "Pink Tide," refers to the election in the last decades of the twentieth and early twenty-first centuries of left and center-left governments in many Latin American countries, including Argentina, Bolivia, Brazil, Chile, Ecuador, Paraguay, Uruguay, Venezuela, and, disputably, Nicaragua. As opposed to the Cold War label, "the Red Tide," that implied the spread of communism from the Soviet Union and China to other parts of the world, this "Pink Tide" is a milder, "less Red," political current. While many of these elected socialist and leftist politicians are sympathetic to their own country's revolutionary past, have voiced open admiration for Cuba's stubborn rejection of US hegemony, and have personally suffered under the military dictatorships that dominated much of the region from the 1960s to 1990s, they are at the same time proceeding cautiously. These new, pragmatic leftists do not follow a single political trajectory and have not attempted to forge a united front. In fact, most seem to be content to remain loosely affiliated ideologically, pursuing policies that benefit their own nations while seeking the broadest level of cooperation with like-minded, and even not so like-minded, neighbors.

Among the elected leaders, Venezuela's President Hugo Chávez is the most outspoken opponent of US policy in Latin America, and has forged close ties with Cuba's Marxist government. Chávez, leading a nation with enormous oil reserves, can afford to be oppositional in a way that, for example, Tabaré Vasquez, president of tiny Uruguay, cannot. In Bolivia President Evo Morales has supported the cultivation and sale of coca for medicinal and nutritional uses, much to the alarm of Washington. On the other hand, since Bolivia has the largest natural gas reserves in the hemisphere, the US has moved cautiously in mounting a critique. Similar to Chávez, with whom he is closely allied, Evo Morales has used the clout of Bolivia's vital energy resources to bargain for better terms of trade with international bodies and for the political space to undertake a social reform agenda, despite objections from the country's traditional ruling circles. Both leaders face powerful opponents inside their respective countries: Chávez from the media, highly skilled petroleum workers, members of the traditional elite, and from the growing middle class. Morales has confronted a separatist movement from the energy-rich eastern provinces. Both leaders have faced showdowns over attempts to amend and change their nations' constitutions and curb democracy, and both have scaled back plans for redistributing wealth in the face of the economic crisis that began in 2008.

Michelle Bachelet, Chile's second socialist president elected since the demise of the military dictatorship in 1990, is one of very few female heads of state in the history of the Americas (Figure 1.1). Interestingly, the other women to head governments have all been in Latin America, rather than the United States: Isabel Perón in Argentina, 1974–6; Violeta Chamorro in Nicaragua, 1990–6; Mireya Moscoso de Arias in Panama, 1999–2004, and Cristina Fernández de Kirchner, Argentina's first elected female

Figure 1.1   Presidents Michelle Bachelet (Chile), Luiz Inácio Lula da Silva (Brazil), and Evo Morales (Bolivia) at the founding meeting of the Union of South American Nations (UNASUR), May 2008 in Brasilia. Leaders from throughout Latin America and the Caribbean attended but formal members at the time were Argentina, Bolivia, Brazil, Chile, Colombia, Ecuador, Guyana, Paraguay, Peru, Suriname, Uruguay, and Venezuela. (*Agência Brasil* photo)

president in 2007. Bachelet's government has made some strides in promoting the rights of women and taking on the issue of income inequality in Chile, but her tenure in office has thus far remained tied to the more moderate wing of the "Pink Tide." In general, progressive governments have found that the goal of providing social benefits to the many poor, unhealthy, and uneducated people in their respective countries must be balanced against the fiscal discipline required to pay off the debt burden they inherited from previous authoritarian and military regimes. Many Latin American observers and political pundits speculate that the leftist rhetoric at the forefront of recent electoral campaigns has given way to economic centrism and political maneuvering.

These new leaders have likewise demonstrated a variety of views on one of Latin America's most enduring institutions: the Catholic Church. Rafael Correa Delgado was elected president of Ecuador in 2006 and assumed office in January 2007. Considered one of the most recent additions to the "Pink Tide" presidencies in Latin America, Correa describes himself as a "Christian on the left" and as a "twenty-first-century socialist." After earning a degree from the Catholic University of Guayaquil, Correa volunteered for a year in a Salesian mission, an order of Catholic priests known for their charity work with young children, and seriously considered joining the priesthood. Instead he opted for a PhD in economics from the University of Illinois and a career in politics, but credits the Church for introducing him to social justice issues. In many ways Ecuador's new president illustrates the variety of positions on religion apparent among the new crop of progressive leaders. For example, Correa has voiced political views in line with those of other left and center-left presidents in Latin America, but does not share Chilean Bachelet's embrace of atheism, nor support same-sex civil unions and reproductive freedoms as do the Kirchners of Argentina, nor has he antagonized the church hierarchy as has Chávez in Venezuela. The new president of Paraguay, Fernando Armindo Lugo Méndez, is in fact a former bishop, as well as a left-wing politician. What Lugo will be able to accomplish is uncertain, since he heads one of the poorest and smallest countries of Latin America. Paraguay is still recovering from 35 years of military rule under Alfredo Stroessner, who came to power in a military coup in 1954 and was subsequently "re-elected" (often by margins of 80 percent or more) over the next 35 years. Stroessner's decisions were funneled through the compliant Colorado Party. Lugo's election brought an end to 61 years of Colorado rule and marked the first time in Paraguay's nearly 300-year history as a republic that a ruling party surrendered power peacefully.

If presidents Correa and Lugo came to politics from a base in Catholic activism, Nicaragua's President Daniel Ortega seems to have moved away from socialism and toward religion. A former guerrilla commander who headed the leftist Sandinista government in the turbulent 1980s, he returned to power in 2007 under a political banner that many argue includes few of the social reform measures or promises of equality, especially for women, sought during the earlier period. The Sandinista coalition recently split under a barrage of accusations of corruption against Ortega and his closed circle of supporters. Because of his acceptance of Christian fundamentalism, or because he simply wants to curry favor with the Catholic hierarchy, Ortega imposed a ban on abortion even in cases where the mother's life is in danger. Oddly, Tabaré Vasquez in Uruguay has voiced the same position, promising to veto reproductive rights legislation that passed in 2008 with widespread backing from Uruguayan citizens. In religion, as in politics and economics, the new leaders exhibit a variety of ideological stances.

Culture and Entertainment

Latin America and the Caribbean is a crazy quilt of nationalities, cultures, and language groups, representing nearly every part of the globe and creating a profoundly heterogeneous society from North to South. This diversity is manifest in many aspects of Latin American culture.

Literature

Archeologists have deciphered over 15 pre-Columbian distinct writing systems from Mesoamerican societies. The ancient Maya had the most sophisticated textually written language, but since texts were largely confined to the religious and administrative elite, traditions were passed down orally. The same was true of other major indigenous groups including, but not limited to, the Aztecs and other Nahuatl speakers, Quechua and Aymara of the Andean regions, the Quiché of Central America, the Tupi-Guaraní in today's Brazil, the Guaraní in Paraguay, the Mapuche in Chile.

The contemporary reincarnation of an African and Indian oral tradition can be found in the *testimónio* literature; the best known, and controversial, example being the narrative of the life of Rigoberta Menchú, a Guatemalan Indian woman whose graphic account of the persecution of her people in the 1980s has been widely read and translated into many languages. Although there have been some questions about the book's veracity, Rigoberta Menchú's story gripped readers' attention, much like Frederick Douglass's narrative of his life as a slave in the South of the US a century earlier, *because* it was a first-hand account. Her testimony brought to the world's attention the persecution of Native Americans in the hemisphere, especially the genocide against the Quiché-Maya of her native Guatemala, where an estimated 200,000 people died during a string of brutal military dictatorships from 1978 to 1996. For her efforts, she was awarded the Nobel Peace Prize in 1992 on the 500th anniversary of the European "discovery" of America.

Latin American literature has been particularly significant in its contribution to the world of letters. Nicaraguan poet Rubén Darío has a place among the greats of the Spanish literary canon as the founder of modernism, a passionate, visual, and stylized form of poetry that broke with romanticism. Chile alone produced two of the major poets of the modern era, both of whom were awarded the Nobel Prize in Literature: Gabriela Mistral in 1945 and Pablo Neruda in 1971. Mistral joins the small handful of women worldwide who have received the prize in over a century of its existence. Other Latin American Nobel laureates include Miguel Angel Asturias (1967), a Guatemalan author whose book *El Señor Presidente* set the standard for depictions of egomaniacal dictators; Colombian novelist Gabriel García Márquez (1982), whose work, especially *A Hundred Years of Solitude*, popularized the "magic realism" literary genre; and

Mexican poet, novelist, and essayist Octavio Paz (1990), best known for *A Labyrinth of Solitude*, a meditation on modern Mexico and the unfulfilled goals of that nation's turbulent 1910 Revolution.

The breadth and depth of literary production in Latin America over the past two centuries is impressive. The list includes Cuba's José Martí, whose journalistic articles, essays, and poems were published in Spanish and English in the US, Latin America, and Europe during his exile from Cuba in the late nineteenth century. Martí epitomized the symbiosis of politics and art that is quite prevalent among Latin American artists and writers, while others, including Argentines Julio Cortázar, Jorge Luis Borges, and Luisa Valenzuela, exemplify artists' concern with individual and existential crises. More overtly political authors whose works are widely read in English include Chile's Isabel Allende, whose novel *The House of the Spirits* is often considered one of the best descriptions of the struggle against patriarchy. Julia Alvarez writes about life growing up in the Dominican Republic and the US and Rosario Ferré captures the impact of US colonialism on the lives of Puerto Rican men and women. The 2008 Pulitzer Prize for fiction went to *The Brief Wondrous Life of Oscar Wao*, Junot Díaz's comment on the heartache and hilarity of adjusting as a Dominican immigrant in Patterson, New Jersey, while keeping one foot back on the island.

Mexican novelist and political figure Carlos Fuentes; journalist and essayist Elena Poniatowska; and Uruguayan writer Eduardo Galeano have produced a prodigious body of work that combines history, lyricism, and sharp political analysis, mainly from the left. At the other end of the political spectrum, Peruvian novelist and politician Mario Vargas Llosa has long been an outspoken critic of the left. Finally, Augusto Roa Bastos of Paraguay shares with the Guatemalan Asturias a talent for capturing the personality of authoritarian Latin American leaders, as seen in his book *I The Supreme*. Brazilian writers Machado de Assis, Jorge Amado, and Clarice Lispector draw on timeless themes in that nation's history, including the treatment of women, the issue of racial and ethnic identity in a multicultural society, nature and realism, and the intersection of African and European-based spirituality in modern society.

Visual arts

While Latin American visual art in the eighteenth and nineteenth centuries borrowed closely from the traditions of Spanish, Portuguese, and French classical and baroque painting, much of it tied to religion, the influence of Africa and indigenous cultures permeates most artistic production. From the works of Colombian master painter Fernando Botero, whose fat cherubs are a biting criticism of Latin America's elite, to the photography of Sebastião Salgado, Brazil's contribution to the use of the photograph as a document, the world of Latin American visual art is as critical and joyfully diverse as its people. Another Brazilian, the architect Oscar Niemeyer, is considered one of the inventors of the modernist style and creator of the use of reinforced concrete for constructing some of the masterpieces of modern architecture, especially the United Nations in New York and, with urban planner Lucio Costa, the futurist capital city of Brasilia (Figure 1.2). In 1996, at the advanced age of 89, he completed the Niteroi

Figure 1.2   Brazilian National Congress being washed by rain. Architecture by Oscar Niemeyer. (Eurico Zimbres photo)

Museum of Contemporary Art, across the bay from Rio de Janeiro. A lifelong socialist, Niemeyer designed an elaborate monument in Salvador da Bahia at the grave site of the country's most famous communist (who had trained as an architect), Carlos Marighella.

Two major schools of painting that distinguish Latin American artists in the mind of the world today are the rich, colorful Haitian paintings that depict the complexity of everyday life, and Mexican murals of the 1930s and 1940s, which project a radical interpretation of history. In bold lines and dramatic colors, Haitian painting shows everyday people involved in commonplace events. Art historians assume this style of painting was common among artists as far back as the early nineteenth century, but it was not marketed commercially until the 1940s. Formulaic reproductions of standard scenes in wondrous colors can be bought from stalls in flea markets and on the streets of many cities of the world where Haitian artists peddle their wares; the highly skilled show their creations in the major galleries of the world, selling for six-figure dollar prices. Similarly, Mexican mural art links popular subjects and high-art world prices. The most famous muralists, Diego Rivera, David Alfaro Siqueiros, and José Clemente Orozco, told the story of Mexico's history from pre-Columbian times to the twentieth century Revolution. They depicted the struggle for modernization and clash of cultures, races, and classes in bold murals commissioned by the government of Mexico. World famous for their political and ideological brashness and competitiveness, the muralists had a strong influence on Mexican and other Latin American art. Likewise, they set the standard for an art form that can be found on the walls of subways, aqueducts, buildings, and fences throughout the world. Frida Kahlo, whose work is today one the most popular products of that era, is famous for her self-portraits that spell out the physical and emotional pain she experienced in life and, some argue, stands as a universalized statement of women's oppression. Although her personal life was troubled, fraught with conflict with her husband Diego Rivera, whose art and fame overshadowed her career during her lifetime, Kahlo's paintings today command the highest prices of any Latin American artist.

The most widely known forms of artistic expression in many Latin American countries are handicrafts. Especially in countries with a large indigenous population (such as Peru, Ecuador, Guatemala, Bolivia, and Mexico), textiles, pottery, embroidery, weaving, crochet, and other crafts are produced in homes and small workshops. In some parts of the country young girls are withdrawn from school after only a few years and put to work sewing, weaving, knitting and otherwise producing the elaborate crafts that fill the markets of small tourist towns, stops along the highways, stores, and the huge open-air markets of capital cities. The sheer quantity, variety, and ingenuity of crafts displayed in any one market can be mind-boggling, while the income from the sale of handicrafts is essential to the livelihood of entire families and regions.

In the 1970s a new handicraft, the *arpillera*, was developed and has since spread to many regions of Latin America. Chilean women imprisoned under the dictatorship of Augusto Pinochet (1973–90) created these three-dimensional textile pictures that depict a scene or tell a story. The women developed the *arpilleras* as a way of communicating with friends and families outside the prison. Into the intricately sewn pictures the prisoners incorporated sticks, pockets, pieces of aluminum foil and other found items, all providing hiding places for messages. The images in the *arpillera*, on careful examination, revealed scenes of the torture, abuse, and suffering that the women were enduring. Prison guards, assuming the *arpilleras* were simple women's sewing, did not suspect that hidden within the folds of the fabric the women were sending messages to the outside world of the repressive conditions in Chilean prisons. The craft form spread from prisons to neighborhoods on the outside, and later became a popular art form in communities in Chile, Peru, and eventually throughout Latin America. Today *arpilleras* represent a significant source of income for women in cooperatives and shantytowns. They narrate life stories, including events such as weddings and festivals, show the day-to-day life in which women live and work, plant and harvest crops, tend animals, cook, clean and care for children.

Music and dance

Latin America's diversity may be most readily apparent in the rich variation of musical and dance forms. The thin, austere chants of music from the Andean Altiplano reflect indigenous sensitivities and invoke the harsh emptiness of the highlands of Peru, Ecuador, Bolivia, and Chile, while the pounding drumbeat and percussion of Brazil and the Caribbean definitely draw their inspiration from Africa. The Americas in general have elaborated on and enhanced the world's repertoire of sound, combining the instruments of Africa with the strings and horns of European musical tradition. Latin

America's contribution includes the samba, marimba, merengue, cumbia, mariachi, reggae (and its contemporary hip-hop permutation, reggaeton), salsa, cha cha, bossa nova, and literally dozens of variations in between. Samba in Brazil and tango in Buenos Aires, as with jazz in the US, traveled a similar route from bawdy, back-alley association with promiscuity and hot sex to popularity on the world stage. Only after gaining acceptance abroad were these musical and dance genres embraced by their own national elites. Today, of course, they are considered the emblematic music of their respective countries, promoted and practiced among all social groups.

A key feature of Latin American music and dance is the intermingling of styles and forms, drawing on the wide variety of folk traditions and cultures developed in the countryside in both African and indigenous societies, from European imports, or blended with the latest in international pop or classical music. One of the earliest names to make its way to the world stage was that of classical composer Heitor Villa-Lobos (1887–1959), who incorporated the native sounds of Brazil into classical European-influenced pieces. The most famous name in Latin American music is probably Carmen Miranda, a Portuguese-born Brazilian who sported wild, fruit-bowl hats in movies and stage acts. Extremely popular abroad (she was the most highly paid actress in Hollywood during the 1940s), her outlandish hats and "hot Latin" image were seen by many Brazilians as a demeaning stereotype.

The 1960s Brazilian movement called *tropicalismo* – developed by Caetano Veloso, Gilberto Gil (later appointed as the Minister of Culture), Gal Costa, Maria Bethânia, Tom Zé and others – was an expression of the fusion of various musical forms, from Portuguese *fado* to samba and bossa nova to contemporary Latin and international rock and pop. Jon Pareles, music critic of the *New York Times*, in an article recommending Veloso's albums *Estrangeiro* and *Livro*, has called Caetano Veloso "one of the greatest living songwriters."

As with Latin American literature, its music has played a central role in criticizing conservative politics and human rights abuses and as a tool for bolstering movements for social change, many of them on the left. Victor Jara, a famous Chilean folk singer who was tortured and killed in the early days of the 1973 military coup against Salvador Allende's socialist government, was part of a Latin America-wide folk revival, the New Song Movement (*la Nueva Canción*). The movement was inspired by the work of Argentine folk singer Mercedes Sosa and Chile's Violeta Parra. The large instrumentalist and choral groups Quilapayún and Inti-Illimani popularized the music of the New Song movement in concerts throughout the world, both during the heady days of the Allende government and later during the Pinochet dictatorship as they traveled the world in exile.

Today's music scene has seen a blending of styles from Latin America, the United States, and Europe. The borders that previously separated the Americas are now porous for both people and music; Latin American rhythms regularly float from mainstream US and European radio. Carried with the migrant culture, Latin pop has introduced new forms of hip-hop that bears the stamp of *plena* and *bomba* styles from Latin America, incorporates the strong social critique often expressed in US rap music and, regrettably, a fair share of misogynist and violent lyrics. The rhythm of Latin music accompanies the migration of people from Latin America into major urban areas and even into the more sparsely settled Midwestern heartland.

Cinema and television

At the 2006 Academy Awards ceremony in Los Angeles, critics were abuzz with commentary on the "Three Amigos," an adaptation of the title of a 1986 slapstick comedy starring Steve Martin, Chevy Chase, and Martin Short. In 2006 the "three friends" were Mexican film directors Guillermo del Toro, Alejandro González Iñárritu, and Alfonso Cuarón. Each had directed and produced movies that were in contention for the top prizes, including Best Picture. That these filmmakers had Oscar-nominated movies was not as novel as the fact that the movies in contention (*Pan's Labyrinth*, *Children of Men*, and *Babel*) were not based in Mexico, nor did they star or pertain to Latin American personalities or themes. Their earlier movies, such as *Y tu mamá tambien*, *Amores Perros*, *21 Grams*, had brought actors Gael García Bernal and Diego Luna to the attention, and admiration, of a young US audience. The fame of today's Latin American directors builds on a line of cinematic achievements stretching back to *Black Orpheus*, the 1959 Brazilian movie by French director Marcel Camus. This adaptation of the classic Greek legend of Orpheus and Eurydice set in Rio de Janeiro during Carnival introduced the world to Brazilian culture, music, and racial themes. It won the Palme d'Or at the Cannes Film Festival, as well as an Oscar and Golden Globe for Best Foreign Film (for France).

The 1960s and 1970s brought international success to Argentine director Fernando Solanas (*Hour of the Furnaces*) and Chilean Patricio Guzmán (*Battle for Chile*), whose powerful political documentaries captured the imagination of young people in the US and Europe. The directors interspersed news footage with a montage of symbols from political struggles in other countries, as well as snippets of acting and drama, to create *cinema verité* documentary films. Argentina had been a leader in the early years of the twentieth century, but suffered under the military government from 1976 to 1983 only to re-emerge with an Academy Award-winning film, *The Official Story*, in 1985. The country has since begun a frenzy of filmmaking, with a number of critically acclaimed movies, including *Social Genocide*, Solanas's 2004 exposé of corrupt politicians who sold off Argentine resources and bankrupted the economy.

Brazil's film industry, the largest and best financed in the region, has produced well-known directors such as Walter Salles (*Central Station*), Bruno Barreto (*Dona Flor and Her Two Husbands*), Hector Babenco (*Kiss of the Spider Woman*), and several well-received films about harsh life in the *favelas* (shantytowns) and on the streets of São Paulo and Rio de Janeiro, including *Pixote*, *City of God*, *Bus 174*, and the most controversial, *The Elite Squad*, winner of various film festival prizes. Finally, Cuban films, such as *Memories of Underdevelopment*, a studied meditation on the role of the intellectual in the early days of the Revolution and the choice between staying in Cuba or going into exile, along with *Strawberry and Chocolate*, *Lucía*, *Portrait of Teresa*, *Before Night Falls*, and *The Last Supper*, have won for Cuba a place in the international cinema arena. This is quite astonishing considering Cuba's tiny size, small capacity for filmmaking, scarce resources, and the intrusive oversight of official censors.

Although film has achieved international commendation, most Latin Americans watch television far more than movies. Not all Latin American households have a refrigerator, but most have a television – essential for watching soccer games, news, and the night-time soap operas or *telenovelas*. The *telenovela*, one of the most widespread expressions of popular culture in Latin America, is a basic staple of both daytime and nighttime programming and the main source of support for many channels. Like soap operas, which some consider a distant North American cousin, the *telenovela* examines personal and family themes. Plots revolve around power relations in work and domestic settings, "bad" women, love rivalries and triangles, and paternity disputes. According to sociologist José Antonio Guevara, the typical *telenovela* theme is the struggle to found a traditional family: falling in love, marrying, and having children. It pursues this theme by showing the contrasting lives of rich and poor, good and evil. From this tension the melodrama develops its plot, which is often based on a projection of reality drawn from an historical event or torn from the pages of the news, like some police, courtroom, and hospital dramas shown on US television. Whereas soap operas never end (unless they go off the air) since the events with which its characters struggle are timeless and cannot be solved, the goal of the *telenovela* is to solve the problems of society, usually in a three-to-four month series, and even to teach a way to resolve the tensions inherent in the progress of human events.

Since *telenovelas* play at night, they are a main source of entertainment for entire families, even entire communities and nations (including millions of US Hispanic households). The plot will be discussed at the office the next day and become part of the analogies, references, and metaphors around which day-to-day life is constructed. The *telenovela*, to borrow a phrase from Italian theorist Antonio Gramsci (1891–1937), is, in terms of entertainment, hegemonic; that is, it depicts and preaches the "shared common sense" of Latin America culture.

Sports

Latin America has a broad and varied array of athletic competitions, although *fútbol* (called *futebol* in Brazil and soccer in the United States) is probably the most widespread national pastime. British sailors introduced soccer to most South American countries in the latter half of the nineteenth century when they played pick-up games while on shore leave, sometimes among themselves and then increasingly with local youths. Charles Miller, the son of a Paulista merchant, is thought to have brought two soccer balls from England to Brazil in the 1890s with the purpose of setting up matches between teams of young British employees of the Gas Company, the London and Brazilian bank, and the São Paulo Railway Company. In Brazil, as in other Latin American countries, European football was eventually absorbed into the lives of working men and boys. A game that can be played anywhere, requiring only a ball and a few eager players, it was easily adopted by the working poor, some of whom made do with less than a ball. Today innovative boys can be seen on vacant lots or in the street, passing wadded up balls of paper or string, crushed cans, or some other makeshift ball with the same fancy footwork one might expect to find in an official game with a regulation ball. Brazil is the only country to have won five World Cups, but its lackluster performance in 2006 and charges of corruption in the coaching and team selection process have led to some disillusionment with the team. As with many teams from Latin America and Africa, Brazil's performance may suffer because the team only plays together during World Cup competitions every four years, since most players live abroad while pursuing lucrative professional careers with teams in Europe, Canada, and the US. Nonetheless, soccer remains the top spectator sport in most Latin American nations, dominating the airwaves and, some might argue, the national psyche.

In parts of the Caribbean and Central America *beisbol* outshines soccer in terms of popularity. The sport took hold especially in the Dominican Republic and Cuba in the late nineteenth century, when sugar companies imported cane cutters from the British Caribbean. The workers played cricket in their free time, but later, during the long periods of US military occupation, cricket gave way to baseball and rapidly assumed widespread popularity, although cricket remains the favorite in the British Caribbean. Baseball has the greatest following in those nations occupied at length by the US military, especially, Nicaragua, Panama, Cuba, Puerto Rico, and the Dominican Republic. These countries have also emerged as sources of baseball talent, since many players hone their skills on local teams, or in "academies" managed by the US Major Leagues to cultivate the most promising young men for their own teams.

Critics charge that the Major Leagues exploit players from poor backgrounds, signing them to contracts at prices far below what US players would command and robbing small, much poorer, countries of their best talent. Others argue that players now negotiate through shrewd lawyers and agents to obtain top-rung salaries. Both baseball and soccer create, nurture, and then export great players for the sports industry in developed countries – a process not unlike that accorded to other Latin American "commodities." Only in Cuba does a top-notch national team compete on its own turf and in international competitions, winning numerous gold medals at the Olympic Games. Nonetheless, even Cuba contributes talent to the Major Leagues, most recently through the defections of players such as José Contreras, and half-brothers Liván and Orlando (El Duque) Hernández. The drain of sports talent, like that of Latin America's skilled professionals, workers and the poor, will probably continue as long as the dramatic income inequalities between the US and countries to the south persist.

All in Latin America is not soccer and baseball, however. A look at the competitions and medal winners at the last few Olympic Games illustrate the breadth of sports in the region. For example, although Argentina is a perennial powerhouse in soccer and produced one of the game's legendary players, Diego Maradona, it was the Women's Field Hockey team that brought home the most Olympic medals from Sydney (2000), Athens (2004), and Beijing (2008). The women returned to Argentina as national heroes, especially Vanina Oneto who scored four goals in the championship match against New Zealand. The Argentine women's field hockey teams are among the best in the world, followed by the men's teams. Peruvian and Brazilian women's volleyball teams are top contenders in international matches, while in wrestling, boxing, and many powerful track and field events Cuban men and women rank first or second in the world.

The Olympics and Pan-American Games have served as a showcase for a variety of talented athletes, although the Olympics were only once hosted in Latin America. The 1968 games in Mexico City entered the history books for several firsts, including the first time a woman, Enriqueta Basilio, a Mexican hurdler, lit the Olympic Torch. It was also the first time that African distance runners swept up the medals, in part because they had trained at high altitudes and were not handicapped by Mexico City's location at 6,000 feet above sea level. The 1968 Olympics elicited the most protests, including the Black Power salute on the winners' block from the US medalists as a mark of solidarity with the African-American Civil Rights movement. Finally, the 1968 games were preceded by a brutal massacre of students in Tlatelolco Square, in downtown Mexico City, a month before they opened. The event drew attention to the repressive single-party government that had ruled Mexico since the 1930s and which had poured massive amounts of money into preparations for the international athletic competition while the majority of Mexicans continued to live in desperate poverty.

Despite Latin American nations having fielded many teams in the Olympics, the games have never returned to the continent and the Olympic Torch only passed through Latin America for the first time in 2004 on its way to the games in Greece. On June 13, 2004, one of the world's foremost athletes, Edson Arantes do Nascimento, known to the world as Pelé, ran through the streets of Rio de Janeiro with the torch before passing it on. Pelé, one of the most skilled players in the history of soccer, led his team to two World Cup victories in the 1960s and is frequently credited with bringing Brazil to the forefront of world competition. In July 2008 at the age of 67 Pelé opened the game in Cape Town, South Africa at a world soccer match commemorating former president Nelson Mandela on his 90th birthday.

Latin America: Past and Present

Today it is impossible to consider the future of the United States without taking into account the countries of Latin America. Whereas politics, wars, perennial crises, major celebrations and commemorations in other parts of the world may take center stage at one time or another, the people and cultures of Latin America remain one of the foremost external influences on life in the US. From concerns over drug trafficking in Colombia and Mexico to the latest Latin American singing sensation, to the never-ending debate over border patrols and immigration policy, the past, present, and future of the United States and Latin America are interwoven, straddling their respective political, economic, and cultural landscapes. For that reason alone it is essential that US students (large numbers of whom trace their origin to the countries of the Caribbean, Central and South America), as well as the general public, learn and understand the history of this vital region of the world.

Latin America is not simply a neighbor to the United States. It has produced world-class athletes, artists, musicians, writers, filmmakers, scientists, inventors, politicians, and more. The fate of its rivers, wetlands, and rainforests, and of the thousands of plants, animals, and natural resources they produce, matters to us all and affects the quality of life on Earth. Latin America is a tremendous repository of resources, but it is likewise a land whose people, along with the languages they speak and the cultures they reflect, are having a major impact on the entire world, not just its northern neighbors.

2 Latin America in 1790

The early history of Latin America was a period of fighting over privilege: to possess it, dispense it, or usurp it. Privilege became the basis for rule according to an unwritten code followed by the rich and powerful throughout most of the hemisphere. These layers of privilege and power were wielded through succeeding historical eras, first by Indian rulers, and then European conquerors and men of European descent; the Catholic Church; the wealthy; the strong; the cunning and resourceful; the physically, mentally, and militarily skillful; and even by the gods of one or another religion.

During the late eighteenth century profound transformations began to convulse societies in Europe and the Americas to their core. Beginning earlier in the century, and reaching intensity in the revolutions of 1776 and 1789, philosophical, political, and social forces combined to produce explosive and irrevocable revolutionary changes. After years of back-and-forth rebellion and retaliation, and eventual armed conflict, the colonies in North America successfully separated from England and formed a new federation of the United States of America in 1788. The following year France exploded in a revolution more profound and far-reaching than anything before known in Europe, precipitating an uprising in the French slave colony of Saint-Domingue (later Haiti). In southern Europe the monarchies of Spain and Portugal were doing their best to suppress the spread of Enlightenment broadsides and revolutionary calls to arms both at home and in their colonies, only to fail as republicanism upended the political balance of power in Spain just as it had in other parts of Europe. In the Americas ideas of free trade, separation of Church and state, and anti-monarchical republicanism were stirring a new generation of Creole nationalists.[1] In Spain, the moribund Hapsburg Empire had given way early in the century to the more dynamic French House of Bourbon, ushering in an era of "enlightened despotism."

The Bourbons set about shoring up the Spanish empire by imposing taxes, reorganizing the colonial administration, eliminating widespread graft and smuggling, and generally seeking to make the empire a viable enterprise. The Bourbon Reforms, begun in mid-century, reached full force by 1790. The Portuguese equivalent, the

Pombaline Reforms (named for their architect, the Marquês de Pombal), followed a similar trajectory. Examining the depth and extent of these reforms opens a window onto the social order that had been in place since the earliest days of conquest, and hints at the dramatic changes that would sweep the Americas in the late eighteenth and early nineteenth centuries. The reforms were, however, a desperate move, and ultimately a futile one, as the same spirit that impelled its North American neighbors to seek independence from Britain, and the French Jacobins to overthrow the *ancien régime* of Louis XVI, gave rise to slave revolts, street rioting, and demonstrations against taxes and high prices in the cities and countryside from the Caribbean to the Southern Cone. The masses of Latin America pushed forward a more radical agenda to replace the reformist goals of Iberian monarchs.

In order to understand the reasons for the eighteenth-century reforms, and the rebellions they provoked, it is necessary to review the colonial world established by the Spanish and Portuguese, especially the use they made of the land, their method of extracting profit and sustenance from labor, and the economic and political regulations that governed the peoples of their empires. As in all monarchies and authoritarian states – of which the Spanish and Portuguese colonial empires in the Americas were prime examples – privilege and power changed hands depending on the outcome of war, conquest, and survival, as well as conditions of ethnicity and gender. In the colonial world, however, power and privilege can be traced through ownership of property, especially land and mines, and control over the labor supply.

Colonial Background

Spain designed the model for colonial administration, and with a few variations Portugal followed a similar pattern. From the earliest days of the Spanish occupation of the Americas, the Crown had moved quickly to establish a vast network of political and economic oversight, since it was soon apparent that the tremendous wealth of the Americas – a wealth that accrued to the colonists who traveled and settled there as much as to the Crown's coffers on the other side of the ocean – could quickly outstrip that of the Old World aristocracy. Hernán Cortes (ca. 1484–1547), a minor noble who had brazenly disobeyed his superiors when he set off on his dangerous trek into the central valley of Mexico, was worth today's equivalent of approximately $2.5 million seven years after capturing the Aztec capital of Tenochtitlán in 1521. Francisco Pizarro (ca. 1478–1541), the illegitimate son of a peasant woman and an absent father who never acknowledged him, became an exceedingly wealthy and powerful man after his conquest in 1532 of the region that would become Peru. At Cajamarca he held hostage the Inca ruler Atahualpa, forcing him to turn over a ransom amounting to 11 tons of worked gold, and then killed the king in a brutal and bold move to demonstrate the Spaniards' power. The $22^{1}/_{2}$ carat gold statuary and religious icons that the Incas provided for the release of their ruler, the Spanish troops melted down into gold bars worth an estimated $17.5 million. For their contribution to the triumph every foot soldier in the regiment was given 500 pieces of gold, a fortune at the time, and an inconceivable booty for the motley band of mostly illiterate, peasant soldiers from the barren plains of Estremadura in southern Spain.

As early conquest evolved into colonization and administration, the acquisition of real gold and silver became increasingly uncommon and Conquistadores began to acquire wealth instead through the *encomienda*, a Spanish feudal trusteeship meaning "entrustment." A controversial institution, and one that would soon come under attack both for its brutality and for the vast wealth it placed into the hands of a very few conquerors, the *encomienda* had developed in the south of Spain. It was a method of extracting labor and tribute from the Muslims (called Moors), who had resided in Catholic Spain before they were expelled in 1492 when the Islamic armies were defeated at the battle for the fortressed city of Granada. This system, intended as a way of rewarding soldiers and moneymen alike who triumphed against the Moors, then traveled to the New World where the Crown granted to the recipient, called an *encomendero*, the right to extract labor and tribute from the Indians who fell under Spanish authority in the wake of the Conquest.[2] Christopher Columbus (ca. 1451–1506) instituted the *encomienda* quite soon after his arrival and settlement on the island of Hispaniola, requiring the indigenous population to pay gold tributes (which were quite scarce) to their masters or face brutal punishment. In return Columbus, and subsequent Spanish overlords, were required to ensure that the Indians were baptized, protected from harm, and had access to the rituals and services of the Catholic Church. The Crown utilized this system of rewards to encourage the settlement and further conquest of the New World.

The Spaniards, including the *encomenderos*, the official government agents of the Crown, and the many hundreds of ordinary settlers who made their way across the Atlantic all sought to reap the wealth of the New World by drawing on organized work routines, the system of tribute collection, and resource management already in place in the indigenous communities. The indigenous communities of the Americas were of many different types, following no single pattern of social organization. It is, therefore, unwise, if not impossible, for historians to describe the interaction between colonists and colonized as a uniform model. Where feasible, however, colonial authorities attempted to build from the pre-existing social structure.

From the time of the Europeans' first landing on the island of Hispaniola (today the Dominican Republic and Haiti), the conquerors would identify an Indian leader whom they called a *cacique*, and it was with him (occasionally her) they sought to negotiate for labor, tribute, and gold. This process of using *caciques* as brokers between the Spanish conquerors and the Indian communities was established in the Caribbean and carried over to the mainland expeditions in Mexico and South America. There is considerable controversy among scholars regarding the contours of this interaction. It appears, however, that in some areas *caciques* resisted Spanish rule, especially when the latter demanded more and more work from an ever-declining indigenous population. A *cacique* who refused to cooperate with the Spaniards was eliminated and a new one was appointed, holding the position so long as he proved useful to the Spaniards.

Caciques, or whomever they delegated to carry out the task, answered to an appointed Spanish official within the royal bureaucracy whose job it was to make sure each and every Indian community turned over a determined amount of labor and wealth to the Spaniards. These officials, called *corregidores*, were granted this privileged position because they came from influential families in Spain, or because they paid the Crown a sum of money in return for the appointment. Either way, they were the linchpins of the system of colonial domination. They served as the intermediary between the Crown, the viceroy at the top of the colonial administration and the wealth of the Americas, ensuring that the fruit of indigenous labor (in mining, farming, sweatshops, or other production) was turned over to the Spaniards. The problem was that the Indians could not meet the impossibly high quotas set for them, especially as they sickened and died in massive numbers to the newly imported European diseases to which they had no immunity. These appointed officials also managed the demands of merchants and landowners anxious to reap the maximum amount of profit from Indian labor. A man in this position served as overseer, census taker, negotiator, slave driver, and Crown official all in one, and was in line to became the richest, most powerful, and most hated (by the Indians) official in the colony.

Although most of the earliest settlers were men, some women also accrued land grants from the Crown through inheritance, the death of a husband, or recognition of their achievements by royal authorities. One interesting case is that of María Escobar, who in addition to holding large plots of lands after being twice widowed, was given a grant of Indian laborers in sixteenth-century Lima as a reward for her aid in the introduction of wheat production in the region. When antagonistic officials tried to take her holdings away because of her gender, she fought through legal means to hold onto her slaves and her property, serving as an example of the ability of some Spanish women, albeit few, to achieve great wealth and prestige in colonial society. The most celebrated *conquistadora* was Inés de Suárez (1507–80), a Spanish woman who traveled to the Americas from a small town in Extremadura, Spain in search of her ne'er-do-well husband. When she arrived in Cuzco and learned that he was dead, she managed to procure a small *encomienda*. She prospered as a baker and apparently had a talent for finding water which she had learned from her mother in Spain. The latter was of no small value in the arid and barren climate of the Peruvian *altiplano*. Inés Suárez became the mistress of Pedro de Valdivia, a high officer in Pizarro's army who had left a wife behind in Spain, and accompanied him on his exploration and eventual conquest of Chile. Known as a skilled and cunning fighter, she participated in the defense of Santiago when the town came under attack from the indigenous Mapuche in 1541. Eventually she married Rodrigo de Quiroga, the Royal Governor of Chile. She outlived most of her companions, and left a diary which has been the source for numerous novels, including one by Isabel Allende.

In 1544 the Crown outlawed Indian slavery for a combination of reasons. On the one hand, the rapid disappearance of the native people alarmed some in the Catholic Church who felt that the Indians were being worked to death, even before the priests and friars could baptize and win to Christianity this enormous population. As a result of the tireless efforts of the Dominican Friar Bartolomé de las Casas (1484–1566) to expose the maltreatment of the native people, the Spanish Crown conducted a famous debate at the Court in Spain to determine the conquerors' right to enslave the Indians. In a book, *A Brief Account of the Destruction of the Indies*, published in 1552, Las Casas detailed the torture of the Indians who were forced to work in the mines of the Caribbean islands and who were sickening and dying. By the time the Crown's ruling reached the Americas and went into effect, so many Indians had died as to make their enslavement impossible in many parts of the realm. African slavery was not prohibited and thus became the preferred alternative among the European colonists, especially in the Caribbean and Brazil.

The original inhabitants of the Caribbean islands disappeared almost completely, as did populations in lowland Brazil, the Amazon, and other areas around the Caribbean Sea. In Mexico anywhere from 50 to 90 percent of the indigenous population was killed off, mainly by disease. In Peru, 82 million people died of disease and overwork in the 250 years from 1540 to 1800. Everywhere there were dramatic declines: in the Caracas Valley of Venezuela a smallpox epidemic wiped out two-thirds of the Indian population, reducing it from 30,000 to 10,000 in a few years around 1580; virtually the entire indigenous population of the Caribbean islands disappeared due to disease, overwork, brutality, and other effects of their encounters with Europeans.

Some argue that the decimation of the indigenous population of the Americas could be considered genocide, which according to the definition developed by the Geneva Conventions after World War II is a crime "committed with intent to destroy, in whole or in part, a national, ethnical, racial or religious group, as such." Although the devastating effect of colonization on the Indians of the Americas does not fit precisely this definition, there have been cases when native populations were intentionally decimated, especially in Argentina, Brazil, Guatemala, and parts of Eastern and Western North America, both during the colonial period and into the present day (see Box 2.1). Scholars note that the full-scale destruction of the indigenous people of the Americas may not technically be classified as genocide, since for the most part their demise was unintentional. Nonetheless, they and their communities were destroyed physically and culturally as a result of the European invasion, which might amount to the same thing.

Although of comparatively short duration, Indian slavery institutionalized in the colonies the custom of ruthlessly exploiting laborers who were not white or European, and not even fully Christian, for the enrichment of a powerful elite that divided control among itself. The *encomienda*, as the first form of slavery in the Americas, therefore was the foundation for the system of relations between laborers and owners, elites and peasants, that has remained unchanged in parts of Latin America today. What is more, while according to the law Indian slavery was illegal after the mid-sixteenth century, it remained in place in many outlying, remote regions of the empire, in some cases into the eighteenth century. Beginning in the seventeenth century, labor was organized under a system of debt peonage and near slavery of Indians, and chattel slavery of Africans, on big estates called *haciendas* or *estancias*, in Spanish America, and *fazendas* and *engenhos*, or plantations, in Brazil and the Caribbean. Having

Box 2.1   "The Pestilence": Couri, 1586

Eduardo Galeano portrays a native call for the rejection of Christianity. This was at least one Indian's subversive solution for the plagues that were devastating his people in Peru.

> Influenza does not shine like the steel sword, but no Indian can dodge it. Tetanus and typhus kill more people than a thousand greyhounds with fiery eyes and foaming jaws. The smallpox attacks in secret and the gun with a loud bang, amid clouds of sparks and sulfurous smoke, but smallpox annihilates more Indians than all the guns. The winds of pestilence are devastating these regions. Anyone they strike, they blow down: They devour the body, eat the eyes, close the throat. All smells of decay. Meanwhile, a mysterious voice ranges over Peru. It treads on the heels of the pestilence and penetrates the litanies of the dying, this voice that whispers, from one ear to another: "Whoever throws the crucifix out of his house will return from the dead."

From Nathan Wachtel, *Los vencidos: Los indios del Perú frente a la conquista española (1530–1570)*. Quoted in Galeano, *Memory of Fire*, v. 1, p. 158

long-established ties and interconnections with Europe, the people of Africa had immunity to many of the diseases that had decimated the indigenous population. Inordinately high death rates continued, however, so that even in the seventeenth century, one of every five miners working under conditions of near slavery in the massive mountain of silver at Potosí (present-day Bolivia) met his death.

Power and Privilege

Authority in the colonial world was divided between the Crown and its state bureaucracy, both in Europe and the Americas. In the first place, in New Spain power and privilege was exerted through the indigenous hierarchy, which – unlike most of America north of New Spain – retained aspects of its interconnected town, labor, kinship, and cultural networks. Secondly, in both America and Europe, the Crown vied for absolute control over the realm with the hierarchy of the Catholic Church. As Holy Roman Emperor, Charles V and succeeding Hapsburg monarchs were in a perennial tug- of-war with ecclesiastical authorities at all levels of the clerical hierarchy.

The Catholic Church represented the second arm of Spanish authority, overlapping and interpenetrating with the state. Priests, as bearers of Christianity, as scribes, notaries, executors of Church authority, and as both advocates for the poor and oppressors of Indians, accompanied every step of the early conquest, settlement, and organization of the imperial project. No colonial village was without a Catholic church, often a huge, cathedral-like structure with elaborate statuary bathed in gold leaf, looming over a collection of modest adobe houses and commercial structures. The Church ministered to the Indians and carried out its part of the "bargain" set down by the Spanish and Portuguese conquerors: the Indians were to provide labor, tribute, and taxes in return for receiving the "one true faith" – Catholicism. As Indian slavery gave way to debt peonage, some of the requirements were lifted, but Indians in towns and those in their own villages were rarely free of the colonists' demands.

The role of the Church in colonial Spain and Portugal has been widely debated. No doubt the debate stems from the fact that the Church, through its many layers of clergy, nuns, and hierarchy, was never one thing for all places and people. Some of the clergy served as parish priests, called "regular" clergy, administering sacraments to the indigenous, mixed race, African slave, and free people of color, as well as those of European descent. Another group, called "secular" clergy, belonged to monastic orders (such as Dominicans, Franciscans, and Jesuits) that fitted within a chain of command both within the broader church hierarchy, as well as within their own orders. The Church's main instrument of regulation and authority, in Iberia as well as in America, was the Holy Office of the Inquisition. Although Indians legally were exempt from the rulings of the Inquisition, the reach of the Holy Office into the life of communities was extensive and served as the final arbiter of moral standing.

Land

From the colonial period onward the ownership and cultivation of land was the most important determinant of wealth and status. The European concept of private property ownership, as opposed to communal use and possession, was a concept foreign to the worldview of the native peoples of the American continent. The significance of land as a commodity increased as more settlers arrived from Europe. In writing about the conquest and settlement of North and South America, historian Michael Rogin remarks: "Land was the major economic resource, the major determinant of social status, and the major source of political power in early America."[3] Landownership, therefore, became the desire and goal of people from all sectors of society, especially those seeking upward mobility. In general those who received the earliest access to land, either through tribute collection or outright land grants, came to be the owners of enormous plots, which in turn furthered their economic advantage, since "regional monopoly of good land and thus of local markets was an effective way of limiting production and thus controlling prices." Owners of large tracts of land quickly became the wealthiest people in a given community, dominating all aspects of life through their influence on agriculture, government, the Church, and the local economy. This was the beginning of the system known in Latin America to this day as *latifundia*, defined as large pieces of land, usually worked by slaves or other unfree laborers. *Latifundia* originated in ancient Rome and North Africa, but today the term is only applied to landownership in Latin America, and is used interchangeably with other words for large estates: *hacienda, estancia, fazenda*.

In addition to *latifundia*, smaller parcels of land, known as *minifundia*, were acquired by people of less importance, particularly in the more remote regions of the empire. For the Crown, which desired the vast frontier of newly acquired territories to be physically settled to the greatest extent possible, land became an incentive to move people away from ports and cities and into the hinterlands. Unlike their elite counterparts, small landowners often led difficult lives, eking out a meager existence and taking nearly half a century to accumulate the capital necessary to pursue any type of mechanization or large-scale production, or to buy slaves or equipment. Finally, property ownership was not limited to entrepreneurial laypeople. The Church, both individual clergy and convents and monasteries, held title to large tracts of land, and most notably in the case of the convents of Mexico City and Lima, accrued fortunes, usually invested in property, made loans and collected rents. At one point in the late sixteenth century, female-headed convents in Lima were the largest property owners in the city.

Finally, indigenous communities maintained possession of villages and the surrounding lands through grants obtained from the Crown or the colonial authorities. The right of Indians to work their lands, free from the infringement of outsiders, came increasingly under threat as the number of European settlers grew during the colonial period. The right to land, and especially to the water needed to farm the land, as well as the right of Indians to resist obligatory labor on the neighboring estates, was a constant source of litigation, strife, and war from the moment the first colonists arrived in the New World. Indians found themselves in need of money to pay for tools, seeds, and other consumer goods and thus needed to enter into commercial relations with the towns. Most importantly, they came under the scrutiny of the Church, entering into considerable debt to pay for baptisms, funerals, and other requirements of the faith. It was nearly impossible for any of the indigenous people of the Spanish empire to ignore colonial institutions. Their villages and lives were poor and on the margins; their livelihood ever more threatened with each decade.

Many large landowners lived in opulent surroundings, though their lifestyle has been exaggerated in the historical imagination and the size of landholdings varied immensely, as did the amount of wealth of each individual. Landowners often spent little time in the rural areas over which they held title, preferring instead to maintain a household in a colonial city or town, and only occasionally visiting their estate to conduct business. Basic tasks in regards to the land, therefore, were undertaken by others, most commonly the plantation overseer, a person of lower rank and often of mixed race, who interacted closely with *caciques* and local colonial officials. Landowners generally sought to live a noble life, as defined by European aesthetics and values, surrounded by imported luxury goods, eschewing manual labor. In general, only those persons in the colonies who held some sort of title from the Crown had special privileges, thus a major drive existed to accrue them through service or achievement. Successful enterprises, such as sugar mills (called *engenhos*) in Brazil and agricultural plantations in Central America, assured the wealth, prestige, and control over society of early *latifundistas*. Over time it became more possible for those who showed aptitude, talent, or entrepreneurship in local bureaucracies to rise in status and wealth, and eventually to acquire land.

Box 2.2   The dowry in colonial society

The mid-seventeenth-century dowry of Doña Lucía de Pastene of Chile provides an example of the extent to which great fortunes could be united through the politics of marriage. Her dowry letter to husband Maese de Campo Don Bernardo de Amara Yturigoyen provided him with:

> 7,000 pesos in cash and the ranch of La Quillota with 1,200 heads of cattle, 1,000 goats, 6,500 sheep, and 12 pairs of oxen all of them valued at 18,190 pesos, without counting the value of the land. The agricultural yield of La Quillota was valued at 23,231 pesos per year. Doña Lucía's dowry also included several houses in Santiago de Chile, which were valued at 8,300 pesos and twenty-seven slaves whose price in the slave market was 10,300 pesos. Doña Lucía brought also as a part of the dowry silverware and silver luxury objects with a combined weight of 277.12 kilos, a personal wardrobe worthy of a queen, jewelry, a collection of paintings by colonial artists, and exquisite linens for beds and tables. If all the above was not enough, Doña Lucía de Pastene owned a small encomienda of twenty-five Indians which also became part of the dowry transferred to Maese de Campo Don Bernardo de Amara Yturigoyen.

From Luís Martín, *Daughters of the Conquistadores: Women of the Viceroyalty of Colonial Peru* (Dallas, TX: Southern Methodist University Press, 1989), p. 121.

Another important attribute of early Latin America, which has come to define its societies into the present, is the continuous consolidation and negotiation of power relationships. According to historian Susan Ramírez in her book *The World Upside Down*, power, prestige, and wealth were concentrated in the ranks of the elite, leaving little opportunity for anyone else to obtain a respectable and prosperous status. A system of land and wealth consolidation quickly emerged amongst the elite in which family played a major role, specifically through deaths and marriages. Women were a crucial component of these power relationships, since a widow could inherit a large amount of land or wealth, which would then be perceived as available to a male through marriage. Similarly, daughters were often married into familial networks with the goal of consolidating land and power. During the colonial period a bride's dowry served as a critical means for the transference of wealth and property (see Box 2.2). Wealthy families sought advantageous marriages for their children to strengthen their prestige, increase their fortunes, and protect their privileged position in society. As a result, marriages often took place between the relatively young daughters of elite families, with sometimes significantly older men with whom parents desired to establish ties for the mutual benefit of the parties. The *compadrazgo*, or godparent–godchild relationship, also represented an important means of creating power relationships, as did the unions of distant – and not-so-distant – relatives.

The major result of intricately planned intermarriages among large landholding families and other people of privilege was the solidification and furtherance of the already emerging grip that elites held over early Latin American society. Even in areas where smaller holdings were more common, the most prominent members of society flexed considerable muscle and exerted their influence through kinship networks. This was the case in the town of Nossa Senhora de Penha e França in 1765 in the Brazilian state of São Paulo, where one figure, Manuel Dias Bueno, had family ties to the wealthiest one-third of the entire population. Since it was not uncommon for a powerful landowner to live in a city or town, influence was often felt through the control of munic-ipal governance systems. In another case, the pervasiveness of landowners' power can be seen in the actions of Don Juan Bonifacio de Seña in Piura, who served at various points in his life in late seventeenth-century Peru as captain of the militia, governor of arms, general and field marshal, military reviewer, lieutenant governor, and *corregi-dor*. In addition to positions of authority, local bureaucracies came to be filled with those having family connections to the wealthiest figure in the region, creating a serious obstacle for upward mobility among those who found themselves outside his (or her) sphere. Many times, the reputation surrounding certain elite families exaggerated their actual financial prowess, and their mystique and celebrity outlived their actual power over those around them.

Colonial Administration

If privilege, power, and ownership represented the key elements in the formation of colonial society, the courts in Spain and Portugal were correspondingly concerned that the colonial elite not outstrip their counterparts in Europe in wealth or power over their underlings. To ensure subservience, the Crown dispatched a retinue of governors, viceroys, royal accountants, notaries, civil servants, and the full bureaucratic hierarchy of Catholic officialdom to the New World. While daring and ruthless soldiers, men, and a few women, of fortune claimed the land of the Americas for themselves in the name of the Spanish monarchs, it was left to the dispassionate calculations of Crown and Church officials to regulate, administer, convert, and police the American holdings. These Spaniards and their family members who were born in Europe were called *peninsulares*. Their positions, and their loyalties, were tied to the enforcement of customs and rules from the Old World.

The Crown's administrative arm was the Council of Indies and the two bodies that served as primary regulators: the *Consulado* or Merchant's Guild, and the *Casa de Contratación* or Board of Trade. Established in 1524 by Charles I, the Madrid-based Council of Indies oversaw all matters pertaining to taxation, administration, patronage, and defense of the newly acquired lands. At the height of its influence, in the mid- to late sixteenth century, the Council served as the court of appeals for civil cases, arranged judicial reviews, censored books and reading materials, and issued the final stamp of approval on papal decrees. The close cooperation of the two institutions ensured for the Crown a monopoly of trade with America, as well as its colonies in Asia. The *Consulado* of Seville, an extension of the medieval guilds established throughout Spain, oversaw the fleets of ships that carried wealth from the colonies to the Spanish coffers. *Consulados* in Peru and Mexico funneled trade from the mineral-rich colonies through few hands, in hopes of holding the lion's share of the royal tithe, or share, intact. Peru and Mexico effectively controlled the licensure of many merchants in the Americas, ensuring maximum oversight for the Crown through its closely guarded coterie of merchant houses and families based in Lima and Mexico City. These guilds guaranteed the exclusive domain of the Crown over all trading relationships, including licensing all those engaged in the colonial trade, issuing contracts, authorizing insurance policies, and arbitrating disputed bankruptcy proceedings.

The *Casa de Contratación* (known as the *Casa*), the other arm of the Council of the Indies, oversaw every detail of the colonial monopoly, including purchases, warehouses, transportation, and routing, and served as the official registrant of the merchants, importers and exporters. The *Casa* sat in Seville and was eventually subsumed under the Council of Indies, with its authority centered on trade as opposed to the other political duties of the Council. One of its key functions was the collection and enforcement of taxes as an aspect of the imperial monopoly. Emblematic of the royal bureaucracy, the *Casa* was obsessed with finding contraband, and since official position offered anyone easy access, the *Casa* ended up arbitrarily repressing and profiting from the vast contraband networks that seemed to sprout directly from the very system of rigid controls the Hapsburg throne sought to enforce for almost three centuries.

By the end of the eighteenth century, charges of corruption hampered the entire Council of Indies bureaucracy, leading to one of the key organizational changes instituted by the Bourbon monarchy, when the Hapsburg line came to an end in 1700. Administratively, the colonial monopoly had functioned through a system of designated ports in Iberia and America, servicing designated ships, owned or managed by designated individuals and companies trading designated goods, including a very extensive trade in slaves from Africa. It was the fate of such a tightly controlled system to eventually break down, despite assiduous efforts on the part of many state functionaries and the Holy Office of the Inquisition, whose role in intercepting and censoring "blasphemous" materials extended to confiscation of reading materials that touched on issues contrary to dogmatic Catholicism and strict adherence to the rule of the Crown. Faced with ineptitude at home, smuggling abroad, piracy on the high seas, and cheating throughout, the poorly managed Hapsburg monarchy fell into increasing crisis as the empire proved more and more unwieldy. When in 1700 the Hapsburg line came to an end and the Spanish throne was turned over to the French-based House of Bourbon, a new era of "enlightened despotism" dictated a change in course.

Enlightened Monarchy

During the eighteenth century a number of European monarchs selectively embraced some aspects of Enlightenment philosophy. The Enlightenment was a set of ideas that swept European intellectual circles and eventually the colonies. This movement called for the defeat of superstition and the triumph of reason and rationality in the realm of politics, economics, and scholarship. The monarchies, however, did not embrace the ultimate in enlightened rationality – an end to their own inherited rule – thus the term for this system of authority is "enlightened monarchy" or "enlightened despotism." They were still absolute monarchs, or despots, but they hoped to maintain their power by adopting some features of capitalist rationality. The Bourbons focused largely on a more rational administration of trade with the colonies and a streamlining of the royal bureaucracy.

From 1759 until 1808 they embarked on a series of innovations and reforms to transform colonial policy, revolving around several key measures, including reorganizing the political administration to replace unwieldy viceroyalties with smaller "intendancies." The new Intendant functioned more as a governor than as an arm of the king. Second, in an effort to undermine rampant smuggling in unsanctioned ports – notably Buenos Aires, which had grown and prospered as a key conduit for contraband entering the colonies – more ports were opened to trade and more merchants were brought into the monopoly. It wasn't exactly "free trade" as some were beginning to demand, but it was a step away from the stranglehold of the royal merchant guilds. Thus, under pressure from a growing population of colonial traders, the Bourbon monarchy opened *consulados* in Manila, Buenos Aires, Caracas, Cartagena, Guadalajara, Guatemala, Havana, Santiago de Chile, and Veracruz, while informal, smaller guilds that essentially functioned as mini-*consulados* were founded in Montevideo and San Juan, Puerto Rico. Eventually, as a part of the Bourbon Reforms, the Board of Trade was eliminated in the late eighteenth century; a few decades later, when independence was won from Spain, the entire colonial network was dismantled. The monarchy's need to raise revenue was behind the third reform: an elaborate system of taxes, raising the sales tax (*alcabala*); imposing new taxes on rum and *pulque* (the common alcoholic beverage of the peasantry and townsfolk); and generally tightening both the tax collection system in the colonies and the transference of riches from America to the Iberian peninsula. A fourth measure opened more ports in Spain to colonial trade, previously the monopoly of Seville, effectively destroying the Andalusian aristocracy's grip on trade with the New World.

Finally, although not exactly a part of the economic and political package, the Jesuits were expelled from the Americas (and much of Europe). This tightly structured and industrious order of priests had established hospitals, universities, and missions throughout Latin America, and because of their efficient organization, sometimes harsh use of Indian labor, and contacts with the sons of the Creole elite in the universities, had gained what their enemies considered to be undue influence and prestige. The Jesuits were expelled from the lands under Portuguese control in 1759 and in 1767 from Spanish America. Their "crimes" against the Iberian crowns illustrate the link between Church and state, and the presence of the Church on many sides of ideological debates of the era, including Indian slavery, the free expression of new ideas, success in commerce and land management. The elite on both sides of the Atlantic perceived Jesuit positions on these issues as a threat.

In a host of ways, the Bourbon Reforms (like the eighteenth-century enforcement of the Navigation Acts in British North America) were intended to reclaim the empire. Effective but hated, the reforms produced mixed results. For a while they did allow for the reconquest of the empire, but in the long run they introduced new views on commerce, politics, and philosophy to such an extent that more and more members of the Latin American elite began to ponder the possibility of independence from Spain. After 1788 and the successful rebellion of the northern American colonies against England, followed by the French Revolution of 1789, the landowners and merchants of South America debated the consequences of following in the path of their northern neighbors. When they took action, the fervor passed through both Spanish and Portuguese America.

The Agents of the Reform

It bears remembering that although momentous social and political forces were afoot in the mid- to late eighteenth century, a number of key figures pushed particular agendas and were responsible for bringing about dramatic changes. José Gálvez (1720–87) who became Spain's minister of the Indies in January 1776, cast a long shadow over the Bourbon program. On the Portuguese side, reforms were the work of the Marquês de Pombal (1699–1782). These two men profoundly influenced the contours of the reform era both on the Iberian Peninsula and in the colonial world.

No official's personal imprint on the reform era was more obvious than that of José de Gálvez. He arrived in Mexico in 1765 on a *visita* (official visit) as the monarch's representative, sent to inspect the management of the Crown's affairs and sit in judgment at hearings on grievances brought against colonial authorities by citizens of all ranks, even very lowly ones. Bearing the ominous title of Inspector-General, Gálvez found the viceroyalty in disarray. He proceeded to reorganize the system of tax collection, consolidate mercantile affairs in the hands of loyal Spanish merchants, imprison corrupt tax officials, and centralize more of the economy in mining enterprises. Intent on bettering relations between the colony and Spain, Gálvez moved decisively and swiftly to isolate troublemakers, especially the independent-thinking Jesuits whose intellectual and entrepreneurial ventures had long aggravated the Holy Office of the Inquisition and other arbiters of religious and political conformity.

After a bout of poor health, Gálvez returned to Spain in 1771, took up a seat on the Council of Indies and within a few years assumed its top position. In this capacity, as the most powerful figure in the realm apart from the monarch (some would say including the monarch), Gálvez spread throughout the Americas the reforms initiated in Mexico, especially collecting taxes, weeding out graft, and repressing smuggling. In response to this tightening of the colonial hold, there were revolts, the most famous of which were the Comunero Revolt in New Granada in 1781 and the rebellion of Túpac Amaru II in Peru in 1780–1. Both were met with intense repression, as Gálvez's strategy was to brook no opposition to his tight-fisted rule. He remained actively involved in administering the realm until his death in 1787.

As minister to the Portuguese Crown the Marquês de Pombal instituted what came to be known as the Pombaline Reforms in much the same way as had Gálvez in Spain. In the mid-eighteenth century Pombal determined to consolidate Portugal's holdings and promote settlements throughout the vast Brazilian territory. He encouraged intermarriage between whites and Indians by rewarding white men with access to office for marrying Indian women. Similar to the formation of the intendancies in Spanish America, Pombal formed "captaincies" in Brazil, solidified the oversight of tax collection, regulated the inspection of goods coming in and out of the ports, and reinforced the dominance of the Portuguese Board of Trade, or *Junta da Fazenda*. The capital of Brazil was moved from Salvador, in the northeast, to Rio de Janeiro in the southeast. Pombal's role in expelling the Jesuits angered the Church, as well as his support for secularizing the court system and basing legal judgments on national laws, as opposed to canon or church laws and regulations. Similar to Spanish America, when the Portuguese Crown expelled the Jesuits, Indians were ejected from mission lands and became prey to local slave catchers and mercenaries in the employ of landowners.

Fundamentally, Pombal and Gálvez were instruments of Enlightenment monarchy, a peculiar blend of eighteenth-century secular freedom and despotism. Both figures sought to reclaim for the central authority in the homeland stricter control over management of the empire's political and economic affairs. Not surprisingly, both of these far-reaching reformers were operating at a time when the French and the English monarchies were concerned with revolutionary uprisings at home, in the case of France, or in its North American colonies, in the case of England. Bourbon and Pombaline reforms were the first stage of a defensive action intent on eliminating the worst excesses of monarchical rule, while preserving the core of feudal military and political power. Furthermore, both of these powerful administrators were emblematic of the transitional nature of the times in which they were living. They each came from modest families of the lower gentry and rose to positions of unparalleled influence in government and society. Both were efficient managers and became powerful despite their modest origins because they seized on new methods of rule at a time when the old order was in crisis. Neither leader had the backing of the Church, and indeed each bucked it; neither relied on royal favoritism, nor did either rise through the ranks of the military or by bravery in the field of battle or conquest, the most common road to upward mobility for the lesser nobility. They were, oddly enough, secular, entrepreneurial and nascent administrators whose purpose was to secure the continuance of the monarchies they served. They each died within a decade of the French Revolution (1789), an event that would irrevocably change the political future of Spain and Portugal, of all of Europe, and of imperial rule. History records them as transitional figures that used, and refashioned, the rules of the old feudal order to govern more efficiently an empire forced to come to terms with the advance of merchant capitalism.

Disorder and Rebellion

As the eighteenth century drew to a close, administrators and ruling elites at home and in the colonies confronted civil disorder involving a wide range of social classes, led often by non-elite Creoles and supported by men and women from the growing urban and rural working classes. Historian Stuart Voss comments that the most remarkable change of the mid-eighteenth century was the appearance of "civil disorder whose participants were from different social strata."[4] Throughout the colonial world, especially in market towns and port cities, the rigid rules of the royal bureaucracy strained under pressure from increasingly nationalist Creoles. Resistance and rebellion erupted on many fronts, including shopkeepers and merchants who felt cut out of the colonial monopoly, an expanding group of mid-level bureaucrats, teachers, professionals, small landowners, and low-ranking clergy, all of whom chafed against the stultifying regulations and capricious enforcement of the weighty royal bureaucracy. New groups whose voices had been silent during the colonial era, at least on the national stage, began to mobilize: women, Indians, urban workers, artisans, slaves, and others dispossessed of land and money.

A string of uprisings punctuated the Andean region in the eighteenth century. In all, 128 rebellions took place, beginning in 1730 and culminating in "The Great Andean Rebellion" of the 1780s. Led by Túpac Amaru II, the Inca name for José Gabriel Condorcanqui (1738–81), thousands of indigenous and mixed-race Andeans demonstrated, destroyed property, and entered into combat against colonial officials in the cities and countryside of Peru and Bolivia for over a year. Taking the name of the last Inca ruler (executed by the Spanish in the late sixteenth century), Túpac Amaru II began in 1780 to lead an uprising of the indigenous people of what is today Peru and Bolivia. His forces attacked Cuzco from January 2 to 9, 1781, but the Spanish military proved too strong for his army of 40,000–60,000 followers. After being repelled from the capital of the ancient Inca empire and intellectual hub of colonial Peru, the insurgents marched around the countryside galvanizing forces. In April Túpac Amaru was captured, taken to Cuzco, and executed the following month, but not before being forced to watch the torture and execution of his wife and family members. Another member of the insurgent force, Túpac Katarí (similarly adopting an Indian name) led a siege of La Paz, Bolivia, in November, but was eventually betrayed and captured. Both Túpac Amaru II and Túpac Katarí were executed by having their extremities tied to four horses driven in different directions, ripping their bodies asunder (Figure 2.1). The remains were left posted on the outskirts of the respective cities as a warning of the consequences of opposing Spanish rule.

A second rebellion shook the area of New Granada (present-day Colombia) that same year. Called the Revolt of the Comuneros, this rebellion erupted in opposition to the increased sales tax (*alcabala*). The disturbance began on March 16, 1781 in Socorro when town residents came together to protest a new tax imposed by the very unpopular Visitador Juan Francisco Gutiérrez de Piñeres. Along with a reduction in the *alcabala*, citizens demanded an end to a series of other measures including higher head taxes,

Figure 2.1   The Execution of Túpac Amaru II, ca. eighteenth century. (Artist unknown)

new restrictions on tobacco cultivation, abuses of the liquor monopoly, and an excessive concentration of public revenue expenditures in the capital city of Bogotá, to the detriment of smaller, regional municipalities, such as Socorro. Although the majority of participants were mestizos, complaints against the treatment of blacks and Indians also figured in the insurgents' demands.

The act that sparked the initial protest and led to the much larger Comunero Revolt over the succeeding weeks was carried out by Manuela Beltrán (1724–?), a young woman of ordinary background who stepped forward to rip the hated tax decree from the wall on which it was posted. Whether Beltrán continued as a leader of the demonstration is unclear. Her name all but disappears from the account, probably for reasons of her gender and social class. According to one of the only reports of this demonstration to survive, Captain Juan Francisco Berbeo (1729–95), a local military officer, stepped into the leadership role at the head of the crowd. The demonstration gained strength in its march from Socorro to Bogotá to the point that a reported 20,000 women and men descended on the outskirts of the colonial capital, demanding a meeting with local officials. Indicative of the fear that this hitherto rare demonstration evoked, the colonial Visitador went into hiding and left the negotiations to Archbishop Caballero y Góngora (1723–96). Assuming the role of intermediary, the bishop negotiated an agreement that met a portion of the *comuneros*' demands. As the crowds dispersed for home, the Archbishop and colonial officers reneged on the accord and ordered the military to pursue and apprehend the insurgents. In subsequent months trials and executions decimated the movement and terrorized the rank and file with public executions of some of the leading figures. However, Captain Berbeo and his co-conspirators from the elite were granted amnesty and returned to their previous positions in society. Under the leadership of a small farmer, José Antonio Galán, a small band of protesters continued to attack government installations for another year. With their capture and execution in early 1782 the revolt came to an end, and for decades remained largely unknown to anyone outside the immediate region.

Scant research into the uprising has left many unanswered questions, specifically pertaining to the identity of those involved and precisely what they intended to do in

Bogotá. Some historians have argued that the Comunero Revolt was an opening salvo in the independence movement that swept the continent during the early decades of the nineteenth century, while others view it as an isolated protest against Bourbon taxation policies. Viewed with the benefit of hindsight, it seems that the actions of the comuneros portended a growing willingness on the part of previously silent social actors to demonstrate their rejection of certain aspects of colonial rule. It began in the provinces, swept through the countryside to the capital, involved participants from across the spectrum of social class, gender, and age, and drew in members from both military and civilian ranks.

Discontent and Disorder in Brazil

Similar to Spanish America, in the early 1790s conspiracies and plots against the Portuguese colonial government erupted in Brazil. In the prosperous mining area of Minas Gerais a local dentist, Joaquim José da Silva Xavier (1746–92), who went by the nickname Tiradentes ("tooth-puller"), conspired with a number of wealthy miners to sever ties with the Portuguese government. When the mines had turned a handsome profit for colonial miners in the early eighteenth century, they had been content to accept the protection and benefits of the Portuguese Crown. Discontent arose in tandem with the exhaustion of the mines. In the face of a diminishing supply of gold and gems, colonists grew angry that the Crown refused to reduce the tithe it demanded or lighten the tax burden on miners. The conspirators met in secret and hatched a plan to declare Minas Gerais independent, their audacity based on the assumption that the other states would follow their lead and likewise declare independence from Portugal. The plan was scuttled when an agent in their midst revealed the plot to the authorities, who captured Tiradentes who had fled to Rio de Janeiro. His decapitated head was returned to the wealthy mining city of Vila Rica (today Ouro Preto) and left to decompose on a post in the main square as a formidable deterrent to others discontented with the Crown's policies.

Six years later in Salvador da Bahia, northeast Brazil's most important city, the Tailors' Conspiracy (*Inconfidência de Alfaiates*) convulsed the city. In this case, educated members of the colonial elite – influenced by principles of the Enlightenment and the outbreak of successful revolutions and independence movements abroad, and fueled by grievances against the Pombaline reforms – along with mixed-race artisans, conspired to overthrow the government and institute free trade and a new independent state. Similar to revolts in Colombia, Peru, and Minas Gerais, the cross-class, multiracial composition of the conspirators divided along class and racial lines on the goals of the uprising. Poor whites, freed persons, slaves, mixed-race artisans, and a few radical upper-class whites wanted to abolish slavery, curb the power of the Catholic Church, end all forms of racial oppression, and establish a government that provided opportunity for all citizens. Their plan was borrowed from the most radical precepts of the French Revolution, which by the 1790s was setting the standard for revolutionary rhetoric throughout much of the colonial world.

When the royal authorities discovered the plot, they moved to jail and execute the conspirators. Similar to the outcome of conspiracies in neighboring states or distant lands, the most severe punishments, including execution, torture, banishment, and long jail sentences, were meted out to poor whites, working people of color, and slaves. Among the white elite, the radicals who joined the Tailors' Conspiracy were influenced by the revolutionary ideals rocking France at this time, whereas those equally discontented with colonial policies, but wary of the power of the lower classes, held back, either refusing to get involved or condemning the conspirators as a threat to the social order. The plot and resultant repression demonstrates the divergent goals that previously silent social groups were bringing to the foreground, and the importance of class position in determining the depth of commitment of individual insurgents.

Changing Gender Roles

Women from all social classes broke into the public arena on many levels: politically, economically, and culturally. By the mid-eighteenth century, and continuing into the nineteenth, women were increasingly participating in the workforce, particularly in the production of cotton cloth and as market traders. In many major textile production centers, such as Querétaro (Mexico) and Cochabamba (Bolivia) and parts of the Chaco in La Plata (Argentina), women were the mainstay of the production process, as was also the case in tobacco sales and cigar making in Cuba and other areas of the Caribbean. The Bourbon Reformers extolled the importance of women, even middle-class "respectable" women, as laborers because of their diligent work habits, especially in arduous and repetitive tasks, which were needed to bolster the lagging economy. As a result of their heightened role in the economic life of the colonies, women were angered along with men – their husbands, brothers, sons, and fathers – at the imposition of new and higher taxes, especially sales taxes that increased the price of necessary household goods. Also, their role as sellers in the marketplace brought many women into direct conflict with restrictive aspects of the Reforms.

Women were a major presence in the Túpac Amaru II revolt in 1780–1. As historian Sonya Lipsett-Rivera notes, the revolt that had begun as a protest against the Bourbon Reforms soon mushroomed into a general rebellion against the colonial government's racist treatment of the indigenous people of the Andean region. "Women, as much as men, were affected by these injustices."[5] Túpac Amaru II's wife, Micaela Bastidas, commanded a battalion of insurgents and was responsible for the uprising in the San Felipe de Tungasucan region. She is often credited with being a superior strategist to Túpac Amaru II, and certainly more daring. Apparently she chided her husband at one point for his timidity and refusal to mount a surprise attack against the Spaniards in Cuzco to catch the weakly fortified city off guard. Instead Túpac Amaru II wasted precious time encircling the countryside in hopes of building up his army. By the time the insurgents attacked the city, the Spaniards had brought in reinforcements and were able to quell the uprising. Túpac Amaru II, Micaela Bastidas, and many others were captured and the rebels dispersed.

At one stage in the rebellion the Quechua speakers, under Túpac Amaru's command, fought together with Aymara-speaking rebels from Puno on Lake Titicaca and on the Bolivian side of the lake. The alliance did not last, however, and the Aymara leader, Túpac Katarí (ca. 1750–81) led his forces alone until his capture in October 1781. His female commander and partner Bartola Sisa continued the resistance, leading a contingent of 2,000 troops for a number of months. Eventually, in early 1782, the Spanish army defeated the rebels in Peru and Bolivia. According to contemporary sources, colonial officials were shocked to find that of the 73 leaders, 32 were women, all of whom were executed, although not publicly.

Manuela Beltrán in the Comunero Revolt, and Micaela Bastidas and Bartola Sisa in the Andean insurgency were some of the more famous of a large group of women who took part in public demonstrations against high prices, poor food distribution networks to outlying areas, racist treatment of Indian people, mounting taxes and ever-tightening controls on day-to-day life in the colonies. Nonetheless, the march of the women of Socorro drew enough recognition that the great liberator of Spanish America, Simón Bolívar, commemorated the event with a speech in 1820 known as the "Address to the Ladies [*Matronas*] of Socorro," which was publicly proclaimed in February of that year. The address refers to the women in relationship with their families, their husbands and children, thus seeing them as mothers, wives, and daughters, yet at the same time associates them with power and heroism. Bolivar's address to "the Illustrious Ladies of Socorro" as "virile women" whom no human power "is capable of subjugating," was a reference that he no doubt hoped would shame the men into like-wise defying Spanish officials. Comparing the bravery of the women of Socorro against the Spanish colonial army, he declared:

> Heroic ladies of Socorro: the mothers of Sparta did not ask for their children's lives, but for the victory of their country; the mothers of Rome contemplated with pleasure the glorious wounds of their family; they encouraged them to achieve the honour of dying in combat. More sublime are you in your generous patriotism, you have wielded the lance, you have taken up position in the columns and you ask to die for the homeland. Mothers, wives, sisters, who could follow your steps in the race towards heroism? Are there men worthy of you? No, no, no! But you are worth the admiration of the Universe and the adoration of the liberators of Colombia.[6]

To be sure, most women who participated in the rebellions received little notice; yet many were active in village uprisings in the waves of protest that preceded the outbreak of independence in the nineteenth century. This militancy among women of the working and peasant classes coincided with the first cracks in the patriarchal system that restricted life for women of all social strata.

On the Road to Independence

The eighteenth century ended with the tug-of-war between the dictates of the reorganized Bourbon and Pombaline leadership and a growing colonial opposition. Whereas Enlightenment philosophy was infusing debates over whether the European Crowns had the right to rule the colonies in America, militant voices began to question the right of *any* monarchy to rule *any* populace, at home or abroad. Radicals debated moderates, pro-monarchy conservatives confronted militant republicans, anti-slavery forces denounced slavery and the parasitical landowning system it supported. Yet, despite sporadic regional conspiracies no Latin American or Caribbean country actively moved to take up independence until the last days of the eighteenth century, following the slave uprising in the French Caribbean colony of Saint-Domingue. Nonetheless, strains of republicanism and calls for universal brotherhood and equality had begun to filter into the salons, cafes, street conversations, newspapers, pamphlets, and books in Latin American and Caribbean capitals and port cities.

The call for freedom, however, would not resonate in all ears in the same way. Longstanding servile peasants, *castas*, slaves, and oppressed people of color were not a part of the discussion among the Creole landowning, merchant, and planter elite. The latter envisioned freedom for themselves, but not for those who served them. The masses, on the other hand, saw no reason to give up their lives for freedom unless they were guaranteed a stake in the independent new society.

Nationalism and American Culture

The eighteenth century saw the flowering of intellectual currents that fused Creole and indigenous Latin American culture, such as *Cuzqueño* (originating in the city of Cuzco) painting in Peru and mestizo art and literature in Mexico. From the earliest encounter between the indigenous people of the continent and the European interlopers – or, it could be argued, from the first moments in which Spaniards enslaved the conquered natives to help in the destruction of their own art, drama, and architectural forms so as to replace them with European forms – indigenous and mestizo cultural expression struggled to survive. Even in the midst of Spanish and Catholic orthodoxy that sought to eliminate, or at least sublimate, indigenous artistry, native expression persevered, and even coexisted, in colonial society. At the end of the eighteenth century trends shifted and mestizo culture emerged as a source of pride, even as a nascent home-grown philosophical justification for Latin American autonomy.

One of the key expressions of mestizo art became synonymous with the Peruvian city of Cuzco, which for a hundred years before the arrival of the Spaniards had served as the capital of the vast Inca empire. Nestled in the highlands, this religious and political center of both Incan and Spanish culture still bears a bit of spectacular Inca architecture in walls and palaces. One of the most intriguing early examples of mestizo architecture can be seen in Coricancha, an Inca palace around which the Dominican

Figure 2.2   Eighteenth-century painting of the Last Supper, Cuzco Cathedral, Peru, by indigenous artist Marcos Zapata. (Courtesy South American Pictures)

order of priests built a monastery, utilizing some of the precisely cut Inca stone walls for both exterior and interior supports. Remarkably, whereas the part of the monastery the Spaniards constructed has been destroyed and rebuilt several times after devastating earthquakes, the Inca walls remain intact.

Under the Spaniards Cuzco was transformed into a dazzling baroque city of churches and colorful colonial streets, while indigenous art maintained a lively presence beneath the surface. Beginning in the seventeenth century, and reaching its apex in the eighteenth, Spanish and indigenous art came together in a form that splendidly fused both cultures. A prime example of mestizo art, the Cuzqueño school was made up of a group of artists led by the Indian painters Diego Quispe Tito in the seventeenth century and Marcos Zapata in the mid- to late eighteenth century. These indigenous artists developed workshops that trained artisans, painters, and sculptors to produce paintings, altar pieces, and many religious and secular artifacts that displayed a harmonious blend of indigenous and European symbols. One of the most famous is the "Last Supper" that hangs in the Cathedral in Cuzco, which depicts cooked guinea pigs (an Andean staple) on the table for the consumption of Christ and the apostles (Figure 2.2).

In Mexico Creole nationalists appropriated and reconfigured for the broader society symbols that had previously belonged only to Spain. The famous legend of the appearance of the Virgin Mary to Juan Diego, an Indian peasant boy, at Tepeyac on the outskirts of Mexico City became the prime symbol of Mexican, mestizo, and Indian nationalism. According to the well-known legend, the Virgin directed the boy to tell the bishop to build a church on the site of her appearance. When the bishop doubted the boy, more for his station in life than from disbelief in miracles, the Virgin left her image on a cloth for the boy to take to the bishop as proof of her request. The story was first popularized in the mid-seventeenth century, over a hundred years after it supposedly occurred, and the image of the Virgin is both dark and Indian in its features, signifying her indigenous roots and power in the face of European Catholicism (see Box 2.3). If, ardent Creole nationalists observed, Mary was indigenous to Mexico, then why did the Mexicans need the Spanish? Centuries later thousands of devout followers continue to worship at the vast, ultramodern cathedral that stands alongside the small original sixteenth-century church, now subsumed into the sprawling environs of Mexico City, while the Virgin's image graces T-shirts, tattoos, rock-and-roll concert posters, and other paraphernalia of the secular world as a symbol of Mexican pride.

Similarly, the appearance of the myth of Quetzalcoatl in an era when Mexicans were beginning to chafe under Spanish rule was no accident, and lent force once again to the assertion that Mexico did not need to depend on a distant colonial power for cultural inspiration. The myth of Quetzalcoatl, the pacificist god of the Toltecs for whom, according to legend, the Aztecs mistook Hernán Cortés, actually entered Mexican mythology in the eighteenth century. If, as the priests had argued, the key virtue the Spaniards had brought to the Indians was Christian salvation and the replacement of the angry god of human sacrifice (Huitzilopoctli) with the benign god of Christian forgiveness (Jesus Christ), then the very fact that the Indians had a god of forgiveness in the person of Quetzalcoatl long before the Spaniards arrived made their Christ of little or no relevance to the salvation of Indian souls. One particularly bizarre twist on the returning god legend was the idea that Quetzalcoatl had actually been a Christian god, if not Jesus Christ himself. According to this logic, the native peoples of America were not indebted to the Spaniards for their faith; rather, the entire process of conversion had actually gone in the other direction. According to this version, Quetzalcoatl was banished from Mexico for his pacifist teachings, somehow ending up in Europe, and then returned with the Spaniards to rekindle Christianity in the land of its origins: Mexico! The logic was that if Europeans could not be credited with ending human sacrifice and bringing Christianity, then their intervention had brought nothing but destruction: disease, malnutrition, overwork, mass death, cultural and political devastation.

In Brazil the cultural, artistic, and intellectual seeds of a nationalist separatist identity proceeded more haltingly than in Spanish America. The preponderance of slavery and its penetration through all aspects of Brazilian society (see Chapter 3) produced an Afro-Brazilian culture, apparent in religion, in dress, food, language, and art. Since slavery was everywhere in Brazil, and slaves performed every type of work, the imprint of Africa on Brazil was profound. African rituals, kept alive in slave quarters, permeated white society as well, while the considerable population of mulattos served as cultural transmission belts from African to Portuguese culture. African religions such as *candomblé* dominated the slave quarters, and found an occasional audience in the Big House as well, while Catholicism remained the official religion. Elements of African cuisine appeared on the table of the masters; tales of Africa resonated through the slave quarters; the rhythm of the drums, the single-stringed *berimbau*, along with language

Box 2.3   The Virgin of Guadalupe

The Virgin of Guadalupe (Figure 2.3) is not only a popular icon in Mexican history, art, and literature, but plays a crucial role in the daily lives of the Mexican people, both at home and in the diaspora. In the words of Mexican Nobel Laureate Octavio Paz, the "Virgin is the consolation of the poor, the shield of the weak, the help of the oppressed. In sum, she is the Mother of orphans. All men are born disinherited and their true condition is orphanhood, but this is particularly true among the Indians and the poor in Mexico."[7]

Made famous by Father Miguel Hidalgo when he carried her image into battle at the outbreak of the independence struggle in 1808, the Virgin has evolved over the centuries from a symbol of resistance against Spanish oppression to an icon of rebelliousness in general. In the 1970s César Chávez, the main spokesperson for the United Farm Workers, an organization overwhelmingly composed of Mexican-Americans in California and the Southwest, carried a banner with the union's crest alongside an image of the Virgin of Guadalupe as he and others fought

Figure 2.3   The Virgin of Guadalupe, a sixteenth-century Katsam painting of unknown provenance, resides in the Cathedral of the Virgin of Guadalupe in Mexico City.

Figure 2.4   "Portrait of the Artist as the Virgin of Guadalupe" by Yolanda López (permission of artist; image courtesy Special Collections, Davidson Library, UCSB).

for basic economic and political rights for migrant farm workers. Likewise, during the 1960s and 1970s Mexican-American student organizations displayed the Virgin on posters and banners at demonstrations as both a symbol of Chicano power and the emblem of their mixed identity.

The Virgin's appearance in present-day pop culture reflects the switch from a sacred religious image in Mexico to a global popular culture icon, especially among Mexican-Americans. She graces the drum set of the Chicano rock band Los Lobos, but surfaces in more unlikely venues as well. For example, in the 1970s the Chicana feminist artist Yolanda López painted the Virgin as an active, contemporary woman in athletic running gear, symbolic of the liberated Mexican-American (Figure 2.4). As explained by Mexican writer Guillermo Gómez-Peña, feminists, gang members, political activists, and a slew of irreverent outcasts embraced the image of the Virgin of Guadalupe as a way of creating something new: "They had reappropriated it, reactivated it, recontextualized it, and turned it into a symbol of resistance . . . no longer the contemplative *mestiza* Mother of all Mexicans, but a warrior goddess who blessed the cultural and political weapons of activists and artists."[8]

and folk tales from the African homeland, infused Brazilian music. Unlike Spanish America, however, the overwhelming dependence on slavery, and the demographic predominance of people of African descent, served as a brake on pro-independence sentiments among the planters and merchant Creoles. The gradual, almost laconic, fusion of European and African cultures did not herald a dismissal of Portuguese political dominance. At the end of the eighteenth century Brazilians thought, looked, talked, and acted in ways dramatically different from the Portuguese. However, cultural confrontations remained in-house expressions of master–slave relations, as opposed to the Creole–Peninsular conflict more typical of Spanish America.

Conclusion

The sweep of events from the moment the Spanish and Portuguese arrived in what they erroneously called a "New World" moved from conquest to management. The Iberian monarchs oversaw an extensive bureaucracy that stretched from ports in Europe into the far reaches of the American colonies. From the onset, the seeds of rebellion and separation from the ways of the "Old World" were apparent.

The strains of Creole nationalism that permeated empires in the eighteenth century had in common a demonstrated fusion of European, native indigenous, and African cultures, essentially transposing one iconography for another and thus, in turn, planting the seeds of a new "American" sensibility. Creole, mestizo, indigenous, and African intellectual and cultural expression foreshadowed momentous political changes, and, notably, found that expression in the religious arena. Creole nationalism came to terms with the powerful religiosity and spiritualism of the masses most oppressed under the colonial order, incorporating and accommodating indigenous and African symbols into Catholic Church doctrine and the Christian cultural milieu. In the nineteenth century Spanish America, in particular, was the staging ground for the emergence of a decidedly separatist and revolutionary agenda, but one rooted and nourished by a distinct American culture that had been developing in fits and starts from the moment of the first encounters between Europeans, Africans, and Indians on the soil of the "New World." This cultural expression legitimized the more powerful economic and political breach that increasingly divided Europe and Latin America.

3 | Competing Notions of Freedom

As the eighteenth century passed the halfway mark, sporadic demands for freedom, sovereignty, equality, and justice began to give rise to organized political actions. However, what different groups meant by freedom – and even whom they viewed as their oppressors – varied according to race, social class, and status, and occasionally gender. Creoles of European background were aware of sentiments for independence emanating from the British colonies of North America, and along with Thomas Jefferson (1743–1826), Benjamin Franklin (1706–90) and others, they were reading, discussing, and disputing the ideas of the Enlightenment. As noted earlier, North America's successful war of independence and the uprising of the French masses against a corrupt and decadent monarchy inspired patriots in Latin America and the Caribbean to take the same road. The Napoleonic Wars following the revolution in France had a particularly strong impact on Latin America. It could even be argued that Napoleon Bonaparte's (1769–1821) invasion of much of Europe, with the intent of deposing monarchs everywhere and establishing his own empire, had the effect of pushing Latin America toward independence from Spain. The Napoleonic invasion of Spain and Portugal in 1807 undermined Iberian authority in the colonies, leading eventually to the outbreak of the independence wars.

Although Latin American Creoles shared many of the same grievances as their counterparts in the British colonies of North America, the land, people, customs, and traditions differed dramatically. From Mexico (which at this time extended as far as the northern border of Alta California), through the islands of Cuba and Hispaniola, to Argentina and Chile at the tip of Antarctica, the Spanish empire was spread over a steep and often inhospitable terrain inhabited by Indians speaking many native languages and rural laborers living in near-feudal relations of servitude to local landlords. At the same time, commerce, intellectual life, and political debate thrived in major cosmopolitan centers from Havana, Mexico City, and Lima to distant Buenos Aires, the latter a city that had developed over hundreds of years as an outpost for smuggling and evading the controls of Church and state. Throughout the Caribbean, in many parts of the lands now known as Mexico, Peru, Colombia, Venezuela, Bolivia, and all of Brazil, slaves labored on huge estates producing sugar, coffee, cattle; as laborers in mines; as well as performing every type of job in the urban areas. In fact the spread of slave labor far and wide in Latin America, into areas traditionally considered Creole, mestizo, and Indian, has only recently been uncovered. Because few people descendant from Africa seem apparent in the populations today of Mexico, Bolivia, Peru, even Chile and Argentina, historians have tended to overlook the extent to which slaves bought from Africa were a key feature of the workforce.

Five Roads to Independence

Independence movements in Latin America and the Caribbean proceeded down five divergent paths, starting in the last years of the eighteenth century and continuing through the late nineteenth. The first broke out on the Caribbean sugar colony of Saint-Domingue (later renamed Haiti), where rumblings of independence from France among planters precipitated a massive slave revolt. By contrast, in Brazil, also a large slave-owning colony, independence from Portugal gave way to an empire in America, and slavery remained intact. A third path was forged in Mexico, where independence progressed irregularly, even erratically, pushed by an uprising from below and met with repression from the fearful Creole elite. The opening salvo in 1810 was a massive uprising of indigenous and mestizo peasants following the call of radical clergy. In response the Creole elite retreated and held back for more than 10 years before declaring independence under an autocratic military ruler. Mexico's social revolution, and a bid to improve the lives of the masses, had to wait nearly another century. The fourth case is that of the South American continent as a whole. There military officers, either wealthy Creoles or supported by them, fought the Crown at the head of armies made up of landless *casta* and indigenous peasants. The effort ultimately left South America free of colonial rule, but in ruins and with little change in the basic class nature of the ruling hierarchies.

Cuba and Puerto Rico constitute a fifth example, in which belated independence movements were stolen out from under revolutionary forces just as patriots had freedom from Spain in their grasp. The anti-colonial struggles, and victories, in Spanish and Portuguese America stirred independence movements on many Caribbean islands, but the Creoles' fear of slave uprisings staved off independence in Cuba, Spanish America's most important Caribbean possession. There, in neighboring Puerto Rico, and on British and other French sugar islands, elites refused to join the revolutionary movement sweeping Latin America, believing that colonial status, combined as it was with prosperous sugar sales and slave labor, was preferable to the risks that independence might entail.

The story of independence in Latin America begins not with Spain or Portugal, but with France and a slave revolt in 1791 in Saint-Domingue, a tiny French colony on the western half of Hispaniola. The explosion that convulsed this Caribbean island brought slavery, an institution that dominated every aspect of life in the Caribbean, Brazil, and many areas of Latin America from the sixteenth through the nineteenth centuries, into a collision course with the anti-colonial struggle. Before examining the slave revolt in Haiti, however, it is important to understand the role of African slavery in Latin America and the Caribbean. At first glance it might seem that this discussion takes us far afield from independence; however, slavery and the systems of privilege it conferred on the Creole elite were the critical backdrops to the independence process.

African Slavery in the Americas

Although slaves of African origin traveled on Columbus's early voyages, it was not until 1501 that the formal trade began, when Spain's Catholic monarchs, Isabella (1451–1504) and Ferdinand (1452–1516), granted to Nicolas de Ovando (1460–1518), the appointed governor of Hispaniola, the right to bring in slaves for sale on the island (Maps 3.1 to 3.4 show the Atlantic slave trade during the period 1451 to 1870). Over the next 350 years the Spanish colonies imported over two million slaves, mainly concentrated along the sugar-producing coastline settlements and islands of the Caribbean, as well as in Mexico and Peru, and otherwise dispersed throughout the Spanish colonies. Brazil maintained a vigorous slave trade with Africa for over 300 years. For nearly the entire first 400 years of that country's existence, slaves, originally from Africa and later born into slavery in the New World, were the main labor force. Throughout Latin America slaves worked as field hands, on sugar and coffee plantations as parts of large gangs, or on smallholdings alongside a farmer who, with one or two slaves, grew corn, manioc, beans, and fruit. Slaves worked in mines in Brazil, Mexico, and Peru, on whaling expeditions as sailors and oarsmen, and in warehouses extracting and processing whale oil. Those brought from the coast of Africa introduced rice cultivation to the Americas, taught fishing techniques to Brazilian settlers, and intermixed with Spanish and Portuguese explorers and indigenous captives to create the backlands' cowboy-frontiersmen *bandeirantes* of Brazil and *gauchos* of Argentina. As opposed to the US South, where slaves were mainly rural field hands, in both urban and rural areas of Latin America slaves filled *all* jobs. They worked as skilled laborers, domestic servants, wet nurses, field hands, in the military, and occasionally even supervised other slaves. They were hired out as prostitutes, offered as parts of wedding dowries, as prizes in church lotteries; they served at Mass, lived as concubines, and transported any type of produce, animal, mineral, or person in conveyances ranging from wagons and buggies to sedan chairs.

Slaves, amply replenished through a brisk trade from West Africa, were worked to death in less than five years on Caribbean sugar islands and in 8–10 years on the plantations of northeast Brazil. In no place in the Americas did the slave population reproduce itself in large numbers except, curiously, in the United States. The reason was that the new US republic, in its pre-cotton boom era, ended the external slave trade in 1808, a feature of the compromise that had ensured the ratification of the Constitution 20 years earlier. With the invention of the cotton gin in 1792, which breathed new life into cotton production, US planters embarked on a strategy of slave breeding to replenish the supply internally. By 1860 and the outbreak of the Civil War, the entire US slave population had been born in America, numbering almost four million. Although the US, in both

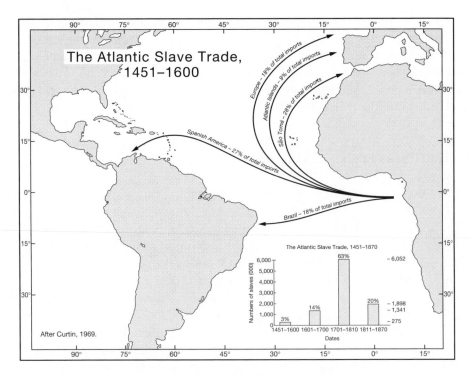

Map 3.1 The Atlantic slave trade, 1451–1600. (Based on Cathryn L. Lombardi and John V. Lombardi, *Latin American History: A Teaching Atlas* ca. 1983. By permission of The University of Wisconsin Press.)

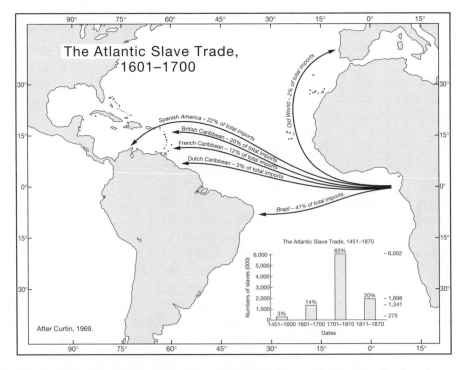

Map 3.2 The Atlantic slave trade, 1601–1700. (Based on Cathryn L. Lombardi and John V. Lombardi, *Latin American History: A Teaching Atlas* ca. 1983. By permission of The University of Wisconsin Press.)

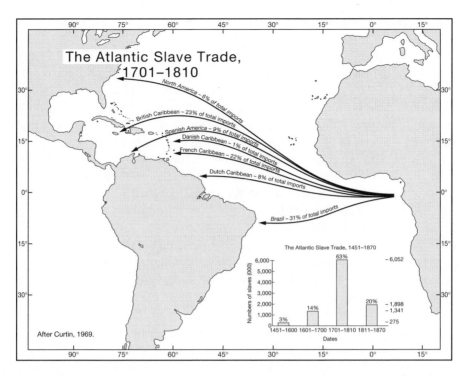

Map 3.3 The Atlantic slave trade, 1701–1810. (Based on Cathryn L. Lombardi and John V. Lombardi, *Latin American History: A Teaching Atlas* ca. 1983. By permission of The University of Wisconsin Press.)

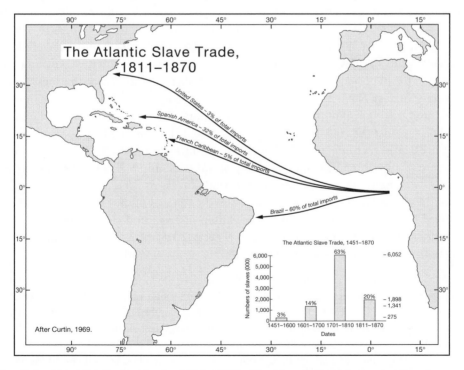

Map 3.4 The Atlantic slave trade, 1811–1870. (Based on Cathryn L. Lombardi and John V. Lombardi, *Latin American History: A Teaching Atlas* ca. 1983. By permission of The University of Wisconsin Press.)

the colonial and post-colonial eras, imported an estimated 523,000 humans – less than five percent of the total number of Africans sold into slavery in the Americas – it had one of the largest slave populations in the hemisphere by the time of abolition. By contrast, Spanish America imported approximately 2.5 million slaves, slightly more than 20 percent of the total Atlantic slave trade, and Brazil alone imported some 4 million, representing 35 percent of the entire trade, during the nearly four centuries in which slavery existed in the Americas. A particularly stark comparison can be seen in the cases of Cuba and the United States. Cuba brought in more than 595,000 slaves in the last 50 years of the trade (1816–67), or 70,000 more than the US ever imported.

High death rates, combined with larger numbers of runaways and greater levels of manumission (granting a slave freedom), meant that Latin American and Caribbean societies had fewer slaves than the US at any given time. However, throughout the colonial period, and later in Brazil, the slaves of Latin America were frequently African-born, more prone toward rebellion, less assimilated into Spanish or Portuguese language and culture, and comprised a much higher percentage of the total population. In 1827, near the end of the Spanish American rebellions, census data listed 18.2 percent of the population as white, compared with 81.9 percent people of color, divided among Indians, blacks, mestizos, and mixed-race black and white, or mulattos. For Portuguese America the difference was nearly the same, with whites comprising 23.4 percent of the population and people of color 76.7, divided among blacks, Indians, mulattos, and *caboclos* (Brazilian term for European–Indian mixture). Given the limitations that had been imposed on people of color since the early colonial period – slavery, debt peonage, marginalized and restricted access to public space, poverty, and humiliation – the grievances of the latter group were directed not at distant imperial centers in Madrid and Lisbon, but instead at local planters, *hacendados*, merchants, and the slaveholding clergy. Wealthy Creoles weighed the extent of their grievances with the Crown against their need for the royal military that held their societies in the order that best served their class interest. Not without reason, they feared the uprising of the masses of Indians, slaves, and the poor of all racial and ethnic groups should there be any outbreak of hostilities against the rule of the *peninsulares* (people born in the Iberian peninsula).

If slaves did everything, white masters did very little to support their own livelihood, take care of their homes, children, or the world they inhabited. The French colony of Saint-Domingue had an estimated 500,000 slaves, or 15 slaves for every white person. Not only did slaves perform all labor on the island, but they were driven so hard, and died so frequently of overwork, starvation, disease, and sleep deprivation, that the entire African-born population turned over every 20 years. As C. L. R. James explained in his classic study of the Haitian Revolution, in terms of work,

> no white man did any work that he could get a Negro to do for him. A barber summoned to attend to a customer appeared in silk attire, hat under his arm, sword at his side, cane under his elbow, followed by four Negroes. One of them combed the hair, another dressed it, a third curled it and the fourth finished . . . At the slightest slackness, at the slightest mistake, he boxed the cheek of the unfortunate slave so hard that often he knocked him over . . . The same hand which had knocked over the slave closed on an enormous fee, and the barber took his exit with the same insolence and elegance as before."[1]

Slavery and the Countryside

Because of the importance of sugar exports to the local economies of Brazil and the Caribbean islands, over 70 percent of slaves worked on sugar plantations and adjacent mills. They also worked in the production of tobacco, rice, cotton, fruit, manioc, corn, beans, and other staple crops. Although the majority of slaves brought to the Americas were men, women were brought to Caribbean slave plantations for the same reasons as African men – to provide labor. Many plantations had absentee planters, who lived in Europe and left overseers (themselves slaves or freed people of color) to manage the plantations. In the Caribbean, with mainly absentee planters, there were few massive plantation houses, such as the antebellum mansions of the US Deep South and thus less need for female house slaves. Not only did the overwhelming majority of female slaves, therefore, work in the fields, but almost half of all field hands were women. This was the case, despite the reduced number of women. Female slaves cut cane, weeded and fertilized the plants, fed the cane stalks into the mill grinders, looked after children, and tended the garden vegetables that supplemented the slaves' meager diet. Men cut cane and worked in the mill; they also worked as carpenters, blacksmiths, valets, drivers, overseers, and even as part of the plantation's militia.

After the 1808 slave revolt and revolution in Haiti, Cuba became the foremost sugar-producing area of the Americas, with coffee and tobacco adding to planters' wealth. Travelers report scenes of more than 500 slaves at a time working on the large Cuban estates, with hundreds of men and women feeding the stalks into the huge mills and hauling away the boiling juice. Slavery had existed in Cuba since 1700, but doubled in the years before 1810 and increasingly supported a resident planter elite. Because of the comparatively late start of sugar production, it developed as a more highly capitalized enterprise; many slaves worked in steam-powered mills, along with the large numbers working in the fields, and in slaveholders' homes in both urban and rural areas.

In Mexico, Peru, Venezuela, and Brazil, women more frequently worked in households, cooking, cleaning, washing and repairing clothing, and caring for the planter's children while overseeing slave children. On the ranches slaves worked alongside free laborers and freedmen, tending cattle, cultivating cocoa beans, herding sheep, and were sometimes beyond the oversight of the owners for extended periods. In terms of pure inhumane labor, time in the mines of Brazil, Mexico, or Peru was probably the worst job of all. For the slaves who worked the pits, mining was sometimes a death sentence. They stood in water panning for gold or diamonds all day, were given very little to eat, worked long hours, and suffered from constant fevers and lethargy resulting from toxins in mercury and other minerals used in the processing of gold and metals.

Slavery in the Cities

Africans and their freed descendants were responsible for building the infrastructure of American societies, working as skilled and unskilled laborers, fishermen, on docks, on ships, and in construction. Travelers to Brazil frequently reported that there were few carts or wagons drawn by horses and mules in the cities. Instead slaves "are the beasts of draught as well as of burden. The loads they drag, and the roads they drag them over, are enough to kill both mules and horses."[2] Cargo was moved on the backs of slaves or in parcels and carts dragged along the ground. Since in Africa people traditionally carried huge, heavy loads on their heads, slaves introduced the practice to America. Travelers marveled in their diaries at the sight of rail-thin slave women transporting on their heads cotton, textiles, jars of water, sometimes while carrying a baby strapped to their bodies. Platoons of slave children and adults of both sexes scurried through city streets balancing enormous tubs filled with the daily slop and human excrement collected from homes and workplaces and conveyed to dumps. One observer in Rio de Janeiro compared the work of slaves with that of oxen: "A week ago I stood to observe eight oxen drag an ordinary wagon-load of building stone for the Capuchins up the steep Castle hill; it was straining work for them to ascend a few rods at a time; today I noticed similar loads of stone discharged at the foot of the ascent, and borne up on negroes' heads."[3]

Both men and women, along with children, were engaged in all forms of labor in the cities. In Brazil curtained sedan chairs, called *cadeiras*, suspended from a single pole that rested on the shoulders of two or more slaves, were the universal form of travel for white men and women (Figure 3.1). "You meet with captains of ships, English and American sailors, fashionable ladies, bishops and fat priests, passengers from emigrant ships, the old and the young, the lame and the blind, all riding about in these cadeiras."[4]

BRAZILIAN SEDAN

Figure 3.1   This engraving from the 1800s shows two slaves carrying a woman in her sedan chair, with her attendants walking behind. The slaves are in formal attire, to indicate the high status of the woman, but are barefoot, to indicate their enslavement. (Thomas Ewbank, *Life in Brazil*, 1856)

Masters set female slaves to work as prostitutes, many at a very young age. Prostitution was a lucrative source of income for slave owners. Moreover, far from the watchful eye of "polite society" and the church hierarchy, priests in Cuba, Hispaniola, and remote (or not so remote) areas of Brazil frequented slave prostitutes, forced sex on their female slaves, and kept concubines. In addition, slave women were used as wet nurses for the babies of their mistresses, since in elite circles it was considered indelicate for a woman to breastfeed her baby. Sometimes mistresses rented out their wet-nurse slaves to others. Little is known of the fate of these women's newborn children, but historian Robert Conrad speculates that in Brazil the infants may have been taken from the slave mothers to orphanages or perhaps sold. Newspapers were filled with advertisements such as this one: "For rent, a wet nurse with very good milk, from her first pregnancy, gave birth six days ago, in the Rua dos Pescadores, No. 64. Be it advised that she does not have a child."[5] In Mexico, Peru, Brazil and wherever there were slaves, wealthy mistresses had personal attendants. Secluded in their townhouses or isolated on rural plantations, elite women relied on personal slaves as their closest confidantes and often their only company. It was not unusual for enslaved wet nurses, nannies, and house servants, male and female, to grow fond of the infants and children they tended and even to develop a loyalty to their mistresses and masters. Such loyalty had its rewards. A valued personal servant who served a family faithfully for many years could be granted his or her freedom later in life. Nonetheless, the short lifespan of slaves in Latin America indicates that overall slavery was brutal, and likewise points to the futility of disputing whether masters in one country or another were kinder. C. L. R. James offers the most succinct appraisal: "There were good and bad Governors, good and bad Intendents, as there were good and bad slave owners. But this was a matter of pure chance. It was the system that was bad."[6]

Treatment and Punishment

By law in any slaveholding society of Latin America masters could either punish their slaves on the plantation or bring them to police stations, where for a fee the slave would be whipped for serious crimes such as running away, striking an overseer, or theft. For the most part slaveholders meted out punishments on their own estates, since towns were distant and often inaccessible. There is little evidence that women were treated better than men, in Brazil or elsewhere. Although women were probably not whipped as often as men and were instead placed in chains or stocks, there is every indication that they were severely abused. A house guest at a plantation reported watching the master pin a female house servant to a tree post by driving a huge nail through her ear because she had broken a plate. Left there overnight, the young woman escaped by tearing the head of the nail through her ear. She was found the next day, returned to the plantation, and whipped for attempting to escape.

Some planters were concerned about the treatment of their female slaves, especially to protect their ability to bear children. Pregnant women worked cutting cane until five or six weeks before giving birth and returned about two or three weeks afterwards, although there are reports, mainly from the Caribbean islands, of women forced to strap their babies to their backs and return to the fields in a few days. Planters on Saint-Domingue used the "four post" to punish pregnant women, a method in which a hole was dug in the earth to accommodate her belly while lashes were "laid on" her back. A heavy iron collar with tentacles extended all around was specifically reserved for women suspected of aborting the fetus, or killing a newborn child to save their offspring from the horrors of the slave life. The collar was not removed until the woman had produced a child. Again James offers a prescient observation: "Undoubtedly there were kind masters who did not indulge in these refinements of cruelty and whose slaves merely suffered over-work, under-nourishment and the whip."[7]

Slavery and the Church

Rarely did the clergy in Spanish or Portuguese America raise an outcry against the enslavement of Africans. The Church's position toward the enslavement of Africans was very different from its role in opposing Indian slavery. Several Catholic friars, most notably Bartolomé de las Casas, whose work is described in Chapter 2, were instrumental in seeing the harsh *encomienda* system and Indian slavery abolished because it had contributed to the drastic decline of the Indian population. At the core of this difference in approach was the fact that Africans had been enslaved in Europe since ancient times, and were not considered to have the childish "innocence" the Church attributed to the indigenous people of the New World. Africans, the logic went, had had the opportunity to accept Christianity and had rejected it, and thus could be dominated and enslaved according to the principles of "just war."

On the other hand, Catholic doctrine accepted Africans as children of God, and the Church mandated that all slaves be baptized, administered the sacraments, and permitted to attend weekly Mass. In addition, owners were required to allow slaves the Christian "day of rest," which in truth interfered little with productivity on plantations, since slaves used that time to tend to their gardens and repair clothing. Whereas slaves in the United States were not allowed to marry, in Latin America the Catholic Church made marriage a requirement, and the couple could not be "honorably" separated, although it certainly may have happened. Nonetheless, there is scant evidence of the Catholic Church speaking out against slavery, with the exception of occasional reprimands against particularly sadistic masters, rebukes to owners who refused slaves the sacraments, or, infrequently, admonishments against the widespread practice of masters keeping slave concubines.

More often the Church was subservient to the slaveholders, especially in Brazil where planters built chapels on their plantations and retained priests to attend to the spiritual needs of their households and slaves. Priests and nuns had personal slaves, and brotherhoods, monasteries, and convents had large numbers of slaves working for them. One of the largest convents in Mexico City bordered the slave market, where nuns purchased their own personal slaves or those that toiled in the convent. In colonial Peru convents were large establishments, inhabited by rich and worldly women who chose to live a sequestered life rather than to accept a distasteful marriage partner. Inside these convents, elite women kept personal slaves, who tended to their luxurious quarters, helped with their wardrobe, and ran errands to the outside world.

A particularly revealing indication of the Church's participation in the slave system is a record of lottery prizes from the Santa Casa de Misericórdia in the city of Ouro Prêto, Brazil. Slaves as young as one year old, others 6, 8, 16, and 32 years of age, along with leather couches, an English writing desk, a musket and "horse bridle of fine silver" were listed as prizes in a fundraiser for this Catholic charity.[8] Brazil's leading abolitionist, Joaquim Nabuco, offered a stinging indictment of the collusion of the Church with the system of slavery: "No priest ever tried to stop a slave auction; none ever denounced the religious regimen of the slave quarters. The Catholic Church, despite its immense power in a country still greatly fanaticized by it, *never* raised its voice in Brazil in favor of emancipation."[9]

African Medicine and Religious Practices

The extent to which the Catholic clergy administered to slaves varied depending on locale, the proclivity of individual priests and planters, and the receptivity of the slaves toward Catholicism. In general, slaves adopted Catholicism loosely and incorporated its outward rituals into their own system of African religious belief and practice. Despite wide variations, most African religions practiced in slave quarters centered on the idea of a supreme being, a set of non-human gods usually associated with natural forces (water, sun, crops, corn, etc.), ancestor worship and the use of charms, devices, and potions to alter one's life on earth, and sometimes to provide for happiness in the afterlife. Despite the immense efforts of the Catholic Church – and whatever one thinks of its methods or motives, the Church took seriously its responsibility to convert African and Indian "heathens" – it was largely unsuccessful. In the realm of religious belief, far and above any other aspect of life, African culture still flourishes in many areas of Latin America and the Caribbean.

Religion was the one area of a slave's life that was truly his or her own; thus the continued practice of African religious traditions, in defiance of planters and the Church, became a method of resisting slavery. The 1791 slave rebellion on Saint-Domingue, which grew into the largest and most successful revolt in the Americas, began in the clandestine ceremonies of a voodoo priest named Boukman. Decades later, in 1835, in northeastern Brazil Muslim slaves inspired the Malé Revolt. Malé, the Yoruban word for Muslim, was an uprising led by Muslim religious leaders slated to begin on January 25, the day of a Catholic holiday that corresponded with the end of the holiest Muslim holiday of Ramadan. Although the police uncovered the plot before it began, over 500 slaves participated anyway, fighting for much of a day before being defeated by the local police and militia.

In keeping with their role in West African culture, slave women in Latin America played a prominent role in religious ceremonies and held the position as medical prac-titioners, or *curanderas*, in the community. The practice of superficially worshipping the

Christian God and praying to the saints allowed the slaves to substitute their African deities and develop syncretic religions such as *Santería* (Spanish America) and *candomblé* (Brazil). The syncretic Christian–African religions that developed out of the slave quarters called on a spiritual force to facilitate human interaction with the saints who in turn were the intermediaries with God. Devotees carried out various rituals and participated in ceremonies involving dancing rhythmically, smoking cigars, re-enacting religious stories, and, at its peak, entering into a trance, the latter as the ultimate demonstration of human submission to the power of the high spirit. Different from the male hierarchy in Christianity, women were priestesses and at the center of African-based religious practice. Three former slave women founded the first *candomblé* center outside of the slave quarters in 1830 in the northeast city of Salvador. Throughout the Americas, slaves, similar to the practice of indigenous people of the Americas, often became Christians on the outside, but continued to practice their native religions in private. Even planters who sought to convert all their slaves admitted that many were not really Christians.

Religious and medical practices overlapped in Africa, as well as among slaves and freed persons in the Americas. Since European medicine in the eighteenth and nineteenth centuries involved emptying the body of its affliction by "bleeding, blistering, purging or puking," undoubtedly the herbal remedies of the African priests were more successful, or at least they did not do as much harm as opening a vein to drain out blood from the sick person, administering purgatives and applying leeches. Doctors who traveled to the Caribbean islands or Brazil's sugar and coffee regions derided the slaves' use of medicinal herbs as the work of sorcerers and witches and warned against the "unusual effect" the slaves' remedies could produce. Quite likely many among the whites feared these "effects," especially slaves' claims that they could bring down hexes and bad luck on cruel masters. Given that European medicine was little more sophisticated in some of its theories until the late nineteenth century, there is every reason to believe that whites who lived in a highly superstitious world were prone to fear, as well as to actually feel, the aches and pains the slaves wished on them. Certainly they had reason to fear being poisoned. Finally, although slaveholders voiced disdain for the slave's medicine, many whites who consulted the healers of the slave quarters claimed to have found relief from the African medicines. In the slave cabins of the Caribbean and Brazil, following African custom, age conferred respect, lending the elders, both men and women, positions of leadership in the community, in secret societies, and in regulating and governing the social order. Post-menopausal women were held in especially high regard since they were no longer chained to their biological role and thus able to assume political and cultural leadership of the village, equal to men.

Resistance and Rebellion

Scholars have long recognized that slave rebellions were most intense in societies with a large percentage of slaves newly arrived from Africa. Slaves retained close ties to African religion and traditions; they were most likely to run away, form maroon communities, called *quilombos* in Brazil and *cimarróns* in Spanish America, and reinstitute African practices. And where the traditions of Africa persevered, revolts were common. Brazilian slave quarters were alive with the languages, religions, and rituals of Africa. Slaves came from different areas of Africa, although a large number were of the Yoruban ethnic group from Nigeria and Benin, while others were Bantu-speaking people. The language and cultural differences that separated the slaves initially made it difficult to communicate with each other in the diaspora. Over time, however, African customs blended together to form an Afro-Brazilian culture, within which the strongest influence was Yoruban ritual and practice. For almost the entire seventeenth century in the interior of the state of Pernambuco, Brazil had the largest runaway slave community in the Americas, known as the *Quilombo de Palmares*. "Palmares," meaning the land of the palm trees, had over 11,000 inhabitants at its height living in a fully functioning African community in terms of language, customs, religion, and even African forms of slavery. Until its final defeat in 1694, Palmares repelled hundreds of colonial and Portuguese military assaults. Despite its defeat, the spirit of the *quilombo* lived on. Over a century later in 1809 a group of Aja-Fon and Yoruba slaves ran away from sugar plantations in Bahia and formed a *quilombo* from which they attacked a nearby village to get food. They controlled the village of Nazaré for several months before being defeated by troops sent from the capital.

In contrast with the United States, where slaves' direct knowledge of Africa was minimal after a generation or two, nearly every slave community in Spanish, Portuguese, and French America had members within it who spoke African languages, practiced African religions, played African musical instruments, cooked food in the style they knew in Africa, organized their families and their gender relations according to the ways of their homeland. As late as 1864 Cuban colonial authorities thwarted a slave rebellion intended to kill all the whites. The Spanish court where the conspirators were tried was compelled to bring in translators because the defendants only knew their African language.

Another factor contributing to the likelihood of slave revolts – and definitely feeding the paranoia of the planter class – was that slaves, along with free people of color, far outnumbered whites in many areas. In Brazil, by 1808, slaves made up 38 percent of the total population of about three million, with the rest spread fairly evenly among whites and free people of color. That meant that in Brazil 63 percent of the population was comprised of slaves, former slaves, or the descendants of slaves. In the Caribbean islands slaves and people of color far outnumbered whites: Saint-Domingue in 1789 had 459,277 slaves and free people of color, and only 30,831 whites. Other French islands such as Martinique and Guadeloupe had similar ratios. Over half of Cuba's population in the mid-nineteenth century was slaves and free people of color, out-numbering the whites. The sheer number of non-whites afforded cover for runaways and left slave owners in constant fear of revolts.

The Caribbean society with the largest number of slave revolts, Jamaica, had 310,000 slaves and free coloreds in 1800, compared to 30,000 whites, while in 1834 the divide between the two groups had grown to 356,200 to 20,000. Jamaica had more slave revolts than all other British islands combined, and, with the exception of the Haitian Revolution, involved more slaves in uprisings than any other Caribbean island. The sugar economy on Jamaica was very dynamic, resulting in large numbers of estates. When planters established new sugar plantations, they imported hundreds of slaves all at once to stock it, usually directly from Africa. The arrival of a shipload of African slaves lent itself to violent uprisings, often sweeping neighboring plantations as well and sometimes involving thousands of slaves.

In Spanish America, especially Peru and Mexico, systems of forced labor varied. Indigenous communities were required to contribute laborers to the haciendas, while maintaining residence in their own towns, or, more commonly, entered into a kind of widespread sharecropping relationship with Creole or Spanish landowners. In addition, many Indian towns entered fairly easily into the market economy the colonists established, since such a method for buying and selling foodstuffs, crafts, and labor was consistent with practices of the pre-colonial era. As the decline in indigenous population lessened in the late seventeenth and eighteenth centuries, more Indians and mestizos were available for work and became incorporated into the religious, political, and economic life of the Spanish cities and towns.

This extensive discussion of slavery and labor systems is important to establish the basis for the onset and the outcome of independence movements in Latin America. In the early years of the nineteenth century there was discontent with the rule of the Iberian monarchs, but very little outright opposition. Independence was not on the agenda anywhere. Even the most rabidly anti-colonial Creoles were aware that the extreme differences in class and access to wealth would affect any major upheaval. In addition, the huge numbers of people living and working under conditions of coerced labor on plantations, rural estates, and in the cities, who were of Indian, African, and mixed-race backgrounds, far outnumbered the Creole elite. Nonetheless, the Creoles protested their suffocation under the colonial monopoly and the humiliation they suffered at the hands of the *peninsulares* and colonial authorities, fully realizing that they needed the support of the masses if they hoped to launch a rebellion.

The merchants and planters of Latin America complained that the Crown prevented their access to political office, imposed taxes, fines, and petty restrictions from afar, limited the markets with which they could trade, and sent corrupt and inefficient colonial agents to lord over them. Although grievances against the British in North America were similar to those in the Latin American colonies, the outcome of the two revolutionary wars was very different. Slavery was abolished in Spanish America in the wake of independence, as a necessary condition for conscripting an army of adequate size and strength to combat the Spanish. By contrast, the republicans who shaped the new United States sidestepped the question of abolition for a hundred years, only to have it divide the states in civil war from 1861 to 1865, or what some historians have called the "second American revolution."

The Sugar Colony of Saint-Domingue

In a completely unexpected turn of events, the struggle for Latin America's independence can be traced to the sugar-producing island of Saint-Domingue. As a French possession, accounts of the slave revolt on Saint-Domingue, usually referred to as the Haitian Revolution, have warranted only a marginal role in histories of Spanish and Portuguese America. It should hold a more central place because its importance to the narrative of independence in the Americas is indisputable. First, the slave revolt on Saint-Domingue represented most graphically the limitations of the Enlightenment and the revolutionary ideals of *liberté, equalité,* and *fraternité* that were so central to the anti-colonial and anti-monarchical designs of Latin America's Creole elite. Secondly, the slave insurgents did what no other independence struggle in the Americas had done before it, or would afterward. They secured their independence by proclaiming their own freedom, a move that laid bare the prevailing hypocrisy of the white elites' notion of sovereignty for slaveholders, but not for slaves. For their audacity the Haitians paid a dear price. The only black republic of America was isolated, invaded, boycotted, embargoed, and in every way undermined and punished for its revolution. The racism and subterfuge of the European colonial powers of Spain, France, and England, as well as hostility from the young US republic, set the standard for the world's policy toward Haiti in the revolutionary and post-revolutionary era. Finally, the specter of slave revolts and the brutality of the uprising and subsequent war on all sides served as a brake on independence movements in other slaveholding societies, especially Cuba, Santo Domingo, Puerto Rico, and Brazil.

At the time, Saint-Domingue, one of the smallest of France's possessions in the late eighteenth century, was the largest sugar producer in the Americas, surpassing Brazil and Jamaica. Sugar was planted, tended, harvested, and shipped entirely by men, women, and children who worked under some of the most abhorrent, inhumane, and life-threatening conditions of any slave society. In addition to a large number of slaves, the island population was divided into three castes comprised of a tiny group of whites (*grands blancs*) who held all the power and much of the property and lived mostly in France; lesser whites (*petits blancs*) who held local political office and maintained the militia, worked as artisans and small entrepreneurs, and resented the *grands blancs*; and a third group of free persons of color. In Saint-Domingue, the slaves were very African, and the planters very European. Mulattos, meanwhile, controlled nearly all property and wealth not in the hands of large planters, and were for that reason despised by less affluent whites. The mulattos represented many generations of descendants of the widespread practice of intercourse between slave women and white men. They had obtained their freedom due to their master's guilt or generosity, or were skilled laborers who had purchased their freedom. As punishment for their hard work, thrift, and ultimate prosperity, they were subjected to a humiliating and endless set of petty restrictions designed to keep them "in their place."

The revolutionary events in France in 1789 rumbled in waves onto the colonies, affecting each caste in a different way, but the cumulative effect was as a match to a powder keg. When revolution broke out in France, overturning the monarchy, the planters of Saint-Domingue immediately cheered, since they saw the revolution – especially the pronouncements in favor of greater commercial freedom – as a way to end the colonial monopoly and thus further enrich themselves. From 1789 until 1791 the island men of property and standing argued and negotiated with each other, and with the political clubs of Paris, over the distribution of economic and political rights, especially the granting of full equality to mulattos, and even began to broach the issue of the abolition of slavery.

The Slave Revolt

In 1791 a slave revolt led by Boukman, a voodoo priest, erupted in the north of the island, spread in three days to the south, and soon enveloped the entire colony, pushing hostilities between mulattos and whites, the homeland and the colony, to the backseat. Given the brutality of the slave system, it was no wonder that the uprising was from the beginning extremely bloody. From 1791 until the end of the revolts and the war with France (and other European powers), hundreds of thousands of blacks on the island died. They fought with abandon at first and then as a disciplined army under the leadership of former slaves turned military strategists, since as the campaign unfolded returning to slavery became the most repellent of all options. No part of the island and no section of the population, slave or free, man, woman or child, was left untouched. In the few accounts that have survived, written exclusively by planters, there is repeated mention of fighting by female slaves and the ferociousness of these women in battle (Figure 3.2).

By May 1794 the uprising was under the skillful leadership of Toussaint L'Overture (1743–1803), a former slave who had learned to read and write and studied both

Figure 3.2 *Neg Mawon* or *Marron Inconnnu* (The Runaway Slave) is a sculpture located across from the National Palace in Port-au-Prince, Haiti. It was designed by Albert Mangones in 1959. (Tiana Markova-Gold photo)

Enlightenment philosophy and military tactics. His task, however, was overwhelming, since Toussaint and his army of former slaves found themselves not only facing the planters' small militia, but also caught in the international intrigue among world powers – all of whom wanted to meddle in this war to obtain some advantage. Spain supported the slave uprising in hopes of winning back the French colony and joining it to Santo Domingo on the eastern part of the island, from which it had split off a century earlier. Fearing the revolt would spread to other slave societies in the Caribbean and the mainland United States, Britain jumped in on the side of the Saint-Domingue whites, while the US looked on nervously and refused to admit any ships from the French colonies to southern ports lest word of the rebellion reach the slaves in the US.

The slave revolt triumphed and Toussaint tried to reorganize the plantations and convince former slaves to return to their jobs so that sugar sales could generate sufficient revenue to rebuild the country. But political intrigue among former planters and mulattos and resistance from ex-slaves to return to the hated plantation routine eventually stymied the country's progress. General Napoleon Bonaparte (1769–1821), the new leader of the French Republic, recognized Toussaint as "captain-general" of the colony, only to betray him shortly thereafter, ordering an invasion to restore the rule of the white planters, a move that won full support from the United States and England. French property holders, whose goal was the overthrow of the French monarchy and the installation of men of business to run society, found themselves in a quandary. At first France's revolutionary government had denounced slavery, but the property-holding "revolutionaries" then remembered their bank accounts. It had been on the backs of slaves on distant sugar estates that the new class of French capitalists had grown rich, and it was this wealth that had emboldened them to overthrow the decadent monarchy. The bourgeoisie now had bills to pay at home, armies to outfit, and peasants, shopkeepers, and the entire emerging middle class clamoring for an end to the heavy taxes. Without the profits from sugar-producing islands, based on the servitude of slaves who worked the plantations, republican France was in jeopardy. There was, of course, no end to the justification for this double standard. Supporters of Saint-Domingue's slave system from among the revolutionaries in Paris argued that "these coarse men [the blacks] are incapable of knowing liberty and enjoying it with wisdom," and as such need to be held in bondage until such time as they understand.[10] Ultimately, the white governments of Europe and America chose to protect their property, inanimate and human alike, rather than extend "the rights of man" to blacks.

Probably no other action more belied racial and class solidarity than the duplicity of the imperial powers' alliance with France. Although nearly at war with Napoleon's armies throughout Europe, England found the French army preferable to the enlightened Toussaint L'Ouverture, while the US, only just free of its own colonial oppression, opted to ally with the colonial powers of England and France rather than give aid to Saint-Domingue's anti-colonial struggle. It was, in fact, in their views toward the Haitian Revolution that North America's revolutionary leaders demonstrated the limits of their Enlightenment philosophy. In 1791 George Washington (1732–99) urged that the new United States republic come to France's aid to "crush the alarming insurrection of the Negroes in St. Domingo." Thomas Jefferson in 1799 referred to

Toussaint L'Ouverture and the other leaders of the slave uprising as "the cannibals of the terrible Republic."

The Revolution Betrayed

In 1802 Napoleon's brother-in-law General Charles Leclerc (1772–1802), leading a force of 20,000 soldiers including Swiss and Polish conscripts, launched an invasion of Saint-Domingue with the intention of re-establishing the colonial empire. He then captured Toussaint and sent him to France, where the latter died in prison on April 7, 1803. With the full support of its European and US allies, the Napoleonic army slaughtered the insurgents, only to find themselves in turn defeated both by a combination of blacks' resistance and disease, especially yellow fever. Leclerc died of disease, as did thousands of his soldiers. Succeeding armies fought on, racking up tremendous losses, untold atrocities, and expenses so massive that Napoleon sold the huge Louisiana territory to the US to raise revenue to defray his military losses. The French forces lagged in the face of untiring assaults from the black army under the leadership of Jean-Jacques Dessalines (1758–1806), a skillful military officer of dubious integrity who had fought with Toussaint, had at one point betrayed him to support Leclerc, and then returned to the rebels' side against the French. French invaders found themselves facing a guerrilla force they could not pin down. The term "guerrilla" (small war) had been coined in Spain during Napoleon's invasion and occupation of the country. There, irregular bands of Spanish fighters attacked the occupiers and beat them, just like Dessalines' army on the other side of the ocean.

In the 22 months that Napoleon's army battled on the island, it had lost over 40,000 troops. As the army retreated to the coast, its soldiers destroyed the island, setting fire to cane fields, leveling towns and villages, and killing every man, woman, and child they encountered. Fearing that the news of the successful slave rebellion would spread to their other Caribbean colonies (news had already reached Guadeloupe and inspired a revolt), the French government had ordered the military to eliminate every black who had tasted freedom. In January 1804 Dessalines declared victory, renamed the new country Haiti (supposedly its Arawak name of old), tore the white middle from the French tricolor flag and raised the red and blue banner of the new nation. Whether the small white square, added later, bearing a coat of arms symbolizes the reduced status of whites is only speculative. In a few short years Haiti moved from the most productive land in the Caribbean to an impoverished, ecologically ruined outpost whose population was afforded no way to rebuild a new economy on the ashes of the destroyed sugar monoculture. Universally illiterate, devoid of agricultural and technological know-how, exhausted from a war that had taken thousands of lives and nearly all the young, able-bodied men, the remainder of Haiti's people turned to digging in the soil with sticks to eke out a subsistence.

Although the leaders of slaveholding societies attempted to prevent tales of the Haitian revolt from spreading to their own lands and inspiring similar actions, the events on the French island spread rapidly throughout the Caribbean. Laurent Dubois's history of the impact of the Haitian Revolution in the Caribbean, aptly entitled *Avengers of the New World*, tells of many instances wherein news about Haiti and the struggle of the slaves there served as both a battle cry of freedom and an instrument for the spread of Enlightenment ideology among slaves. For Latin America's Creole elite the lesson of the Haitian Revolution was clear: insurgency against a colonial power was a risky business. Among planters in the US, the opinion was much the same. President Jefferson's secretary of state Albert Gallatin (1761–1849) argued against entering into trade with the newly liberated Haiti, even going so far as to say that the right of self-determination should be denied to other peoples on occasion, especially if the population was not white.

Brazil's Independent Empire

Like their counterparts throughout the Americas, Brazilian Creoles were aware of the era's revolutionary movements and shared many of the grievances against the Crown that had prompted change in distant lands. Nonetheless, word of the slave uprising in Saint-Domingue, and the fate of the white planters there, instilled caution, if not out-right fear, among planters who chafed under Portuguese restrictions but were aware that their own society, worked as it was by slave labor, was infused with the same resentment, anger, and potential for widespread rebellion as the former French colony. Conspiracies to overthrow the Portuguese-led government had come and gone in the late eighteenth century, and most were notable for their reluctance to involve the poor, free, or unfree persons in their plans.

Brazil's road to independence began in November 1807 when the Portuguese Court of the House of Braganza fled Napoleon's invading army for the colony in Brazil. Sailing under the protection of their British allies, the monarch and the 10,000 courtiers in his party stopped briefly in Salvador da Bahia on the northeast coast, which they found too cramped and poor, and moved a month later to Rio de Janeiro further south. When the Court arrived in Rio de Janeiro, it elevated the colonial capital to the status of seat of the empire. Even when the Portuguese military managed to drive Napoleon's army from Portugal, the future King João VI (1767–1826) remained in Brazil, possibly reluctant to trade Rio's tropical splendor for Lisbon. Finally on December 16, 1815, after spending 13 years in Brazil, the Prince Regent declared that Brazil had equal status with the homeland, joining them into a single united kingdom. Six years later, under threat from the Lisbon Cortes and according to the mandates of the new Portuguese constitution, which stated that he would lose his imperial throne entirely, João VI returned to Portugal, leaving behind his son, Pedro (1798–1834), as the Prince Regent of Brazil. A little less than half of the Court and military that had accompanied the king to Brazil a decade earlier returned with him.

In 1822 the Portuguese Cortes sought to end the dual kingdom status and recon-stitute Lisbon as the sole center of the empire. It demanded that Dom Pedro give up his throne in Rio and return to Portugal, and that Brazil once again assume its subordinate status. With support from the Brazilian aristocracy – anxious to preserve their considerable landholdings, from which they exported sugar, coffee, and cotton – and with the backing of the British, who were eager to monopolize trade with Brazil, Dom Pedro moved to secure Brazil's autonomy from Portugal. On the banks of the Ipiranga River on September 7, 1822, the monarch declared Brazil's independence with what came to be known as the Cry of Ipiranga: "Independence or Death!" On December 1 the 24-year-old monarch had himself crowned Emperor Pedro I – a title more in keeping with French conqueror Napoleon Bonaparte than anything in Portugal's monarchical tradition. Two years later he promulgated the first constitution. Brazil did not fight a long and bloody war to separate from Portugal, unlike its neighbors in their campaign for independence from Spain. There were small uprisings among Portuguese military units in the northeast who remained loyal to the seat of government in Lisbon, but little open combat. Instead, Brazil experienced smoldering discontent among native-born Brazilian merchants, planters, and lower-level bureaucrats against the privileged and arrogant Portuguese who had elbowed their way to the top of the former colony's economic and political life. This hatred of the Portuguese courtiers and their many allies, especially in urban areas, added to class and regional tensions and eventually disturbed the peace.

The new empire was not without its detractors; by 1830 Dom Pedro I's popularity had begun to wane, due especially to his authoritarian style of governance and lavish lifestyle. Sugar planters in the northeast voiced the greatest discontent with the new government, but felt that their grievances went unheeded by the court in Rio. The planters were losing their share of the international sugar market to the more efficiently produced Cuban variety, a situation compounded by the high cost of slaves, since the 1830 treaty with Britain abolishing the slave trade drove up the price. Merchants, urban entrepreneurs, and liberals were angered at the monarch's favoritism toward Portuguese courtiers, many of whom were seen as nothing more than worthless hangers-on and obstacles in the path of Brazilian autonomy. Moreover, Brazil had suffered a humiliating defeat in a territorial war with Argentina in 1825–8, further undercutting the aspirations of the nationalist Brazilians. In 1831 Dom Pedro I abdicated his throne and returned to Portugal. Like his father, Dom Pedro left behind his son, then five years old, under the protection of a three-man council. The council, or Regency, governed in the name of the emperor until the youth's 14th birthday in 1840, when he assumed the throne as Pedro II (1825–91). Brazil functioned under an independent empire until 1889 when, after finally abolishing slavery in 1888, republican military officers seized the government. The Republic replaced the empire, and the aged Dom Pedro II returned to Portugal with the remnants of his royal court.

Independence in Mexico

Independence in Mexico followed a third course, but with important similarities to the struggles in Haiti and Brazil. In the end, Mexican independence in 1821 was the result of the residual militancy from an 1810 radical peasant uprising, during which hundreds of thousands of Indians and mestizos rose up to demand their rights to land and an end to burdensome taxes. The road to independence began in a small village in the rural country north of the capital, Mexico City. Historian Eric Van Young has pointed out in his book *The Other Rebellion* that the rebellions were entirely rural, never garnering support from urban areas. In 1810 Father Miguel Hidalgo y Costilla (1753–1811), a local priest in the impoverished Indian town of Dolores near Guanajuato, along with Ignacio Allende (1769–1811) and a few other Creole intellectuals, met in secret to plot the overthrow of local Spanish officials. On September 16 Hidalgo rallied thousands of local peasants, mostly Indians and *castas*, in the cause of independence, under the banner of the Virgin of Guadalupe. They marched en masse on the provincial capital of Guanajuato. Hidalgo's exact demands were unclear and his military tactics even more so, but as a priest he commanded a huge following. Priests formed a part of what historian Stuart Voss refers to as the mainstay of colonial society, organized under the "traditional triad of the family, parish, and community" and dominated by the "patriarch, priest and local official."[11] Hidalgo drew on his prestige to pursue his belief that the Church should serve the people and take the side of the downtrodden.

The intensity of Hidalgo's anti-monarchical stance, combined with the violence of the peasant crowds aroused by his message, horrified the Creole elite, many of whom had initially supported the anti-colonial cause. When Father Hidalgo rang the church bell in Dolores to signal the beginning of the revolt, it seemed that only impoverished Indians and mestizos responded, sending the anti-colonial elite scurrying back into their houses to bar their doors. Before the revolt came to an end and Father Hidalgo was captured when his march faltered outside Mexico City, he had managed to separate from Allende's army and lose control of many of his peasant followers; he also proved unable to control widespread looting and killing in the countryside. Moreover, the professional Spanish army outmatched the priest's forces of over 100,000 peasants, armed only with machetes, sticks, and crude homemade weapons. Hidalgo's head, along with Allende's and those of other rebel commanders, were posted in metal cages at the corners of the entrances to Mexico City. The ferocity of the rebellion was matched only by the government's response. Hidalgo's revolt clearly demonstrated the intensity of class and racial antagonisms that the colonial regime had engendered, but lacked planning, strategy, and organization.

In the months after Hidalgo's death another priest, José María Morelos y Pavón (1765–1815), took up the standard of rebellion. Unlike Hidalgo, Father Morelos defined a revolutionary program calling for independence from Spain, the creation of a republican government in which all the Mexican people would participate, the abolition of slavery, and elimination of divisions between races and ethnicities. Though a priest, Morelos recognized the suffering of the poor at the hands of the Church. He called for termination of the Church's special privileges and the compulsory tithe exacted from the poor parishioners, and demanded partition of the large estates, to be distributed among the people. If Hidalgo's uprising had shocked wealthy Creoles, Morelos' political program increased their hostility. Through four campaigns in which the insurgents drew together thousands of followers – and then lost as many in the face of assaults from the Spanish military – Morelos's forces roamed throughout the western coastal and central areas of the country. Eventually, as a result of weariness, lack of military materiel, and betrayal, Morelos retreated in the face of a reinforced Spanish army. He was captured outside Cuernavaca in 1815, tried, placed before a firing squad and shot. As a mass uprising destined to redress the years of wrong and the cumulative grievances of the poor and downtrodden, the Mexican independence movement came to an end. In its later reincarnation, it would emerge under the careful military and political control of the Creole elite, content to replace Spanish tyranny with native-born Mexican tyranny, in the name of an independent Mexico.

Ironically enough, it was events in Spain that precipitated revolt in the colonies. In 1812 the Spanish Cortes (the advisory council to the throne) installed a liberal constitution, putting into place a program similar to what the revolutionaries in Mexico had demanded. Thus the Spanish colonial elite, representing the interest of the Crown in Mexico, no longer benefited from their ties with the Crown and joined with the Creoles to crush the masses and declare independence. In 1821, under the leadership of General Agustín de Iturbide (1763–1824), a military officer whose promotion to general resulted from his distinguished service in repressing the Hidalgo and Morelos uprisings, Mexico separated from Spain. General Iturbide elevated himself to emperor in May 1822, a position he was able to assume as a reward from the families of property and standing for declaring the nation independent. The honeymoon was short-lived; the Creole elite, who had been too fearful to align with the Mexican masses earlier, now found themselves out of power completely and once again subservient to a new authoritarian ruler. Within a year of crowning himself emperor, Iturbide dissolved congress, presided over the arrest of more than 60 political officials, and embarked on a personalist regime until his forced abdication and exile to Italy the next year. Convinced to return in 1824, Iturbide's hope of reclaiming his throne proved illusory. He was captured, court-martialed, and executed.

South American Independence

The pattern of independence wars in Spanish South America was similar to those in Mexico and the Caribbean. Stretching from Cartagena on the Caribbean Sea to Buenos Aires at the mouth of the Rio de la Plata (River Plate), the South American campaigns were led by Creole military officers, many of whom have streets, plazas, cities, and countries named for them today, and whose statues – nearly always a figure mounted on horseback – adorn the plazas of cities and parks. Collectively, their exploits have earned them the title "Liberator." Foremost among them was Simón Bolívar (1783–1830), liberator of the North, an elite Creole whose idealism and belief in republican values, learned in the best schools and universities of America and Europe, came into conflict with his distrust of the masses and pushed him ultimately to rely on military solutions. He led armies, penned letters, shouted proclamations, and defeated the royalists on long marches through the lands that became Venezuela, Colombia, Panama, and Ecuador. Andrés Bello (1781–1865) was one of the main influences on Bolívar's intellectual formation. The two traveled to England together in 1810 where, under Bello's tutelage (despite the fact that the two were nearly the same age), the future liberator was introduced to the intellectual currents coursing through Europe's salons and political gatherings of the era. Upon their return, Bello remained in the world of politics and scholarship, while Bolívar opted for the military road. Possibly one of the leading intellectuals of his day, Bello formulated many of the theoretical justifications for Latin American independence. Outliving most of the military leaders, Bello died of old age in Chile after a successful career as a scholar and statesman. He left behind an inspiring set of works calling for Latin American political and cultural sovereignty.

The liberator of the South was José San Martín (1778–1850), an Argentine general who led an army made up of former slaves and poor peasants on a heroic march across the Andes to defeat the Spanish royalists in Chile at the Battle of Chacabuco. He then marched on to Lima and declared independence in July 1821. Others were Bernardo O'Higgins (1778–1842), San Martín's subordinate whom he left to drive the Spanish from Chile, and Antonio José de Sucre (1795–1830), Bolívar's closest lieutenant, who led the campaign in Bolivia. The Latin American masses fought with the liberating armies; and even at times with the Spanish royalists. Their loyalties depended on very local factors, such as promises of freedom, waivers of prison or debt sentences, pay, force, the reputation of a general, personal loyalty, or the promise of food and clothing. From beginning to end, the liberation proceeded unevenly, from 1810 when the Creoles of Venezuela openly defied the Spanish, until the last royalist army was defeated at Callao (the port serving Lima) in 1826. The rebellions were ideological, political, and sometimes personal. When they were over, America was free from Spain but the continent was in shambles.

In contrast to events in Mexico, where the uprisings began tumultuously with thousands of poor mestizos and Indians marching on Spanish garrisons behind the banner of the Virgin of Guadalupe, the tenor of revolution in Spanish America proceeded more slowly. The spark came from Napoleon's 1807 invasion of Spain and deposition of the Spanish Crown. In response, many key colonial capitals formed *juntas* – local councils or assemblies – to govern in the absence of the king; or in his name, depending on the royalist sympathies of the particular junta. For example, the Montevideo junta, formed in 1808, was loyal to the king and sought to carry on the monarchy even in the face of the monarch's deposition. Conversely, juntas in Lima, Buenos Aires, Quito, Santiago de Chile, Caracas and other cities sought to govern autonomously from the Crown, or at a healthy distance. Most juntas bypassed colonial officials, changed rules that placed the colonies in economic and political subservience to the Crown, and rolled back measures the colonists most abhorred. They opened the ports to trade with ships from many countries, eliminated the sales tax (*alcabala*), abolished the slave trade, and ended the Church's right to exact tribute. In some areas the power of the Church was dramatically curtailed, Spanish clergy and officials loyal to the Crown were expelled, and steps were taken to separate the affairs of the state from the Church. Both from Spain and from outposts in the Americas, the loyalists responded. At places such as Buenos Aires, Asunción, and intensely royalist Montevideo, they refused to accept the authority of the new Creole juntas.

For nearly two decades armies fought up and down the expanse of South America, gaining and losing ground until final victory. The two best-known liberators, Bolívar and San Martín, despite differences of approach, attempted to mold the disparate states of the continent united into a loose federation. They failed. San Martín resigned his command and left for self-imposed exile in France after having been victorious in liberating most of the Southern Cone. Bolívar went on to help his closest lieutenant, Antonio de Sucre, win at the battle of Ayacucho in today's Peru, but stood by as the latter claimed much of modern-day Bolivia as his own.

From 1826 to 1828 Bolívar pursued his plan to unite Spanish America into a federated republic. His attempts to form a constitution met with opposition from regional forces, since the battlefield of the independence struggles was extended over extremely rugged terrain separated by thousands of miles. At one point Bolívar ruled as dictator in his attempt to quell intrigue and splits among and between the generals who had defeated the Spaniards. This move proved disastrous, generating as it did even greater distrust and hostility toward the Liberator. Bolívar, to his fault, was not a warm and charismatic leader who engendered great personal loyalty. He could be cold, aloof, ruthless, and his aristocratic demeanor sowed distrust among the hardscrabble troops and officers who came up through the ranks of local armies. Likewise, he appeared to trust few others, and refused to share power and ultimate command of the army with San Martín, or anyone else. He was mismatched with his army of lower-class recruits, many of whom fought in return for the promise of social reforms, access to land, abolition of slavery, and an end to the forced payment of tribute. In 1830 he stepped down from his post as leader of the constitutional process and chose to go into exile. Before leaving, however, he fell sick and died in December, a few months before his 47th birthday. Even as Bolívar lay dying, he was dealt two mortal political blows that no doubt undercut his resolve to live on. Ecuador pulled out of the fragile union he was attempting to form and Venezuela betrayed him, refusing even to allow him to return to the country of his birth. In June Bolívar had sent Antonio Sucre, in a last-ditch effort to save a unified Gran Colombia, but Sucre was killed by an unknown assassin, probably a political opponent of the federation, on his way back to report to Bolívar the news of his failure. Over the next few years the entire unity plan dissolved.

At the mid-point of the century Latin America stood in shambles (Map 3.5). The long and bloody conflict had exacted a tremendous toll on its people, fragile political institutions, and already weak economy, as well as on the social cohesion of the new states. Trade and communication was disrupted, mines were flooded and equipment destroyed, livestock slaughtered or ill-fed and dispersed. There were few stable governments, no uniform and trusted currency, inflation was rampant, capital had disappeared, property was confiscated, and economies lay in ruins. Apart from Indian villages, the majority of people lacked titles to land and few non-Indian inhabitants of rural areas had the skills required to manage their holdings and restore trade lines to markets. Similar to the train of events in Haiti after independence, individual peasants and rural Indian communities attempted to return to the pre-independence way of life. No central government capable of uniting the factions of generals emerged, and the dream of a United States of Latin America dissolved. After Bolívar's death, San Martín despaired of leading recalcitrant Creoles to carry out reforms, such as ending slavery, dividing land among the peasantry, and controlling the Church. He left Peru after the

Latin America in 1830

Santo Domingo gained its independence from
Spain in 1821. Occupied by Haiti in 1822,
it finally regained its independence in 1844.

Mexico
Veracruz
Cuba – Spanish
Puerto Rico – Spanish
Belize – British   Jamaica – British

The United Provinces of Central
America was dissolved by 1839

Trinidad – British
Caracas
British Guiana was founded in 1831
by uniting Berbice, Demerara, and Essequibo.
Bogotá
Guiana – French
Quito
Surinam – Dutch

Lima

Salvador

Rio de Janeiro
São Paulo
Asunción

States with date of independence

Argentine Confederacy 1810–1816

Santiago

Mexico – 1821
United Provinces of Central America – 1823
Haiti – 1803
Gran Colombia – 1819–1830
Peru – 1821
Bolivia – 1825
Brazil – 1822
Paraguay – 1811
Uruguay – 1828
United Provinces of La Plata – 1816
Chile – 1817

Montevideo
Buenos Aires

Patagonia

Map 3.5   Latin America in 1830. (Courtesy Cathryn L. Lombardi and John V. Lombardi, *Latin American History: A Teaching Atlas* ca. 1983. By permission of The University of Wisconsin Press.)

fall of Callao, retired to Europe and never returned to the lands he had fought to liberate from Spain. Other military commanders and their Creole allies divided the spoils, and eventually their strongholds emerged as the countries of Latin America. For the masses who had fought for independence against Spanish tyranny, the face of power looked the same. Whites born in the Americas dictated to the masses, just as whites born in Spain had done in the past.

Post-independence Changes in Racial and Gender Status

Women had participated in the independence armies, moving with the troops, preparing food, sewing and repairing uniforms. They worked as nurses, messengers, spies, and sometimes as soldiers (see Box 3.1). Some women joined the effort out of ideological conviction; others did so because they needed protection in the face of the marauding army of the other side, and many were forced into sexual servitude against their will. The economic and political instability that permeated the era mitigated against steady employment. When men joined the ranks of the military as a way of earning a wage or being assured of daily rations, women stayed behind and took jobs the men vacated, or managed the crops on landholdings ranging in size from tiny plots to large estates. As frequently has occurred in times of war, women filled the gap in production left by men, and in so doing came away from the war with a heightened sense of self-worth, stronger incorporation into the national body, and demands for greater equality. Although nationalist sentiments and the hardships of battle opened up new roles for women, including the first murmurings of female suffrage, at war's end patriarchy was reasserted. The fragmented states of the post-colonial era fell under the governance of powerful male leaders, cutting off any claims for sharing power with the subordinate classes, races, and genders that had attempted to carve out a space for equal treatment under the law.

Box 3.1   1812 Cochabamba

It was on May 27, 1812 that the women of Cochabamba fought the Spanish army. In commemoration of their heroism Bolivia today marks May 27 as Mothers' Day:

> From Cochabamba, many men have fled. Not one woman. On the hillside, a great clamor. Cochabamba's plebeian women, at bay, fight from the center of a circle of fire. Surrounded by five thousand Spaniards, they resist with battered tin guns and a few arquebuses; and they fight to the last yell, whose echoes will resound throughout the long war for independence. Whenever his army weakens, General Manuel Belgrano will shout those words which never fail to restore courage and spark anger. The general will ask his vacillating soldiers: "*Are the women of Cochabamba present?*"

From Nathaniel Aguirre, *Juan de la Rosa*. Quoted in Galeano, *Memory of Fire: II. Faces and Masks*, p. 106.

One of the main accomplishments of independence was the abolition of slavery, everywhere but Brazil, whose independence from Portugal had not precipitated armed conflict. Because many slaves had taken advantage of automatic manumission in return for joining the army of either Spain or the independence forces, when peace was declared the system of slavery was far too undermined to return. Bolívar's commitment to abolition is said to have come from his contact in Haiti with Alexandre Sabès Pétion (1770–1818), a mixed-race ally of General Dessalines. As president of the southern half of the country after Dessalines' death in 1806, with Henri Christophe (1767–1820) claiming the northern half, Pétion is known for his (only partially successful) attempts to distribute land to the peasants and to establish a democratic government. Pétion welcomed Bolívar in 1816 as the latter was returning, destitute, from exile in Jamaica on his way to the northern coast of South America to relaunch the campaign. For the seven ships, 250 men, guns and provisions that Pétion provided Bolívar for his campaign, the Haitian leader demanded that Bolívar liberate the slaves in whatever land he took from Spain.

A final accomplishment of the independence struggle was a new sense of nationalism, or what one might call "Americanism." The Creoles no longer saw themselves as tied to Europe and its institutions of domination, especially the Church. They enacted laws to separate Church and state; seize church property; install public, non-religious educational institutions; and end the practice of forced tithing for Crown and Church. For the remainder of the nineteenth century Church and state wrangled over the latter's attempts to hold ecclesiastical authority in check and to formulate a secular doctrine to govern the civil societies of the new republics.

The Last Holdout of Slavery in Spanish America

From the northern border of Mexico to Tierra del Fuego, Latin America had thrown off the shackles of colonialism. Most telling, however, were the places that remained in the hands of Spain: Cuba and Puerto Rico in the Caribbean. In fact, these valuable sugar-producing islands only entered into importance, to Spain and to the world economy in general, as a result of the demise of Haiti. The chaos and devastation Haiti endured, and the impoverished state in which it was left after independence, was sufficient to consolidate the hold of slavery and colonialism in the remaining, and nearby, Spanish possessions. In her history of race and nationalism historian Ada Ferrer summarizes the sentiments of the Cuban planters as they absorbed the fate of their counterparts on Saint-Domingue: "Cuba, they said, would either be Spanish or it would be African; it would be Spanish, or it would be another Haiti. For those with the power to decide, the answer came without hesitation: Cuba would remain a Spanish colony."[12] It would take Cuba and Puerto Rico until century's end to raise the banner of independence, and even then the struggle would be long, difficult, and ultimately incomplete. When the war ended in 1898, Cuba and Puerto Rico found themselves free from Spain but in the grip of a new power, the United States.

Slavery lasted longer in Cuba and Brazil than in any other American society, for slightly differing reasons. In Brazil, slavery went unquestioned until the early nineteenth century. The debate over slavery that raged in the capitals of Europe, North America, and in other Latin American nations went largely unheard in Brazil until several decades into the century. Up and down the continent slavery had ended by the mid-nineteenth century as a part of their struggles for independence from Spain and following the Civil War in the United States. Abolition in Cuba, Puerto Rico, and Brazil stalled for several reasons: the peculiar course of the independence struggle; the extreme dependence on slaves to carry out all productive work in these societies; the flexibility in the system, whereby many slaves obtained their freedom or lived separately from owners who rented them out and took a share of the slave's wages as compensation; and the coexistence, especially in the Caribbean, of slavery alongside Asian indentured servants.

Although the Spanish Court set the date of final abolition as 1888, slavery in Cuba had ended in practice, if not in law, two years earlier. Abolition came about, as the planters had predicted, as a result of the struggle for independence, but without the fireworks that characterized the Haitian Revolution. Instead, a remarkable coalition of whites, free people of color, and ex-slaves fought together in an army against Spanish colonial forces in three stages over 30 years, from 1868 until 1898. As historians have noted, 60 percent of the rank and file and 40 percent of the commissioned officers in the Cuban independence army were Afro-descendant. Had Cuba been able to remain autonomous, and had the US military not intervened and recolonized the island at the behest of powerful sugar trusts and politicians, Cuba may well have emerged as a remarkable multiracial society, governed by a diverse range of whites, blacks, and people of mixed race, including a large number of Chinese who had been brought as indentured

Box 3.2   Modern-day "slavery"

Although formal, legally sanctioned, state-sponsored slavery ceased to exist nearly everywhere in the world by the end of the nineteenth century, many workers still live in conditions so coercive as to be considered a new "modern" slave system. In 2005 the Brazilian government estimated that 25,000 people were held in unfree labor conditions, but independent observers have placed that number far higher. Hardly spoken of around the world, nonetheless the Swiss-based International Labor Organization calculates that at the beginning of the twenty-first century 27 million people are held in slave and "slave-like" conditions, bound to jobs and lands they cannot leave, tricked, or coerced, sold and captured into sex-slavery throughout the world. The largest numbers are in the Middle East, Pakistan, sub-Saharan Africa, and at least 10,000 in the United States. Although history has ample records and analyses of ancient slavery in Greece, Rome, Egypt, China and much of Africa, along with the Atlantic slave trade and New World slavery from the fifteenth through the nineteenth centuries, very little mention is made of slavery in the contemporary world, despite the remarkable fact that more people are held today in coerced labor conditions from which they cannot leave than at any time in history.[13]

servants in the mid-nineteenth century. Frequently lost in the explanations of the Spanish American war – which is generally understood as an act of imperialist aggression engineered by yellow journalists and powerful industrialists – is the fact that neither the US, which was entering into the height of its Jim Crow era, nor Europe, where racist eugenicist theories justified white colonialism, wanted to allow Cuba to thrive as a successful multiracial republic. The planter elite clung to their colonial status. We will take up the Cuban and Puerto Rican independence movement in Chapter 5.

Latin America in a Changing World Order

European merchants eyed warily the developments in Latin America as conflict turned to peace, and the independent republics struggled to rebuild. Great Britain's influence was strongest in Brazil, because of Portugal's traditionally close alliance with Britain. For example, in 1808 the Portuguese court had earned Napoleon's enmity by refusing to bar British ships from its ports; the departure of the House of Braganza to Brazil was carried out under the protection of the British fleet. When in 1825 Portugal demanded £2 million sterling (equal to about $7 million) as compensation for the loss of its colony, British banks had secured the loan, thereby sealing the new nation's fate in much the same way that Portugal's had been sealed by the many agreements tying Portugal to England since the 1703 Treaty of Methuen.

In response to growing pressure at home, England ended the transatlantic slave trade in 1830; trading in slaves was seen as the most abhorrent aspect of slavery by a growing body of abolitionists making their case before the British Parliament, in street rallies, and in a barrage of newspaper articles and pamphlets. England in turn required Brazil to end the external slave trade in return for favorable commercial agreements and full recognition of the latter's independence. Although the slave trade continued – with the full knowledge of the Brazilian government – the bombardment of ports and seizure of slave ships on the high seas pushed up the price of slaves, contributing to the eventual demise of the system. After several years of back-and-forth negotiating, Brazil finally outlawed the external slave trade on March 13, 1830. In an attempt to stem the ongoing trade in contraband slaves the following year, the government passed a law freeing any slave who entered Brazil, a rule that was admittedly hard to enforce.

Independence from Spain had fulfilled the dreams of the prosperous Latin American Creoles. Merchants began to ship minerals and agricultural products, cotton, sugar, tobacco, henequen, beef, wool, and other goods out on British ships, which docked at ports where the British were installing better facilities, financed by British banks, with an export–import trade insured by the superior resources and organization of British financial houses. The planters and *latifundistas* saw no reason to wrest trade from the British, since they profited so handsomely from the exchange. They called it Progress, or Civilization. The economies of the newly formed republics, no more than personal territories carved out by victorious generals in some cases, were in dire straits. Given this instability, traditional forms of labor and hierarchy soon re-emerged. The large estates began to produce for export, relying on the work of indebted laborers, many of whom returned to their jobs on the pre-independence haciendas where they had previously toiled. No longer under the restrictions of Spanish colonial rule, the new nations began to establish new markets for their goods.

England's close relationship with Portugal, and subsequently with the independent empire of Brazil as the latter's chief export market, had a contradictory effect on the persistence of slavery. Primarily it was Brazil's lucrative trade in slaves, coffee, and other export commodities that made it an attractive nineteenth-century ally and neocolonial trading partner for Britain, and one the great power eagerly nurtured. Britain exerted its influence in a number of ways, including forcing its own manufactured goods, especially textiles, onto the Brazilian consumer – thereby undermining the thriving domestic textile manufacturing of the colonial period. Paradoxically, while Britain profited from the sale of cheap cotton, wool, and minerals from Brazil – all produced with slave labor – its Parliament was under heavy pressure to end slavery and the slave trade. After Brazil agreed to shut down its trade in slaves in 1830, smuggling continued for at least another two decades and the country accounted for 60 percent of the slave trade from 1811 until it finally came to an end in 1852. Cuba and Puerto Rico absorbed the bulk of the slaves coming into Spanish America; Cuba's slave trade continued until 1867. Thus British citizens were able to purchase inexpensive sugar, coffee, and textiles while denouncing slavery, the practice that kept commodity prices low. The situation is reminiscent of modern-day campaigns in the US and Europe to end slave-like labor conditions in sweatshops, while consumers continue to expect low-priced consumer goods.

Conclusion

The struggle for independence in Latin America and the Caribbean originated with the 1791 slave revolt in the French colony that would become Haiti, and swept through Mexico in fits and starts, culminating in 1821. The armies of the great Liberators, San Martín, Bolívar, Sucre, and others had secured the independence of the rugged, geographically, politically and culturally fragmented Spanish American territories, finally pulling in a reluctant Peru in 1824. Cuba, one of the most important colonies and the jewel of the Caribbean holdings, along with the smaller island of Puerto Rico, remained loyal to Spain until the end of the nineteenth century. Independence arrived in Brazil through the most circuitous of routes, ending in the proclamation of an independent empire in 1822. Brazil's status as a monarchy meant that it did not suffer from the regional fragmentation that plagued the former Spanish colonies. There were a few secessionist movements in some areas, but for the most part Brazil maintained political cohesion, under the rule of slaveholding elites, throughout the nineteenth century.

As Eduardo Galeano points out, independence did very little to improve the lot of the masses because the system that began with the first conquistadores, based on exploitation of the many by the few and centered on large landholdings, remained in place. Brazil worked slaves on its sugar plantations; Argentine *estancieros* raised herds of cattle and sheep; Peru had mines and sugar plantations; Mexico had livestock, mines, henequen (rope), sugar and silver, among a wide variety of export products. Vast estates dotted the Latin American landscape. Fortunes survived the wars of independence intact. Inequalities were not swept away in the fires of revolution, despite the promises of freedom that the Liberators and generals used to entice the masses onto the battlefield. The nineteenth-century debate pitted the legacies of a semi-feudal colonial order – based on corporate holdings, church and state protection of Indian rights – against the emerging doctrine of liberalism rooted in a belief in free trade, low tariffs, and individual rights. Although championed as the epitome of freedom, liberalism did not necessarily benefit the majority, especially Indians.

Independence had left in its wake an economically devastated, politically fractured, and culturally divided continent under pressure to build autonomous states. The post-colonial world stretched ahead, serving as the field upon which the struggle over class, ethnic, gender, racial, and religious tensions would take place.

4 | Fragmented Nationalisms

From his deathbed Simón Bolívar is said to have declared: "America is ungovernable." Whether the Liberator's pessimism stemmed from the remote distances that separated the population of the immense continent or the disparate cultures, languages, ethnicities, and races of its people, or simply the lack of political unity, is not clear. Certainly any or all of these factors were sufficient to give pause to anyone hoping to unite the now sovereign territory. Vast expanses separated the old colonial cities, while new trading centers were geographically remote from one another, separated by impassable mountains, high deserts, and arid plains, linked by unnavigable waterways and rudimentary roads. All of these factors were to some extent responsible for the fragmented states that emerged in the wake of the wars of independence.

This chapter examines nation building during the nineteenth century, with a focus on certain influential political, economic, and cultural forces and trends. Liberating Latin America from Spain was simpler than governing the independent states. Bolívar died on his way into exile in Europe; San Martín died in exile in Paris, never returning to Argentina; while José Gervasio Artigas (1764–1850), a reformist general who had led an army of cowboys in pursuit of land and rights for the peasants on the Uruguay and Argentine border, died in exile in Paraguay. The pitiful disillusion experienced by the "Liberators" has served as rich material for Latin American novelists, but their failures sealed the unenviable fate of the continent's masses.

Searching for Political and Economic Unity

In Latin America, as anywhere in the world, the state-building process did not proceed down the same path nor conform to a single mold. Thus post-colonial Peru or Mexico, Argentina or Colombia were not simply failed variations of the nation-building project long underway in Europe. Florencia Mallon notes that in Europe the concept of freedom, especially the notion of "freeborn men," was shaped in the context of the *lack* of

freedom – colonialism and slavery – that Europe had imposed on subjugated populations around the globe. If Europeans championed "universal" equality and liberty of
ideas for themselves, or if they took pride in their "citizenship" as members of a nation,
they barred access to freedom and democracy for much of the rest of the world, and
most definitely to the people in those areas they directly controlled.

It is appropriate that students understand that many of the people from all social
classes, ethnic and racial groups who participated in the independence wars felt they
were deserving of freedom, equality, and the exercise of sovereignty. Others, however,
in both Europe and America, did not assume that such rights as liberty, equality, and
fraternity should be extended to the masses. Thus, we cannot assume that the failure
to consolidate democratic reforms in the new nations was solely the fault of their
peoples. The fate of post-independence Haiti stands as a case in point, especially the
disdain with which the so-called champions of Enlightenment rights in the United States
and Europe showed toward the former slaves when the latter expressed the same aspirations. According to the eighteenth- and nineteenth-century Enlightenment thinkers,
liberty and equality were concepts reserved for Europeans, and ultimately white
Americans, but denied to the majority of people of color in both North and South America.
The status of elite women complicated the terms of citizenship everywhere, causing the
matter of women's rights to develop as something of a wild card. As we will see in this
and later chapters, gender equality was an inconsistent and incomplete concept in independent America, just as it had been during the colonial era. White women, for example,
could have great power over black slaves or matters of their own household, while at
the same time have no real voice in the management of the broader society.

Economically, independence affected disparate regions differently. Previous trade
routes disappeared, and new towns in secondary regions with new population centers
emerged. These areas had come into existence as a result of the encampment of roam-
ing revolutionary armies that often included women and children, and sometimes
entire communities. Towns grew up near the long supply lines stretching between pre-
existing villages or from urban areas to distant front lines. Some of the recently formed
towns shut down once the army left, while others hung on and morphed into new communities. European and North American demand for sugar, coffee, cacao, and hides
had increased dramatically by mid-century, but it was this external trade that the
new republics were most unprepared to handle. They had no ships, and port facilities
were inadequate; even a supply of hard currency was hard to come by. British, and
some other foreign and domestic entrepreneurs, however, were anxious to step in and
supply the means to further develop Latin America's trade.

New World "Feudalism"

A key feature of post-colonial life that exemplified the nature of class relationships in
Latin America was the progressive concentration of wealth in a few hands, especially
wealth measured in the form of land. In fact, it was in the nineteenth century that the
concept of the *latifundia*, or very large tracts of land, shifted into the vernacular of the

newly independent nations. In much of Latin America land tenure became even more unequal following independence. Land granted to members of the army in reward for service usually ended up in the hands of speculators and powerful local bosses. The latter operated as regional rulers and were referred to as *caudillos*, literally meaning "strongmen." In the backlands of Brazil they were often called "colonels," since they wielded the authority of military chiefs, despite their civilian status. But many *caudillos* were, in fact, former military commanders who derived their prestige and following from the independence wars and the disputes that broke out during the period of instability following the treaties that ended formal hostilities.

Caudillo strongmen came in many varieties: some were more progressive than others, for example José Gregorio Monegas (1791–1858) and his brother José Tadeo Monegas (1785–1868) alternately held the presidency of Venezuela in the 1850s and abolished slavery in 1854, more out of expediency and an (ultimately unsuccessful) attempt to win political support than from a genuine commitment to social equality. A few *caudillos* were known for their nationalist programs, building infrastructure and attempting to strengthen local enterprises. Nonetheless, the general stamp of authoritarianism marked the *caudillo* era. Just as the precise terms for large landholdings varied, so too did the extent to which the *caudillos* controlled their subordinates. In sum, uneven relations of production characterized the era: indebted laborers, called debt peons, produced goods on large rural estates, laboring under conditions more akin to feudalism than capitalism.

Although nineteenth-century estates were self-contained, they were not necessarily self-sufficient. Inventories of haciendas in the interior of Argentina, the remote countryside of Mexico, and many places in between revealed the presence of large quantities of imported luxury and essential goods. According to Argentine historian Carlos Mayo, remote nineteenth-century *estancias* on the pampas had stocks of imported silver and linens from Europe, perfumes and soaps, furniture and household accessories, all of which had long been assumed to be present in wealthy homes in capital cities – but not on distant estates located inland. A single owner or family, employing laborers working at subsistence-level wages, controlled the archetypical estate through autocratic rule. Unlike Cuba and Brazil, labor on the large estates of most of Latin America was free in name, but seldom in practice. Together the *latifundio* system and *minifundios* (smallholdings where peasants worked their own plots and sold their produce to the *latifundista* or at local markets) kept the majority of rural people in conditions of perpetual impoverishment and created a landscape in which large-scale landowners exercised near complete control over rural resources, especially water, and the entire production process (Figure 4.1).

If a map of landholdings in mid-nineteenth century Latin America existed, it would show little or no change from the colonial period. In 1830 in Argentina, for example, 21 million acres of public land was taken over by 500 private individuals, giving them each an estate of about 42,000 acres. By the mid-nineteenth century the Anchorena family controlled 1.5 million acres. Similarly, in northern Mexico the Sanchez Navarro family consolidated and expanded holdings during the independence wars and the long period of strife that followed. By 1848 they controlled 17 haciendas encompassing more

Figure 4.1   Plantation of Senator Vergueiro with house, barns, storage sheds and a row of slave cabins, ca. 1800s. (James C. Fletcher and D. P. Kidder, *Brazil and the Brazilians*)

than 16 million acres of land. An English traveler to Mexico wrote in awe of the incredible wealth of local landowners:

> This beautiful hacienda is 30 leagues in length and 17 in width [about 1,800 square miles], containing in this great space the productions of every climate, from the fir-clad mountains on a level with the volcano of Toluca, to the fertile plains which produce corn and maize; and lower down fields of sugar cane and other productions of the tropics.[1]

These immense estates became self-contained enclaves employing carpenters, black-smiths, bakers, seamstresses, candle-makers, mechanics, and even their own priest or estate chaplain. Wealthy landowners became a fixture on the Latin American land-scape, ruling entire provinces through their own personal armies, enforcing their own laws, collecting taxes from rural peasants who were tied to the land, in debt, illiterate, and ignorant of any rights that distant constitutions might have won for them. The *caudillos* ruled as patriarchs, making all decisions, dispensing "justice," determining what was produced, when and by whom. Most maintained city homes, where their wives and families lived for a part of the year and to which they made occasional trips. Alone in the countryside, far from the restraining eye of the Church, "polite society" and their families, *caudillo* patriarchs took advantage of young women on their estates, sometimes to cook and keep house, or to serve in whatever ways they might desire.

Most workers on plantations and estates did not leave that world their entire lives. They never saw a government official, a city, a church outside the chapel on the estate; never went to school or learned the basic rights of citizenship. Even those who had been freed as payment for serving in the independence armies were confined in a status close to enslavement in Bolivia, Colombia, and rural areas of Argentina once the revolution ended. The majority was bound to the land by virtue of debt to the *patrón*, lack of education and ignorance of life away from the estate, as well as the absence of marketable skills that would allow a worker and his family to make a living in the city. Considering that in the nineteenth century the majority of Latin America's population lived far from urban areas, such isolation was the norm for all but a comparative few. In Mexico, for example, 90 percent of the country's eight million people dwelled in rural areas at the end of the independence wars. Cut off and ignored, the peasantry had little knowledge of, or concern for, events outside their villages, leading lives consumed by desperate attempts to find enough to eat and conserve the resources of a bare livelihood. By the end of the nineteenth century, only 10 percent of Mexican peasants were literate, and the life expectancy of a rural worker stood at 24 years.

Much of the information we have on life in Mexico comes to us from the diaries of the Marquesa Frances Calderón de la Barca (1804–82) who traveled through Mexico in the 1840s and recorded her observations about Mexican life in both rural and urban areas. Born in Scotland, Calderón de la Barca, known as Fanny, and her family moved to Washington DC in the 1830s, where she met and married the Spanish Ambassador to the US, Angel Calderón de la Barca. She traveled with him when he became Ambassador to Mexico in 1839. Her journals and letters were compiled into a book, *Life in Mexico*, published in Boston in 1843 by author, journalist, and Mexico observer William H. Prescott. In 1861, after the death of her husband, Fanny became the governess and companion to the Spanish royal family, and was eventually given the title of *marquesa*.

One of Calderón de la Barca's comments explains the reasons why in the mid-nineteenth century many Mexicans, not just the poor, may have seemed uneducated:

> There are no circulating libraries in Mexico. Books are at least double the price that they are in Europe. There is no diffusion of useful knowledge amongst the people; neither cheap pamphlets nor cheap magazines written for their amusement or instruction; but this is less owing to want of attention to their interests on the part of many good and enlightened men, than to the unsettled state of the country; for the blight of civil war prevents the best systems from ripening.[2]

Depending on the country, era, and/or geographic region and terrain, the center of the landed estate was the Big House, the *casa grande* or *hacienda*. It varied in size, degree of luxury, and accoutrements of wealth and fashion according to the region and prosperity of the landowner. In Brazil it was typically a two-story dwelling, but those in Mexico, Colombia, Argentina, and other places in Latin America were sometimes rambling one-story structures. The house had separate parlors to greet guests, large dining rooms and, occasionally, ballrooms. There were many bedrooms, both for the family and to accommodate travelers who came and stayed on as guests of the *patrón* and his family. The ground floor had a pantry and a kitchen – although kitchens were sometimes separate from the house to contain the smells of butchering game and preparing food. Estates, especially those far from municipalities, often boasted their own chapel where a resident member of the clergy held services in which the family, slaves, and laborers partook according to their station. Many homes had separate or attached small houses or rooms for storing linens, kitchen supplies, and goods for furnishing and cleaning the house, as well as storage areas for food, wine, and the produce of the estate. The houses generally had a large porch or veranda from which the *patrón* oversaw his estate, greeted guests, and meted out punishment and reward to laborers. Indeed, much of the business of the estate was conducted from the veranda.

Standing amidst other buildings that serviced the estate, the Big House represented the pinnacle of power in rural society, and symbolized the authority the patriarch wielded over his environs. In stark contrast, workers were housed in small shacks near the fields, barns or behind the Big House, usually adjacent to their places of employment. Entire families lived in a single room in ramshackle buildings the workers themselves constructed and maintained with whatever scrap materials they could salvage.

While systems of production in urban areas have changed dramatically over the centuries, large landed estates and the coerced labor force they employ have remained a permanent fixture in many countries. The legacy of the colonial and immediate post-colonial period is apparent today: 60 percent of rural Mexican households are landless, as are 66 percent of Colombians and 70 percent of Brazilians. In Chile, a country that underwent a number of land reforms in the twentieth century, and continuing into the twenty-first, most of the fertile central valley remains in the hands of three percent of the country's landowners. The *latifundistas*, whose modern-day embodiment in some areas (especially Brazil and parts of Mexico) is corporate agribusiness, have been able to influence national politics and prevent meaningful enforcement of reforms for those who work the land.

Post-independence Politics

Political alignments and realignments left a permanent imprint on the post-colonial era. In most studies of Latin American history the post-independence decades have been viewed as a time of perpetual upheaval. As Peter Bakewell puts it in his comprehensive history of Latin America: "although it would be foolish, and wrong, to dismiss the post-independence decades as simply a period of indescribable chaos, political calm was notably absent from a time when it was much needed."[3] Historically, neither the process of forging a new nation, nor of creating a sense of loyalty to that nation – nationalism – can be seen as following a single ideological trajectory. Nationalism is at home on the left or the right; embraced by the radical freethinker or the conservative, by the forward-looking reformer or the backward-looking traditionalist. Latin American nationalism and particular definition of national identity varied over time and place, rested on competing notions of power, and depended on the rights accorded to, or taken by, Indians, blacks, mestizos, and mixed-race people. In the hands of *caudillos* one or another racial group was restricted or promoted, one or another conception of manliness or femininity stood as the ideal, alongside standard symbols and rituals – flags, anthems, language, and customs – that drew the community together. An emerging authoritarianism,

Box 4.1   Gabriel García Márquez on the ultimate *caudillo*

The Colombian novelist, famous for his absurdist portrayals of Latin American tyrants, refers in this excerpt from his Nobel Prize acceptance speech to the antics, and savagery, of a few leading military men:

> Our independence from Spanish domination did not put us beyond the reach of madness. General Antonio López de Santana, three times dictator of Mexico, held a magnificent funeral for the right leg he had lost in the so-called Pastry War. General Gabriel García Moreno ruled Ecuador for sixteen years as an absolute monarch; at his wake, the corpse was seated on the presidential chair, decked out in full-dress uniform and a protective layer of medals. General Maximiliano Hernández Martínez, the theosophical despot of El Salvador who had thirty thousand peasants slaughtered in a savage massacre, invented a pendulum to detect poison in his food, and had streetlamps draped in red paper to defeat an epidemic of scarlet fever. The statue to General Francisco Morazán erected in the main square of Tegucigalpa is actually one of Marshal Ney, purchased at a Paris warehouse of second-hand sculptures.

From Gabriel García Márquez, "The Solitude of Latin America" (Nobel Lecture, December 8, 1982).

epitomized by the personalist *caudillos*, stamped the post-independence era as one of excessive individual greed and power, based on distrust of foreigners and foreign governments. Some *caudillos* were self-serving, backward-looking, authoritarian, and anti-intellectual, while others were progressive and reform-minded. Some *caudillos* abolished slavery, instituted educational structures, built railroads and other transport systems, and sought to forge economic units capable of driving hard bargains with entrepreneurs representing European and US firms. Because the *caudillos* did not fit into a single mold nor represent a single political vision, and because they tended to rise to power through networks of personal loyalty, some historians have characterized them as "populists." Admittedly populism is a frustratingly vague and imprecise label that has meant different things in different historical periods, but the flexibility of the term may help to define the *caudillo*. As a "strongman" the *caudillo* tolerated little or no opposition, and relied on armed strength to maintain his power (see Box 4.1). As a "populist," the *caudillo* drew his power from those who were loyal to him, many of whom were small producers beholden to his beneficence and the patronage he doled out to ensure their loyalty.

Argentina and the Tyrants

The archetypical *caudillo* Juan Manuel de Rosas (1793–1877) rose to power in Argentina in 1829 and ruled until 1854, drawing his support from the *estancieros* south of Buenos Aires, the capital. Rosas began his career in the military, following a path common to many ambitious young men active in the drive for independence. Cousin to the wealthy landholding Anchorena family, Rosas's military career and influence helped to build the dynasty's resources in the province. Rosas is known for developing a mini-government and system of authority on his estate that eventually spread to the surrounding region. He demanded absolute respect, obedience, loyalty, and diligent work from the Indians, mixed-race debt peons, and *gauchos* (cowboys) in return for employment on his ranch or membership in his personal army. Rosas rejected attempts from the capital to centralize authority, modernize and build the export market, or enforce other measures intended to serve the country as a whole. Although he sometimes expressed staunch adherence to a federalized system and local control, Rosas was mostly concerned with absolute authority centralized in himself and those loyal to him. In 1828 he began a guerrilla war against the country's leadership and eventually launched a successful assault on the capital, backed by an army of *gauchos*, peasant militiamen, and assorted vagrants he had mobilized into a fighting force. By the end of 1829 he controlled the governorship of Buenos Aires province, a post he used as a steppingstone to leadership of Argentina that he held until his defeat and exile to England in early 1852.

Over his more than two decades of rule, Rosas epitomized *caudillismo*. After using rural forces from the *estancias* to bring himself to power, he sent them back to the land from which they had come and relied instead on the regular army, paramilitaries who did his extra-legal bidding, and the police and law enforcement bureaucracy. Initially he attempted to win support from domestic enterprises and artisans by imposing strict duties on imported goods in hopes of reviving national industry. The effort failed, forcing him to lift the ban on essential imports, especially textiles, and open the door to British manufactures in order to meet Argentina's consumer demand. Rosas maintained control of the legislative branch, denying it resources and ensuring a rubber stamp for his many edicts; the legislature served mainly as window-dressing for foreign visitors and dignitaries. Rosas maintained his popularity through patronage and tight control of the press and organs of public relations, but mainly he relied on repression: jailing, exiling, or killing those who opposed him. This method, particularly his ironfisted rule over Buenos Aires, the export–import market, the police, and the military allowed the general a monopoly hold over the seat of national power for nearly 20 years – but it did not ensure peace throughout the country.

Writer Domingo Sarmiento captured the rivalry and jealousy among *estancieros*, as well as the discontent among liberal, cosmopolitan urban dwellers, in the epic chronicle *Facundo*, published in 1845 and later translated as *Life in the Argentine Republic in the Days of the Tyrants; or Civilization and Barbarism*. Sarmiento (1811–88) used the character of Juan Facundo Quiroga as the archetypical barbaric *caudillo*. Although Sarmiento described the backwardness of the rural *caudillo*, his stereotype extended to the landless peasant as well, casting a racist pall over the intelligence of the rural dweller in a classic "blame the victim" account. Rosas certainly derived support from fellow *caudillos* and a segment of the rural poor, but also from urban merchants and complacent legislators, who often profited from his authoritarian rule.

By the late 1840s and early 1850s Rosas's authority was under threat from *estancieros* in other parts of the country who desired better access to regional markets and local shipping lines, as opposed to the funneling of all trade through the port of Buenos Aires. The period was almost a repeat of the call for free trade and an end to the colonial monopoly that had galvanized independence forces and local strongmen a half-century earlier. In 1852 Rosas found himself under attack politically and militarily. He lost to an invading army comprised of forces from Brazil and Uruguay, in addition to rival regional armies within Argentina itself. The British, who had benefited from Rosas's reliance on English monetary support in return for assured British control of the export/import market, hurried him to a ship and into exile in England, where he eventually died.

Populist *Caudillismo*: Paraguay and Bolivia

Rosas's career was a case study in *caudillismo*, a phenomenon that relied on outside support from largely foreign financial and mercantile interests. It likewise illustrates that the privilege of liberalism in Europe was anchored in colonial and neocolonial authoritarianism, despite the self-righteousness and moral superiority claimed over much of the rest of the world. Nothing demonstrates that contradiction better than a comparison between the life, career, and eventual fate of Juan Manuel Rosas and that of José Gaspar Rodríguez de Francia in Paraguay. Francia governed Paraguay from 1811 to his death in 1840, a period that coincided with *caudillismo* in Argentina and elsewhere in Latin America. Although sometimes included in the list of strongman rulers of the era, Francia used his power to attempt to establish a very different form of society, based on communal principles and local control rather than centralized authoritarianism. Sometimes counted among the dictators of his era, contemporary history has presented a revised view, seeing Francia as an honest, populist leader, who promoted sovereign economic prosperity in war-torn Paraguay. An austere man, simply dressed, modest, efficient, a Doctor of Theology, the Scottish travelers John Parish Robertson and William Parish observed that Francia had the respect of all parties; that he "never would defend an unjust cause; while he was ever ready to take the part of the poor and the weak against the rich and the strong."[4]

Throughout the colonial period Paraguay was a backwater of the empire, the people there a mixture of Guaraní Indians and early Spanish settlers who for generations lived a fairly simple agricultural existence. After independence land that had belonged to the Church and the Spanish state reverted to the government. Rather than use it for himself as the other liberators had done, Francia established state ranches and rented out the land to those willing to till it for a nominal fee, aiming to rebuild the communal Indian society that had existed in Paraguay before the arrival of European settlers. Shunning the favors of the landed elite, the Catholic Church, and foreign investors, Francia used his authority to rearrange society according to the demands of the poor. He nationalized the Church, abolished the tithe, declared religious freedom, and put the clergy on the government payroll. Allowing working and landless peasants the opportunity to earn a living on the state-run *estancias* angered the *estancieros*, who had long relied on local peasants as a cheap and ready source of labor. Francia also closed down municipal councils that were in the hands of the traditional landed elite, or severely restricted their authority, but allowed local councils to continue in areas where small producers, artisans, skilled and unskilled laborers were in the majority. He established state-run iron and textile works, livestock and small handicraft industries, from which a wide swath of the ordinary population derived a modest living.

It was Francia's disregard for wealthy landowners, merchants, and the Church, and his interference with the paternalistic, all-encompassing power of the ruling elite that sparked opposition to his policies. He was accused of anti-clericalism for curbing the absolute authority of the Church, but he actually used state funds to construct new churches, support religious festivals, and tend cemeteries. He likewise ordered a state takeover of the management of social welfare services (such as orphanages, hospitals, and care for the indigent), which had previously been under the auspices of the Church and the beneficence of the local elite. Moreover, under Francia, much to the dislike of powerful Argentine *estancieros*, Paraguay prospered. A fairly lively trade maintained through an overland route to Buenos Aires. If the old-line Spanish elite and Catholic hierarchy denounced Francia for his dictatorial treatment of them, the majority of Paraguayans cheered his measures. Never having received any particular support or benefit from the established ruling classes, and having suffered under the burden of high tithes to a clergy that required payment for sacraments and burial plots in Catholic cemeteries, the mass of Paraguayans found in Francia a sympathetic and honest leader.

At the time of Francia's death in 1840, Paraguay's prosperity was also linked to its policy of vigilant neutrality toward its large and powerful neighbors: Argentina and Brazil. Subsequent administrations weakly followed Francia's path, expending efforts to expand railroad and telegraph lines, upgrade the educational system, and renovate the capital city of Asunción. But in a particularly ill-conceived move, Francisco Solano López (1826–70), president from 1862 to 1870, interceded on the side of neighboring Uruguay and declared war on Argentina and then Brazil. After a trip to France as a young man, López apparently became enthralled with Napoleon's exploits and fancied himself the "Napoleon of South America." Both were military men, but the comparison pretty much stopped there. López led thousands of soldiers to their death in a futile and senseless war against Argentina, Brazil, and Uruguay, who formed what was known as the "Triple Alliance" and unleashed armies that ravaged tiny Paraguay from 1864 to 1870. At the behest of powerful merchants, the British government financed the war, in part out of fear that Paraguayan economic independence might prove contagious. Brazil, Uruguay, and Argentina did the dirty work, waging a war of extermination against Paraguay and its people. In six years untold numbers of Indians were eliminated; 90 percent of the male population in the country between the ages of 14 and 65 was killed, and Paraguay lay prostrate. Any semblance of the prosperity and independence initiated by Francia was destroyed.

Some historians argue that López was a David fighting the Goliath of his larger and more powerful neighbors, but most conclude that he led Paraguay into a war that it could never win, and which nearly destroyed it. Indisputably, López resorted to the most brutal tactics, wiping out any sign of opposition among his countrymen, including his own family and closest advisors. Thousands died in battle, but hundreds more were tortured and killed by López and his henchmen in his paranoid pursuit of personal glory.

While Paraguay suffered greater losses than any of the other Southern Cone countries, the War of the Triple Alliance probably benefited England the most. British traders profited handsomely from the destruction of competition from domestic producers in Uruguay, Argentina, Brazil, and Paraguay as the countries squandered valuable human and industrial resources on a senseless war. In the name of economic liberalism, Britain dealt the final blow to the remnants of Francia's populism and assured for its own burgeoning working class and hungry factories on the other side of the Atlantic a ready supply of hides, dried beef, wool, and agricultural goods.

Manuel Isidoro Belzú (1808–65), who governed Bolivia from 1848 until 1855, bore some similarities to Francia. A populist *caudillo*, Belzú attempted to modernize a small, landlocked country by dividing the nation's wealth and rewarding the work of the poor and dispossessed. His efforts earned him admiration from the masses and enmity from wealthy Creoles. During the seven years he held the presidency, Belzú instigated protectionist economic policies to defend small, indigenous producers and enacted a nationalist mining code that retained the nation's resources in the hands of Bolivian companies – thus provoking the ire of influential British shipping and mining interests. Despite his popularity in many sectors, Belzú had many powerful enemies (he supposedly survived over 40 assassination attempts), many of whom wanted to destroy the state-run projects that benefited a nationalist program, but likewise improved the public sphere on which the country's poor were reliant.

Like Francia, Belzú was attracted to communal, state-sponsored, social welfare projects that struck a responsive chord with Indians in particular, since communalism was more representative of indigenous values than the private property and international trade proposals favored by urban Creoles and British merchants. Belzú left office in 1855, after presiding over the first civilian census in Bolivia's history. He remained abroad and out of the public limelight for several years, but began to consider returning to the presidency in 1861, only to be gunned down by one of his rivals. Francia's policies endured longer than Belzú's, probably because the former's were based on a more fundamental reordering of Paraguayan society. Although attempting to enact a similar program, Belzú was unable to create a lasting legacy, and his populist programs largely died with him.

After *Caudillismo*

The personalist nature of *caudillismo* worked against the long-term social changes required to lay the foundations of a flourishing civil society for two reasons. It imposed a tradition of authoritarianism, and thereby set the stage for subsequent rebellion as the only way to eliminate powerful dictators. Whether the *caudillo* improved the lot of his people (like Francia and Belzú) or stole from and abused the people and the lands he governed (like

Rosas and López) he did not alter the undemocratic form of governance inherited from the colonial era. The widespread emergence of *caudillismo* postponed and prevented the construction of social institutions accountable to the citizenry and managed by capable experts – legislators, intellectuals, entrepreneurs. Thus *caudillismo* may matter as much for what it forestalled – independent democratic institutions – as for the legacy of personal strongman rule it embodied.

Caudillismo filled the vacuum left by colonial rule, serving as a bridge between political and economic power, on the one hand, and personal, kinship-based cultural arrangements, on the other. The best of the populist *caudillos*, the "good patriarch," claimed prestige and obtained the trust of followers on the basis of his willingness to confront outsiders and anyone he perceived as endangering or exploiting the village, the region, or the entire nation (depending on the extent of his influence). Rosas, for example, opportunistically denounced British financiers and entrepreneurs as interlopers and purveyors of dangerous foreign influences, while at the same time relying heavily on support from the British government to suppress internal opposition.

Secondly, *caudillismo* existed hand in hand with regionalism, manifested in the persistence of isolated, parochial local rule. Historians speak of the *republiquetas*, or "little republics," that punctuated the continental landscape in the nineteenth century, transforming large estates into politically autonomous entities. Geographically dispersed settlements allowed local strongmen to evolve into national leaders, establishing a pattern of rule that characterized – or plagued – much of Latin America throughout the twentieth century. The situation was far from Bolívar's dream of a United States of South America and tragically remote from the goal of nurturing an active citizenry that would determine the course of the continent's future. Moreover, the small size of some of the *republiquetas* made them vulnerable to the overpowering influence of foreign investors. Neocolonial economic relations were established on the foundation of local, isolated – and often, tyrannical – political formations.

Thirdly, the post-independence era witnessed important alterations in the sovereign status of indigenous communities, as well as in the demographic and cultural influence of non-whites in relation with whites. If *caudillismo* was personalist and paternal, its intersection with liberalism led to a shrinking of the safety net that had protected Indians under colonial rule. Never a consistently uniform ideology, nineteenth-century liberalism trumpeted individual choice, freedom of thought and speech, the rule of law, and adherence to a market economy. Obviously the authoritarianism of *caudillo* rule was inconsistent with many of the founding principles of liberal thought, especially free and open elections. On the other hand, liberalism favored aggressive free-market tactics and accommodated the rugged *caudillo*, under whose rule indigenous communal towns came under attack.

Creoles and their nineteenth-century descendants asserted their power over people of color who made up the majority of Latin America's population. The percentage of white to non-white (indigenous, African and Afro-descendant, *mestizo*, and *casta*) varied widely from country to country in the nineteenth century, as it still does today. In the latter half of the century two major social changes affected the pre-independence racial balance. On the one hand, improved living conditions in urban areas, including sanitation and health care, combined with better diet, led to population growth. On the other hand, European immigration contributed to both population increase and to *mestizaje*, or race mixture. Both of these trends are considered in more detail in later chapters; here we examine changes in racial composition, the impact of the wars of independence on the racial make-up of the new nations, the role of race in the development of national identity, and changes in the racial balance of power in the new social order.

Finally, *caudillismo* exemplified classic patriarchal relations, according to which men ruled over their families and communities in a form that was elsewhere dissolving into what political theorist Carole Pateman terms the "brotherhood of men."[5] In northern Europe by the end of the seventeenth century, the rigid command of fathers over sons that had prevailed in the medieval era began to give way to a looser social contract of undifferentiated male authority (which could also include powerful female monarchs) over all institutions of the social order. Late nineteenth-century Latin America underwent a similar process; it remained a patriarchal society, especially in the countryside, where a *specific man* was all-powerful. In succeeding generations the single patriarch/ *caudillo*, immortalized in the writings of Gabriel García Márquez, Miguel Asturias, Isabel Allende, Rosario Ferre and other novelists, gave way to a restructured patriarchy in which social institutions – the economy, politics, religion, and rules governing social behavior – persisted under masculine authority. The post-independence world combined rigid patriarchy in the countryside with the emerging rule of the more modern "brotherhood of men" in urban areas. Nevertheless, it bears mention that such male domination, personalist or institutional, was, and is, complex and in no way implies that women did not on occasion play the demagogue, nor that their influence was not strong, especially as guardians of "acceptable" social conventions.

Race, Race Mixture, and Liberalism

Liberalism and its attendant principles of free trade, political sovereignty, and protection of property had varied effects on racial balance and race relations. Latin America's population has long been divided by race and ethnicity, both of which are socially constructed categories that have undergone many definitions throughout history. Therefore, as understanding of race and ethnicity changed over time, separating people and communities for unique and differing reasons (religion, language, physical characteristics, social conditions), the process of defining "race" became increasingly difficult. Despite the fact that terms such as "racial difference," "racism," "racial oppression," and "color blindness" are widely used, it would be hard to provide a definition of race that would stand the test of historical change. The Spanish and Portuguese explorers of the fifteenth and sixteenth centuries embraced the biblical premise that all people were descended from Adam and Eve and therefore comprised one race. Africans, who the Iberians knew well from long contact with North Africa, were thought to have descended from Noah's son Ham, and bore the curse of his outcast. In this case scripture, not skin color, determined the difference. Some Native American groups in regions that are today the United States and Canada assumed that a Creator had devised different races for various parts of the universe, placing each in a specific corner of the world (or their known world), while some Mesoamerican pre-Columbian groups believed that the Creator had developed humans in a process of trial and error, with some of the "errors" taking up residence in the world as different racial types. For centuries scientists debated whether race developed as a geographical adaptation or, conversely, was an expression of pre-existing adaptations in people who had been cast asunder because of their violation of a religious doctrine, such as being cast from ancient Babel. In summary, what race actually meant in one society or another can be hard to nail down.

Nineteenth-century scientific debate revolved around the importance of natural selection, placing racial and ethnic difference within a hierarchy of fitness, and used specific characteristics such as skin color and hair texture – as opposed to height, weight, eye and hair color or any of the hundreds of other ways people differ physically from each other – as scientific determinants of race. Perception, or what people see in one another, has also changed over time. Early in the nineteenth century Irish immigrants to North America were considered another race, and were even seen as black. Today in parts of Belfast in Northern Ireland, Protestants and Catholics refuse to venture onto the "wrong" side of Falls Road, because the residents of each side see a difference, ascribed with racial connotations, that is completely invisible to outsiders. Hence, as notions of race have varied over time and place, people have perceived race in myriad ways. Obviously, drawing racial lines has been one of the most contortionist enterprises humans have undertaken; if it had not been so destructive, one might find it laughable. But the genocide of Jews, Armenians, Tutsis, Kurds, and the ongoing strife in many parts of the world carries a racial imprint so varied, complex, and inconsistent that neither science nor social science can codify its characteristics. Therefore, although we think we know what we mean when we refer to race, racism, or racial purity, historically these terms have applied to a variety of groups, people, and events. Race and race theory rests on attempts to explain what perceived differences meant to widely disparate people in varied times and places.

Since Latin American history was from the start an encounter between assorted groups who differed by what we will call race, ethnicity, religion, and culture, two phenomena occurred quite rapidly. First, each group ascribed a value to the other, seeing the peculiarities of these strangers as "barbaric" or "uncivilized" or "unnatural," usually within a hierarchy capable of explaining domination. Secondly, the members of each group began to intermingle and intermix, by choice or not, immediately creating a hybrid of themselves. The intermingling of the races (which were themselves products of centuries of mixture in Europe and America) did not, however, mean that race lost its significance as a determinant of difference. If people of supposedly unlike races were intermingling and creating more and more variations on themselves, should not the original reason for seeing themselves as distinct have faded away? Perhaps so, but this was not the case; in fact, the opposite occurred. The more that Americans mixed and recreated themselves in diverse forms, the more rigidly did they define race, the more stridently did they debate its significance, and the more actively did they use it as a tool of domination and subordination.

The nineteenth century was a formative era in the development of new theories of race, most of which were extensions and variations on pre-existing notions and thus carried with them the prejudices and values used to explain difference since the beginning of time. The liberal patriots who promoted independence envisioned citizenship in the hands of the men of property and standing: educated, freeborn, and white. Although the wealth and education of some men (but never women) of color qualified them for inclusion in the upper echelon of society, commonly the new leaders were of European heritage, with little or no non-white ancestry. Interestingly, in his early writings Simón Bolívar considered the diversity of Latin Americans as an asset, remarking that they could take pride in their mixed racial origins. That his great-grandmother was said to have been part black may have affected the optimism of his early writings. However, as he became more discouraged in the face of fragmentation and dissent among the newly independent lands, the Liberator instead argued that their "impure" origins weighted down the people and marred their future prospects. He called for rule by strong authoritative governments until such time as the descendants of indigenous, African, and mixed-race people were uplifted, educated, or otherwise "prepared" to accept citizenship.

The new ruling elite took for granted their privileged status, championing individualism and the benefits of unfettered free trade, separation of Church and state, an end to the traditional protection of Indian lands, and the abolition of slavery. Even in Brazil and Cuba, where slavery would not end until late in the century, abolitionists invoked liberal principles. For indigenous communities, however, the effect of free-market individualism was to deprive Indians of their claims to the land. Liberals heralded individual self-sufficiency, democracy, secularism, and the progressive free market as the road to prosperity and a modern economy, and claimed that Indian communal lands were an impediment to the forward march of progress. Many even considered Indians, as a people, to be an obstacle to the development of a modern state. Under the banner of liberalism, thousands of Indians were turned off their land and forced to fend for themselves in a world that made no attempt to understand their languages, disdained their culture, and offered only the most menial employment. In the name of progress, landowners laid claim to Indian lands – sometimes legally, often not. Independence was in most ways a disaster for the indigenous people of Mexico, Guatemala, Ecuador, Peru, and Bolivia, where they were most heavily concentrated.

Victimized by liberal economic policy, Indians were penalized as well by liberal philosophy. Observers and theorists of the time embraced various brands of "scientific" racism that divided the world between greater/whiter and lesser/darker races, attributing apparent human differences to "biological" or "natural" inadequacy. Spread from Europe to the elite of much of the world through societies and publications, eugenicists diverted blame for the unequal conditions in the world away from the policies of colonialism and domination attached to the white nations and people of Europe, and toward biology – a supposedly immutable "fact of life" about which little could be done. Accordingly, they contended, Europeans and their descendants in Latin America were winners in the natural selection process while Indians, Africans, and their descendants were losers. Eugenicists in many countries, including the United States as well as Latin

America, embraced a variety of policies including sterilization of people of color, the mentally disabled, and others considered unfit; stratified educational systems based on racial criteria; and forced destruction of Indian communities and deportation of laborers to distant estates. The thinking of these various Social Darwinists and eugenicists was divided. Some argued that all non-elite men of any race, and all women, could be trained and uplifted so as to qualify for citizenship, while others felt that the poor and those deemed racially, culturally, or physically unfit would never advance, and simply had to be managed or even eliminated.

In the end, the racist premises that triumphed after independence and were integral to liberal individualism eliminated the little protection Indians had managed to hold onto for the first 350 years after the arrival of Europeans. The Indian population declined in the post-independence era, while European and mixed-race populations increased, both through waves of immigrants arriving in every country (especially Brazil, Argentina, Uruguay, and Chile) and as a result of continued race mixture. As the Indian and black population decreased in proportion to whites, the urgency of improving the conditions of former slaves, Indians, and *castas* declined, and was, for the time, all but abandoned in governing circles.

Gender and Liberalism

If only propertied men were deemed qualified for citizenship, then liberalism served to exclude women for many of the same reasons that it excluded the majority of men. Women lacked autonomy and were, like poor men, tied to the land, in debt, enslaved, or in some way not free. Deirdre Keenan, in speaking of the generations of architects of racial theory, remarks: "Whether they located racial difference in the body or in the body politic, or whether they accounted for racial difference by divine appointment or natural selection, all of these theories were created, codified, and institutionalized by men."[6] Hence, it is impossible to demarcate racial boundaries apart from gender, since both rest on an explication of the patriarchal order that was such an important feature of *caudillismo* and survived, in a sometimes altered form, under liberalism.

During and after the wars of independence patriarchy was contested in many societies. In post-independence Venezuela, civil laws governing marriage – especially as they intersected and coincided with Catholic Church doctrine – relied on a particular ideal of femininity that was restricted to wife, mother, housekeeper, and called for general confinement to the domestic sphere. This remarkably stable construct in Venezuelan society, which lasted from independence to the early twentieth century, influenced the freedom accorded female citizens in the context of the economic and political transformation that marked the post-independence period. Whereas the Venezuelan Constitution was the first in Latin America to espouse liberal ideals of liberty, equality, individual rights, and citizenship, these rights, as was the case everywhere in the world at that time, were limited to propertied, mostly white, men. In Venezuela, as elsewhere, "the issue of women's rights was not part of the political discussions, nor did the Constitution grant women any specific rights."[7]

The new liberal doctrine ensured that women, the poor, and most people of color were excluded from nineteenth-century republicanism; however, their exclusion was played out on a field of defined masculine values that asserted male dominance and excluded female participation. Several studies of the general contours of gender relations in Latin America have concluded that women actually lost rights when the new states adopted liberal reforms. Elizabeth Dore refers to "counter-reforms" to describe what happened to women, as land was privatized and colonial law secularized in the wake of independence. As the newly formed nations sought to adopt the European model of private property and individual rights, laws promoting the break-up of communal landholdings and large estates, as occurred in Mexico under its mid-nineteenth-century "Reforma," adversely affected women. In her study of debt peonage in nineteenth- and twentieth-century Nicaragua, Dore differentiates these forms of patriarchy as falling into two categories. She argues that "patriarchy from above" is the rule of the state through masculine authority, while "patriarchy from below" is the rule of the father over his family. Both, she shows, were detrimental to all forms of economic and political progress.[8] In Argentina, despite the verbal proclamations of rights and liberties, liberals used "scientific" theories to prove female inferiority. Women and girls were seen as weak of body and mind, prone to emotionalism and hysteria, and incapable of deciding for themselves and meeting the challenges of an aggressively individualist society.

The buzzword of the era was "private property," under which guise many medium-scale landholders were able to increase the size of their estates, or to lay hold of Indian communal lands. The large estates attracted the bulk of the labor force, drawing workers away from smaller, less profitable properties. The state sought to ensure an ample supply of cheap labor for the landowners and other elites by enacting several laws that diluted parental control over children, lowered the age of majority, and relaxed restrictions on child labor. Another free market reform was the institution of mandatory, partible inheritance, or inheritance divided among heirs. In most countries previous laws had required property transmission to favor the eldest son, or sometimes the eldest daughter if there were no male heirs, in a primogeniture system. Women were able to inherit a small sum in this way, but their ability to manage and invest the money, buy and sell property, and so forth was so restricted that very few women could hope to turn a modest inheritance into real wealth. Pressure on women to marry for reasons of economic security remained extreme, and their potential for earning a living outside of marriage became even more remote. The only professional job available to women in the nineteenth century was teaching, which became an important female occupation when localities determined that they could pay unmarried women less than men. The market economy thus provided some jobs and opportunities for women, but most females remained under the strict control of their husbands or other male relatives.

The new secular republics sought to break the Church's hold over all determinations pertaining to marriage, annulment, sexuality, and legitimacy of birth. Rather than a shift that would have allowed women to control their own lives, the state appropriated the Church's power over women for itself, and in turn handed that authority over to fathers and husbands. Under the banner of liberalism, patriarchy was reinforced. For example, before independence the Catholic Church had exclusive power over enforcing the sanctity of marriage and determining the legitimacy of heirs (even if the Church chose to ignore the many illegitimate offspring belonging to men of high standing). When marriage laws were secularized after independence, women did not necessarily gain greater freedom. They were still controlled by husbands who might now abandon them even more easily, since marriage was no longer, in the eyes of the state, an enforceable moral obligation; rather it was simply a legal contract. In addition, the Church always prohibited adultery by husbands or wives, since it was a sin against the sanctity of marriage, regardless of which partner was at fault. However, post-independence civil laws decreed that adultery was not illegal for men, but was a capital offense for women. In Mexico, Argentina, and Nicaragua a husband's infidelity was neither criminalized nor considered grounds for divorce unless he created a public scandal, or dishonored the daughter of a powerful family. By contrast, if a husband discovered that his wife was unfaithful, and he killed her, he could usually escape prosecution. Court cases in Brazil in the late nineteenth and early twentieth centuries reveal that men were seldom prosecuted for killing their wives and their wives' lovers when found in adulterous affairs. Thus the authority of the state and new liberal laws in some cases reinforced patriarchy.

There were a few bright spots for women, however. Single and widowed women were allowed authority over, and responsibility for, their children. This right was not extended to married women, since to do so would have impinged on the authority of husbands. Nonetheless, it was the first time in modern Latin American history that women were allowed control over another freeborn person. New laws also provided for female equality in primary education, prohibited violence against women and children, and laid the foundations for greater equality before the law in some civil cases. As many studies of nineteenth-century liberalism suggest, the record of equality for men and women was contradictory. Court records pertaining to women's claims of wrongful treatment at the hands of abusive, adulterous, cheating, and extortionist husbands, partners and even parents indicate that women were empowered to object. They occasionally protested in court and attempted to extend the rights reserved for men to themselves, demonstrating, even as their cases failed, that they were far from passive observers of the liberal order that excluded them.

Intersections of Gender, Race, and Class

In some cases, during the independence wars, women who were left behind to manage estates, mines, or small plots of land became decision makers and exerted more authority; however, the shortage of men in the post-independence era was not to women's advantage. When men left to find work on distant estates and mines after losing their source of livelihood, marriage choices and marital arrangements became more complicated for the single women left behind since there were fewer choices of partners, at least among their own age group. Also, in areas undergoing a transition from one nationality or seat of power to another, as happened after the wars of independence, negotiating marriages became more problematic. For example, in the mid-nineteenth century, in the northern provinces of Mexico that moved from Spanish to Mexican to United States ownership, civil and ecclesiastical laws came into conflict as elite families sought to arrange marriages using racial and economic criteria alone, in contrast to the Church that sought to enforce adherence to religious principles.

Arranged marriages of very young girls to much older men demonstrate the marriage mandate for both men and women that persevered among property-holding members of nineteenth-century society. Except for those entering religious orders, marriage was expected of women from the middle and upper classes – most decidedly because of the property consolidation that the marriage bond ensured. Only rarely would a member of an elite family remain single. For men, marriage choice was not a great inconvenience – even if they were less than enamored with the spouse chosen for them – since marriage, while expected, did not mandate fidelity to one's wife. Social convention allowed men to take a mistress, have a concubine, or engage in short-term dalliances. For example, it was not unusual for a planter in Brazil, Cuba, or any rural area to establish his concubine near, or even in, the family home. His illegitimate children were accorded a favored place among the retinue of slaves or peasants on a plantation and, if necessary, he would expect his legal wife to take care of his children by other women. Finally, men were even free to show their preference for a mistress over a wife, although the Church and "polite society" frowned on such behavior.

One of the main restrictions on a woman's marriage choice was the dowry. Her ability to contract a favorable marriage depended on her family's ability to offer a substantial dowry. For his part, the groom promised to meet the financial obligations of supporting his wife and family for the rest of their lives. In the late nineteenth century the process of giving dowries underwent considerable change among the elite. Dowries were smaller, less of a proportion of the parents' estate, and by the end of the nineteenth century began to disappear. Not only was the marriage of a daughter or a son no longer such a substantial investment for the wealthy family as in earlier times, but, if a dowry were offered, it increasingly consisted of consumer goods rather than property or productive assets. Dowries were never a major concern for poor girls, just as marriage in the Church or a recognized civil institution was less common among poor, working-class whites, or among free and slave people of color, than among the white elite. The main reason was that both Church and state charged exorbitant fees for civil and ecclesiastical licenses and ceremonies. Thus many people entered into common-law marriages, which is still true in many parts of Latin America today.

According to Göran Therborn, the major Swedish sociologist of family structure throughout the world, the family in twentieth-century Latin America is distinguished by the absence of officially sanctioned and sanctified marriages. He calculates that during the nineteenth century, one-third to one-half of the population of northeast Brazil never married, instead living in conjugal union. In the Rio de la Plata region of Argentina, out-of-wedlock births were four or five times as common as in Spain or Italy. In Mexico in 1900 as many as four out of five sexual unions, stable or otherwise, were maintained outside any formal marriage ceremony. Therborn attributes this astounding contrast with the rest of the world to the high cost of marriage in Latin America, especially the weighty fees extracted by the Church.[9]

Throughout Latin America marriage placed limitations on a woman's status and power, particularly when gender intersected with class, as it did for the most elite women whose participation in the public arena was carefully circumscribed. But those who managed farms and small businesses with their husbands enjoyed considerable equality with men. In Mexico women sold *pulque* (a common alcoholic beverage consumed by the poor and working class), maintained stands in the marketplace, tended gardens and sold their produce. Among non-elites, women became heads of household when men died or deserted the family, often assuming the full management of businesses, farms, and even mines. A number even prospered; however, those women who found themselves alone and with limited resources faced grim prospects, including prostitution.

According to many scholars, it was during the mid-nineteenth century that the concept of male honor became associated with service to nation and work, as opposed to the narrow world of family, clan, and community. For women, denied citizenship and lacking legal rights outside the home, the concept of service to nation remained defined as service and obedience to men – father, husband, brother, cleric, and grown son. However, as civil society restrained the hold of the Church over education, charity, and public welfare, women stepped in to provide crucial service functions, including formal education of the young, and their introduction to social norms and values. Upper-class women, in particular, engaged in fund-raising to support new state-sponsored and private hospitals, orphanages, workhouses, homes for "wayward" women, and a host of other educational and charitable institutions. Women increasingly inserted themselves into the broader spectrum of society's concerns, both to perform a needed service and for the example they set as virtuous representatives of republican morality.

In conclusion, a hierarchical economic and social order influenced – and sometimes dictated – the way people lived, interacted with each other, and made choices about their own future and that of their children. Gender, race, class, and social position came together to provide the field upon which economic and political interactions and transactions were played. Nonetheless, the social norms and expectations varied among individuals, within regions, and over time. This variation left much of Latin American society twisting within a paradox. Societies sought to demarcate family lines, property holdings, racial lineage, and community ties through a complex set of rulings that restricted the social movement of individuals and families. Yet the freedom that patriarchy granted to men to produce illegitimate children increasingly blurred racial categories and dictated the passage of laws that placed the growing number of mixed-race women at the mercy of white, powerful, men. So long as the power of the wealthy and landowners remained uncontested, the patriarchal order held firm. It was reinforced in myriad institutions of elite power, including kinship, godparenthood, nepotism, and clientelism, along with dowries and arranged marriages. At the same time Latin America in the mid-nineteenth century was the heyday of the *caudillo* – a man who epitomized patriarchal authority in an all-embracing expression of economic and political power.

Nationalism

Little about *caudillismo* conjures up a world of high art and culture; indeed, from Domingo Faustino Sarmiento's perspective, it plummeted society to the depths of barbarism. However, counterbalancing forces in the newly independent worlds of art, music, and literature were emerging. With independence, Latin America embarked on a new aesthetic, replacing the stultifying scholasticism of the colonial period (a dogmatic belief in the Church's revealed "truth") with romanticism in the early decades of the nineteenth century, and with realism later in the century. Romanticism, epitomized in Sarmiento's classic story *Facundo, Civilization and Barbarism*, appeared as the counterweight to the reality of disorganized federalism dominated by *caudillo*s. Art and literature drew on human emotions, more understandable in the midst of a political world that lacked stable models, while architecture expressed the independent nations' fascination with European neoclassical grandeur. In imperial Brazil the capital city of Rio de Janeiro sported new libraries, theaters, and operas in the image of Europe, while Buenos Aires had emerged as the most European of Latin American cities by century's end. Art, music, and architecture of the time suggested a set of nations searching for independent identity, while at the same time clinging to established forms of European civilization.

The nineteenth century swayed back and forth between romanticizing indigenous peoples and the bedrock peasantry for its oneness with American soil, to trading the integrity of America for European neoclassicism inherited from the colonial period. By century's end, realism had increasingly replaced romanticism, most apparent in the writings of Cuba's José Martí (1853–95) and Brazilian journalist Euclides da Cunha (1866–1909). Both spoke out against the legacy of dogged emulation of European and North American concepts of civilization, while searching for a genuine Latin American identity. For Martí, Latin America's future depended on the cultural unity the nations of "our America" would forge with each other (Figure 4.2). Elaborating on a theme that Bolívar had raised early in the century, Martí strove not so much for political unity in a single federation, but for cultural unity and political and economic cooperation as a bulwark against the expansionism of North America. In his many writings from the United States, where he lived in exile for decades, Martí repeated the theme that Latin America's sovereignty rested with its ability to find its soul, define its identity, and forge its own unique community (see Box 4.2). He was killed at the age of 42 as he participated in the first battle for Cuban independence in 1895. He never saw the island liberated from Spain, nor, mercifully, did he witness its de facto colonization and subsequent humiliation at the hands of the United States at century's end.

Conclusion

Latin America at the end of the nineteenth century was virtually independent, enjoyed trade and political relations with the world at large, and, in spite of cultural fragmentation and geographic separation, was forging a new national identity.

Figure 4.2   "Cuba and Martí Present at the Moncada" by Rafael Morante. (Courtesy Lincoln Cushing, *Revolución: Cuban Poster Art* ca. 2003)

Box 4.2   José Martí and the American identity

The essay "Our America" by José Martí has long been considered one of the most important declarations of the need for Latin America to take pride in its heritage and assume its place on equal terms with the United States and Europe. The following passage excerpts some of the essay's key concepts:

In what lands can men take more pride that in our long-suffering American republics, raised up among the silent Indian masses by the bleeding arms of a hundred apostles, to the sound of battle between the book and processional candle? Never in history have such advanced and united nations been forged in so short a time from such disorganized elements . . .

And the able governor in America is not the one who knows how to govern the Germans or the French; he must know the elements that make up his own country, and how to bring them together, using methods and institutions originating within the country, to reach that desirable state where each man can attain self-realization and all may enjoy the abundance that Nature has bestowed in everyone in the nation to enrich with their toil and defend with their lives. Government must originate in the country. The spirit of government must be that of the country. Its structure must conform to rules appropriate to the country. Good government is nothing more than the balance of the country's natural elements . . .

How can the universities produce governors if not a single university in America teaches the rudiments of the art of government, the analysis of elements peculiar to the peoples of America? The young go out into the world wearing Yankee or French spectacles, hoping to govern a people they do not know. In the political race entrance should not go for the best ode, but for the best study of the political factors of one's country . . .

To know one's country and govern it with that knowledge is the only way to free it from tyranny. The European university must bow to the American university. The history of America, from the Incas to the present, must be taught in clear detail and to the letter, even if the archons of Greece are overlooked. Our Greece must take priority over the Greece which is not ours. We need it more. Nationalist statement must replace foreign statement. Let the world be grafted onto our republics, but the trunk must be our own. And let the vanquished pedant hold his tongue, for there are no lands in which a man may take greater pride than in our long-suffering American republics . . .

There can be no racial animosity, because there are no races. . . . The soul, equal and eternal, emanates from bodies of different shapes and colors. Whoever foments and spreads antagonism and hate between the races, sins against humanity.

From José Martí, "Our America," *La Revista Ilustrada*, New York, January 1, 1891.

Nevertheless, many of the same inequalities persisted that had separated people by race, class, gender, religion, culture, language, and geography at the start of the century. On the isolated highlands and vast rural plains, peasants exchanged landlords formerly subservient to Spain and Portugal for others that wielded authority as local strongmen, looking toward England and the US for economic and, often, military support. The privileges of citizenship remained off-limits to many, probably most, of the continent's residents, while the Creole elite held firm to the reins of political and economic power. Women had little authority because they lacked the right to participate as independent actors in society – although wealthy women enjoyed the comforts and amenities of their class despite the limitations imposed by husbands, fathers, and male authority in general.

If the Creole patriots who emerged victorious at the end of the independence wars did not see themselves as particularly concerned with the plight of the humble, neither were they all complacent about the poverty all around them. The men in charge in post-colonial Latin America were a varied lot. Indeed some were tyrants, just as Sarmiento described them; others were not, but still accepted the "scientific" theories of the era that discounted the possibility for advancement of society's poorest and most marginalized, as well as their own wives, sisters, and daughters. They trusted liberalism, championed individualism, and some even presumed that the communal-minded Indian would one day flourish as an independent farmer. While the best of the Creole elite were anxious to build prosperous independent nations, the strife of future centuries would demonstrate the shortcomings inherent in their liberal doctrine.

5 | Latin America's Place in the Commodity Chain

"The deed is done, the nail is driven, Spanish America is free, and if we do not mismanage our affairs sadly, she is English," declared George Canning (1770–1827) in 1824. The British Foreign Secretary from 1822 to 1827 was not expressing a desire on England's part to recolonize the newly independent states. Rather he was speculating on the potential for foreign trade, markets for British goods, and access to Latin America's extensive natural resources in minerals and agricultural products, which he envisioned flowing on English ships to English seaports to be processed in English factories and resold throughout the British Empire.[1] Indebted to England for the cost of waging the independence wars, weakened by long years of political upheaval, and facing chaotic conditions at home that interfered with the orderly establishment of internal affairs, the new states of Latin America welcomed the opportunity to sell to Britain. Although by the twentieth century a sector of the ruling elite was chafing at the domination Britain and other foreign powers exerted over Latin American economies, during the first years after independence – and in some countries for a long time thereafter – Latin America embraced free trade policies. Domestic *latifundistas* and merchant capitalists sold raw materials and some manufactured goods abroad, in return for investment in the infrastructure and industrial base that would promote development at home.

Because the greatest wealth was to be gained from exporting cash crops, as opposed to growing and consuming diversified agricultural products that would lead to self-sufficiency, the estates focused on one or two crops, a system known as monoculture. Latin America was well situated to feed the growing European population: its exports ranged from Brazilian coffee to fruit and other agricultural products from Central America, sugar from the Caribbean islands, and meat, hides, wheat and other grains from Argentina, Uruguay, and southern Brazil. The region also exported minerals and ores from Mexico, Chile, Bolivia, and other areas, guano from Peru, and ultimately oil from Venezuela and Mexico. New forms of economic control, known as neocolonialism, replaced the old constraints imposed by colonialism. In addition, the export economy created a demand for roads, port facilities, transportation and communication networks, all of which required large capital outlays. Rather than investing revenues from exports into the generation and expansion of a dynamic infrastructure, many countries relied on the resources and technology that could be supplied by England, and subsequently the United States. This combination of monoculture and an export-led economy pulled Latin America away from self-sufficiency and internal stability toward an economic model based on capital infusion from the outside and dependence on fluctuating international demand. Finally, economic historians have argued that commodity exports need to be considered as a "two-way bridge," with production at one end and consumption at the other. As such, goods from Latin America entered into a broad, international commodity chain, producing goods for consumption abroad, the demand for which could fluctuate widely.

This chapter seeks to explain both the benefits and the pitfalls deriving from the pursuit of economic liberalism, which fostered individual over state ownership, using several country and commodity examples: Peru and the guano boom of the nineteenth century, when a single, tremendously lucrative export tipped the balance toward domestic self-sufficiency for a time, but ultimately discouraged diversification and domestic enterprise; Brazil and a series of boom-and-bust cycles that elevated one regional economy, only to have the boom go bust and prosperity move to another region (with the exception of São Paulo, which remained prosperous). The mining of nitrates in Chile and coffee cultivation in Colombia provide examples of commodities that have maintained modest levels of prosperity although not without outside and domestic government assistance. In Mexico we look at a different phenomenon, wherein a nascent hide and tallow trade in the cash-poor distant northern territories led to the landowners' reliance on the expanding US market. Among the smaller Central American and Caribbean nations, autonomous economic development never got off the ground. Small nations found themselves overrun by the powerful sugar, fruit, railroad, shipping, and mineral monopolies of the North American trusts in an era characterized by "robber barons."

The Guano Boom

The harvest and export of guano (bird dung used for fertilizer) from islands off the southern coast of Peru offers a story of intense regional economic prosperity, followed by sudden decline. Whereas coffee cultivation in Brazil, sugar in Cuba, and a host of other examples demonstrate the effects of persistent reliance on a single (or very few) export crops, harvesting guano exemplifies the economic and social impact of a spike in demand followed by precipitous decline.

Over centuries bird droppings had accumulated in layers hundreds of feet thick on the Chincha Islands off the coast of Peru, producing a substance that proved to be a highly rich plant fertilizer. In the mid-nineteenth century Europe entered a heightened agricultural boom, offering an ideal market for processed guano fertilizer, resulting in the transformation of a small local trade into a fabulously lucrative international export commodity for Peru. From 1841 to 1879 guano was Peru's most important export; revenues were in the hundreds of millions of dollars, providing a healthy infusion of capital into the depressed, post-independence economy. Since guano fertilizer was known for boosting the productivity of a range of crops, including turnips, tobacco, grains, and vegetables, and since it was relatively inexpensive, European demand at first appeared to be boundless. Peruvian guano was instrumental to Europe's nineteenth-century agricultural revolution and ensuing population increase. As quickly as it began, however, the trade declined when Chilean nitrates and other forms of fertilizer replaced guano, especially as the latter became increasingly scarce and harder to collect and transport. By the mid-1870s the much-celebrated "Age of Guano" was ending, leaving in its wake a devastated economy. In 1876 Peru defaulted on its foreign debt and the region entered a crisis from which it would not soon emerge.

Although the guano trade was highly lucrative, assets were very unevenly distributed throughout Peruvian society; most revenues accrued to the government and in turn to a small group of capitalists engaged in the trade. The Peruvian government controlled the guano fields, granting to a few individual companies the rights to handle sales. The private merchants were not required to – and did not – return their profits as investment into the local economy. Neither did the Peruvian state ensure that guano revenues poured into the betterment of the nation as a whole. Consistent with liberal economic policies popular at the time, Peru had drawn heavily on loans from British financiers to build the infrastructure, transportation, communication and other service networks needed to advance the trade, offer credit to new businesses, and increase government programs – but not to raise the educational level and standard of living of the populace. From the 1840s to the late 1870s both the state and private-sector bureaucracies expanded rapidly, including government offices, financial markets, commercial and real estate networks.

By the 1860s, when guano sales climaxed and before the slide downward, guano alone had brought in over $500 million in export earnings from the sale abroad. Nonetheless, not every part of the economy profited equally and some parts suffered, rather than benefited, from the guano boom. Small agricultural producers, artisans, and domestic manufacturers, unable to compete with the cheaper and higher-quality imported goods that began to flood the market, went out of business. The sectors that grew tremendously were linked directly or indirectly to foreign trade and positioned to benefit from British financial generosity.

When guano went bust in the 1860s, Peru's government and a small coterie of private entrepreneurs found themselves heavily in debt and no longer able to meet debt-servicing payments. As the country entered a crisis, the social strife that resulted from Peru's failure to address social inequalities and hardships left over from the colonial and independence war eras, compounded by the unequal distribution of benefits from the guano boom, came back to haunt the country in full force. The government had not used the increased revenues to raise living standards, train a core of local technicians, entrepreneurs, and domestic intelligentsia capable of advancing a diversified economy. In the midst of social upheaval, strikes, and demonstrations the Peruvian government desperately looked for a way to build national unity and gain a share in extracting nitrates, the next major fertilizer business. Peru, in alliance with Bolivia, went to war against Chile in 1879 over control of a disputed area of the Atacama Desert. Peru's loss pushed it further into debt, while Chile used its victory in this conflict, known by the grandiose name "War of the Pacific" (1879–83), to take from Bolivia the tiny strip of land through which the latter had access to the sea. The Chilean government sold off the nitrate processing business to private, mainly foreign, companies and kept for itself the revenue from the export tax on sales. With a hold on the largest nitrate deposits in the world, Chile's tax revenue alone was so high as to provide nearly half of the government's total income in the last years of the century.

Nitrates in Chile

The exploitation of nitrates from the Atacama Desert picked up as guano supplies dwindled, and some foreign investors transferred their operations from Peru to Chile. Like guano, nitrates were primarily destined for use in fertilizers for the North Atlantic market, but also for the United States, especially plantations in the South. Nitrates could also be used in explosives, and thus commanded a broader, more flexible, market share. The Chilean government's decision to lease nitrate exploitation to foreign firms has been criticized for following the same path as Peru just decades earlier. There is some truth to this charge, but recent studies of nineteenth-century commodity chains point out that Chile may well have benefited as best it could from the arrangement, given its limited means of reaching foreign markets on its own. Another, perhaps more valid, criticism focuses on the way that the Peruvian and Chilean governments invested the profits from these boom economies. The influx of revenue was, for a few decades in Peru and many more in Chile, an opportunity to build infrastructure, promote public education, and generally benefit their respective societies, building an autonomous and prosperous citizenry. This opportunity was largely ignored; neither the government nor the few elites benefiting from the export booms saw fit to spread the wealth in the interest of national development.

From outside the country, European and US entrepreneurs, many of them modern-day "conquistadores," roamed the southern hemisphere looking for lucrative returns on quick investments. Henry Meiggs (1821–77) was a colorful entrepreneur who personified the imperialist and expeditionary views of the nineteenth century. Born in Boston, Meiggs moved to Chile in 1854 after a stint in California, where he reputedly made and lost millions of dollars in several schemes. Undaunted by past failures, Meiggs set about raising funds to build a railroad in Chile. He succeeded in constructing a line from Santiago to the south and another one from Santiago to the port of Valparaiso. With the fortune he amassed in the railroad business, he built an elaborate mansion in Chile. Soon restless, he left Chile in the 1860s and moved to Peru, where he invested in the guano trade, and then used his profits to build a railroad from Lima to the Altiplano at a height of 14,000 feet. One might argue that Meiggs's railroads benefited the economies of both Chile and Peru, and so they did in the short term. On the other hand, Meiggs's investments promoted the development of infrastructure to service the export economy rather than domestic development. Secondly, although Meiggs was known for paying local workers at rates above domestic entrepreneurs, his enormous profits largely left the country. So long as neither the Peruvian nor Chilean governments had the political clout to recoup revenues, through income and corporate taxes, to support internal development, the system of "robber barons" so well known in the US in this period functioned yet more freely in South America.

Sugar and Coffee

Brazil's boom-and-bust export cycles were both similar to and different from those in Peru and Chile. First, Brazil was so large that one or another part of the country could be prospering while another was undergoing decline (see Map 5.1). Thus

Map 5.1 Comparative size of Brazil and the countries of Europe. (Based on E. Bradford Burns, *A History of Brazil*, 2nd edition, ca. 1980. By permission Columbia University Press.)

Brazil can be seen as moving through a series of boom/bust cycles, a phenomenon that stretched back to activities of the first Portuguese settlers who exported brazil wood in the 1500s, a lucrative trade that gave the country its name. When permanent settlements appeared along the northeastern coast, they relied on sugar cultivation on plantations worked by slaves from Africa to generate wealth. By 1650 Brazil's northeast was the world's largest sugar producer, exporting 2.5 million pounds a year, making it one of the richest single regions of the Americas. The lucrative sugar trade attracted the attention of other European powers, especially the Dutch who occupied the northeast and profited from the sugar trade from 1630 to 1654. When the Portuguese reclaimed the territory, sugar exports were facing competition from several sources, including English colonies in Jamaica and Barbados and the French colony at Saint-Domingue. By the 1780s Caribbean plantations were out-producing those in Brazil, where mills stood in disrepair and the soil at many plantations was nearing exhaustion. Between 1650 and 1715 Brazil's income from sugar declined by two-thirds. One of the richest areas of agricultural production on the entire planet in the early seventeenth century had gone bankrupt in less than one hundred years. The northeast experienced a brief recovery in the 1790s, immediately after the Haitian Revolution, only to be outdone by Cuban sugar producers, who profited from that country's richer soil and more efficient mills in the nineteenth century.

The reasons for the precipitous decline in Brazil were several. Initially the big planters, or *senhores de engenho*, saw little reason to make the sugar mills and plantations more efficient, relying as they could on a steady supply of slaves for most of the seventeenth and eighteenth centuries. As it became clear that Brazil's share of the international sugar market was declining rapidly, many planters, especially in the state of Pernambuco, attempted to modernize, employing paid laborers alongside slaves, renting out land to sharecroppers from whom they could draw some income rather than letting it lie fallow, and experimenting with steam power and better technology in the mills. Nonetheless, their efforts came too late and proved to be inadequate.

Second, the heavy reliance on a single commodity for a limited market abroad brought the sugar planters to the same fate as Peru's guano merchants. Demand for Brazil's sugar fell when Europeans began importing sugar from their own island possessions on a large scale, but a boom in beet sugar cultivation in Europe diminished demand for the more expensive cane sugar products, reducing further the narrow profit margin for Brazilian planters. Finally, and again similar to what happened with guano and, later, nitrates in the Andean nations, the sugar boom had not introduced a diversified, self-sustaining economy that could prosper after sugar's decline. Foreign capital was used to finance roads, rail, and communication lines constructed to connect sugar plantations with the point of embarkation for exports, not to lay the foundation for a regional transportation network servicing domestic trade. Moreover, as in Peru, planters used their profits to purchase consumer goods from Europe (textiles, furniture, and fine crafts), thereby limiting demand for goods produced by domestic manufacturing and artisanal enterprises.

The Growth of São Paulo

Latin America turned much of the world into coffee drinkers, providing inexpensive-grade coffee for mass consumption, combined with finer-grade Costa Rican, Colombian, Guatemalan and other varieties for more specialized markets. By the mid-twentieth century, Brazil would supply 80 percent of the world's coffee. The story of Brazil's pre-eminence as a coffee producer and exporter largely unfolded after independence from Portugal in 1822; by the 1840s coffee was by far the leading export commodity. Today coffee cultivation bears some of the characteristics of the old plantation system, but also shows signs of modern agricultural methods. First introduced in 1727 into the far northern state of Pará with some seeds from French Guiana, coffee reached Rio de Janeiro by 1770 and flourished in the Paraiba Valley before moving west when the soil of the coastal hills became depleted. By the mid-nineteenth century the coffee tree found its home in the states of São Paulo, Minas Gerais and as far south as Paraná.

The effect of coffee cultivation on the nation's economy, especially in shifting the vital center from the northeast to the southeast, played a tremendously important role in Brazil's history. Coffee production attracted foreign capital and generated domestic profits that were poured into manufacturing and commercial ventures in São Paulo. It facilitated the introduction of new technologies, encouraged railroad construction, and opened up new areas of Brazil, to the west and south of São Paulo state. Some operators managed enormous estates worked by many slaves, while others relied on a few slaves or a combination of wage and slave labor to cultivate a modest amount of land. In general, planters experimented with crop rotation, fertilizers, and innova-tive agronomy methods to increase production, as well as investing in new technology rather than simply relying on longer working hours for their slaves and free laborers. Coffee introduced far-reaching political, economic, and social changes in Brazil, including the construction of rail lines from the fields to the port in Santos; industrial development, especially in the state of São Paulo; and an influx of immigrants. Following emancipation in 1888, coffee planters began to use immigrant labor on a larger scale, even subsidizing the cost of transporting them from Italy, and later Japan. The important role played by government-sponsored immigration in Brazil and elsewhere in Latin America is a major topic of the next chapter.

The impact of the coffee economy on Brazil's southeast was dramatically different from that of sugar in the northeast, mainly because coffee revenues stimulated urban and industrial development, whereas sugar revenues had not. Yet coffee replicated several of the features associated with the sugar economy: production on large plan-tations; dependence on a single crop; heavy reliance on slave labor in the years before abolition; and the flourishing of plantation systems governed by a patriarch whose influence over family, community, and workforce was largely unquestioned; as well as reliance on foreign merchants. Some coffee estates were worked by more than 200 slaves, making them far larger than most northeastern sugar plantations (Figure 5.1). Since coffee trees have a life span of 20 years, but take four to six years to mature, a single plantation has trees growing at various stages of maturity. The investment in

Figure 5.1 Slave men and women sorting and transporting coffee beans, ca. nineteenth century. (Hoffenberg Collection)

labor, trees, and extensive acreage means that large-scale production for export is expensive, although small coffee farms have always existed alongside larger plantations and Brazil's coffee regions have always supported a number of smaller operators who produce cheaper coffee for the local market, along with cassava, manioc, and other staples.

According to historian Bill Albert, in his book *South America and the First World War*, at the turn of the twentieth century foreign merchants, mainly British, controlled about 60 percent of Brazil's foreign coffee sales. Operating through a few dozen tightly controlled firms, foreign merchants assumed a powerful position linking rural planters with the world of trade abroad. Albert explains that British firms' contacts on the world market, control of credit, and increasing interest in processing and warehousing agricultural products gave Britain considerable authority over Brazil's foreign trade. Brazil's economic dependence on both the export market and foreign investors, in turn, strongly influenced the autonomy of the industrial elite. Relying on foreign investors allowed Brazil's own entrepreneurs to avoid taking risks with their own profits. Likewise the government did not have to have sufficient credit reserves to bail out failing investors in the early, and precarious, stage of capitalist expansion. In short, large-scale Brazilian planters and merchants could get very rich very fast by tying themselves firmly to the coat-tails of powerful British trading houses, investors, and middlemen.

This dependence had shifted by the 1920s, when more and more of the world coffee supply originated from just 10 exporting firms in Brazil that by the mid-twentieth century were supplying nearly 80 percent of the world's coffee. Only then did the Brazilian government assume a central role in subsidizing coffee profits and ensuring that the market share of sales remained firmly under the control of Brazilian entrepreneurs.

Colombian Coffee

The nineteenth century saw the emergence of new regional economies that were carving out niches for specific commodities in the expanding export markets. In Colombia coffee cultivation spread into previously uncultivated highland regions, producing a particularly savory type of coffee bean. Coffee exports boomed from the 1880s onward and would by the 1920s account for 70 percent of Colombian exports. Unlike Brazil, where coffee had been cultivated on large plantations since the beginning of the boom in the nineteenth century, in Colombia most coffee plantations were small-scale operations. This had both positive and negative effects. In the first place, growers on small farms, and some on larger plantations, became a powerful segment of the economically and politically active citizenry. It seemed, for a while at least, that Colombia might develop a large middle class made up of small producers, which would tend to generate a more equitable distribution of income. The problem with the smallholdings, however, was that cultivation under these conditions made for a very rich, aromatic coffee, but the product was more expensive to grow and ship. Since coffee trees mature over five to six years, and then produce only for a limited amount of time, plantations that cover large amounts of land can more efficiently rotate through the trees in various stages of maturation. The modest plantations in Colombia had a difficult time competing with the huge estates in Brazil, Guatemala, and El Salvador. In the latter three cases giant corporations such as the United Fruit Company, and other major coffee producers, kept the price of coffee high by controlling large tracts of land, and holding it untilled in reserve.

Another positive effect can be seen in the stimulus that profits from coffee exports lent to Colombia's broader economic prosperity. Coffee production in Colombia contributed to the development of an infrastructure, especially roads from the coastline to the expanding coffee groves in more distant areas of the country. Railway construction, however, was not as successful in Colombia as it had been in Argentina, where the flat plains facilitated the spread of rail transportation from the port to the interior. In addition to coffee, other agricultural goods became prime exports, including flowers, fruits, and bananas, as well as livestock. By the 1920s coffee was enjoying the status of a fixed-demand commodity, meaning it was always consumed, even in times of economic downturn. In addition, the primary market for Colombia's coffee was the United States, which was a stable market compared, for example, to Europe, where imports were interrupted during World War II. Coffee, as well as textiles, hides and leather, fruits and flowers, would have seemed to provide Colombia with the means to develop a healthy economy free of some of the perils of *latifundia* that plagued other countries in the region. Indeed that was the case until the 1940s, when declines in foreign revenues combined with particularly virulent political rivalries between the Liberal and Conservative parties dragged Colombia into years of political chaos and poor economic performance.

The Rubber Boom

If coffee serves as an example of steadily expanding sales on foreign markets, the story of Brazilian rubber exports illustrates the other end of the spectrum. Rubber provided an enormous amount of wealth to a relatively small group in Brazil's Amazon region beginning in the 1870s, but then collapsed completely after 1910. Called the "rubber boom," this period was actually a "boom gone bust" in the span of just 50 years. During its heyday, the rubber trade attracted laborers, speculators, and merchants from all over the world. It opened a region of Brazil that had been largely ignored, except by missionaries and naturalists, since the earliest exploration of the country. It also paved the way for the extinction of the remaining Indians, who had lived far removed from modern society and the diseases and destruction that befell the vast majority of indigenous people in the Americas.

Long before the arrival of Europeans, people had been extracting a milky white fluid called latex from the *Hevea brasiliensis* tree that grows wild in the Amazon tropical rainforest. The exact uses they made of the natural rubber, which they formed into objects after smoking it over a fire until it coagulated, is not clear. Early Portuguese explorers wrote in their journals of this strange substance, which they eventually used to make crude boots. The boots never became a large enterprise, since "tapping" the latex from the tree, a process of scoring the trunk and letting the latex substance drain out, was highly labor intensive and fairly slow. This changed in the nineteenth century, however. By the 1840s British and US scientists had discovered a way to stabilize raw rubber through a process call "vulcanization," and the mini-boom began. Industrializing countries wanted rubber for bicycle and wagon tires, insulation, and other industrial uses. Demand skyrocketed, as did the number of migrants pouring into the Amazon region in hopes of making a fortune collecting and selling the latex. Others came to provide food, services, entertainment, and other amenities in demand in the new boom-towns. First Belém, at the mouth of the Amazon River, and then Manaus, a small outpost far upstream, became main entrepôts for the shipment of huge balls of rubber from Brazil to the world outside. British steamboats plied the river trading with local firms that formed the rubber balls, exporting rubber in exchange for food, tools, and supplies. The riverboats connected with ships at the port of Belém, from which the rubber was shipped abroad.

The rubber boom created instant millionaires or "rubber barons." The population of Manaus soared from a scattering of settlers to nearly 100,000 people in 1910. Wealthy rubber barons, anxious to demonstrate their grasp of high culture to the world, built a magnificent opera house constructed with imported materials (Figure 5.2), in addition to the first electric street lighting of any city in the country, piped water and gas, and an elaborate system of floating docks. In 1912 the Madeira–Mamoré Railway, further upriver, was completed to connect Brazil and Bolivia. Despite the grandeur of

Figure 5.2   Teatro Amazonas, Manaus, Brazil. Completed in 1892, this theater and opera house was intended to showcase the wealth and culture the rubber boom brought to the Amazon territory. The Italian architect Celestial Sacardim was commissioned to design the theater in the Renaissance style, employing building materials from Paris and England; marble for stairs, statues, and columns from Italy; and up-to-date design including electric lights. The roof is adorned with a dome covered by 36,000 ceramic tiles painted in the colors of the Brazilian national flag. (Pontanegra photo)

the opera house and the riches rubber provided, Brazil's place as the rubber capital did not endure. Aware that rubber trees could grow outside the Amazon region, British scientists managed to hide some seeds in parcels and bring them to England, where they reproduced the plants in the British Royal Botanic Gardens at Kew. British traders then transported the seedlings to plantations in their colonies in Ceylon (Sri Lanka) and Malaya (Malaysia), thus sparking a lively, competing trade. South Asian rubber plants, cultivated on plantations rather than harvested from wild trees, produced a higher yield, destroying the market for Brazil. By 1910, a major economic enterprise had folded. During World War I scientists developed a synthetic substitute and the use of natural rubber declined dramatically, although a limited market for natural rubber still exists.

Expanding Exports

Other aspects of the boom–bust production cycles characterized Brazil's development. Gold, and then diamonds, were discovered in Minas Gerais in the 1700s. After initial frenzied speculation, however, gem mining declined, becoming a stable enterprise but not generating the vast fortunes originally expected. In the late nineteenth century cacao trees were planted in various parts of Brazil, such as Pará and Rio Negro in the Amazon forest, and eventually in the northeastern state of Bahia. Immortalized in the classic tales by Jorge Amado (1912–2001), one of Brazil's most popular novelists, the wars among the cacao barons hold a place in the national psyche analogous to the shoot-outs in the Old West of the United States. The promise of great wealth panned out for only a few of the most powerful planters, although the myth lived on long after the decline in cacao cultivation and exports. Ecuador, a longstanding cacao producer, held the pre-eminent position past World War I, outstripping Brazil and Venezuela. In the late twentieth century, cacao was being produced in other areas of the world, many of them outside Latin America. Thus, cacao, and the chocolate produced from it, may be one of Latin America's great contributions to world cuisine, but it was not the sole contributor.

Brazil's boom–bust cycles contributed to a pattern of unstable growth, and of decentralized and erratic political power centers, as products boomed in one place, then declined, and the center shifted to a different locale. Nevertheless, individuals involved in the trade and subject to the rise and fall of the demand for rubber were neither passive participants nor victims. According to Barbara Weinstein, in her history of the rise and fall of the rubber boom, rubber tappers did all they could to adapt to the shifting demand, roamed over large expanses of land, opened up new areas, and innovated to the extent possible in the extraction of more latex, while merchants sought to find new markets. While Brazil lost out to competitors in the international commodity chain in the sale of rubber, it maintained its position and ultimately excelled in the production of coffee.

Contemporary historians look back to the experience of nineteenth-century British hegemony, when the small island exerted unparalleled economic, political and cultural influence over much of the globe, and draw comparisons with other empires. Inevitably focus centers on the subsequent rise of the United States as a similar global powerhouse in the twentieth century. Both Britain and the US rose to prominence as industrial giants, a fact that differs from the Spanish, French, and Portuguese, whose success as world colonial powers occurred in the pre-industrial era. There were, however, key differences in the early stages and in the ultimate outcome of English and US influence, especially as regards Latin America. For all its global reach, Britain never sought to annex territory in the Americas, holding only those colonies in the West Indies and on the rim of the Caribbean – mainly Guyana, Trinidad, Jamaica, Barbados, Belize – it had taken in the earlier pre-industrial era. The United States, on the other hand, played a stronger political role in the hemisphere, overtaking and eventually annexing a large swath of Mexican territory and absorbing Cuba, Puerto Rico, and a slice of the Virgin Islands into its political sphere as formal or informal colonies.

It is of no small importance to understand the difference between relationships of trade, even unequal trading relationships, and imperialism, especially as regards the direct political and military acquisition of territory. No matter what role Britain may have played in other parts of the world, especially in Africa and Asia, it was never a major imperial power in the Americas in the same way that the United States eventually was. The narrative of dominance and dependence, that posits Latin America as sequentially overpowered by a series of outsiders – Spain, Portugal, France, and a few others in the sixteenth through eighteenth centuries, then Great Britain in the nine-teenth, and lastly the United States in the twentieth – is too simple. In each specific era the relationship of Latin American nations with the rest of the world was complexly intertwined in a maze of political, economic, even cultural ties. Moreover, at no point through all the centuries could one say that colonizers, merchants, investors, and military officers operated without the consent of at least a section of the domestic ruling elite. Similarly, no country submitted without a fight, at least for very long, from a large swath of the population.

Mexico and US Expansionism

If South America was drawn more closely into the web of English trade and manufac-ture – and the unstable development pattern such investment produced – Mexico fell prey to the expansionist designs of the US. Emerging from the independence war with Spain broken and bankrupt, the country's seat of government in Mexico City held little control over the extensive territories in the far north, an area that was inviting settlement by Yankee explorers, farmers, miners, and the general spillover from the early nineteenth-century influx of European immigrants into eastern US cities. Mexico, for its part, had never encouraged European immigration on a large scale, and was thus less compelled to push out settlements into the far reaches of its territory, except for a few colonization projects in New Mexico and Arizona. The northern provinces in particular, encompassing northern California, present-day Colorado, and Texas, were sparsely settled and had been explored only by Jesuit and Franciscan missionaries set on converting the remote indigenous population to Christianity.

From the outset there was tension over the goals of the Spanish, and subsequently Mexican, governments and the Church, especially in the more distant territories. Priests had argued throughout the colonial period that soldiers and settlers constituted a corrupting influence on the Indians they sought to convert, since the settlers were made up of unruly peoples of mixed race whose presence, according to clergymen sent directly from Spain, impacted negatively on the Indians. Nevertheless, colonial authorities recognized that in order to maintain military and political control over a huge territory that was coveted by England, Russia, and the United States, Spain needed towns with women and the potential for permanent settlements.

In 1777 Spanish settlers established the first town at San José and the second at Los Angeles, a half-day's walk from the existing San Gabriel mission. Others continued up the coast, followed by settlers and soldiers enticed northward by the promise of con-siderable plots of land upon retirement from service. When the first round of soldiers retired in 1784, Spanish governor Pedro Fages doled out land grants, including 43,000 acres to Juan José Dominguez, a 65-year-old soldier; a 36,000-acre grant to José Maria Verdugo; and the largest, 75,000 acres, to Manuel Perez Nieto. Between 1784 and 1821 colonial authorities issued about 30 land grants to retired soldiers and a few more to newly arrived settlers from other parts of New Spain. Indicative of the humble background of these suddenly land-rich grantees, only a very few were able to sign their name to the land title with anything but a simple cross. According to records from the era, Manuel Perez Nieto, owner of the "great Los Nietos rancho," signed a betrothal agreement in the late 1780s with the mark of an illiterate: "+".

After Mexico achieved its independence from Spain in 1821, many of the settlers in the far northern areas felt greater affinity for the US than for the distant government in Mexico City. They welcomed Anglo migrants into their territory and entered into commercial relationships with banks and trading houses originating in the eastern US. As explained by historian Alberto Hurtado in *Intimate Frontiers*, since many Mexican ranchers, like Nieto, were "land-and-cattle rich, but money-poor," they readily entered into trade with the Anglo immigrants, who were increasingly settling illegally in Mexican territory. Despite the Anglos' questionable right to do business in Mexico, their access to cash coincided with the ranchers' needs. In addition, the daughters of Mexican ranchers were sought after as marriage partners by the newly arrived Anglos, many of whom were anxious to transform their cash resources into landholdings and become a part of the local gentry. For their part, the Mexican ranchers – who were overwhelmingly mestizos and from the least educated strata of society – looked on a marriage between their daughters and white Anglos, who were usually literate (although not in Spanish), as a chance to enter the white elite. Land-rich families often married off at least one daughter, usually before her fifteenth birthday, to an Anglo man who was sometimes 10 to 20 years her senior and about whose background they knew very little – so long as he converted to Catholicism.

According to Arcadia Bandini Brennan, a woman who lived through this transition, "as California changed one country's rule to another, family holdings had to be protected, as well as the women." Arcadia Bandini was married in 1825 at the age of 11 to Abel Stearns, a 45-year-old Protestant Yankee from Boston, a man even older than her father, Juan Bandini, one of the largest landowners in Mexican California. Arcadia explains in her memoirs how "Don Abel" brought back presents for her from his trips, including "some beautiful bisque dolls from Paris, whose eyes opened and closed and limbs and head moved. One was a baby doll."[2] The marriage, a business transaction between two men, the Mexican Bandini and the Anglo Stearns, had economic and political ramifications: Stearns got land from Bandini while, according to Arcadia, her husband "fixed things for him [her father] in a very nice and legal way" when the Anglo courts annulled Mexican land grants after California was admitted as a US state. The match had met the needs of both sides, and since Arcadia was too young to determine her future or object to the determination made for her, her own views were deemed of little importance. For most Mexican landowners, however, their relationship with the Anglo settlers would not prove advantageous.

The North American Invasion

For Mexico the mid-nineteenth-century loss of its northern territory following war with the United States was dramatic, brutal, and shocking. Finalized in the 1848 Treaty of

Guadalupe Hidalgo, the transformation and loss had begun over 20 years earlier. Impoverished and lacking unity after the War of Independence against Spain (1810–21), most Mexicans, including wealthy owners of land bordering the United States, concentrated their energies on subsistence agriculture and trade. Beginning in 1821, a transplanted Missourian, Stephen Austin, obtained from the Mexican government the right to settle in Texas 400 families, a number that soon multiplied when others sneaked across the border from Louisiana in hopes of establishing cotton farms, with slaves, despite the prohibition against slavery that Mexico had enacted following independence from Spain. Soon the lucrative cotton cultivation in Texas, along with the prospect of adding a huge pro-slavery territory to the US, led expansionist President James Polk (1795–1849) to launch an attack on Mexico, using as an excuse the drubbing that Texan forces had received in the famous battle of the Alamo in San Antonio (1835). In 1847 Polk sent the US army, under the command of General Winfield Scott (1786–1866), not only to the independent republic of Texas but deep into Mexican territory, all the way south to the capital city. Despite the valor of *Los Niños Heroes*, the young cadets who fell at Chapultepec on the outskirts of Mexico City in a heroic effort to hold out against the invaders, the Mexicans lost. Humiliated, overrun by a superior armed force, and woefully lacking in leadership, Mexico surrendered.

By the terms of the 1848 Treaty of Guadalupe Hidalgo Mexico settled for $15 million, in return for ceding two-thirds of its northern territory to the US (Map 5.2). In one fell swoop the US obtained most of the southwest and California, a state that would one day be the richest and most populous of the Union. The war concluded in 1848 is referred to in US history books as the "Mexican American War," but in the Mexican texts it is called, more accurately, the "War of the North American Invasion."

Notably, the saga of Mexico and the United States exemplified the full gamut of equal and unequal interaction from trade to settlement and eventually war, wherein victors and losers were determined according to relationships of race, class, and gender. The fate of many wealthy Mexican landowners in the territories acquired by the United States was particularly tragic, if ironic. Lulled into believing that their future could be tied to the new American nation with its seat in Washington DC, rather than with distant Mexico City, wealthy Mexican ranchers had joined with Anglos in pursuit of an independent Texas and, for a short while, an independent California. When the latter proved elusive or unworkable, Mexicans who had a few decades earlier welcomed the Anglos into their territory now found themselves in precarious circumstances. Anglos used the US courts and blatantly racist criteria against their Mexican neighbors, who were stripped of their possessions, lost the titles to their ranches, were disenfranchised, and demoted from the highest ranks of society to the status of outsiders in their ancestral land. Mexican landowners who thought that intermarriage with whites had won for them elite status became targets of racial discrimination on the part of newly triumphant Anglos anxious to take their land.

Map 5.2   Mexican territory lost to the United States. (Courtesy Lynn V. Foster, *A Brief History of Mexico*, revised edition, ca. 2004. By permission Facts on File, Inc.)

General López de Santa Anna

The chief figure in Mexican politics during this era was the colorful general Antonio López de Santa Anna (1794–1876). His long military and political career encapsulated the various sides of *caudillismo*, ranging from a heroic defense of the fatherland, in his best moments, to periods of autocratic rule, for much of his career. He was president of Mexico nine times and the most important political figure from 1821 until 1855, abdicating the office from time to time to pursue a military career. In 1836 he led the Mexican assault on the Texas insurgency, defeating the rebels at the Alamo, but was subsequently pursued and forced to concede Texas territory to the independent Lone Star Republic. In what became one of his most memorable exploits, Santa Anna lost a leg during the 1838 defeat of a French invasion, and then presided over the leg's burial in a state funeral some years later. Local residents reportedly would know of the general's stopover in a town because he would leave his artificial leg at a blacksmith's shop to have the silver ornaments polished while he relaxed in a nearby tavern. The leg was just one of the many quirks contributing to his reputation for drama. He was a passionate fan of cockfighting and had many roosters that he entered in competitions with fighting cocks from all over the world. A legendary gambler, he spent thousands of dollars on the games and on acquiring particular fighters. Santa Anna reached heroic status in the war with the United States in 1846, only to descend into humiliating disgrace after the 1848 loss. Following a short return to dictatorial rule from 1853 to 1855, he retreated into political obscurity, where he remained until his death in 1876.

One particular story seems almost too emblematic of Santa Anna's penchant for snatching defeat from the jaws of victory. By 1855 the former military leader had fallen out of favor with every section of the Mexican political class, including his formerly staunch conservative supporters. He left the country and traveled on and off from his base in Cuba to the United States and Europe, dabbling in various gambling and business schemes in hopes of finding riches or glory. On a trip to New York City in the late 1850s, he is said to have brought with him the first shipment of *chicle*, a substance that would later become the base of chewing gum. Santa Anna had no plans to develop chewing gum; rather he had tried, unsuccessfully, to convince US wheel manufacturers that *chicle* could be adapted into a substance for buggy tires. Meanwhile, James Adams, an American who served as an official US government escort for Santa Anna when he was in the US, began to experiment with *chicle*, transforming it into a substance he named "Chiclets". This product was then sold as the first chewing gum. There is no record of Santa Anna expressing any interest in what happened to the *chicle* he introduced to the United States, nor did he make any money from the product he inadvertently helped to launch.

Despite ups and downs, Santa Anna left a strong impression on the tumultuous mid-nineteenth-century Mexican politics, a fame shared by only two others who held national leadership: Benito Juárez (1806–72) and Porfirio Díaz (1830–1915). Defeat at the hands of the North Americans and loss of such a vast amount of Mexican territory in such a shameful (and in the eyes of many international observers, illegal) fashion, left Santa Anna discredited, along with the Church and conservative landowners who had supported him. It was no secret, in fact, that a number of powerful Mexican landowners had sided with the US, and even considered the idea that the US should take over Mexico.

The New Age of Imperialism

In the rest of Latin America, the late nineteenth century was an era of intensified capital investment. In Europe and the US manufacturing accelerated during a time of political and economic stability, following the winding down of several major wars and civil strife on both sides of the Atlantic. The restoration of trade between France and the US, the slow modernization of post-serf Russia and other areas to the east, and the opening of new markets in the Far East and Latin America contributed to global economic expansion. However, England, more than any other nation, was poised to command the seas and flood other nations with its manufactured goods. Spain had tottered and fallen from a vast empire to possessing only a couple colonies in the Americas, which also would be lost by century's end. Portugal had long ceased to have more than a token role in the colonies, having ceded its influence over Brazil to England well before independence in 1821. France was recovering from the effects of the 1848 uprising and rebuilding its economy after the long Napoleonic wars. Great Britain, the most advanced manufacturing center, began to sell a wide range of goods in traditional trading centers in Latin America, such as Rio de Janeiro, Buenos Aires, Mexico City, and Lima, while exploring the feasibility of flooding smaller regional markets with cheaper manufactured goods, especially textiles. Absorbed with supplying a huge home market, the United States remained an infant in international trade until the end of the century. No competitor to England in Europe and Asia, the US began instead to flex its economic and political muscle in relation to the neighboring states of Mexico and Central America, the islands of the Caribbean, and eventually, all of South America.

Central America and the Panama Canal

The countries of the Central American isthmus – Guatemala, Nicaragua, Belize, Honduras, El Salvador, Costa Rica, and Panama – have struggled to maintain sovereignty in the face of fairly concerted outside interference during much of their modern history. Fragmented and, with the exception of Costa Rica, desperately poor, these republics have been prey to bullies from abroad and tyrants at home. For much of the nineteenth and early twentieth centuries a variety of international governments and private firms focused on one or another plan to construct a water route across the narrow landmass. Although interest in cutting a canal through the jungle of the isthmus to facilitate shipping between the Atlantic and Pacific Oceans stretched as far back as the sixteenth century, it was never considered very seriously. When presented with the possibility, King Philip II of Spain reportedly dismissed the plan with the admonition that "What God hath joined together, let no man put asunder," extending the biblical precept for marriage to geography. However, the 1848 discovery of gold in California heightened interest in developing a shorter route to the US West, reducing the time required to circle as far south as Tierra del Fuego, or to continue the cumbersome and costly process of unloading cargo, portaging across the isthmus and reloading on the other side – the only alternatives available at the time.

After the Union's success over southern planters in the Civil War, the newly unified US republic embarked in earnest on a long-held expansionist dream of connecting the country from coast to coast. The need to supply the Pacific coast with goods, settlers, and entrepreneurs from the burgeoning East and Midwest again raised the urgent need for a canal through Central America. The lucrative investment potential was not lost on the major powers of the time, since whoever controlled the canal would reap considerable financial and political benefit. Thus US, French, and British companies were all interested in building a canal, and sent private surveying teams through the jungle in hopes of mapping out the most favorable route, while likewise seeking to secure the backing of a local *caudillo*, or whatever government happened to be in power. US shipping magnate Cornelius Vanderbilt (1794–1877) had secured a concession from the Nicaraguan government in 1840 to survey and build a canal through that country. Navigating Nicaraguan politics was actually as ticklish as attempting to build a water route through the inhospitable terrain. The government was in the hands of one or the other faction of the Liberal or Conservative parties, and politics represented familial or clan feuds more than any distinctive views on political and economic policy. As a result, Vanderbilt's agreement with the Liberals lasted only as long as their party held power, while the subsequent Conservative government fielded offers from British firms.

The back-and-forth was interrupted by one of the more peculiar episodes in the history of US intervention. In 1855 William Walker (1824–60), son of a Tennessee fundamentalist Christian preacher and one-time abolitionist, led an invasion of Nicaragua with 300 mercenaries left over from the US war against Mexico, with the intention of establishing himself as President (read "dictator") of Nicaragua. With the complicity of the Liberals and despite many protests from the Conservatives, who at that time controlled the Nicaraguan government, Walker re-legalized slavery and installed himself as emperor. If the US government ignored Nicaragua's protests, Cornelius Vanderbilt did not. The latter sent his own set of mercenaries into the once-sovereign nation to overthrow Walker, much to the delight of Conservatives. Work proceeded on the canal through Nicaragua, but was soon defeated not by politics, war, or finances, but by yellow fever. Workers imported from China and the West Indies, along with some natives of the region, died in such numbers that Vanderbilt was forced to call a halt to the embattled Nicaraguan route.

Meanwhile, the French company Ferdinand de Lesseps, which built the Suez Canal, began digging in Panama, which was at the time the northernmost province of Colombia. Under the direction of the engineer Phillip Bunau-Varilla (1859–1940), the company began to dig a sea-level canal but soon abandoned the project because it was far too expensive, a construction nightmare, and ultimately unworkable. In 1889 the New Panama Canal Company took up the project in the same area. Supplied and even led by US military officers, a small group in Panama led a rebellion against Colombia, ultimately declaring war on their own government for the dubious purpose of achieving their "independence" as a province. The absolute hypocrisy of this claim was all the more apparent when it became clear that the so-called "rebellion" was nearly over before the government in Bogotá had even learned of its existence. Hastily amassing an army to quell the secessionist movement, Colombian forces arrived too late and found themselves confronting not a small provincial insurgency, but the US army.

There was, in fact, no unified Colombian army capable of responding to the seizure of the northern province, even had Bogotá gotten the news earlier. From October 1899 until November 1902 the two main parties in Colombia (Conservatives and Liberals) fought each other in a conflict that came to be known as the "Thousand Days War." The struggle between the two parties built on ongoing factional warfare that had punctuated the Colombian landscape since the time of independence, the reasons for which have never been entirely clear. As mentioned in an earlier chapter, the post-independence era saw a continuation of regional and personalist rivalries that began as far back as the initial fighting against Spain. With an economy based on the production of various agricultural products, and each producer attempting to negotiate the most favorable trade deals with foreign markets, Colombia was by the end of the century a nation of localized economic and political centers supporting enclaves of pro-ducers in coffee, textiles, livestock, and fruit production. Thus, the rivalries between Liberal and Conservative factions did not represent strong ideological differences as much as competing economies. In *One Hundred Years of Solitude*, García Márquez presents a "docudrama" of how the struggle was understood by ordinary Colombians. The residents of the fictional town of Macondo initially professed their loyalty to either the Liberal or Conservative Party by painting their houses in dramatic colors representative of one or the other side. As the war dragged on, and everyone became increasingly confused as to what each side represented, they all painted their houses the same undefined color, demonstrating the failure, at least in terms of ideological clarity, of either party to offer a well-defined alternative. So it was in the mythical land of Macondo and, García Márquez suggests, so it was throughout the land.

The fact that Colombia was engaged in civil war contributed to the ease with which the US was able to intervene and strip away the northern province. After various attempts to end the conflict, a peace was signed on the US battleship *Wisconsin* on November 21, 1902 in the harbor off Panama. At the time of the signing US engineering teams were surveying for a canal through the isthmus. Colombia's thousand days of civil war thereby came to an end just at the time and place that Washington had designated for the construction of the canal. It might seem serendipitous; it was not. In an exercise of Theodore Roosevelt's "Big Stick" diplomacy, army gunboats docked off the harbor while the US government promptly recognized the sovereign nation of Panama, whose first president was none other than Phillip Bunau-Varilla, the canal engineer and a French citizen. In one of its first acts, the New Panama Canal Company, located in the recently formed "country" of Panama, signed a treaty authorized by US Secretary of State John Hay, paying Bunau-Varilla $40 million to build the canal, for which favor Bunau-Varilla delivered to Washington in 1903 an agreement granting to the US the right "in perpetuity" to control the Panama Canal. Despite Colombia's vociferous objections to the terms of the Hay–Bunau-Varilla treaty, and the entire fiasco, the United States guaranteed the independence of Panama and secured a perpetual lease on a 10-mile strip for the canal. The newly created surrogate state of Panama was compensated with an initial payment of $10 million and an annuity of $250,000, beginning in 1913.

Actual construction of the canal proved to be a massive undertaking, far more difficult, deadly, and expensive than the construction of the Suez Canal through desert sand. Jungle and rock excavations cost thousands of lives, many of them workers imported from the West Indies. So dangerous was the work that the project for a while gener-ated a sordid, but nonetheless "legal," sale in cadavers from Panama to medical schools in the US, the profits for which sale accrued to the Panama Railroad Company that

shipped them off. One doctor was rumored to have accumulated, bleached, and cata-
logued a wide range of skeletons for so-called "scientific study" of the many nationalities
that had participated, and died, in the building of the canal. The waterway through
the Canal Zone opened in 1914 and remained under US control until the 1970s, when
Panamanian President Omar Torrijos (1929–81) and US President Jimmy Carter
(b. 1924) negotiated a new agreement whereby the administration of the canal
reverted to Panamanian control on December 31, 1999.

Ecuador and the "Panama" Hat

Curiously, apart from the canal Panama may be most associated with a hat. Actually,
the hat belongs not at all to Panama, except that it stands as a symbol of the entrepreneurship, the importance of new international trade routes, and the political
wheeling and dealing that surrounded the history of the canal. The canal was, after
all, an engineering wonder and a laborer's nightmare, or at least a creative marvel for
which those who executed the plan (the workers who dug it) were inadequately compensated. So too are the hats. These finely woven, light cream-colored straw hats have
been carefully sewn, blocked, and shaped in a few towns in the highlands of Ecuador
and some other areas of the Andean Altiplano for centuries. The first written reference
to the "woven straw hats" appears in the accounts of the Spanish conquistador Francisco Pizarro in the sixteenth century when he met the people of what is today Peru.
Today most genuine Panama hats are produced in Montecristi and Cuenca in Ecuador
(Figure 5.3).

Famous for their fine weave, which provides ideal protection from the tropical sun,
the hats were prized for their utility, comfort, and style. The US army bought 10,000
Ecuadoran hats for the men stationed in Cuba at the turn of the century, while other
thousands were sold by itinerant peddlers in Colombia and other countries adjacent to
Ecuador throughout the nineteenth century. The Ecuadorian hats became identified
with Panama when travelers passing through the isthmus on their way to and from
the gold fields of California purchased them and brought them to both ends of the US
continent as a "souvenir of Panama." By the time the canal was being dug in the first
decade of the twentieth century, the straw hats from Ecuador were standard on the
heads of workers depicted in photographs of the gigantic construction project that
appeared in newspapers throughout the world. On his November 1906 visit to the canal
excavation, then-President Theodore Roosevelt was photographed at the controls of
a huge Bucyrus steam shovel wearing a "Panama" hat, as were the other workers and
onlookers in the picture (Figure 5.4). No matter how many corrections and clarifications
from Ecuadorians, then as now, the hat would forever be associated with Panama.

In many ways the story of the hat parallels the history of uneven exchange char-
acteristic of most Latin American exports. A master weaver can take as long as eight
months to weave a hat, using for the finest hats the best fronds from the toquilla
palm tree. Many of the best weavers, who live in villages as far as 100 miles from
Montecristi, sell a single hat of the highest quality to buyers for approximately $200.

Figure 5.3   Saint James the Great as a Moor-killer (Santiago de Matamoros), painting by an unknown artist of the Cuzco school, presumably seventeenth century. The painting, and others that survive in Ecuador and Peru, show the early conquistadores wearing headgear that was later dubbed a "Panama" hat.

Figure 5.4 US President Theodore Roosevelt at the construction of the Panama Canal.
The *New York Times* photograph of Roosevelt wearing a white hat while on a steam shovel
at the Panama Canal on November 15, 1906 appeared in newspapers throughout the world,
supposedly giving rise to the label "Panama hat." (Courtesy Theodore Roosevelt Collection,
Harvard College Library)

The hat then passes through five more people who finish the brim, shape it, remove imperfections, bleach the straw, and add interior and exterior bands. Since a classic woven hat retails outside Ecuador for anywhere from $450 to $10,000, depending on the quality, the best hats sell for two to five times more than one master weaver is paid for his *eight months* of work. Given the time and skill involved, and the encroaching competition from low-quality copies made in China and other parts of the world – and, interestingly, that the market for Panama hats in Ecuador has lost out to the ubiquitous baseball cap – the production and sale of high-quality Panamas is disappearing. A fine craft and the livelihoods of a line of artisans and other entrepreneurs in the commodity chain are likewise coming to an end. What, one might ask, will replace the creations and the trade in hats from the towns of Ecuador for the next generations?

Independence at Last? Cuba and Puerto Rico

The Panama Canal and the Ecuadorian hat that has since been associated with it illustrate nineteenth-century changes in hemispheric political and economic relationships. If Latin America suffered from fragmentation, localism, and weak central governments, the US was poised to take advantage of the disunity in the South. A consolidated post-Civil War US with capital to spare looked to its own territory and that of neighbors to feed its ravenously hungry industrial appetite. In fact, one of the most egregious examples of US gunboat diplomacy was its late nineteenth-century war with Spain to acquire that nation's possessions in the Caribbean and far Pacific. The most important was Cuba, a country that President John Quincy Adams had voiced an interest in annexing since as early as 1823. That was the year of the Monroe Doctrine, a US statement that claimed the hemisphere for the Americans, warning out European interference. Its use over the centuries has been to promote US dominance more than exclude European intervention and as such demonstrates the difference between Britain's role in the Americas and that of the United States. Even if England's trading and investment relationship with Latin America, especially Argentina, seemed to place the latter at a disadvantage, it was an interaction based on trade. For the US in the nineteenth century, securing stable and reliable trading partners began to merge with direct political intervention.

Throughout the nineteenth century US business interests were intensely involved in Cuban affairs, mainly because from 1850 onward the small island was the world's leading sugar producer and the US its most important customer. US capital was heavily invested in Cuba's mills, transportation and communication networks, and all aspects of the sugar economy. When Creole planters moved to end the parasitical control that Spain held over the island, preferring instead to develop their own trading partners, the power vacuum that resulted opened opportunities for more direct US intervention. Taking advantage of a naval revolt in the Spanish port city of Cadiz that resulted in the temporary overthrow of the Spanish monarchy and installation of a republic, Cuban patriots declared independence on October 10, 1868. Despite Spain's weakness, the imperial power refused to accede to the Cuban Creoles' demands for self-rule, instead launching a strong retaliatory force against the independence movement and playing on fears among Creole elites that Cuba without Spain would become another Haiti. The Ten Years' War raged from 1868 until 1878, cost the Cubans over 250,000 lives, inflicted major damage on the sugar industry, and – except for beginning the gradual abolition of slavery (met with ambivalence by many Creole planters) – ended with no significant change in the colonial relationship.

One key result, however, was increased interest by US sugar trusts in restoring the island's profitable exports. The initial independence movement was quashed during the patriots' defeat in both the Ten Years' War and the subsequent *Guerra Chiquita* ("Little War") from 1875 to 1880, but the events brought to prominence a number of important Cuban leaders, foremost of whom was José Martí, considered the "Father of the Cuban Nation." From exile in New York, the charismatic poet, essayist, literary figure, and political activist had waged a tireless war in the pages of US newspapers, calling for independence from Spain. He was the founder of the Cuban Revolutionary Party in 1892 and participated in the patriots' 1895 invasion of the island, where he died in a skirmish with Spanish forces. The most important military commander was General Antonio Maceo Grajales (1845–96), the man known as the "Bronze Titan" in reference to both his military genius and his African heritage. General Maceo led an army of mainly Afro-Cuban soldiers against far larger Spanish forces, chalking up impressive victories with a guerrilla warfare strategy for over 20 years. He entered the rebel army as a private in 1868, rising to the rank of general and chief military officer in a less than a decade. Despite Creole fears that independence would result in a black republic on the Haitian model, and unfavorable comparisons with the black generals of Haiti, Maceo maintained his command because he was an expert officer. Like Martí, General Maceo died in battle, killed in a Spanish ambush in 1896. While interpretations that place the entire course of history on the shoulders of individual figures should be viewed with great caution, Cuba may be the exception. Both Maceo and Martí were tremendously important political figures whose reputations as patriots, and whose political and military expertise, earned them enormous respect from their followers. Their leadership and stature might have been capable of offsetting the conservative Creoles' eventual surrender in the face of the US intervention. It was not to be, however.

In the midst of the renewed Cuban independence struggle, powerful US interests sought to acquire Cuba. Pushed by President William McKinley's expansionist Republican Party, urged on by sugar interests, and propagandized widely by the William Randolph Hearst newspaper conglomerate, the US declared war on Spain after a dubious incident that resulted in the explosion of the US battleship *Maine* in Havana harbor. The cause of the explosion remains unclear – whether a spark in the ship's powder magazine, a harbor mine, or sabotage by provocateurs linked with the US sugar interests or the Hearst newspapers – the result was the same. The jingoistic "yellow press," especially Joseph Pulitzer of the New York *Tribune*, screamed for revenge; Teddy Roosevelt sought to use the incident as a political platform from which to oppose McKinley; and demonstrations erupted in the streets of American cities calling for war with Spain.

Exhausted after over 20 years of war, Spain was able to mount little resistance against the fierce onslaught of Cuban independence forces. Indeed, the Spanish were widely regarded to be on the verge of defeat when the US intervened in what the Secretary of

State called "a splendid little war." Teddy Roosevelt finally got the recognition he craved by leading his volunteer troop of Rough Riders on the island, although his "triumphant" seizure of San Juan Hill (resulting in the loss of 76 percent of his combatants, three times the losses of the Spanish) was opposed by the regular military officer in charge. Despite their competence on the battlefield, the US excluded Cubans from the formal peace negotiations, and signed the Treaty of Paris with Spain on December 10, 1898. Washington declared its own terms, which included controlling Cuba as a self-governing protectorate, forcing on the latter all the administrative burdens but none of the benefits of sovereignty (see Box 5.1). US Army General Leonard Wood was appointed governor and charged with overseeing the terms of the new Cuban Constitution, a document that only met with US approval after the addition of the Platt Amendment. The latter granted the US the right to intervene at will to maintain whatever government it chose on the island and required Cuba to sell or lease land for US military bases. This was the origin of the Guantánamo military base at one end of the Cuban island, which housed an infamous US federal prison after the September 11, 2001 attacks on the New York World Trade Center.

The tiny island of Puerto Rico was a neighbor to Cuba and experienced a similar turn of historical events. As one of Spain's earliest possessions, it developed into a prosperous sugar and tobacco colony over the succeeding 400 years. Like Cuba, Puerto Rico imported African slaves to work on sugar plantations and, in the mid-nineteenth century, brought in increasing numbers of Chinese indentured servants as laborers, especially in tobacco. The independence movement in Puerto Rico also paralleled Cuba's, but owing to its much smaller size was never as powerful or ideologically cohesive. In the *Grito de Lares*, September 23, 1868, a group of Creole planters under the leadership of Ramón Betances rose in revolt against the Spanish Crown. But just as Spain was ready to grant Puerto Rico functional sovereignty, including representatives to the Spanish Parliament and an elected governor, the US intervened in Cuba and declared war on Spain. Although Puerto Rico already had a sovereign parliament in session on July 17, 1898, and an elected governor, the US invaded the southernmost city of Ponce, raised the Stars and Stripes, and declared Puerto Rico to be free from Spain – a colonial power that was essentially no longer even claiming it. According to the terms of the Treaty of Paris that ended the "conflict," Puerto Rico became a possession of the United States.

Determined to prevent Cuban independence fighters from obtaining control over their homeland (highlighting the unfortunate vacuum in Cuban leadership wrought by the deaths of Martí and Maceo), General Wood installed in power the most conservative planters: Creoles who had resisted independence from Spain, opposed the abolition of slavery, and were comfortable with US domination so long as their profits were secure. The US army patrolled a compliant Cuba, ushering the small country even more fully into the economic sphere of its powerful northern neighbor.

To their credit, some from within the ranks of US political and intellectual circles heard the protests of the Cuban patriots and voiced their disapproval of this new, heavy-handed US imperialism. The eloquence of Carl Schurz (1829–1906), a founding member of the Republican Party, stands in sharp contrast to the malleable McKinley or the

Box 5.1   Yellow journalism

The US public formed its impressions of Cuba and other parts of Latin America through many articles and cartoons that depicted the Cuban people as needing US intervention to "save" it from Spain. The cartoon shown here (Figure 5.5) depicts Cuba as an unruly (black) child recklessly shunning Uncle Sam who holds a well-behaved (white) Puerto Rican child, docilely accepting US protection.

UNCLE SAM to PORTO RICO: **"And to think that bad boy came near being your brother!"**
Chicago Inter Ocean, 1905.

Figure 5.5   Discontent with Cuban political and business leaders led to a rebellion against the first independent government in July 1906. The US media claimed Cuba – here depicted in a racist stereotype as a reckless gunslinger and a child – was unable to govern itself, while Puerto Rico – which was under direct US control – is seen as docile and stable.

Box 5.2   1898 San Juan Hill: Teddy Roosevelt

Eduardo Galeano wrote of these events:

> Brandishing his Stetson, Teddy Roosevelt gallops at the head of his "Rough Riders;" and when he descends San Juan Hill he carries, crumpled in his hand, a Spanish flag. He will take all the glory for this battle which opens the way to Santiago de Cuba. Of the Cubans who also fought, no journalist will write a word . . .

> To make a quick end to the Cuban war, Teddy has proposed that a North American squadron should flatten Cadiz and Barcelona with its guns; but Spain, exhausted from so much warfare against the Cubans, surrenders in less than four months. From San Juan Hill, the victorious Teddy Roosevelt gallops at top speed to the governorship of New York State and on to the presidency of the United States. This fanatical devotee of a God who prefers gunpowder to incense takes a deep breath and writes: *No triumph of peace is quite so great as the supreme triumph of war.*
> Within a few years, he will receive the Nobel Peace Prize.

Quoted in Galeano, *Faces and Masks*, II, p. 248.

grandstanding Teddy Roosevelt (see Box 5.2). Schurz declared: "We hold that the policy known as imperialism is hostile to liberty and tends toward militarism, an evil from which it has been our glory to be free. We regret that it has become necessary in the land of Washington and Lincoln to reaffirm that all men, of whatever race or color, are entitled to life, liberty and the pursuit of happiness."[3] The writer Mark Twain (1835–1910) suggested that the US should remake the flag befitting its new role in the world: remove the traditional stars and stripes, paint the white stripes black, and replace the stars with a skull and crossbones. Piracy reigned again in the Caribbean, but the new pirates were bearing the flag of a powerful expanding nation.

At the opening of the twentieth century, the Monroe Doctrine, President James Monroe's 1823 assertion that the United States would oppose European imperialism and recolonization schemes in the Americas, had become a vital tool for US interference in the internal affairs of the sovereign nations of the hemisphere. The most conspicuous sign of the US "coming of age" as an emerging power on the world stage was President Theodore Roosevelt's speech in 1904, proclaiming US hegemony in the Americas. This statement, known as the "Roosevelt Corollary," came to be seen as an additional rationale for the principles contained in the Monroe Doctrine. Latin American nations had always viewed the Monroe Doctrine with suspicion – especially since Great Britain, not the US, had supported their anti-colonial struggle. However, the Doctrine had little bite so long as their northern neighbor remained a minor power. When the US emerged from the Spanish–American War with the might, and the hubris, to hold the European nations in check, it became clear that business and political interests intent on intervening in Latin America's affairs now had the upper hand.

Conclusion

This chapter has presented a few examples of commodities whose production and sale transformed the society that produced them. We have seen that as opposed to a bare export–import statistic, there is a social history associated with the production of a commodity in a given time and place, just as there is a corresponding social history associated with its consumption. One of the key components of the commodity chain was the rise of the United States as a major consumer power. The imperial muscle from the United States proved a formidable obstacle to Caribbean and Central American sovereignty, as nationalism ran aground under the weight of its northern neighbor.

Similarly, economic and political forces that benefited from the alliance with the emerging US elite stood at the Latin American end of the "two-way bridge." The Peruvian government oversaw an impressive influx of revenue during the guano boom, but failed to remain prosperous, losing out to Chilean nitrates by century's end. Coffee became a staple of Colombian and Brazilian exporters, providing for Brazil sufficient revenues to finance heavy industrialization, when combined with foreign capital investment. In Colombia coffee exports generated income in specific regions that led to a more dispersed economic development and federated pattern of political power. Mexico struggled to create an independent republic only to lose over half of its territory to the expanding US. The next chapter examines the dramatic social and demographic changes that arose in countries that were increasingly urban, industrial, and contentious.

6 | Immigration, and Urban and Rural Life

During the final decades of the nineteenth century and early years of the twentieth, the countries of Latin America underwent significant demographic changes, similar to those that swept the United States and Canada. According to Thomas Holloway, from the 1880s until 1930 approximately 10 million immigrants from Europe and the Near East entered Latin America, arriving from Italy, Spain, Portugal, and Germany, along with Christians from the old Ottoman Empire states of Syria and Lebanon (who were, and still are, misnamed "Turks" from the time they arrived in the new lands). Leaving behind poverty, civil strife, persecution, and hunger in hopes of finding a better life in the "New World," most immigrants poured into the Southern Cone countries of Argentina, Uruguay, and Chile, as well as southern Brazil and to a lesser extent other Latin American and Caribbean nations. By 1895 more than 80 percent of laborers in Buenos Aires were foreign-born, as was a quarter of the nation's entire population of 4 million. Over the next few decades, from 1890 to 1916 – with the exception of World War I (1914–18) when emigration from Europe was suspended – 2.9 million immigrants entered Argentina, mainly from Italy.

Uruguay was the only country of Latin America that had attracted an earlier wave of immigrants, mainly from Spain, France, and Italy, so that as early as 1850 the population of Montevideo was over half foreign-born. In addition, Uruguay underwent explosive population growth in the late nineteenth century as a result of immigration, a high birth rate, and low death rate. Sparsely populated at the start of the century, Uruguay grew from a total of 70,000 inhabitants in 1830 to 450,000 in 1900. Like neighboring Argentina, Uruguay continued to attract immigrants during the late nineteenth and early twentieth centuries; however, the percentage of foreign-born remained lower because of the rapid rate of natural increase. Nonetheless Uruguay also became a country whose population increasingly traced its ancestry back to Europe, rather than to indigenous roots, like Mexico and the Andean nations, or to Africa and Asia, like Brazil.

Between 1890 and 1920 the city of São Paulo in southern Brazil grew nearly tenfold (from 65,000 to 600,000) with the arrival of immigrants from Portugal, Italy, Spain, the Middle East, and Japan. Motivated by a desire to "whiten" the population and hold in check demands for higher wages following the abolition of slavery in 1888, Brazilian private organizations, with government backing, encouraged European immigration. The Society for the Promotion of Immigration in São Paulo and the Rio de Janeiro Central Immigration Society, among others, publicized opportunities for workers in Brazil by distributing handbills in villages and towns in Italy and other countries rimming the Mediterranean, offering free passage and steady work at good wages in Brazil's coffee fields to potential emigrants. Chile also attracted about 100,000 immigrants, especially to the port city of Valparaiso and the capital, Santiago.

Asian Immigration

Apart from those who came from the Middle East, the principal non-European immigrants to Latin America came from China (destined for Cuba, Central America, Mexico, Peru, and Brazil) or Japan (to Brazil and Peru). Following the abolition of black slavery in the 1830s, both the British and Dutch colonial governments imported indentured servants from South Asia to British Guiana (renamed Guyana after independence in 1966), Trinidad & Tobago, Surinam, and Curaçao with the intention of depressing the price of labor and quelling demands for better working conditions among recently freed slaves. Walter Rodney, in his study of the Guyanese working class, points to a colonial policy of taking land from black freed persons and giving it to Indians after the latter had completed their indenture, thereby literally "robbing Peter to pay Paul." When East Indian immigration to the Caribbean ended in 1917, some 250,000 had settled in Guyana; others were brought to Martinique and a few of the French islands, but did not stay. By 1940 the Dutch colonial government had settled 33,000 Javanese indentured servants in Surinam and Curaçao, bringing them from their colonies in Indonesia. Tensions between the descendants of African and Indian immigrants have played a significant role in the political and economic life of both Guyana and Trinidad & Tobago.

During the second half of the nineteenth century about a quarter of a million Chinese, overwhelmingly men, migrated to Cuban sugar plantations where they worked as indentured servants alongside African slaves. Similarly, Chinese "coolies" worked in the guano fields of Peru and on the construction of the Andean railroad. Some of these laborers eventually left the minefields and rural estates to take up work in urban areas as tradesmen, in restaurants, and in the service sector, where, given the extreme gender imbalance, they married non-Chinese women and eventually were absorbed into the mestizo population. As the US began to limit Asian immigration in the early twentieth century, proceeding to cut it off entirely in the 1920s, Chinese immigrants re-routed to Mexico, heading there directly from China or after a stop in California. By the second decade of the twentieth century, over 25,000 Chinese had entered Mexico, where they achieved moderate success in small businesses, intellectual circles, and the government bureaucracy. As more Chinese achieved middle-class status, resentment arose among other Mexicans and outbreaks of anti-Asian rioting erupted, reaching a high point in 1929 when the entire Chinese population was expelled from the northern state of Sonora.

Japanese immigration to Peru and Brazil took place at the turn of the nineteenth and twentieth centuries, crested during the years between World Wars I and II, and then tapered off in subsequent decades, but did not end until the 1960s. Similar to the pattern established earlier by the Chinese, Japanese migrants worked as indentured servants, although their contracts were shorter; the migration process was more closely monitored by the home government in Japan to avoid the most egregious abuses; and, while small in number, women migrated along with men. Having greater opportunities to form marriages among themselves, fewer Japanese intermarried with the Peruvian and Brazilian population, resulting in a more intact transmigration of culture and language from Japan to the new homelands. Free immigrants, not coming under indentured contracts, also entered Peru and Brazil until the Japanese attack on Pearl Harbor in 1941 halted migration. Under pressure from the United States, Peru even expelled over 1,300 Japanese from its territory, sending them to internment camps in Texas during the war.

The greatest flow of people from Asia to Latin America was the movement of Japanese to Brazil. Prompted by planters anxious to recruit low-wage workers in the wake of abolition, politicians from the state of São Paulo prevailed on the Brazilian government to lift an earlier ban on Asian immigration. Between 1908 and 1961 approximately 250,000 *nikkei* (first-generation Japanese migrants) settled in the states of São Paulo, Paraná, Mato Grosso, and Pará. Today their numbers have increased to 800,000, making the community the largest concentration of Japanese outside their homeland. Return migrants from Brazil currently comprise a sizeable number of recent immigrants to Japan (Figure 6.1).

European Immigration

Other distinct migration patterns emerged at the turn of the last century. From 1902 until 1916 approximately 400,000 mainly Spanish immigrants entered Cuba, which likewise received large numbers of Chinese. Paraguay, for its part, attempted to attract settlers in hopes of building up its population after the losses incurred during the War of the Triple Alliance (see Chapter 4). Paraguay encouraged settlements of French, English, Russians, German Mennonites, and others, offering tracts of free land and free passage from the old country. However, in the face of Paraguay's devastated post-war economy, very poor administration, and limited ability to incorporate new arrivals into a country lacking public services, regional markets, road networks, communication and rail lines, most of the immigrant communities failed as rural settlements. Large numbers of the new arrivals either returned home or moved on to cities in Argentina, Brazil, and Uruguay (see Figure 6.2).

The pattern of internal migration from the countryside to cities was more pronounced in some countries than others, depending often on the prosperity, or lack thereof, of the rural area in question. In many cases the landholding elite blocked the passage

Figure 6.1   The Torii gate at the entrance to Liberdade (Liberty), the Little Tokyo neighborhood of São Paulo, Brazil. (Barbara Weightman photo)

of land reform legislation that would have divided the big estates, offering unused portions of land to immigrants for settlement. In others, governments made land available, but the lack of roads and infrastructure limited its appeal to all but the most intrepid. As a result immigrants were discouraged from making a go of it on their own, forced instead to work on the large estates and accept whatever meager wage was offered. Nonetheless, the harsh climate, isolation, and semi-feudal working conditions in the *pampas* (flat plains) of Argentina, the coffee plantations and rural areas of Brazil, and on ranches in Uruguay and Chile encouraged migrants to abandon the countryside and move to cities to take jobs in manufacturing, transportation, and communication networks; on urban development projects; and in the expanding commercial and government sectors. The cities grew, along with a new urban culture, beginning a trend toward urbanization that stands as one of the key features of Latin American societies today.

The Southern Cone

The impetus for the growth of manufacturing, and the migration of millions of people from Europe and Asia to fill jobs in the Americas, stemmed from the dramatic transformation underway in the industrial economies of Europe and, to a lesser extent, North

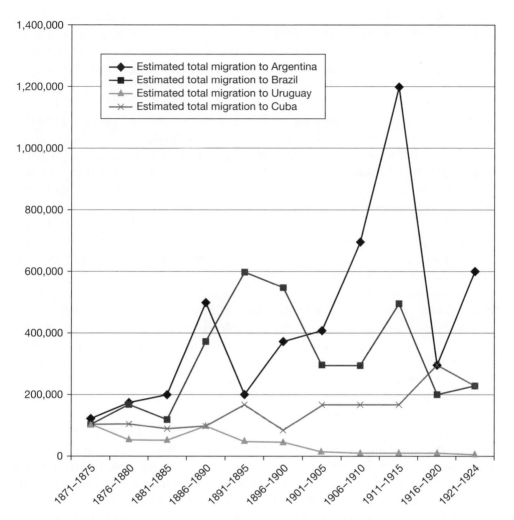

Figure 6.2   Migration to Argentina, Brazil, Cuba, and Uruguay, 1871–1924.

America. When the patriots met in Tucumán in 1816 to form the new Argentine nation – then named the United Provinces of the River Plate – England stood ready to supply the new state with goods, talent, capital, and people. Very much in need of hides for leather goods and shoes, as well as machine belts for factories, wool and cotton to feed the mills of its burgeoning textile industry, and meat and grain to feed its rapidly expanding population, England viewed Argentina as a crucial trading partner.

Unlike Germany and France, which had greater access to agricultural goods within their borders, Britain could not feed and clothe itself autonomously – especially because for generations the peasantry had been moved from the countryside into the city to labor in the "workshop of the world," as the seat of empire was known. Moreover, England stood in stark contrast to the United States, a rising power that was developing its industry and trade from its own ample supply of cotton, hides, grains, and foodstuffs, obtained from the land it was conquering "from shore to shore." Likewise, the US had a natural market for processed goods among the immigrants pouring in to participate in that settlement, as well as displacing the Native Americans. By contrast, England was a tiny island nation that looked out beyond its borders, took from afar, sold to the world, and in so doing claimed the sea as its own domain. Eric Hobsbawm has remarked that Britain was, at its height, the most globalized of world powers and "in some senses even more global than the US now, as it single-handedly controlled the oceans to an extent to which no country now controls the skies."[1]

A sign on the Delaware River Bridge outside Trenton, New Jersey reads: "Trenton Makes – The World Takes." Now an anachronism for the twenty-first-century rust-belt city that stands as a mere shell of what US industrial might used to signify, that terse phrase cuts to the heart of international trade from the perspective of an advanced capitalist state. A variation on those words could have graced a billboard outside Leeds, or Sheffield, Manchester or London in the nineteenth century: "Britain Makes – The World Takes." No Latin American nation complemented England's expansionist, free market, neocolonial designs as well as Argentina. The country seemed tailor-made to fit into England's economic, political, and cultural milieu as a supplier of primary goods and recipient of finished manufactures. Buenos Aires was Argentina's lone city of significant trade and enterprise in the nineteenth century; the rest of the country was, and to some extent still is, an expanse of flat plains. Smaller provincial cities served as collection points for goods, which were then passed on to the port of Buenos Aires over roads that spread out like spokes from the hub at the port to distant provinces. Argentina, it must have seemed, was a land sitting in wait for the call of the industrializing world on the other side of the ocean.

Post-independence Argentina was a geographical, political, and even cultural unit with enormous potential to complement Britain's needs. After 1825 Anglo-Argentine trade was conducted on the "most favored nation" principle, allowing England the greatest advantage in availing itself of Argentine goods. Under the strong-arm rule of Juan Manuel de Rosas, governor of Buenos Aires and later dictator on and off from 1826 until 1852, Argentina became firmly established as an export-oriented agricultural economy. Ranchers, or *estancieros*, consolidated their control by century's end, under the political leadership of Julio Argentino Roca (1843–1914), also known as "the Fox." Roca (not to be confused with Rosas, although they shared a penchant for dictatorial rule), along with other regional *caudillos*, launched a genocidal "ethnic cleansing" to clear the indigenous people from the plains, much like their counterparts in North America. The Argentine campaign that ended in 1880 came to be known as the "Conquest of the Desert," and resulted in Roca selling off or giving away large tracts of land to his military officers and supportive *estancieros*.

But unlike the process in the western US, removal of indigenous people from the Argentine *pampas* was not accompanied by a homesteading policy to settle individual farmers on arable plots of land. Instead, Roca's late nineteenth-century giveaway to the ranchers effectively sealed off the prospects of establishing a class of small farmers linked to the domestic economy, capable of supporting self-sufficient urban growth. What resulted, however, meshed perfectly with British trade and investment designs, as well as the interests of the landowning elite. Argentina's immense grasslands were capable of providing an endless supply of foodstuffs, hides, and wool, so long as Europe supplied technology, capital, and labor. The introduction of steam vessels cut the shipping time between the ports of England and Buenos Aires in half. Added to that, newly developed refrigeration methods allowed for the transport of fresh meat in place of the jerked and salted beef that had previously been the only method of preserving perishable foodstuffs during the many weeks of voyage. British banks and investors readily stepped in with financial assistance to build the infrastructure and manufacturing base, including railroads, roads, port facilities, banks, insurance firms, packing houses, and utilities.

The final obstacle standing in the way of Argentina's entrance into the commodity chain was an adequate supply of labor. Work in the traditional ranching sector had required little labor, mainly a few cowboys (*gauchos*) to oversee thousands of acres of land. But processing raw materials for export; the manufacture of foods, beverages, and textiles; and the construction of railroads and buildings called for thousands of workers, of which Argentina was in short supply. Thus began the massive influx of European immigrants who over the next decades overwhelmed the mestizo and Afro-Argentine population, at least in the coastal zones, to the point of disappearance. Sixty percent of Argentina's population growth was from immigrants, pushing the population upward from1.8 million in 1869 to 8 million in 1914. Five million immigrants poured into Buenos Aires and coastal cities, provincial towns, and some farms, leaving Argentina with a population that traces its origins mainly to northern Italy and Spain, with a smattering of other nationalities, including French, Germans, and Russians (the latter mainly Jews). By 1880 the Carnival flags of Italy, Spain, and other European nations had replaced the banners of the black clubs (see Figure 6.3).

Life on the Pampas

Although most immigrants settled in Buenos Aires (residents of which are called *porteños*, or port dwellers) and a few other urban centers, some of the original immigrants attempted to make a living off the land. Escaping desperate poverty in Italy, immigrants in the 1880s were mainly illiterate, unskilled men who traveled two to four weeks in the bottom of a crowded boat, with little food and poor sanitation, to work during the harvests. Many came as tenant farmers, working either as sharecroppers or as paid laborers for absentee landowners on large, isolated plots of land far from the coast and urban centers. Some of the laborers moved back and forth between Italy and Argentina, their steerage-class fares costing about two week's wages. Called *golondrinas* – meaning swallows, for the bird that is known to return to the same locale each season – these men hailed from small villages in northern Italy and eventually settled down on one or the other side of the Atlantic.

Life on the pampas was dismal and lonely; thus it is no wonder the majority of settlers eventually migrated to cities for more permanent employment, if they stayed in Argentina at all. The transient laborer built his dwelling of mud within a rectangle

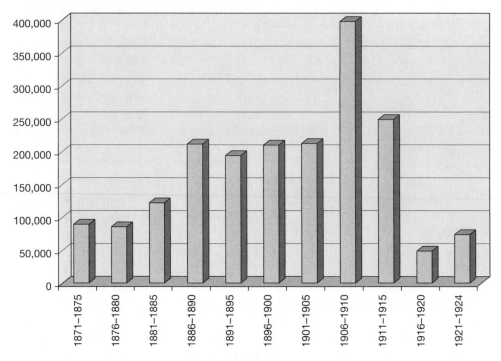

Figure 6.3   Italian immigration to Argentina, 1871–1924.

measured out on the ground; saplings marked the poles of the four corners to provide a makeshift frame, and walls were plastered with a mixture of dirt, water, and manure, with straw woven into the mix for stability. Topped with a roof of straw thatch (replaced in subsequent years by galvanized steel), this dwelling of 10–12 square feet with a door, and maybe a couple of openings for windows, served as the new immigrant's home, often for a season and sometimes for a whole year. A few of the men paired with indigenous and mestizo women from the few settlements scattered on the pampas and raised families. Little is known of these families since they left almost no settled communities with schools or stores, and only occasionally attended church. With little chance of owning property, most immigrants moved to cities or returned to Europe. A tiny fraction managed to buy land, and even prospered, but they were the exception. Overall, Argentina's history of immigration is associated with urban growth and city life, where the new arrivals found opportunities, jobs, education, and social life, all of which were absent in the rural areas.

British Investment

Except for periodic worldwide depressions in the 1890s, the Anglo-Argentine alliance worked out well for both sides. In 1889 British capital in Argentina accounted for nearly half of that nation's entire overseas investment. For its part, in the late nineteenth century Argentina rose to be the foremost corn exporter in the world, second in wheat and near the top in mutton, wool, hides, and beef. From 1860 to 1914 Argentina's GDP (gross domestic product) grew at an annual average rate of at least five percent, one of the longest recorded rates of sustained growth. But over the long term this period of growth did not prove to be completely advantageous to Argentina, or at least not to a majority of its citizens. The country's traditional elite was more interested in overseeing vast country estates, attending horse races and polo matches, and entertaining themselves than in taking on the complicated and sometimes messy task of running the country, building infrastructure, and ensuring an autonomous future. The label "Argentine Playboy" might have been the precursor to today's "jet set," while the phrase, "rich as an Argentine" entered the lexicon in Europe and America in reference to the Argentine oligarchy's demonstrative pride in having the richest jockey club in the world and horse races with the finest thoroughbreds.

Buenos Aires flourished as a result of both foreign investment and the vitality that immigrants brought to its economic and social base. From 1900 to 1929, more than one-third (35 percent) of Argentina's total fixed investment came from foreigners, mostly English banks and private firms. Immigrants to cities took jobs in urban construction, built new buildings, paved streets, widened avenues, and helped to construct an impressive system of parks, plazas, and pathways. In the manufacturing sector immigrants filled jobs in processing plants and packing houses, both inside the city and in the suburban industrial belt cropping up around it. Finally, the influx of such an enormous number of people stimulated internal economic growth as the domestic demand for food, clothing, transportation, housing, household goods, and other necessities of daily life kept pace with urban expansion. Nonetheless, growing dependence on foreign investment disturbed political nationalists who foresaw the danger of tying the nation's economic health to outside interests. But their voices were drowned out in the euphoria of seemingly endless prosperity.

Uruguay, Argentina's neighbor across the Rio de la Plata estuary, likewise attracted large amounts of British investment capital, which grew more than fivefold in less than 20 years, from an estimated £6.5 million in 1884 to £40 million in 1900. Although Uruguay was not a large-scale recipient of capital in comparison with Britain's other investments, the impact of British money was significant when compared to domestic capital investment. With little competition, English firms were able to dictate favorable concessions from the government for constructing rail lines to designated *estancias* in the interior that provided mutton, hides, and wool to the export market. In Argentina, Brazil, and Uruguay British companies largely built the railroads and financed the urban infrastructure, including water, transit networks, telephone, gas, and tram lines. In Montevideo foreign firms bankrolled most government expenses involved in managing the expanding commercial and political bureaucracy. Unlike Argentina and Brazil, however, a large sector of Uruguayan society and members of the government became fearful of losing the nation's autonomy to the British overseers quite early on. In the face of criticism of the high cost and inefficiency of public services, by the beginning of the twentieth century Uruguay's political elite instituted strict controls over foreign investment, passed protectionist legislation, and encouraged domestic manufacturing.

The Changing Cultural Landscape

In addition to their impact on the economy, the large-scale presence of immigrants had a decisive effect on the cultural landscape of many Latin American countries. Recent arrivals poured into ramshackle tenements in the largely Italian neighborhood of La Boca in Buenos Aires, after a long day's labor frequenting and running small grocery stores, shoe repair shops, cafés and bars, barbershops, card parlors, dance halls and brothels.

Music and dance

On the streets of La Boca was born one of Argentina's best-known contributions to world culture: the tango. Developed in lower-class Italian immigrant dance halls, it was shunned by the *porteño* elite and barred from being performed in downtown social gatherings because its sensual moves and lascivious lyrics were considered far too bawdy for the general public (meaning the aesthetic of the refined upper classes). Around 1905 Argentine émigrés to France are known to have introduced the tango in the cafés and dance halls of Paris, where it became quite popular. A so-called "tangomania" gripped European cities by 1914 and the onset of World War I. Acceptance in Paris, along with the spread of sheet music to Argentina, led to a reintroduction of tango to the Buenos Aires elite. In keeping with their proclivity to ape anything approved in Europe, the cultivated *porteño* upper and middle classes embraced tango music and dance, moving it from the back streets of working-class barrios to the front parlors of apartments and clubs in the wealthy neighborhoods of Recoleta and Barrio Norte (Figure 6.4).

A similar pattern of rejection, followed by ultimate acceptance, occurred with the Brazilian samba. Born in the slave quarters of the Brazilian northeast and spreading to the cities of the coast, especially Salvador da Bahia and Rio de Janeiro, the rhythmic dance and music flourished in the social milieu of former slaves during the early decades of the twentieth century. In the *favelas* (shantytowns) and working-class neighborhoods that cropped up in Brazil's expanding urban centers, blacks came together at private parties and outdoor bars, affectionately called *botequims*, to play music on an assortment of homemade instruments. The first formal organization of samba dancers, singers, and instrumentalists was established in 1928. The organizers called it an *escola de samba*, or samba school, probably in hopes of establishing legitimacy for the dance and musical form by associating the concept of a dancehall with a school, a place of discipline, hard work, and learning. These clubs, or schools, became the foundation from which samba emerged as a major cultural force in all urban areas, but especially in Rio de Janeiro. The schools grew out of the loose network of revelers called *blocos de sujo*, literally "groups of dirty ones," who paraded through the streets at Carnival time, the week before the onset of Lent. As Afro-Brazilian musical culture grew, it attached

Figure 6.4   Tango Dancers in San Telmo, Buenos Aires. (Nancy Borowick photo)

itself to the pre-Lenten parties that were a tradition among the Portuguese, Italian, and other Catholic immigrants from Europe.

Not everyone from the white elite and immigrant communities welcomed the entrance of Afro-Brazilian culture on the national scene. In urban areas former slaves who poured into cities to get away from the drudgery of the countryside were met with hostility from whites. One particular method of driving out black culture, if not the people themselves, was passage of a number of laws that sought to prohibit the practice of non-Christian religions and any public expression of black music and dance. This prohibition coincided with efforts by immigration authorities to exclude or actively discourage non-white immigrants from entering the country. Nevertheless, in the early 1930s the samba schools were officially recognized as participants in the citywide Carnival festivities. The mainly black and poor *sambistas*, organized into samba schools, joined the citywide festival dominated by the pre-existing mainstays of Carnival: the *grandes sociedades*, or great societies, in which the city's elite paraded. Eventually, the elite parades died out, and samba became the preferred dance of Brazilians and a growing stream of international tourists who came to partake in the pre-Lenten celebration for which Brazil is now famous. Similar to Argentina's tango, once samba enjoyed worldwide acclaim, resistance among the Brazilian elite dissipated and they embraced it as though it had been their creation in the first place.

Sports

Out of the barrio developed another passion: soccer, known as *fútbol* in Spanish and *futebol* in Portuguese. Introduced by British sailors, and merchants alighting in Buenos Aires in the 1870s, the sport was picked up by dockworkers and other laborers and was soon the rage among men and boys in the poor neighborhoods of port cities such as Buenos Aires, Montevideo, and Santos in Brazil. As mentioned in Chapter 1, an Englishman named Charles Miller (1874–1953) is thought to have introduced organized soccer to Brazil. The son of Paulista merchants, Miller organized a couple of teams made up of young British employees of the São Paulo Gas Company, the London and Brazilian Bank, and the São Paulo Railway Company. They played their first game in 1895 and the sport remained a pastime in elite British clubs that primarily hosted cricket matches. In Brazil and Argentina soccer was also introduced as a diversion among British managers and technicians in some textile plants, but eventually spread to the workers, who struck up matches with the owners, or each other, during breaks. Because of the ease with which soccer can be played, requiring no more than a level field or street, and one ball, the sport spread through working-class neighborhoods in many Latin American cities, becoming more of a passion for young men (not women or girls, at least as participants) of the lower class than it had been for the British elite who introduced it. Working-class youths also grew to be far superior players. Eventually, soccer was transformed from a street sport to one played by organized clubs, facing off in local, citywide, national, and international matches. Historian Greg Bocketti has shown that in Argentina and Brazil soccer teams and club competitions (in addition to unions and cultural organizations) served as a conduit for Italian immigrants to incorporate into the broader urban society.

Recent scholarship has shown that local politicians, even hierarchical *caudillos*, were unable to dictate policies to all citizens. In Argentina crowds used civic festivals, church feast days, sporting events, and localized celebrations to exhibit allegiance to one political party or another. Local leaders, and *caudillos* such as Juan Manual Rosas, not only participated in community festivals; they actively used the events to garner political support. Citizens sported ribbons and uniforms declaring their political sympathies and used the opportunity of public events to wrest concessions or promises from leaders. Citizens in Mexico, Argentina, Peru, Brazil, Uruguay, and other locales were able to temper the most authoritarian regimes. In fact, no *leader* was able to rule through repression alone, but had instead to provide patronage appointments and respond to the demands of petitioners for pay and benefits from the state.

Urban Renewal

By the end of the nineteenth century, both old-line, native-born elites and late-nineteenth-century middle-class reformers were expressing concern over the more sordid facets of urban growth: crowding, squalor, unhygienic living and working conditions, disease, poverty, crime, and vice. The urban elite of Buenos Aires blamed the victims for the squalid conditions into which they were thrust, including the outbreak of a yellow fever epidemic in 1871. It was a pattern reminiscent of Yankee elites who despaired at the sight of the Irish, southern and eastern European masses pouring into Boston, New York, New Orleans, and Philadelphia. Epidemics of yellow fever, malaria, smallpox, and influenza periodically ravaged the major cities of these rapidly expanding regions. Since ships called at many ports on a single voyage, including Recife, Rio, and Santos in Brazil; Montevideo, Uruguay; Buenos Aires, Argentina; Callao, Peru; and Valparaiso, Chile, captains were loath to risk encountering a disease in one port and carrying it to others, thus infecting personnel over a wide swath of the continent. During epidemic seasons port officials refused entry to any ship whose last stop was in a city recently known to have been in the throes of an epidemic; sometimes ship captains simply refused to dock ships during the summer months in ports known for their insalubrious conditions.

A combination of disease and the tenements and their poor residents that filled downtown districts motivated city and national governments to embark on urban renewal projects that transformed many Latin American cities into copies of European cultural refinement, while simultaneously combating tropical diseases. One such project in Buenos Aires eliminated yellow fever – along with the poor inhabitants who had contracted it. As new buildings replaced older, run-down structures, rising property values in downtown districts forced lower-income residents to move to distant suburbs or into the already horrendously crowded tenements in the largely Italian immigrant district of La Boca.

Fortified by Social Darwinist conceptions of northern European superiority over those of so-called "uncivilized" (Mediterranean, indigenous, and African) background, city leaders sought to develop a division of urban space that segregated residents by both race and class. A system of streetcar and rail lines installed with British money and expertise allowed workers to reach their places of employment.

Brazil's capital city of Rio de Janeiro underwent a renovation at much the same time. Rio was geographically well situated to service ships passing from the Brazilian northeast to Montevideo and Buenos Aires further south; the harbor was wide, deep, and sheltered from the ocean by a large bay and the city was then, as now, breathtakingly beautiful. Nevertheless, an obstacle in the path of further development was the poor state of public health: Rio de Janeiro, a tropical city whose residences, government offices, commercial, financial, and cultural institutions rested on narrow strips of land wedged between sharply rising hills, the ocean, and the bay proved to be especially unhealthy. The land flooded during the rainy season, when water from the bay rose above ineffective retaining walls and poured into the streets. Because the drainage system was so inadequate, neighborhoods remained marshy even after the rainwater receded. Worse, for much of the year stagnant water stood in pools throughout the city, providing an ideal breeding ground for mosquitoes carrying yellow fever and malaria. A British traveler described Rio in the late nineteenth century as a "labyrinth of narrow streets, some not more than seven yards wide. West and north of the busy and squalid port area the city is built around marsh and swamps. Here where the poorer inhabitants congregate, is a happy hunting-ground for the yellow fever scourge."[2]

In Cuba and Central America US military forces and health officials had pioneered effective, if often ruthless, vaccination and sanitation programs during the army occupation, with the intentional side effect of cleansing areas to make them safe for trade and investment. Following the Spanish–American War of 1898, Carlos Finlay (1833–1915), the chief scientific officer of Havana's Yellow Fever Commission, discovered the link between stagnant water, mosquitoes, and epidemics. Finlay's discovery led to widespread sanitation campaigns in Havana and other Cuban cities, under the auspices of Walter Reed (1851–1902) and the US Army Corps of Engineers. In Central America William Gorgas (1854–1920) copied the Havana program to clear the way for construction of the Panama Canal. The campaign against yellow fever involved destroying the breeding grounds for the *Aedes aegypti* mosquito and its larvae and draining all pools of stagnant water. In many countries of Latin America, especially in crowded urban environments, public health and pest control teams swept through densely populated barrios, killing rats and using vaccines and serums to stop the spread of plague, smallpox, and a host of diseases that were by that time already rare in many areas of the developed world.

In March 1903 Brazilian president Rodrigues Alves (1848–1919) appointed Oswaldo Gonçalves Cruz (1872–1917) director general of public health, and Cruz began to address yellow fever. Along with the sanitation of Havana and other tropical and semi-tropical cities, including Hong Kong, Cape Town in South Africa, and Kingston in Jamaica, the full-scale assault on yellow fever in Rio de Janeiro stands as a landmark in the record book of disease prevention and control. Dr. Cruz's public health crews, who earned the name "mosquito inspectors," moved throughout the city, spraying, killing rats, ordering the demolition of all unsanitary housing, and systematically implementing various aspects of the new code. Following a plan similar to the one used in Buenos Aires, itself patterned on Georges-Eugène Haussmann's (1809–91) famous renewal of Paris in the late nineteenth century, Rio's sanitation/renovation plan resulted in the relocation of the city's poor from city centers to distant suburbs and company-style towns rimming the outskirts. In subsequent years the poor took up residence in the *favelas* that soon began to dot the urban landscape of Rio and other Brazilian cities. By 1905 downtown Rio de Janeiro had electrical lighting, while most of the areas where the poor and working class lived had yet to be connected even to the existing system of gas illumination. Unfortunately the pattern adopted in Rio de Janeiro was reproduced in many cities of Latin America, where the mass of urban residents enjoyed limited access to lighting, sanitation, clean water, and health care or the beaches extolled in tourist literature. Government inattention to food and housing shortages, poor transportation service, and deplorable sanitary conditions have provoked discontent, and rioting, in working-class neighborhoods and the shantytowns of many cities of Latin America throughout the twentieth century and into the twenty-first.

Mexico and Benito Juárez

The history of Mexico in the nineteenth century differed from that of other areas of Latin America in that it was not affected by immigration and did not grapple with either slavery or the struggle to abolish it. Instead, Mexico confronted the effects of the disastrous war with the US: mainly the need to rebuild a nation in the wake of the loss of over a third of its territory. Thus the main issues of the century – modernization, industrialization, inequality, state versus Church and domestic versus foreign domination – occurred against the backdrop of a deeply fractured nation. Mexican sovereignty hinged on an ability to unify and to construct a Mexican identity capable of encompassing rural and urban areas, and indigenous, European, and mestizo cultures. Although Mexico had, and still has, a large Afro-descendant population along the Gulf coast, the main issue of national identity in the nineteenth and most of the twentieth century rested with integrating the indigenous society into one based on European values. The two figures of the nineteenth century who presided over this nation-building project were Benito Juárez, from 1857 to 1872, and Porfirio Díaz, from 1876 to 1911.

Benito Juárez (1806–72) extended the secularization of Mexico begun under a series of liberal governments after the defeat of Santa Anna. Under Juárez, Mexico did away with *fueros*, the privileged exemptions that allowed the clergy and military to avoid civil and criminal prosecution; ended church control of vast amounts of property; and consolidated state power over taxation and the regulation of births, marriages, deaths, cemeteries, adoptions, and family matters.

A Zapotec Indian born in 1806 of humble, rural origins, Juárez obtained an excellent education and law degree by pure dint of his brilliance, hard work, and the recognition of his exceptional mind and character from influential members of the Church and secular world. He rose to the governorship of the state of Oaxaca, gaining notice for his participation in the Revolution of Ayutla in 1855 that deposed Santa Anna and sent him into exile in Jamaica (from which he never returned). As President of Mexico, Juárez instituted reforms to break the stranglehold of conservative landowners, fortified by their alliance with the Catholic Church, who held the vast majority of Mexican rural laborers, Indians, and the small urban proletariat in poverty and ignorance. Although admired by the poor, as well as by modernizing liberal elites, Juárez ran into trouble when he tried to privatize "corporate property," which by definition included the vast estates of private *latifundistas*, extensive holdings of the Catholic Church, and Indian communal lands, called *ejidos*.

According to laws laid down in Juárez's "Reforma" and the Constitution of 1857, *ejidos* fell into the category of "corporate holdings," even though they were lands attached to Indian villages. Most were used for common grazing, with individual parcels worked by members of the community. Some liberals in the reform government nonetheless considered it essential for the progress of Mexico to divide all estates into small, single-family farms – whether they had been guaranteed for the use of the indigenous people since the days of the Conquest, or were in the hands of church and corporate landowners. The strategy failed, serving only to alienate Juárez from the indigenous peasantry, a constituency from which he should have received support. Ironically, the first Indian president of Mexico passed a law that contravened the ancient customs of its indigenous people.

French Invasions

Plagued by war, near constant Conservative revolts, and political intrigues, Juárez was deposed in 1864 when French Emperor Napoleon III (1808–73), at the invitation of Mexican Conservatives, crowned Austrian Archduke Ferdinand Maximilian von Hapsburg (1832–67) as head of state. In 1862, in an attempt to rekindle its empire, France launched an invasion of Mexico. Their attempt to take the city of Puebla, a short distance from the capital at Mexico City, was repelled by General Ignacio Zaragoza on May 5. The victory was particularly sweet, since the Mexican force was made up of conscripts with little training, while the French had a professional army that outnumbered the Mexicans three to one. Two years later the French were successful, but the heroes of May 5, 1862 are remembered, particularly in Puebla, for their valor. (Although only a local holiday in Mexico, "Cinco de Mayo" has become very popular in the United States, where many non-Mexicans erroneously think it is Mexico's independence day.)

The misguided, and certainly misinformed, Maximilian, along with his disoriented wife, Charlotte of Belgium known as Carlota (1840–1927), arrived in Mexico and, much to the surprise of his backers, embarked on a plan of *noblesse oblige* to elevate Mexico's standard of living. In his short time at the helm, Maximilian introduced modern, liberal reforms including a free press, freedom for political prisoners, living wages, and other measures his conservative and church backers had no intention of supporting. Isolated from much of the Mexican populace, who saw the French monarch as yet another European interloper in league with the conservative elite, Maximilian eventually lost the support of the Church and conservatives as well, because he failed to pander to the latter's interests. Under pressure from the US, the French withdrew the regiments they had dispatched to prop him up, allowing Juárez to reclaim the presidency. Once back in office, Juárez showed no mercy toward the confused old man and ordered Maximilian's execution.

The short-lived reform era ended abruptly when the president who succeeded Juárez, Lerdo de Tejada, was overthrown in 1876. Benito Juárez's legacy was as a leader who attempted to steer Mexico onto a modern path, limit the domination of the Catholic Church in most civil matters, and push ahead with reforms such as public education and distribution of land to the peasantry, all of which served to anger the landed elite and the Church. Porfirio Díaz (1830–1915) was the man responsible for Lerdo's overthrow and the politician who would dominate Mexican politics for the next 30 years.

The Rise of Porfirio Díaz

Porfirio Díaz rose to political prominence as a hero in the war against the French occupation and a defender of the rule of law in the face of extra-legal maneuverings identified with Juárez and his successors, as the Reforma deteriorated. Ultimately, however, Díaz proved to be more autocratic than the forces he initially had opposed. During his first term in office, beginning May 5, 1877 and scheduled to end in 1881, Díaz enacted a number of progressive reforms, including laws ensuring greater competition for political office and competitive bids from foreign companies seeking to invest in Mexican oil, mining, and industrial enterprises. He left office as promised, but after a short stint as governor of his home state of Oaxaca, re-entered national politics as a very different leader. The new Díaz outlawed all opposition and ruled through force until overthrown after the 1910 election. From the 1890s onward he wasted no time overturning the reforms and rescinding the progressive measures enacted as part of the 1857 Constitution. In fact, one of the rallying cries of the 1910 rebellion – when a broad coalition of urban and rural poor workers, domestic landowners and entrepreneurs, intellectuals and democrats joined together to oust Díaz – was a call to return to the 1857 Constitution. Porfirio Díaz's tenure in office is often remembered as a period that transformed Mexico into one of the safest countries in the world for business, foreign capital, and the wealthy; but among the least safe for Mexico's masses, especially the rural poor and Indians.

Díaz's transition from heroic defender of the fatherland to autocrat can be traced through the biographical background of Emiliano Zapata, the legendary hero of the revolutionary forces that deposed the man then known as "the old dictator" at the outbreak of the revolutionary war. José Zapata, young Emiliano's great-uncle and the revered village elder in the hamlet of Anenecuilco, had fought with Porfirio Díaz in the

1866–7 war against the French invaders, founded one of the first "Porfirista" clubs in the village, and until his death in 1876 the older Zapata had turned out the vote for Díaz, even when the latter betrayed the will of the common folk. Indicative of both Díaz's reputation and the esteem a village elder commanded, many poor peasants remained loyal to Díaz purely on the basis of his early heroism. By 1910, however, disaffection among the ranks of a new generation of peasant leaders was widespread, and whatever status Díaz had achieved through his earlier exploits could no longer excuse the tyranny he imposed on the nation. The full details of the Mexican Revolution are taken up in Chapter 7.

Intellectual Theories: Positivism and Eugenics

Porfirio Díaz relied extensively on a group of scientific and technocratic advisors who were imbued with Positivist thinking. Mexico was not alone in advocating such theories. They were based on the philosophical Positivism popular in Europe and America at the time, especially Auguste Comte (1798–1857) in France and Herbert Spencer (1820–1903) in England. As a school of philosophy, Positivism became quite popular in Latin American scholarly circles because it provided a technical, seemingly achievable, path to modernization. If all progress in society was, as the Positivists argued, acquired through science, as opposed to resulting from an act of God or divine intervention, then societies mired in poverty, inefficiency, and primitive tools and technology could be improved. The poor peasant, digging in the ground with a stick, eating a diet lacking in proper nutrients, bearing children year after year only to have many of them die from the combined effects of poverty and disease, could be reformed through technology. He or she could be taught modern agricultural techniques, introduced to a better diet, modern tools, private property, and even the basics of family planning. Some of the leading Positivists were advocates of secular education, mandatory vaccination, and government programs to promote efficiency in farming, manufacturing, urban planning, and government programs to advance progress. Positivists tended to support a strong state that governed with technocratic efficiency, a strictly rationalized tax system, a business environment that invited foreign investment, individual ownership of land and resources, and a judiciary that served for life as a way of eliminating corruption.

While some Positivists and *científicos* in Mexico favored science over superstition as the best tool for solving society's problems, their theories and the ways they were implemented fell short. First, Positivists looked at a static world rather than one in which social class, race, and gender were socially constructed. Indians, for example, were not poor because they failed to fit into the European notion of scientific behavior, but because society at that time placed little value on communal ownership of property, for example. That is, Positivists failed to see that their own prejudices and consciousnesses determined the values they favored for any society. Secondly, not only did Positivists fail to challenge their own assumptions; they believed science was a cure-all for society's wrongs. While it is true that education, proper health care, and other benefits play a positive role, the Positivists felt that these techniques alone would resolve all of society's problems. They did not believe that a society could function well in a variety of ways, quite different from their own. They rejected the beliefs and culture of indigenous people, seeing them as backward and antithetical to civilized society. They rarely accepted religion as the glue that held some communities together regardless of its rational or irrational character, although they correctly branded the Church as a bastion of conservatism.

While not all Positivists were consciously racist, any more than many other intellectuals of the time, Positivism promoted a concept that the world of plants and animals, human development and evolution, was in some part deterministic. The *cientificos* were dismayed that the Indian resided on the bottom rung of society's ladder by virtue of his or her incompletely evolved status, but could only uplift indigenous people by forcing them to abandon everything that made them different from the European.

Mexico's *cientificos* were only one wave of an ideological current that intellectuals in Latin America, and much of the world for that matter, embraced in the late nineteenth and early twentieth centuries. Other intellectuals pointed to Charles Darwin's (1809–82) statement in the *Descent of Man* as evidence for their philosophy: ". . . at some future period, not very distant as measured by centuries, the civilised races of man will almost certainly exterminate, and replace, the savage races throughout the world."[3] Despite this statement, Darwin is not thought to have championed such a theory; rather, the concept of racial determinism was promoted through eugenics societies throughout the world. Its proponents argued that white, northern Europeans were at the pinnacle of the human pyramid – the fittest – while the black African and the American Indian were at the bottom – the least fit – an argument reminiscent of colonial times. At various stages in between were Asians, Jews, Mediterranean and Slavic people, the Irish, and others whose inclusion on the list varied depending on who was doing the defining.

Nancy Stepan's work on the eugenics movement in Latin America shows that there was both a fatalistic side to eugenics (people who are poor and non-European are destined to be scientifically weeded out in the evolutionary process) and an optimistic side (humans can take control of their destiny and, through science, raise the level of the outcast and incorporate him or her into civilization). This debate that pitted theory against practice in the project of "uplifting and civilizing," as the intellectuals, medical personnel, and politicians saw it, played out in a variety of ways. In Brazil, for example, during a hotly debated campaign to require mandatory vaccination against smallpox in 1904, some Positivists advocated the implementation of forced vaccination and public health programs because they epitomized the use of science to eliminate disease; while other Positivists eschewed vaccination because it interfered with the natural selection process by allowing the poor and "racially inferior" to survive.

Beginning at the turn of the century, Bolivian public health officials and medical experts embarked on a series of projects designed to curb disastrous health problems ranging from yaws and dysentery to yellow fever, typhoid, smallpox, pneumonia, whooping cough, and a host of others. Historian Ann Zulawski explains the limits of health policies in the hands of experts – be they scientists from the Rockefeller Foundation or local Bolivian doctors – who held indigenous people, women, and the poor in low regard. Bolivia, as Zulawski shows, is an excellent example of the way an underlying disdain for the patient, based on racist and sexist assumptions, interferes with the delivery of health care and limits the effectiveness of programs designed to pull the nation forward. Although practicing scientists, Bolivian health professionals insisted on linking disease to race and ethnicity, thereby consciously or unconsciously assuming that Indians, who make up half of Bolivia's population, were unable, unprepared, or simply unwilling to embrace a program of personal hygiene. All the evidence, however, was to the contrary. In those cases, admittedly rare, when doctors took an interest in indigenous medicine and attempted to understand the logic of indigenous thinking regarding health, or when they recruited indigenous health care practitioners to government medical teams beginning in the 1930s, they were more successful.

After the Nazi experiments of World War II, where the racist expression of eugenics theories was fully incorporated into a national policy, resulting in the extermination of six million Jews, along with the disabled, homosexuals, gypsies, and any others deemed unfit for the "Master Race," eugenics lost its appeal, and notions of race-based superiority became increasingly discredited. Thus, to view the *científicos* as a particularly Mexican phenomenon would be a mistake. They were a high-profile manifestation of Positivist philosophy in action, wedded to a particular government administration. In part the *científicos* could lament the state of the impoverished Mexican *castas* by attributing their demise to their own inability to adapt to the ways of science and the rationales of the white leadership.

Conclusion

The nineteenth century was as much about creating the Latin American identity as about striving for political and economic sovereignty. In the last chapter we examined the search for economic viability through trade and export markets. This chapter looked at the other side of the equation: the arrival in Latin America of millions of immigrants to provide the backbone of the workforce. Immigrants from Europe and Asia brought with them new traditions, languages, religions, and pastimes, changing forever the cultural landscape of both rural and urban countries. While most immigrants settled in the Southern Cone nations, especially Argentina, Uruguay, and southern Brazil, nearly every nation of the Americas welcomed at least some migrants from Europe and Asia.

Mexico's search for social cohesion occurred against the backdrop of seeking reconciliation between the traditions of indigenous communities that had lived and survived in ways starkly at odds with European traditions. The task of the nineteenth-century political leaders was to find a way to reconcile communal values with the modernizing reforms of the capitalist world. That it fell to Mexico's only indigenous president, Benito Juárez, to attempt a land reform that would curb the power of the corporatist Church and the large landowners, but ultimately disrupt the indigenous way of life, was both ironic and ultimately tragic. Mexico's attempt to forge a unified nation came more as a result of Porfirio Díaz's authoritarian rule than Juárez's comprehensive land reform.

Philosophers sought to break with the static superstitious dogma of Catholicism which had served as the guiding principles since the colonial period. In keeping with the modernizing and scientific ethos of the time, various combinations of Positivism, Social Darwinism, and adherence to eugenics were debated in both government and intellectual circles. The mottos and flags adopted by the new nations reflected the vision that order and progress were the watchwords of modernization, as was the urban renewal and "civilization" of urban areas. However, it was never a progress that could encompass everyone, leaving in place, or even exacerbating, racial, class, and gender divisions.

7 | Revolution from Countryside to City: Mexico

If cities such as Rio de Janeiro, Buenos Aires, Lima, Montevideo, and Mexico City were undergoing major transformations, life in the countryside in Latin America largely remained mired in traditional class relationships. As a result, predominantly rural Mexico entered into one of the most intense periods of economic and political struggle of any Latin American country. The conflict engulfed the agrarian sector, where longstanding inequalities were deeply resented by the majority of the rural population but reached urban areas as well.

At the beginning of his classic study of Emiliano Zapata (1879–1919) and the Mexican Revolution, John Womack wrote: "This is a book about country people who did not want to move and therefore got into a revolution."[1] The revolution was rooted in the issue of land rights, and one of its primary causes was the objection of the peasantry to their forced removal from the lands they had worked and struggled to retain since colonial times. But it was about other things as well. Many authors who have written since Womack's book appeared in the late 1960s have detailed the various grievances fueling this conflict that convulsed Mexico from 1910 to 1920 and probed the motives of the various social forces, and ethnic, gender, and racial groups that participated. The conflict was indeed so widespread and the issues it addressed so vast that one might argue that most cultural, economic, and political issues at stake in Latin America were in some way and at some time addressed in the course of the Mexican Revolution.

Womack vividly describes the rural people of the small state of Morelos, in southern Mexico, who took up the revolutionary cause in order to defend, or restore, the titles to their lands and homes, titles many of them had guarded for generations. However, under Zapata's leadership the peasants of Morelos first joined the Revolution in 1910 over an issue far removed from their immediate concerns: an irregularity in the process of presidential succession. But resolving the immediate political issue – preventing Porfírio Díaz from once again stealing an election – did nothing in the long term to address the peasantry's underlying problem.

Events in Mexico came together to produce the first modern social revolution of the twentieth century. It began as a political dispute in 1910, but gradually evolved into a demand for a deeper social transformation, and eventually culminated in the writing of a new Constitution in 1917. Interspersed throughout the entire period of upheaval was a cultural transformation that altered most facets of Mexican society, from the superficial to the fundamental. Few people – male, female, adult, child, white or *casta*, Indian or black – from any social class were left untouched by the events of these tumultuous decades.

The *Porfiriato*

At the start of the twentieth century Mexico was an agrarian country. Issues of land-ownership and struggles over land reform were central to Mexico's political formation. In 1900 over 77 percent of the population lived in the countryside, and the man who ruled over that land was General Porfirio Díaz. Although he had come to power vowing to side with the people (the *pueblo*, in Spanish), this promise proved to be nothing more than a transparent ploy to appease the expectations of those who had placed great hope in the reforms of Benito Juárez and thought that Díaz would make good on those promises. Instead, during the 34 years he stood at the helm of a compliant Mexican state, either directly or through a surrogate who ruled at his behest, Díaz exerted such over-whelming political, economic, and cultural dominance that the era itself bears his name: the *Porfiriato*.

Díaz claimed to be modernizing Mexico and in many ways he did, but most of the changes he enacted benefited primarily his close supporters and foreign investors. He was known to have cultivated an elaborate patronage system through which he doled out favors. Nonetheless, the technological innovations undertaken during the Porfiriato were impressive: a tenfold increase in railways, steam-powered locomotives, a railroad from Veracruz to Mexico City, telegraph lines across the country, steam-powered factories in Mexico City and other industrial centers. These improvements were mostly financed by foreign capital; Díaz showed less concern for the exploitative conditions Mexican workers endured in foreign-owned companies. Ruling through a policy known as *pan y palo*, which in English we call "carrot and stick," Díaz was a master of cooptation and coercion, backed up by repression. He appointed state governors and gave them free rein to rule over the local population and enrich them-selves, so long as they did not interfere with his own authority.

Díaz's technological and scientific modernization policies accompanied, rather than opposed, as might seem logical, a land policy that consolidated large estates in fewer and fewer hands. Through a series of laws passed from 1883 to 1894, the way was opened for a few individuals to win control over a large amount of land that had been declared "vacant." Although frequently inhabited, occupants' proof of ownership or tenancy (such as a title or agreement) was ruled invalid in courts. In other cases powerful lawyers working for landowners were able to wrest the land from its rightful occupants by enmeshing disputes in prolonged court battles. Finally, on those occa-sions when powerful interests were unable to win in court, they called in the *rurales*, Díaz's appointed rural militia, to clear the land, thereby compelling dispossessed peasants to embark on an uphill, and generally futile, attempt to win back their land through the courts or petitions to state authorities. Often illiterate, unable to hire a lawyer, and unused to the complicated bureaucracy of local and regional courts, the country people stood little chance of emerging victorious, no matter how legitimate their claim. One of Díaz's friends obtained 12 million acres in Baja California for nothing more than a bribe to local judges, who simply declared the land to be vacant. In some cases, when occupants resisted they were killed or captured and sold to plantations in Cuba and the Yucatán as slaves. Alternatively, powerful landowners and political bosses diverted, or cut off entirely, the water supply to villages, thereby forcing the rightful owners to crowd in with relatives or move to other communities where water was still available; relinquish title to the land and sell themselves into debt peonage, even slavery; or to give up and move to the fast-growing cities. By 1900 over 90 percent of the communal land of the Central Plateau had been sold off or expropriated, forcing an estimated 9.5 million peasants off the land and into peonage at the service of the big landowners.

The cultivation of exportable commodities such as coffee, tobacco, henequen (for making rope), and sugar predominated on the estates, leaving almost no land for the production of basic foodstuffs, such as corn and wheat, or livestock. Most of the time the new owners either used the land inefficiently or left it to lie fallow as a means to drive up the price of the maize or cotton crops they were cultivating on other estates. When not engaged in speculation themselves, Mexican *latifundistas* found a ready market for land among US speculators. As a result of the overwhelming emphasis on export-oriented agriculture and concomitant inattention to meeting subsistence needs at home, hunger gripped the countryside at unprecedented levels. Meanwhile, the refining of *pulque* (a strong alcoholic drink made from the maguey cactus plant) and other cheap alcoholic beverages increased. In the midst of hunger the number of bars in Mexico City rose from 51 in 1864 to 1,400 in 1900, and the rate of death from alcoholism and alcohol-related accidents outstripped that of most other areas of the world.

By 1911 US companies had controlling interests in Mexico's copper, gold, lead, and tin mining, monopolizing not only above-ground refining and processing works, but subsoil rights as well. Mexico's oil industry, which was by the end of the first decade of the new century the third largest in the world, was sold to the North American Rockefeller consortium. Profits in all industries were very high while, regardless of whether the enterprise was foreign-owned or domestic, wages and working conditions were terrible. Men and women left the land to take up urban jobs as factory laborers, where women earned a fraction of the salary paid to men. The typical workday was 12–15 hours long; men were paid 75 cents, women and children as little as 11 cents, for a day's labor. Many were never paid in cash, instead receiving vouchers that could only be redeemed at the company store for food or housing in the company towns that encircled plants and mines. The large number of women and girls who entered the workforce in the later years of the century took up typically female jobs as maids, cooks, nannies, laundresses, street vendors, and prostitutes. For some jobs, such as rolling cigars and the least-skilled work in textile mills, owners hired more women and children than men, in hopes that their level of desperation would make them less likely to unionize and cause trouble. Regardless of gender or age, the vast majority of workers were unable to resist the horrendous working and living conditions they faced. Whether in the countryside, recent arrivals to the city, or longtime urban dwellers, Mexico's poor lived out their lives in miserable conditions, forced into debt from a young age and confined to a state of perpetual dependency on the factory bosses, landowners, and mine operators.

Opposition to the *Porfiriato*

Not surprisingly, by the early 1900s the *Porfiriato* was confronting a chorus of opposition from a range of political tendencies. From within the ranks of the Mexican Liberal Party (PLM), organized by Ricardo Flores Magón (1873–1922), came persistent calls for a return to the electoral process, for the judiciary to serve the interests of society, including members of the elite and middle class who were not firmly within Díaz's grasp; and for the extension of rights to workers in rural and urban areas. Mexican landowners who had rejected, or were never offered, the favors the dictator bestowed on his closest cronies began to voice audibly their opposition. In addition, Díaz's pattern of increasingly favoring US investors, mining companies, and industrialists rankled sectors of the Mexican bourgeoisie who wanted to maintain a better balance between national and foreign capital investment, or who thought playing off US investors against British and other European capitalists was a more prudent way for Mexico to maintain control of its natural resources. A growing proportion of the urban-based, liberal elite found Díaz's old-style corruption embarrassing and injurious to Mexico's image and standing as an independent nation, and thus sought his defeat in the electoral arena.

Finally, more and more unrest began to surface among rural laborers, landless indigenous peasants, and labor unions. Discontent among peasants and workers, as historian John Tutino has pointed out, was nothing new, since the poor had repeatedly protested against the Church, landowners, industrialists and the governments they controlled for over a century, from 1810 until 1910. Likewise, the poor had generally gone down in defeat, since the elite remained steadfastly "united in defense of privilege and profit to crush the insurrection of the independence era – and to prevent a movement toward social reconstruction."[2] Under Porfirio Díaz rapid development and unbridled foreign investment, combined with corruption at every level of state and local government, provoked discontent with the prevailing order.

Initially, the most dramatic signs of opposition to Díaz's brand of politics came from organized labor in the form of two key strikes. When workers in the Cananea Copper Company in the northern state of Sonora went out on strike in 1906, they were lobbing the opening salvo in a revolution that would disrupt all of Mexico for years to come. In the tense atmosphere of the early twentieth century, the conflict at Cananea represented more than the articulation of workers' grievances and management's responses at one workplace. Founded in 1896 by William Greene, a US entrepreneur who obtained concessions from the Díaz government, the copper company's history epitomized Porfírio Díaz's sellout of Mexico's resources to foreign interests. The concession enabled Greene not only to build up the Cananea copper mine into one of the most important mining operations in Mexico, but also to add control over land and cattle, transportation networks, lumber mills and a wide range of services, giving him absolute dominance over a vast stretch of Mexican land, as well as over the laborers who worked in his various enterprises.

Beginning on June 1, 1906, 5,400 Mexican miners struck along with a core of anarcho-syndicalist workers from the United States who labored in the mines as well. The company brought across the border from Arizona a band of hired vigilantes to reinforce the Mexican federal army, which was already actively repressing the strike by beating up and dispersing workers. The strike's bloody, violent conclusion, along with the presence of US mercenaries on Mexican soil employed as the private military force of a US company to beat, and even kill, Mexican workers, stirred up anger toward the government that condoned these practices. Similar sentiments arose during a second labor dispute, this time at the French-owned Rio Blanco textile factory in Orizaba, Veracruz. There a strike for better wages and working conditions grew into a factory occupation and eventual takeover of the town by several thousand angry workers. Supported by Flores Magón's PLM in both cases, the worker uprisings served to consolidate a powerful opposition to the policies of the Díaz government and its foreign allies.

Constitutional Opposition

In 1909 the PLM and other opposition forces coalesced around the candidacy of Francisco Madero (1873–1913) to run against Díaz for the presidency. Madero, a prosperous landowner and banker from the northern state of Coahuila, ran on a platform calling for the end to Díaz's practice of succeeding himself as president, a return to civil government as called for by the Constitution, and a program of moderate concessions to peasants and workers – which he considered essential to stop the spread of anarchist ideas. Gathering support from all regions, and from every social and economic stratum of the country, Madero appeared to be sweeping into office when Díaz interrupted the process and tried to place his adversary under virtual house arrest. Madero escaped and fled across the border to San Antonio, Texas, where he began to raise an army of followers to ensure his victory, even at the risk of armed combat against President Díaz and his supporters. From Texas Madero announced the Plan of San Luis Potosí, named himself as provisional president, and, with the tacit support of the US government (which had suddenly had a change of heart toward Díaz when he opted to favor British over American investors on a new enterprise), unleashed a military campaign.

From various parts of the country Madero began to draw supporters, who came to be known as the "Constitutionalists". Among them were Pascual Orozco, a muleteer from Chihuahua (who would abandon Madero a couple years later), Francisco "Pancho" Villa (1878–1923), an erstwhile social bandit turned revolutionary with a strong following among landless peasants in the north, and Emiliano Zapata, a well-respected leader of indigenous and mestizo farmers in Morelos, a state to the south of the capital. By the spring of 1911 the Constitutionalists had gained a considerable following, although many poor, illiterate, and destitute recruits had only a cursory understanding of the conflict ahead. Villa, an adept military commander and astute political organizer, captured many of the northern towns, including Ciudad Juárez across from El Paso, Texas, where the wily commander and arms trader was able to buy weapons to supply his growing army.

In the south, Zapata's army swelled with insurgents who for years had been fighting against the sugar *hacendados* who had been usurping land belonging to ancient Indian villages. Zapata, who was not known for making rash decisions, weighed carefully the pros and cons of joining forces with Madero and Villa, personalities quite different from each other and unlike his own. Eventually Zapata opted to support Madero because he agreed with the land reform provisions of the latter's platform, as laid out in the Plan de San Luis Potosí. For many who took up weapons and swelled Zapata's army the choice was less intellectual. Anthropologist Oscar Lewis interviewed Pedro and Esperanza Martínez, young peasants from a village in Morelos, about Pedro's decision to join the Zapatista army. According to Esperanza, her husband joined "because they offered to give him food . . . he said at least he would have something to eat and furthermore they would pay him." Initially resistant to the prospect of her husband abandoning her and their children to join a distant fight, Esperanza eventually warmed to the idea because "he promised to send me money."[3] The lofty goals of the revolutionary struggle drew sustenance from a rural peasantry placed in dire straits by the policies of the *Porfiriato*.

Fearing the support the rebel armies were amassing, as well as the possibility of full-scale revolt from the working class, Díaz made a deal with Madero in the spring of 1911, after which Madero won the election and assumed office as president in November. Once in office Madero proved disappointing, showing little concern for the long-held grievances against factory owners and large-scale landholders that had won him the support of the workers and peasants in the first place. Madero followed a disastrous course of action; much the opposite from the one Porfirio Díaz had pursued. Whereas the latter ran his entire administration by granting favors to his friends and supporters, Madero seemed to forget his supporters entirely once he was in office. Whatever the Plan of San Luis Potosí had promised to rural laborers, it was quickly forgotten. Under pressure Madero introduced a program that allowed peasants to purchase some land, while simultaneously opposing any reform that would alienate the *hacendados*. The result was massive disaffection, and ultimately rebellion, by those who had previously supported him.

Under the leadership of Pascual Orozco (1882–1915) in the northern states of Sonora and Chihuahua, Emiliano Zapata in the south, and Pancho Villa in Chihuahua, peasants began to occupy the lands and carry out their own agrarian reform. Although the majority of estates were Mexican-owned, hundreds of thousands of acres belonged to US citizens, a fact that brought the US government and army into the precarious balance of forces. Late in 1911 Zapata announced the "Plan of Ayala," which stated that the restoration of land usurped during the Porfiriato was the most immediate goal of the revolution, along with the establishment of rural cooperatives and measures to ensure that the land stayed in the hands of its rightful owners. It is fair to say that Zapata was furious with Madero for reneging on land distribution and willing to throw in with Orozco, and eventually Villa, to fulfill the program articulated in his Plan de Ayala. At the other end of the political spectrum, the *hacendados* and industrialists were outraged at even the very few reforms Madero proposed, such as granting workers the right to strike and the peasantry the right to take their grievances to new courts where redress would supposedly be more balanced.

Madero Assassinated

Madero thus faced opposition on two fronts and found himself politically and, more importantly, militarily powerless. By the late fall and winter of 1912 Madero's government was in crisis. Fearful of alienating the conservative landowners and industrialists, Madero failed to side with the workers who had taken to the streets to demand higher wages and the right to organize, nor did he try to meet even the most reasonable calls by peasants to return usurped land to its rightful owners.

In one of the bolder instances in the long and tawdry history of US intervention in Mexico's internal affairs, American Ambassador Henry Lane Wilson (1859–1932) summoned Madero's military commander, General Victoriano Huerta (1850–1916), to the US embassy where they hammered out an agreement between Huerta and Félix Díaz (1868–1945), Porfirio's nephew and Washington's favored contender for the Mexican presidency. Under the thinly veiled guise of "protecting American interests," the ambassador signaled the US intention to recognize a new government that would replace Madero. Although Wilson and his superiors in Washington intended that Félix Díaz and his supporter Bernardo Reyes actually take office, General Huerta engineered his own rise to power and the subsequent assassinations of President Madero, Vice-President José Pino Suárez (1869–1913), and other government officials.

Firmly in office and enjoying the support of Mexico's powerful northern neighbor, President Huerta set about restoring order to the countryside, his only hope for holding onto power. Orozco's disaffection with Madero pushed him into Huerta's camp, leading to his ultimate political demise, but the brutal murder of the elected president and unabashed manipulation by the US ambassador only served to galvanize nationalist forces against the new dictator. United opposition by Constitutionalists – comprised of the armies of Villa, Zapata, and new additions Venustiano Carranza (1859–1920), governor of the northern state of Coahuila, and Álfaro Obregón (1880–1928) of Sonora – resulted in a shaky alliance that, over the next few years, would determine the course of the revolutionary struggle.

US Intervention

With the situation in Mexico growing increasingly unstable, US owners of mines, land, and timber companies, along with others holding substantial investments in Mexico, began to have reservations about Huerta's ability to restore order. General Villa, commander of one of the largest armies and one bordering on Texas, enjoyed the loyalty of many Texas businessmen who profited from supplying his army and its large retinue of camp followers. Because revenues from US investments and friendly relations with arms dealers along the border were essential to the maintenance of Villa's army, the general provided protection to Americans in Mexico and ensured that their property was safe. Nonetheless, powerful industrialists in New York, and their allies in Washington, were apprehensive about the nation's instability and sought to restore a safe investment environment, while politicians were alarmed about insecurity along the border. On April 21, 1914, the US Navy attacked Veracruz with the intention of influencing the course of the Revolution. Washington assumed it would be able to gain the upper hand by destabilizing Huerta and choosing the next president from among the existing cadre of leaders – thereby eliminating, or diminishing, the influence of Villa and Zapata from the outset. As with other such interventions in Latin America (and elsewhere) the US misjudged popular reaction in Mexico to its 1914 invasion. Washington's military action served more to unite Mexico than divide it, forcing the US to take more extreme measures in its quest to secure a compliant government on its southern border. By year's end the US had thrown its support behind Carranza, who, as a member of the landed gentry with close political ties to the industrial elite, seemed a far more attractive ally than either Villa or Zapata, both of whom represented the interests of the poor and working class. Over the next few years the revolutionary forces sparred across the expanse of Mexican territory.

Ultimately, despite their political affinity, Villa and Zapata were unable to forge a sustained united front to promote their more progressive program. The conservative wing of the Constitutionalists maneuvered to contain the demands of the urban working class, peasantry, miners, small businessmen, and farmers. Especially in the south, in the Federal District of Mexico City, and in states bordering on the capital, labor organizers were calling for new rights for the working class. Centralized in the *Casa del Obrero Mundial*, (House of the World Workers), a federation of over 100,000 members of industrial and service unions, radical workers were joining their demands with the mobilized peasantry. The *Casa* was headquartered in the House of Tiles and the Palace of Fine Arts along the Alameda in downtown Mexico City, where meetings and strategy sessions took place around the clock, coordinating the growing strike waves of 1915 and 1916. By early 1916 striking workers had shut down petroleum works, textile companies, construction sites, and several mines, demanding better wages, more worker control of the production process, union recognition, enforced safety standards, and other benefits.

Women in Combat

The core of an army – whether of revolutionaries trying to overthrow a government or the military in defense of a state – has traditionally been male. Mexico was no exception. But during the Revolution, women traveled with the armies as cooks, gunrunners, nurses, laundresses, prostitutes, spies and much more, as is frequently the case during insurgencies. They also served as soldiers who fought on the front lines (Figure 7.1).

Some were *soldaderas*, a term that means "the one who takes the soldier's pay" (*soldada*) and uses it to buy supplies for him. While the men rode horseback, the women usually walked, carrying weapons, food, supplies, cooking utensils, pots and pans, medicines, and children. Because they walked, the *soldaderas* arrived at camps after the men, but set to work immediately preparing the food, nursing the sick, and caring for the young. According to Elizabeth Salas, the ranks of *soldaderas* included women from a male soldier's family, but also others who joined with the troops as a way of getting food for themselves and their children, and earning some money, especially in areas where the fighting had disrupted farming and the absence of men had placed women in precarious circumstances. Other women joined to provide logistical support, as well as to fight as soldiers because they believed in the revolutionary cause. In essence, *soldaderas* joined the armies for the same reasons as male soldiers: to get food, earn money, and support the cause.

One regiment of the Mexican army in 1914 listed 3,559 officers and soldiers, 1,256 *soldaderas*, and 554 children. In the post-revolution era, women were barred from accompanying troops, serving as soldiers, or providing logistical support, and the history of their contribution to the Revolution was rewritten. The official story was that *soldaderas* in the military camps were the wives of soldiers, not combatants; or, conversely, women who insisted on tagging along, usually referred to as camp followers, or were there as prostitutes. The term "camp follower," in fact, came to mean prostitute, even though many camp followers were not. Finally, in Mexico, as elsewhere in times of war, women who were forced into prostitution to escape poverty were considered entirely disreputable, while the men who used the prostitutes, or even raped in the course of fighting, were not. Only very recently have governments and international agencies passed laws stating that the use of sex slaves and the practice of rape in the course of war must be considered a violation of human rights.

Carranza as President

When Venustiano Carranza assumed the presidency in 1917 his goals were to pacify and repress the revolutionary ardor burning in the labor movement and sever the growing linkages between the industrial working class and rural peons. For Carranza (see Box 7.1) and other Constitutionalist landowners and industrialists, the essential work of the Revolution was over. Porfírio Díaz and his crowd of military men were out of power; the US could now be appeased, a moderate land reform initiated, the Church brought under the control of the state, and labor conditions improved. Whatever Carranza may have desired in terms of meeting the demands of the *Casa del Obrero Mundial* – decent wages, an end to mandatory conscription of workers for mines and estates, company stores, and the near-slave labor conditions owners imposed on the poor – he never followed through. Such measures would have upset the economic elite. The weak

Figure 7.1   This rare photo gives the names of three *Soldaderas*, "Srita Hilda Sanchez, Srita Maria Gonzalez, and Srita Anita Cantu (?)," as "The Women who led the attack on Matamoros," a town near the northern border with the United States. (The Robert Runyon Photograph Collection, courtesy of The Center for American History, The University of Texas at Austin)

Box 7.1   Revolutionaries in profile

Three of the most important figures of the Mexican Revolution – Emiliano Zapata, Francisco "Pancho" Villa (see Figure 7.2), and Venustiano Carranza – represent diverse and interesting personalities, each different from the others in demeanor and in the principles they brought to the Revolution. The following excerpts provide a study in contrasts.

Emiliano Zapata

If he dandied up on holidays and trotted around the village and into the nearby town of Villa de Ayala on a silver-saddled horse, the people never questioned that he was still one of them. Despite his fine horses and suits, Anenecuilcans never referred to him as Don Emiliano, which would have removed him from the guts and flies and manure and mud of local life, sterilizing the real respect they felt for him into a squire's vague respectability. He was one of their own, they felt in Anenecuilco, and it never

Figure 7.2   General Francisco Villa, in the Presidential chair, seated next to General Emiliano Zapata. The revolutionary leaders are surrounded by Constitutionalist militants in the Presidential Palace, ca. 1915. (Library of Congress)

made them uncomfortable to treat him so. "Miliano," they called him, and when he died, *pobrecito* – poor little thing. To them he was a neighbor, a younger cousin who could lead the clan, a beloved nephew as rough and true as seasoned timber.[4]

Francisco "Pancho" Villa

Villa was an outlaw for twenty-two years. When he was only a boy of sixteen, delivering milk in the streets of Chihuahua, he killed a government official and had to take to the mountains . . . His reckless and romantic bravery is the subject of countless poems. They tell, for example, how one of his band named Reza was captured by the *rurales* and bribed to betray Villa. Villa heard of it and sent word into the city of Chihuahua that he was coming for Reza. In broad daylight he entered the city on horseback, took ice-cream on the Plaza – the ballad is very explicit on this point – and rode up and down the streets until he found Reza strolling with his sweetheart in the Sunday crowd on the Paseo Bolívar, where he shot him and escaped. In time of famine he fed whole districts, and took care of entire villages evicted by the soldiers under Porfírio Díaz's outrageous land law. Everywhere he was known as the Friend of the poor. He was the Mexican Robin Hood.[5]

Venustiano Carranza

It was Venustiano Carranza, a man of upright life and high ideals; an aristocrat, descended from the dominant Spanish race; a great landowner, as his family had always been great landowners; and one of the Mexican nobles who, like a few French nobles such as Lafayette in the French Revolution, threw themselves heart and soul into the struggle for liberty. When the Madero Revolution broke out Carranza took the field in truly medieval fashion. He armed the peons who worked upon his great estates, and led theme to war like a feudal overlord . . .'[6]

federal government met the massive general strike in May 1916 with promises to end unfair working conditions and curb the worst abuses in the system, such as the practice of paying wages in near-worthless script. The *Casa* negotiated an agreement, sent its 90,000 members in the city back to work, and then watched as management reneged on every single demand. In response to further labor militancy, Carranza called in the army, ultimately dispersing the workers in the city through jailings, beatings, even death – the same tactics he had used to defeat leaders in rural areas.

Venustiano Carranza was elected president of Mexico, but he ignored most of the laws (including the new Constitution through which he ruled), alienated his previous supporters, and galvanized his enemies. He was ousted in a military coup in 1920 led by his former ally, Álvaro Obregón (1880–1928), the general from Sonora who held the presidency until 1924. Although faced with a rebellion at the end of his term, Obregón managed to install his chosen successor, fellow Sonoran Plutarco Elías Calles (1877–1945), a more liberal president and one whose efforts to carry out land reforms and curb the power of the Church angered both the Catholic hierarchy and the US government.

The Constitution of 1917

The 1917 Constitution is the main record of the gains of the Mexican Revolution, although the document may have seemed premature since formal hostilities did not draw to a close until the late 1920s. Not until 1940 did a president enter and leave office peacefully, when Lázaro Cárdenas (1895–1970) departed after a six-year term during which he enacted some of the greatest social reforms in Mexican history. Thus despite the election of Carranza in 1917 as the first constitutional president since Madero's brief, abortive tenure in 1910–11, and despite the writing of the Constitution that same year, violence characterized the revolutionary process and interfered with the peaceful transition of authority. Without a doubt the laws, ideology, and mandates expressed in the Constitution were more symbolic of the direction that many of Mexico's key political leaders, activists, and intellectuals wanted the country to follow, than where it was actually headed. Certainly all constitutions are mere pieces of paper that lack importance outside the force of law; however, the Mexican Constitution was that and even more. It was the product of some of the country's chief agrarian reformers, who had thrown their weight behind General Obregón, a man who understood that the basis for power in Mexico rested in the countryside. President Carranza, it has been argued, would have returned Mexico to a land tenure system not different from that of 1910, and would have reinstated the reform constitution of 1857 with a few cosmetic changes, such as preventing a president from succeeding himself, since that had been his chief complaint against Porfirio Díaz. Without offering any details, Carranza called for the vague outlines of "legislation for the improvement of the condition of the rural peon, the worker, the miner, and in general the proletarian classes." However, because the masses had been mobilized, they saw things differently.

When the group of reformers came together in Querétaro in 1916, they set about writing an entirely new document, amounting to a wish list for the achievements of the Revolution. When Carranza assumed the presidency in May 1917, as the war came to an end, hopeful forces turned their attention toward institutionalizing the most important feature of the revolutionary process: agrarian reform. The result was Article 27. At 2,500 words the article was a discourse on the principles, and failures, of private property. As the central tenet of the Constitution, the land reform article was a far-reaching prescription for the equitable distribution of land, written by the most radical segments of the new government. But it lacked Carranza's approval, as well as any inclination on his part to follow through by transforming the redistribution plan into reality. In a sweeping blow to landowners and private property, the law nationalized all land and water and declared that all individual property rights derived from the national patrimony. Whereas individuals and groups could own land, neither the Church nor foreigners could own the subsoil. Article 3 placed responsibility for education in the hands of the government, which was mandated to provide free and secular education to all from childhood. The cornerstone of Article 3 was the elimination of the Catholic Church's monopoly on the educational system, a modern reform that so infuriated the church hierarchy that it immediately began to conspire to overthrow the government and restore ecclesiastical authority.

Another highly controversial provision was contained in Article 123, which guaranteed some of the most progressive labor legislation anywhere, including an eight-hour workday, a minimum wage adequate to cover a worker's basic needs, double pay for overtime, equal pay for equal work, social security and workers' compensation. Employers were also required to provide housing, as well as medical and educational facilities. Discrimination by race and gender was outlawed, although, oddly, women did not get the right to vote. They would wait until 1954 for the franchise, making Mexico, with all its revolutionary rhetoric, one of the most conservative countries of the Americas with regard to women's rights. In contrast, workers (mainly men) gained some of the most progressive rights of the time: they were granted the right to strike and organize, meaning the Mexican labor movement obtained as a constitutional guarantee the rights other laborers in Europe, the US and elsewhere were still only demanding.

Aftermath of Struggle

Constitutional gains aside, for the mass of rural Mexicans the Revolution was a time of hardship, widespread hunger, dislocation, and arbitrary violence. Esperanza, the peasant woman interviewed by anthropologist Oscar Lewis, remembers it as a ". . . dreadful time. We suffered a lot. I no longer had clothing and I wore a soldier's khaki shirt. For Pedro [her husband] I had to make a shirt of some heavy unbleached muslin." She recounts their constant travels because Pedro had fought with the *Zapatistas* as a result of which they had to leave their village to avoid the authorities. In their wanderings from one village to another in search of relatives to take them in, the children suffered the most. Esperanza resorted to a series of transitory house servant positions in different towns, remembering:

> I would take my two children along so they could be at my side in the master's house. We had another boy, Manuel, but he died of smallpox in Azteca. Then María and Gonzalo also died on me and I was left alone. The girl died of a sickness. She got very thin and as it was the time of the Revolution, there was no doctor to go to and she died without medicine. The boy died of a scorpion sting.[7]

After the Revolution the small family, now with a new child and another on the way, returned to their original village where "Pedro began to work in the fields. He planted the *tlacolol* [a primitive form of agriculture done with a rough stick] and hired himself out as a field hand and in the dry season he made rope."[8] More than eight years after their first contact with the Revolution, the Martínez family returned to their original village, having withstood hunger, life-threatening illness, the loss of three children and the birth of two others, and took up work that was unchanged – except perhaps for the worse – from the time of the outbreak of conflict. The lives of Pedro and Esperanza Martínez mirrored those of millions of others.

Although the Constitution of 1917 embraced some of the most radical reforms of any government document anywhere at the time, the problem of enforcement was real. Carranza is said to have greeted the new constitution with the old Spanish adage from the days of the Conquest: "*obedezco pero no cumplo*" (I obey but do not comply). This saying is attributed to the Conquistadores who, far from the oversight of the Iberian Crown, refused to carry out the New Laws of the sixteenth century banning Indian enslavement. Similarly, their twentieth-century counterparts ignored the provisions guaranteeing equal distribution of the nation's most valuable resource: its land. Nevertheless, some change occurred. The *ejido* (communally held land belonging to indigenous towns) was allowed to continue, the power of the Church was greatly restrained, foreign companies no longer ruled supreme, and the resources of the Mexican nation were held proudly as a part of the national patrimony. The reforms met with fierce opposition from the Church and the ruling elite, but it was not until the 1990s, in the aftermath of a profound economic crisis, that Articles 3 and 27 were significantly rolled back. The Mexican government agreed to allow the Church broader ownership rights through an agreement with the Vatican in 1992, while subsoil rights and access to Mexico's substantial oil reserves were relaxed to allow US stewardship. Nonetheless, at the time gains by Mexican reformers placed them squarely in the camp that was adopting socialist practices; although the latter were carried out unevenly, they still represented a significant break with the past.

Violence marred the political process, despite the lofty words of Mexico's progressive Constitution. The goals of freedom and equality advanced by Villa and Zapata that had rallied the common foot soldiers, along with women, children, and men of the countryside, to the revolutionary cause proved elusive. Zapata fell into a trap set by Carranza in 1919, while Villa eluded his captors for years in a cat-and-mouse pursuit through the dry and sparsely populated northern states, only to be killed by Obregón's men in 1923. Obregón then ousted Carranza (and had him killed) as one faction sought to eliminate the other in a bloody quest for power. Only several years after the end of hostilities did Mexico settle into the peaceful transition of power; and then its political elite embraced stability with a vengeance, or so it seemed. Consolidated within the Revolutionary Institutional Party (PRI, *Partido Revolucionário Institucional*), from 1946 until 2000 Mexico was governed by a corporate-technocratic-pro-US political system that – curiously, given the struggle of 1910 – re-elected itself with no substantial opposition for the next half-century. At the dawn of the twenty-first century, new parties on the left and right, along with new social movements, sought to establish a political discourse separate from the PRI's empty revolutionary slogans.

Agrarian Revolts in Latin America

While Mexico underwent a full-scale revolution, smaller rural rebellions broke out in many Latin American countries in reaction to political changes in distant capitals. Sometimes disorder erupted in opposition to poorly understood and inadequately explained mandates from remote capitals. People distrusted leaders in urban areas as well. In cities the mass of people were physically close to their government, but poverty, illiteracy, class and racial segregation held the mass of people at a distance from their government. In both rural and urban areas, the masses were frequently distrustful and wary of change, even if it was supposed to improve their lot.

As the Mexican Revolution drew to a close, a different type of rebellion erupted in the state of Jalisco against the liberal gains this very conflict had won. From 1918 until peace returned in 1929 people from rural areas outside the city of Guadalajara, southwest of Mexico City, united in protest against restrictions on the authority of the Catholic Church imposed by the new Constitution. The insurgents were called *Cristeros* because they claimed to be acting in the interest of the one true (Catholic) Christ. They attacked Protestants, burned government buildings, and marched against local authorities, following the direction of activist clergymen who railed against the secular authorities. What on the surface appeared to be a rebellion of devout peasants, being manipulated by conservative landowners and Catholic priests opposed to the reforms of the Revolution, was actually more complicated. As recent scholarship has shown, many of the rebels were actually objecting to the government's agrarian reforms (or lack thereof) that deprived the peasantry of their rightful title to the land. Religion was for many who joined the rebellion a tangential issue that provided an umbrella under which longstanding grievances against land policies favoring the rich and robbing the poor of access to land could be addressed. Some ardent Catholics supported the government and its reforms, while the religious ties of others were fairly tenuous.

The Mexican government ignored the peasants' demands, denounced their claims as illegitimate, and argued that superstitious rural dwellers were being terrorized by priests into believing that the secular reforms would damn the devout to hell in the hereafter. In 1926 President Calles retaliated against the clergy in Jalisco by ordering the churches of the area to be bolted shut, in which state they remained for the next two years. He ignored peasants' demands that the government enforce the agrarian reform act of the Constitution and redress grievances dating back to the mid-nineteenth-century Reforma. Calles probably found it easier to punish the priests than to meet the demands of the peasantry. After all, the Church invoked little sympathy from many quarters of Mexican society, evidenced by the surprisingly feeble response that church closings engendered among most Catholics. Eventually the Catholic Church withdrew its demands, fearing that the mass of the faithful might grow accustomed to the absence of the clergy and cease to require their services. The complaints of rural dwellers likewise died out but, according to Mexican historian Jean Meyer, resurfaced in succeeding decades.

The Cristero Rebellion was not unique among rural, and even urban, uprisings that appear on the surface to promote a backward-looking agenda, but on deeper probing reveal rational economic and political grievances. In the Brazilian state of Pernambuco from 1893 to 1897, self-declared prophet, Antonio Conselheiro (the "Counselor"), called upon his followers to withhold taxes and, eventually, to overthrow the newly installed republican government in Rio de Janeiro, and demand the return of the monarchy. Denounced as a reactionary, anti-modern, and superstitious uprising of religious fanatics, the government in Rio de Janeiro launched four full-scale military assaults against the settlement of Canudos, where Conselheiro and his followers were gathered. Further investigation of the Canudos rebellion shows that, like the Cristeros in Mexico, the backlanders' demands went beyond religious devotion and were more complicated than a tax revolt and general denunciation of distant authorities. Since its installation in 1889 the Brazilian Republic had backed the incorporation of land in the northeast into the hands of what were considered to be "productive" landowners. Simultaneously, rural laborers were forced into the employ of the landowners at whatever wage was offered. The Republic – and nineteenth-century liberalism – held no place for the landless, eschewed genuine land reform with the potential for nurturing small farming communities, and relied instead on an easy rejection of the backlanders' demands by dismissing the protesters as superstitious, backward monarchists.

In the last days of the nineteenth century a rebellion in the highlands of Bolivia pitted indigenous peasants against modernizing industrialists intent on building the import–export market. The Indian leader Pablo Zárate Willka (?–1905) organized a mass uprising of those peasants who were being thrown off their land in the northern Altiplano. Neither of Bolivia's two major political parties gave an ear to the demands of the indigenous population. The Conservative Party represented the landowners and silver-mining elite and the Liberal Party backed industrialization, private property, and an expanded market economy. No one in power cared that the much-heralded "progress" and "civilization" did anything for the Indians who formed the vast majority of the population and were losing their land to capitalist land and mine owners. The Zárate Willka uprising exploded into a massacre of all whites regardless of their economic status. The political forces in distant La Paz and Sucre condemned the Indians as barbarians, claiming that the latter were incapable of joining the body politic of a modernizing nation. In the face of the indigenous uprising, the Liberals and Conservatives buried their differences and united in a brutal fratricidal repression of the Indian peasantry.

Neither the Cristeros in Jalisco nor Conselheiro's followers in Canudos nor the participants in the Zárate Willka rebellion were all of one thing or the other. In Brazil and Mexico undoubtedly many of the insurgents were motivated by religious devotion, even fanaticism in some cases, but they were also participants in rebellions that are not uncommon during periods of transition. In Bolivia, a Spanish-language requirement for voting meant that over 50 percent of the population was ineligible to legally participate in the management of their own affairs. Moreover, historians estimate that from 10 to 15 percent of the population had access to nothing but the barest mechanisms of the political system. As governments changed hands and declared new priorities, most of the people were left behind. Debates over "reform" and "liberal" agendas, heated political rivalries over the road to economic development, went on in far-off capitals and even foreign lands. The poor, isolated, and purposefully left ignorant masses used whatever mechanisms were available to them to seek redress for their grievances. Unfortunately, more often than not, distant, impersonal governments and constitutions failed to come to their aid.

Conclusion

As the twentieth century got underway, Latin America was a study in contrasts. Its vast agricultural regions, the produce of which is often considered the continent's greatest resource, turned out a wealth of commodities for the international market but many parts of the countryside remained unaffected by the wealth and promise of growing export–import markets. As mentioned in earlier chapters, there was a story at each end of the commodity chain bridge, and for Latin America that story was paradoxical. In the countryside, previous forms of coerced labor, patterns of land distribution, and patriarchal authority persisted in some areas and came under attack in others. Mexico was host to a revolutionary transformation that affected the peasantry, miners, and industrial and service workers. Revolution rolled through the countryside and reached urban dwellers as well, building from the original calls for fair elections and a return to constitutional law until it reached a crescendo of demands for greater equality and social justice across ethnic and class lines. Standard bastions of conservatism – the Church, landowners, their allies among the political and intellectual elite – fought to hold on to their traditional privileges while women, the poor, workers, and the dispossessed sought to widen democracy.

The search for a better life was not solely the goal of Mexicans, rather it was a goal of men and women in other countries at other times. Historians have long investigated popular uprisings that on the surface appeared as futile, even misguided, only to discover on deeper investigation that events such as Canudos or Zárate Willka were genuine and determined attempts to redress profound social inequalities. The revolts in Mexico, Bolivia, and Brazil touched on here provide snapshots of the actions of both leaders and ordinary people in playing a part in transforming the world in which they lived.

8 | The Left and the Socialist Alternative

The Mexican Revolution originally centered among rural peasants and miners, spilled over into the cities and drew in urban workers, the emerging middle class, intellectuals, professionals, artists, and masses of displaced rural and urban dwellers. In other countries of Latin America, where manufacturing was contributing to an expanding and prosperous economy, the working class (many of them immigrants with experience in European labor struggles) likewise began to organize itself into trade unions, mutual benefit societies, ethnic and social clubs, and city-wide labor federations as mechanisms through which to defend their class interest.

Socialism on the World Stage

By the end of World War I – or the Great War, as it was called – left-wing alternatives, including socialism, anarchism, and anarcho-syndicalism (a trade unionist form of anarchism that advocated the unity of all workers and their sympathizers into one big union or federation of unions), predominated in labor movements throughout the world. With the triumph of the Russian Revolution in 1917, communist parties formed in most European countries in support of the Bolsheviks. In 1919 socialists in the Soviet Union and Europe formed the Comintern (sometimes called the Communist, or Third, International), a meeting of all Marxist socialist groups in the world. The Comintern became the representative body uniting hundreds of socialist parties, as well as thousands of socialist and anarchist individuals and small groups, local and regional Marxist study circles, newspapers, and other unaffiliated left parties and tendencies, into a disciplined international movement. The Argentine Socialist Party changed its name to the Communist Party in 1918 and voted (through an Italian proxy) as a founding member of the Comintern, the only Latin American party represented. Socialist parties in Chile, Uruguay, Brazil, Mexico, and Cuba followed suit; by the end of the 1920s communist parties existed in every Latin American country.

Between World War I and World War II, Latin American trade union movements were the site of intense ideological debate between communist, socialist, and anarchist tendencies regarding the best alternative for the future of the labor movement, and society in general. Although disagreements were at times intense among leftist parties, socialism was a widely recognized choice among labor militants and social activists for creating equitable societies. By the end of the 1930s, fascism emerged as socialism's most formidable opponent in many parts of Latin America, especially Brazil and Argentina, and, as in Mussolini's Italy, began to win over a segment of the middle class, the manufacturing and commercial bourgeoisie.

It is not possible to delve into the intricacies of these ideological debates here. It can be said, however, that for the most part some form of left-wing option, clustered around Marxist and/or Marxist-Leninist principles, held sway among a considerable portion of the Latin American labor movement throughout the twentieth century. They followed directives from Moscow and frequently parodied the Soviet line. In the early years of the twenty-first century socialism was, and still is – even after the breakup of the Soviet Union and the end of the Cold War – one of the most widely recognized alternatives to capitalism and the status quo embraced by movements for social change. Communist parties have taken a back seat on the world stage since 1990, and all but disappeared in many parts of Latin America. But communism with a small "c" and its associated socialist, leftist ideals remains as an overt strategy in social movements and an acknowledged player in Latin America's ongoing class conflict. The contemporary "Pink Tide," of left-leaning governments in many Latin American countries today contains elements of political movements that hark back more than a half-century. This issue will be examined more fully in the final chapter.

Social Reform and the Middle Class

The coalescence of immigration, industrial expansion, dynamic trade, prosperity, and a rapidly expanding government and commercial bureaucracy made Argentina, particularly Buenos Aires, an important arena for new forms of class conflict. Immigrants brought with them from the northern regions of Italy a familiarity with socialist and anarchist principles and a sense of class-consciousness that made them aware of their own role in the nation's prosperity, and of the validity of their demand for a share in it. If the political and economic elite was heralding Argentina as one of the world's richest countries, and financing opera houses, boulevards, concert halls, parks, and the accoutrements of fine European living for themselves, it was only logical that workers would join together to demand a share of the nation's wealth as well. Since the traditional landholding elite had shown little interest in meeting workers' demands, or even in understanding the new immigrant culture dominating the urban landscape, a party largely representative of the middle class emerged with the political will to both ameliorate class conflict and define a political line between the extremes.

The middle class had grown considerably with the formation of a large government and entrepreneurial bureaucracy, and included a considerable number of professionals, shopkeepers, and managers. Middle-class activists pursued a program of social reform in hopes of expanding opportunities for everyone in society, and thereby enlarging the prospects of a political class that could challenge the power of the old oligarchy. Largely as a result of pressure from middle-class reformers such as Domingo Sarmiento (1811–88), schooling was made mandatory in 1884 and primary instruction was removed from the authority of the Catholic Church – no small feat in a country with a Catholic majority – and immigrants who needed to send their children into factories, not to school, to help support the family. With an 80 percent literacy rate by 1914, Argentina became the most educated country of South America. Under the leadership of Hipólito Yrigoyen (1852–1933), the Radical Civic Union (UCR) developed as the political organ of the middle class and the means through which Yrigoyen won the presidency for the first time in 1916 and served two terms (although not consecutively). Despite the UCR's claim to stand for democratic institutions, universal male suffrage, and educational and labor reforms, the Radicals never succeeded in mediating between the power of ranchers and large landholders on the right and the increasingly powerful labor movement, coalescing under the anarcho-syndicalist banner, on the left. The Radicals' hold was always sporadic and transitory, not unlike middle-class experiments in other Latin American countries.

Anarchism, Socialism, and Anarcho-syndicalism

In contrast to the loose affiliations of middle-class reformers, the working class formed a demographically much larger group and held the potential for demanding greater equality, a better standard of living, and an active role in national governance. Since the Argentine working class has been the most organized industrial labor force in Latin America, it often stands as the main example of trade unionism and radical, socialist, and anarchist urban politics on the continent. It had the largest labor confederation, in the *Federación Obrera Regional Argentina* (FORA, Regional Federation of Argentine Workers), in which nearly a quarter of the Buenos Aires workforce was enrolled by 1918, the year that the Argentine Communist Party (PCA) was founded.

Argentina was not alone. Militant and leftist labor organizations proliferated during this era up and down the continent, where thousands of men and women came together in strikes, worker demonstrations, and community-based protests to demand better living and working conditions. In Brazil the *Confederação Operária Brasileira* (COB, Brazilian Labor Confederation) formed in 1908 in both major cities (Rio de Janeiro and São Paulo), where it was effective in leading opposition movements. From 1917 to 1921 anarchist and communist-inspired trade unions led a series of general strikes in São Paulo for higher wages, better working conditions, an eight-hour workday, and union recognition. The largest occurred in 1917 when women workers at the Rodolfo Crespi textile mill walked out after being turned down for a 25 percent wage increase. The strike soon spread to all workers in the mill, men and women, and from textiles to other industries. Under the coordination of a citywide confederation of labor leaders, the São

Paulo Committee in Defense of the Proletariat, a general strike closed down nearly the entire city in June and July of 1917. The city's leading newspaper, *O Estado de São Paulo*, estimated that 20,000 workers were on strike by July 12 and that most workshops, mills, factories, utilities, and transportation networks were at a standstill. The strike proved very successful. On July 14 the city's leading industrialists met with Committee representatives to offer a 20 percent wage increase, union recognition, no reprisals against those who had been on strike, and a promise to "improve the moral, material and economic conditions of the São Paulo working force."[1]

Women in the Workforce

A very high percentage of immigrants in Buenos Aires at the turn of the century were women, whose rate of participation in the paid workforce surpassed that in most other parts of Latin America. By 1887 the Buenos Aires census recorded that women comprised 39 percent of the paid workforce, often working under terrible conditions. In the last decade of the century Dr. Juan Bialet Masse of the National Labor Department traveled throughout Argentina compiling a record of the living and working conditions of the laboring poor. Although he noted that most laborers endured horrible living conditions, a miserable work environment, and were employed at unsteady jobs for very low pay, he found that women had the worst situation of all. They were paid less, had no job security and no chance of moving beyond the most menial, entry-level positions. Subsequent studies have shown that women in laundries were required to work 11- and 12-hour days, with almost no rest breaks. They were paid 2.60 pesos a day, about half the wage paid to men, and – along with children, who received just one-quarter of what men earned – endured deplorable conditions. Laundries were reasonably profitable enterprises for their owners, most likely because of the extremely low wages paid to the largely female and underage workforce (Figure 8.1). Women suffered from a number of maladies, including rheumatism, sciatica, and menstrual irregularities, in addition to a very high incidence of tuberculosis, which affected the population as a whole.

Notwithstanding their plight, the government pointed to the large number of women at work as indicative of the high level of "culture and progress" Argentine society had achieved, regardless of the miserable conditions under which women labored. Occasional attempts to pass protective legislation, unsuccessfully promoted by the Radicals when they were in office, failed, while the few protections accorded women tended to contribute to their low wages and generally inferior status. Adult married women were considered legal minors and, when not married, no matter their age, were under the control of their fathers. Thus both husbands and fathers, and even older brothers, had the right to dispose of their earnings. They were denied the right to vote and hold office. Argentine women were subject to the paradox common to women in many industrializing societies: they were denied all rights by virtue of their status as the "weaker sex," but were forced into the harshest work for the least amount of pay. Nevertheless, in the early decades of the twentieth century Argentina passed some of the most comprehensive protective legislation for women of any country of

Figure 8.1   The tenement (*conventillo*) patio was the hub of the working-class community in cities. It served as a communal laundry for women who took in washing from families throughout the city, as a playground, and as a communal meeting area. (Harry Grant Olds photographs from Valparaiso, Chile, ca. 1900. In author's possession)

Latin America, comparable to parts of Europe. But, unfortunately, work standards for women and children were universally low.

Throughout Latin America the World War I era (1914–18) was a time of economic instability. Some workplaces ran at full capacity turning out provisions for the European army, while others were forced to slow down production considerably because of the scarcity of, and highly inflated costs for, raw materials. Workers and consumers complained bitterly of inflation, shortages, and price gouging, blaming the government for failure to oversee the equitable supply of basic needs at affordable prices. In response, labor militancy increased throughout Latin America, especially in Colombia, Cuba, Peru, and Uruguay, where labor organizing had been previously less pronounced.

Colombia: Resistance to the United Fruit Company

In Colombia the boom in coffee exports began in the early years of the century and grew from one million bags (60 kilos each) in 1913 to three million bags yearly by the end of the 1920s, making coffee the leading export. Other economically expanding sectors were oil production and the cultivation and export of fruit, especially bananas. Labor militancy and protest broke out first among Colombian dockworkers, but the government, anxious to grow the export sector and to build on the new-found prosperity following years of internal conflict (especially the 1899–1902 Thousand Days War that intermittently paralyzed Colombian productivity), responded by outlawing strikes, invading meetings of labor activists, and closing down nascent organizations. Petroleum workers struck in Barrancabermeja in the mid- and late 1920s, and banana pickers and haulers staged a massive strike and protest in 1928.

The banana workers' strike, and resultant repression, was a major moment in the United Fruit Company's history in Colombia; the "banana massacre" was immortalized for readers around the world in Gabriel García Márquez's novel, *One Hundred Years of Solitude*. The Boston-based United Fruit Company was formed in 1899 as a result of the merger of the Boston Fruit Company and the banana business owned by another Bostonian, Minor Keith. The company's tentacles reached into every corner of the production and export enterprise, earning it the name "*El Pulpo*" or "The Octopus." By the beginning of 1900 it was a major landholder and employer in Colombia. Managers who came to Colombia were largely from the south of the United States and intermingled little with the ordinary, mixed-race workers on their plantations. In an interview García Márquez described his childhood memories of the "banana fever" that overtook his hometown of Aracataca beginning in 1910 with the arrival of United Fruit. He remembered "the wire fences; the ever-neat green lawns; the swimming pools with outdoor tables and umbrellas; the tall, blond, ruddy-faced men in their explorer outfits; their wives decked out in muslin dresses; and their adolescent daughters, playing tennis or going for casual drives in their convertibles around Aracataca." This memory of managers from another country, living in isolation from the people who worked for them, was, he remarked, his first impression of "great-power colonialism." Years later, it would figure in his novel.[2]

Isolated from ordinary Colombians, North American managers had no compunctions about enforcing harsh working conditions for little pay. In response, workers began to organize for improved living and working conditions, including the right to form a union to represent their interests. When 32,000 banana workers struck United Fruit on October 7, 1928, the company initially relied on its own guards to disrupt the picketers, but when these intimidation methods failed, United Fruit called in government troops to put down the strike in Ciénaga (see Box 8.1). The 1928 massacre of banana strikers was a shocking event in Colombian history, prompting calls for an investigation and retaliation against the American conglomerate and the army. A young lawyer, Jorge Eliécer Gaitán (1898–1948), who would reach prominence in subsequent decades, made his reputation in the Liberal Party by calling for an investigation into the 1928 massacre, but to little avail.

Box 8.1   The banana strike

The massacre of the banana workers in *One Hundred Years of Solitude* is a powerfully written, fictionalized depiction of the real historic labor struggle:

> When José Arcadio Segundo came to he was lying face up in the darkness. He realized that he was riding on an endless and silent train and that his head was caked with dry blood and that all his bones ached. He felt an intolerable desire to sleep. Prepared to sleep for many hours, safe from the terror and the horror, he made himself comfortable on the side that pained him less, and only then did he discover that he was lying against dead people . . . Several hours must have passed since the massacre because the corpses had the same temperature as plaster in autumn and the same consistency of petrified foam that it had, and those who had put them in the car had had time to pile them up in the same way in which they transported bunches of bananas.

From Gabriel García Márquez, *One Hundred Years of Solitude*, translated by Gregory Rabassa (New York: Harper and Row, 1967), p. 329.

While the image of José Arcadio Segundo awaking to find himself buried among dead bodies is horrendous, even worse was the outcome of the massacre. García Márquez tells his readers that it began to rain in the mythical town of Macondo for months on end, and when the people emerged from the deluge they were so happy to see the sun they forgot all about the massacre. Hence García Márquez wryly fictionalizes how thousands can die but no one remembers.

The Labor Movement

During the first decades of the twentieth century, labor organizations followed one of two courses, both within the leftist political spectrum. One wing of the movement wanted to achieve socialism through the electoral process, voting for presidents and members of congress, while the other wing dismissed and distrusted the electoral arena, preferring instead to organize directly through trade unions, utilizing general strikes and labor agitation to win support from the masses and take over the government. The anarcho-syndicalists exerted considerable strength in urban areas of Argentina, southern Brazil, Chile (especially the port at Valparaiso), and Mexico.

Like Buenos Aires, Brazil's leading industrial city, São Paulo, had grown rapidly – from a population of 239,820 in 1900 to 1,033,202 by 1934. Social strife compounded as labor militancy accompanied the growth in industries and workers demanded the right to organize and strike if necessary to win higher wages. In response to many urban problems – the city was dangerous, epidemics were frequent, living conditions unsanitary, cramped, unsafe, and often menacing – workers attempted another general strike in 1919, but it did not prove successful. The Brazilian Communist Party formed in 1920 and, although never large, drew to it some of the foremost factory organizers and early anarchist trade unionists who, in turn, played a strong role in raising worker consciousness during the subsequent decade. Nevertheless, demands for higher wages and better working conditions fell on deaf ears. Even in the face of widespread walkouts, industrialists relied on repression, backed by the army, to crush strikes and break up picket lines, following a pattern similar to that in Colombia. Operating on the assumption, or pretext, that labor unrest resulted from the influx of foreigners, rather than issues of working conditions and wages, entrepreneurs and factory owners pressured governments in Argentina, Brazil, Chile, Cuba, and Uruguay to pass laws that made the expulsion of foreign-born workers a common response to strikes or labor disputes. At the same time some governments, with support from liberal, middle-class reformers and the Catholic Church, passed protective legislation ending child labor, restricting women's work in dangerous jobs, and mandating Sunday as a day of rest. Reformist measures of the era ran the gamut from real labor reform to paternalistic, short-term measures introduced to stave off confrontations.

Socialism and the Arts

The transformations sweeping Latin America's political landscape were reflected dramatically in new forms of artistic expression. Among Mexico's cultural workers the battle over the successes and failures of the Revolution continued after formal hostilities had come to an end. Probably more than any other group, Mexico's artists sought to interpret that struggle in terms of class conflict and to present Mexico's history to the world at large through an uncompromising socialist vision, depicting in bold relief the oppression of peasants and the urban working class by one set of rulers after another from the sixteenth century onward. Under the sponsorship of José Vasconcelos (1882–1959), Minister of Education from 1921 to 1924, post-revolution Mexico embarked on an era of unprecedented artistic expression, both at home and on the world stage of revolutionary art. This public rendering of politics into art, along with the pure expression of beauty and color, was unique in the art world of the time.

The words "mural," "muralists," and "muralism" all invoke Mexico and the names most associated with that art form: José Clemente Orozco (1883–1949), Diego Rivera (1886–1957), and David Alfaro Siqueiros (1896–1974). Muralists drew on the sharp political portrayals of the Díaz dictatorship popularized by printmaker José Guadalupe Posada (1852–1913). Posada's animated skeletons enjoyed popularity during his lifetime as inexpensive illustrations for Day of the Dead celebrations in late October and early November, as catchy commercial images on flyers and advertisements, and in newspapers as satirical political commentary on the political and economic elite. Despite the popularity of his images, while he was alive Posada was not considered an artist, or even a serious illustrator, in the art world's more influential circles. Later generations of artists and illustrators, however, especially the muralists whose careers overlapped with Posada's, embraced the satire and themes of picaresque

Mexican street characters represented in his art. Moreover, Posada's skeletal figures have been phenomenally enduring, finding their way into literally thousands of books, calendars, and other publications that portray popular culture or Mexican artwork (Figure 8.2).

The key themes running through the artistic explosion of the post-revolutionary era were nationalism; *indigenismo*; glorification of rural and urban labor and the working man, woman, and child; social criticism to the point of ridicule and mockery; and denunciation of the national and, especially, international ruling classes – all done in bold lines, colors, and shapes. For the muralists, whose politics ranged along the Marxist spectrum from socialist to committed communist, the people of Mexico had nothing to apologize for, no reason to humble themselves at the feet of the world's elite. The oppressed Indian had suffered at the hands of the Spanish, British bankers, Rockefeller oilmen, and armies of repression both at home and abroad. It was, as the muralists unabashedly and graphically declared, time for the oppressed to throw off their chains and assume their place as the decent, hardworking, and worthy salt of the earth. Diego Rivera's illustrated history of Mexico, which graces the walls of the Palace of Justice on the Zócolo plaza in Mexico City, leaves no doubt of his conviction that the purity of Mexico lies in its Indian and peasant masses.

In other works, especially the celebrated murals originally intended for Rockefeller Center in New York City (but painted over when the artist refused to bow to Rockefeller's demand that he remove the favorable images of socialist icons and heroes of the Russian Revolution, Vladimir Lenin and Leon Trotsky), Rivera heralded the redemptive power of the machine. The murals suggested that, put to the use of the betterment of the masses machine technology would ease the drudgery of work, but if left in the hands of the international bourgeoisie, would bring to the world only war and possible annihilation. The mural, which Rivera subsequently reproduced in the *Museo de Bellas Artes* in Mexico City, is a paradox. It was commissioned by the foremost American capitalist, John D. Rockefeller, to grace his monument to capital accumulation on Fifth Avenue in New York, yet it relied on the talent of one of the most highly acclaimed artists of the moment, Diego Rivera, who came from a country long dominated, humiliated, and controlled by the US government and Rockefeller oil interests in particular. But the historical vision portrayed by Rivera in his mural, fired by socialist, anti-imperialist fervor, was found to be unacceptable – even in the country that had long proclaimed itself to be a beacon of free expression. Rivera's refusal to be cowed by the powerful Rockefeller formed a high point in the symbolic, if not always real, affirmation of post-revolutionary Mexico's new-found sovereignty.

Tenentes Revolt and Brazilian Communism

A similar convergence of art, politics, and revolutionary upheaval shook Brazil in the 1920s. Unlike Mexico, however, the uprising did not originate in the countryside and sweep into urban areas; rather the protest mounted by a group of disaffected military officers served as the spark for one of Brazil's most significant insurgent movements.

Figure 8.2   *"Calavera* (skull) of Adelita, the *Soldadera,"* by José Guadalupe Posada.

Since the end of the monarchy in 1889 Brazil's national politics had alternated between control by powerful coffee planters in São Paulo and by dairy farmers and cattle ranchers in Minas Gerais. Loosely referred to as the alliance of *café com leite* (literally "coffee and milk"), the arrangement illustrated the ability of the landed oligarchy, in alliance with urban commercial and industrial elites, to maintain control of national leadership. In July 1922 a group of junior officers, called *tenentes*, took over the garrison in Copacabana in Rio de Janeiro, in an attempt to prevent Artur da Silva Bernardes (1875–1955), the latest president elected by the power elites of Minas Gerais and São Paulo, from assuming office. The *tenentes* denounced the unchecked dominance of the planter oligarchy and called for an end to electoral corruption. Although the young officers fought valiantly, they were easily crushed. Nonetheless, inspired by Rio's *tenentes*, another group of junior officers rose in revolt in São Paulo in 1924, held the city from July 5 to 28, and were joined by angry workers, who raided food warehouses and targeted the holdings of some of the city's leading industrialists (who were considered responsible for keeping food and consumer prices high). In a bloody counterattack the government reclaimed control of the city, resulting in the deaths of over 1,000 residents, nearly 4,000 wounded and an estimated 300,000 temporarily driven to the city's outskirts. Despite its militancy, the uprising was a complete failure that probably accentuated the suffering of the city's poor in the form of destroyed property, food shortages, and increased police repression.

Hearing of the Paulista revolt a young officer, Luís Carlos Prestes (1898–1990), from Rio Grande do Sul in the far South, gathered a group of insurgents to march north in an audacious move to join their comrades in São Paulo. The march, called the "Prestes Column," eventually traveled 14,000 miles through the interior of Brazil from the Argentine border, across into Bolivia in the North, before dispersing. Their travels placed them in contact with the rural peasantry and made the soldiers aware for the first time of the wretched conditions prevailing in the countryside. Increasingly drawn to more radical doctrines, Prestes and his followers expanded their program to include a full range of demands for land reform along with improved working and living conditions for urban workers. Prestes did not, however, succeed in drawing together a movement powerful enough to threaten the dominance of the coffee oligarchy. He went on to become secretary-general of Brazil's Communist Party in later years, playing an important role in the transformation of the Brazilian left (see Box 8.2).

Modern Art Week in Brazil

In a turn of events that echoed political and cultural changes occurring in Mexico, Brazil witnessed in the 1920s the appearance of radical new artistic and intellectual movements. Not comparable to the merger of Marxist politics and art that characterized Mexican muralists, the Brazilian embrace of modernism, nonetheless, represented a stark break with the sentimentalism of earlier artistic expression. Modernism burst on the scene in 1922 when a group of avant-garde artists and writers in São Paulo, called the *Grupo dos Cinco* (Group of Five) organized a week of artistic, literary, and cultural

Box 8.2   Olga Benário Prestes

The wife and companion of Luís Carlos Prestes, Olga Benário was also an active participant in Brazilian communist politics. She was born on February 12, 1908 in Munich, Germany into a family prominent in Social Democratic Party politics. Following in the footsteps of her politically active father, Olga became involved in social struggles at an early age; when she was 15 she joined the Communist Youth International. Through the organization she became romantically and politically involved with fellow member Otto Braun, whom she succeeded in liberating from prison in 1928, after which the two had to flee Germany for Moscow. There she eventually separated from Braun.

Olga Benário met Prestes in 1934 when he visited Russia, and she was assigned to provide him with security on his trip back to Brazil. Prestes and Benário fell in love while traveling across Europe masquerading as a Portuguese husband and wife, on their way to Brazil. They returned to Rio de Janeiro where they partici-pated in the 1935 failed communist uprising, were imprisoned separately, and lost touch with each other. She was deported to Germany in 1936, despite being pregnant with Prestes' child, a fact that according to Brazil's Constitution should have allowed her to stay in the country. Being both Jewish and a leftist, she faced certain incarceration, or worse, upon arrival in Germany. On November 27, 1937, in the Barnimstrasse prison for women, she gave birth to a daughter, Anita Leocádia, who after staying with her mother for a short time was given over to the ward of her paternal grandmother. In 1938 Benário was transferred to the Lichtenburg concentration camp, and later to Ravensbrük as World War II reached full force. At Ravensbrük she became the head of her prison block and set up classrooms, but in February of 1942, she and 200 other prisoners of the camp were sent to the gas chamber. Unaware of what had happened, Luís Carlos Prestes went to Europe to find her after the war.

presentations. Led by novelist, poet, literary and art critic, musicologist, and teacher Mario de Morais Andrade (1893–1945), the group included Tarsila do Amaral (1886–1973), Anita Malfatti (1889–1964), Oswald de Andrade (1890–1954), and Paulo Menotti del Picchia (1892–1988). The writers and artists performed and exhibited work designed to build on Brazilian themes, celebrate aspects of Brazil's indigenous and African cultures, and break with the restrictive and mechanical styles then in vogue. Initially the public viewed the exposition with extreme hostility and ridicule, even damaging some of the paintings and jeering loudly at public readings. Despite initial rejection by the Paulista public, over the next 20 years modernism flourished in Brazil, as both an aesthetic and political movement, until the foremost artists and writers of the century eventually embraced it. Modernism as an art movement is credited not only with bringing Brazilian art and literature into the modern age, but also with showcasing Brazilian talent to the world, especially Europe.

The man heralded as the "Pope of Modernism" was a writer, not an artist. Mario Morais de Andrade exhorted the nation and its people to embrace "the true Brazilian identity," to recognize their "Tupi Indian soul," and to forge a syncretism of European with indigenous and African cultures in order to achieve a genuine national identity. He reproduced and analyzed particular words and speech patterns, especially rough and everyday colloquialisms, to grasp the essence of Brazilian psychology as manifested in language. Andrade's major work was a dense and mystical story, *Macunaima*. Although considered by critics as a masterpiece that defines the soul of the Brazilian people, both the book and the movie made from it in the 1970s rely on a logic and aesthetic that has generally been very hard for foreigners to grasp. Its earthiness and bawdy sexuality were a shocking departure from sentimentalism and considered too bold for most European and US audiences. Brazilian modernism shared with Mexican muralism a call for the expression of a non-European, indigenous, and African identity far from the aesthetic norms adapted from Europe.

Women in the Arts

Several women were at the forefront of the modernist art movement in Brazil and Mexico, although for many years prominent male artists overshadowed their importance. Tarsila and Malfatti were both from the Brazilian upper class, and thus not expected or required to have careers, but were nonetheless encouraged to pursue the study of art in Europe and Brazil. Malfatti is credited with being the first artist to incorporate European and Brazilian themes into paintings, while Tarsila is known for her colorful abstractions of working people and pastoral settings. But the most famous Latin American woman artist – indeed one of the most famous Latin American artists – was Mexico's Frida Kahlo (1907–54). In what Mary Kay Vaughan refers to as "precociously feminist" art, in the 1930s and 1940s Frida Kahlo painted small self-portraits that captured stark images and engrossing, usually female-centered, themes not taken up until many decades later by major women artists such as Judy Chicago. Victim of a terrible bus accident as a teenager that left her with painful disabilities, Kahlo turned the culture's obsession with female beauty and body image into a vast repertoire addressing themes of motherhood, domestic violence, male egoism, and women's reproductive rights. Married to Diego Rivera, and thus subjected to his open infidelities, while engaging in her own extramarital relationships with both men and women, Kahlo might be seen as the precursor to the "personal is political" ideology that swept the modern feminist movement decades later.

In contrast to Rivera and the other muralists, Kahlo did not use the over-painted, grossly bejeweled figure of a bourgeois woman as a symbol of capitalist excess, nor the subdued and hardworking Indian peasant woman to represent Mexican purity. Instead, her small, painfully realistic self-portraits convey a female consciousness that is at once unsettling and shocking, and meant to contribute to the debate over the role of women in society. She relied on clever accoutrements, such as a depiction of herself with shorn hair in a business suit, or a dramatic post-abortion scene, or women infusing each other with blood, to depict the relationship of women to male authority, control over women's bodies, and the importance of female bonding. As Vaughan observes, although the suffering female body that Kahlo painted serves today as a source of "emotional identification," one cannot forget that the source of her turmoil was her own "broken body and anguished mind caught between the cult of motherhood and a man who claimed women's brains were his favorite meal."[3] Not surprisingly, Kahlo's work remained largely on the margins of an art world dominated by the more popular and politically charged male muralists until long after her death. By the end of the twentieth century, and aided by the promotion her work received among celebrities Madonna and Salma Hayek (who played the artist in the 2002 movie, *Frida*), as well as collectors and artists in the US and Europe, Frida Kahlo and her work had reached mega-stardom.

Latin America's most decorated woman of the arts was a poet who, like other artists and writers of the era, was also known for her social criticism. Gabriela Mistral (1889–1957), a Chilean writer who won the Nobel Prize in Literature in 1945, was both an activist writer and the composer of enduring poetry. Born in the Chilean village of Vicuña, she has been described by Langston Hughes and other well-known literary figures as the queen of Spanish-American literature, the honorary mother of Latin America, and the purest embodiment of the most basic and typical essences of her homeland. Although her literary fame has been mostly linked with poetry, for which she won the Nobel Prize in 1945, Mistral's career included equally unique and prolific works of prose, in which she espoused controversial educational and political theories.

Mistral, often referred to simply as "Gabriela," wrote in paradoxes and contradictions, encompassing such a vast array of social and political topics that she is hard to classify. She wrote as a feminist who encouraged women's education and freedom, while at the same time defining women's rightful place in the domestic sphere. She wrote as a socialist and as a religious Christian who took her name from the archangel. She was a pacifist, an anti-colonialist, and a critic of the effects of industrialization on human interaction. The posts Mistral held and the places she lived were equally as diverse, from her position as a local teacher, to working on school reform with the Mexican Secretary of Education, and then representing Chile in the League of Nations, the United Nations Subcommittee on the Status of Women, and as Consul to Brazil, Portugal, Nice, and Los Angeles. Much of her character remains shrouded in mystery, an aura Mistral cultivated by attending award ceremonies incognito, creating a pseudonym, Lucila Godoy y Alcayaga, and never marrying or having children.

It is for this last quality and endless dedication to her region's youth that Mistral is known as the adoptive mother of Latin America. Perhaps her era's most progressive reformer of education, Mistral explored revolutionary methods of pedagogy, including the use of visual aids, of great literature, and of games rather than textbooks. Drawing on her experiences teaching in a desolate region in southern Chile, she infused her writings with themes that emphasized the importance of education. Her most popular poem, *Ternura*, was once sung aloud by 4,000 Mexican children in her honor. The reputed source of her unique voice has contributed to her legendary reputation, something that emerged following the suicide of her fiancé, whose body was discovered with a postcard from his betrothed. It was her reaction to his death that yielded her first and most beloved series of poems and book in 1914 and 1922, *Sonetos de la Muerte* and *Desolación*. The latter is divided into four sections – Life, School, Pain, and Nature – unveiling the story of two lovers who meet, experience intensely passionate romantic love, followed by the man's betrayal of his lover, his subsequent anguish, and suicide. The poem is one of Mistral's most well-known works, most likely because it chronicles the events of her own painful relationship with a man, presented to her audience in a familiar and accessible style. By the time of her death in 1957, Mistral's sojourns in Europe and the United States, her high-profile work for social change, along with her poetry and writing, had rendered her an international icon whose talents were known the world over.

Socialism vs. Capitalism

The worldwide ideological debate between capitalism and socialism inspired Mexican muralists and Brazilian modernists, served as the foundation for the writers of the Mexican 1917 Constitution, and motivated reformers in every sector of Latin American society. Indeed, the most remarkable change of the twentieth century, introduced in the wake of the Mexican Revolution and extending into the social fabric of all of Latin America, was the tension between socialist communalism and capitalist private ownership. The impact on Latin America's nations and people varied according to many factors, not least of which were the levels of urban versus rural development, strength of the labor movement, extent of concepts of unified nationhood, forces of repression, and the role of individual political and intellectual leaders.

Certainly, the debate over socialism and its various forms entered the world stage long before the first decade of the twentieth century; however, the breadth and depth of Mexico's conflict, its long duration, and its appearance on multiple fronts – rural and urban, political and cultural, economic and social – meant that Mexico for the first three or four decades of the twentieth century was the Petri dish for various socialist and communist experiments. Leftist US journalist John Reed (1887–1920) began his career traipsing after General Francisco (Pancho) Villa's army in the north of Mexico and describing for newspaper readers at home the practical, commonsense, but quite radical thinking that came to the surface as Villa attempted to reorganize the conquered territory. Reed would go on to write his most famous work on the Russian Revolution of 1917, an event that truly "shook the world," as he said, and one that was far more intellectually, strategically and politically mapped out than Mexico's "insurgency." For the latter, socialism was a set of practical, seat-of-the-pants strategies for overcoming the gross inequalities wrought by years of capitalist and rural feudalist domination. Villa's army expropriated the large estates of northern Mexico and replaced them with collectively organized, communally run farms, where workers who had never heard of Karl Marx, the Paris Commune, Vladimir Lenin, or the concept of the revolutionary party set about imposing an equal distribution of wealth. In other rural areas, Indian farmers joined the revolution to restore their titles to the communal agrarian *ejidos* that had predominated in rural Mexico, as in much of the world, in the pre-modern era. Although Frederick Engels wrote extensively about the system of primitive communism the *ejido* resembled, certainly none of the *campesinos* (peasants) had heard of him or his books, nor did they see their struggle to reclaim their *ejidos* as part of a worldwide struggle between private and communal ownership.

Finally, there were in Mexico astute and committed socialists and communists, most of whom came together in the "Red Battalions," organized military units of anarcho-syndicalist trade unionists that fought through strikes, demonstrations, and on the battlefield to build a society run by and serving the interests of the working class. Agitators in both rural and urban Mexico rallied the masses, joined the Communist International, and adhered to the (often changing) ideological principles emanating from abroad. Thus, both consciously and unconsciously, the conflagration in Mexico drew from and fed into the international socialist conflict that gripped the world in the early twentieth century.

José Carlos Mariátegui

Probably the foremost socialist political thinker in Latin America of this era was Peruvian essayist José Carlos Mariátegui (1894–1930). Converted to socialism after a trip to Europe in 1919, where he married an Italian woman, Mariátegui convened a salon in his house in Lima that drew together avant-garde artists and writers to discuss and debate the main intellectual ideas of the times. Mariátegui's influential work, *Seven Interpretive Essays on Peruvian Reality*, marked him as the father of Latin American Marxism and one of the main political architects of the particular place of socialist thought in the context of Latin America. Self-schooled, since his poor background had only allowed him a primary school education, but well versed in literature, poetry, and the arts, Mariátegui carved out an eclectic Marxism that incorporated spiritualist egalitarianism with materialist economic equality, anti-authoritarianism and anti-dogmatism with an adherence to socialist principles into a single doctrine. Although he died very young (the cumulative effect of a life of disability resulting from a childhood disease that his impoverished state had left untreated), Mariátegui stands as one of the key figures in the early twentieth-century debate over socialism. His special contribution was the singular task of fitting Marxism into the sharply divergent and underdeveloped Latin American reality. He predicted in 1923 that the economic hardships facing Latin America would give rise to proletarian revolution:

> In this great contemporary crisis, the proletariat is not a spectator; it is an actor. In it the fate of the world proletariat is to be resolved. From it will emerge – according to all odds and predictions – the proletarian civilization, the socialist civilization, destined to succeed the declining, decadent, moribund capitalist, individualist, and bourgeois civilization . . . We are witnessing the disintegration, the agony of a worn-out, senile, decrepit society, and at the same time, we are witnessing the slow and restless gestation, the formation, the creation, of the new society.[4]

Conclusion

The advent of socialism, an ideology born in Europe but adapted to the reality of poor societies in Asia, Latin America, and Africa with varying degrees of success, distinguished the twentieth century from those that came before it. With the triumph of the Russian Revolution in 1917, previously dispersed leftist parties and movements representing labor, agrarian reform, and political and human rights were called on to join into a unified left. By the end of the 1920s, every country of Latin America sported a communist party. Socialist, anarchist and various strains of leftist parties remained active and captured the allegiance of thousands of individuals. While the organized left commanded widespread following among the trade unions, it was in the arena of the arts where Latin Americans began to make their mark. From the Mexican muralists to Brazilian artists, from the writings of essayists such as Mariátegui to the reflective poetry of Gabriela Mistral, the ideology of socialism reached out to the masses.

Nevertheless, debate between left and right continued to permeate the political and economic life in the inter-war years. The rise of fascism as a powerful force in Europe, seeking to destroy the left and to take all democracy with it, influenced Latin America's emerging cadre of socialist and populist leaders. Populist leaders sought to hew a middle ground, hoping to win over the leftist working class while appeasing members of the expanding middle class.

9 | Populism and the Struggle for Change

Quite likely, Mariátegui and other Marxists at the time underestimated not only the rapid rise of the US to pre-eminence in the hemisphere, but likewise the extent to which the northern power would derail attempts at socialist transformation in Latin America. If the twentieth century was the era in which socialism appeared on the world stage with dramatic and earthshaking effect, it was also the "American century"; the era in which the United States became the foremost world power (Figure 9.1).

The trajectory is well known. The United States emerged from World War I as the equal to Britain and in contention with its former colonial master for trade and investment. It surfaced as the unquestioned world capitalist power after World War II, remaining locked in conflict with the communist bloc in the Soviet Union and China for much of the rest of the century. Finally, by the dawn of the twenty-first century, and despite the looming power of China, whose brand of communism was appearing more capitalist by the day, the "West" (the euphemism for capitalist Europe and the United States, but not including Latin America, despite the reality of geography) emerged triumphant over the dismantled communist experiment in Eastern Europe and in a position to dictate harsh economic and political terms, at least for a while, on much of the rest of the so-called "developing world." It was not socialism, however, that rose to prominence in the large economies of Latin America. Populism, revolving around a number of key figures, dominated the era.

Recognition that workers had legitimate demands served as the platform upon which well-known populist political figures built their support in the mid-twentieth century: Getúlio Vargas (1883–1954) in Brazil from 1930 until the mid-1950s; Juan Domingo Perón (1895–1974), who dominated Argentine politics from the late 1940s to the 1950s, and whose legacy has remained influential ever since; and Lázaro Cárdenas (1895–1970), whose 1934–40 presidency implemented the policies of the Mexican Revolution more than any leader before that time or since. Neither Peru's Víctor Raúl Haya de la Torre (1895–1979) nor Colombia's Jorge Eliécer Gaitán ever reached the presidency of their respective countries, but both left an indelible imprint

Accepting the Monroe Doctrine
John Bull gratefully admits that Uncle Sam is the proper custodian of the Western
Hemisphere.
Homer Davenport, *Review of Reviews*, January 1902.

Figure 9.1   By the terms of the Hay–Pauncefote Treaty of 1901 Great Britain ceded to the
United States the right to build a canal through the Isthmus of Panama and recognized the
latter's pre-eminence in the region. In this cartoon, Homer Davenport shows Uncle Sam and
John Bull dividing a world in which Latin America is not even pictured, demonstrating the
way the great powers made decisions with no concern for the leaders or people of the
countries concerned.

on succeeding decades of politics. Haya was the founder of the populist APRA party *(Alianza Popular Revolucionario Americana)*, which produced an influential populist movement in Peru, while Gaitán commanded a broad following among Colombia's popular classes in the 1930s and 1940s until his assassination in 1948. Each of these men figured prominently in political events, left important legacies in whatever political configurations succeeded them, and inalterably influenced the social and cultural landscape, as well as the governments, of their respective countries.

Although we refer to them as "populists," that admittedly imprecise label could have been applied to some *caudillos* mentioned in earlier chapters. This twentieth-century brand of populism differed from the nineteenth-century variety in several important ways. First, it emerged from, and in many ways intersected with, the activist working-class, socialist, and social democratic mass movements described in this chapter. Secondly, while none of these populist leaders were leftists, nor traced their origins to the trade union or socialist movements, they drew on the tactics, honed the rhetoric, and saw the labor movement as a critical social force. Their populist influence relied on a mass base that had been forged in the battle for workers' rights; matured under the tutelage of socialist, anarchist, or communist leaders; and relied on the organizational apparatus of left-leaning political parties.

As a political force, populism can move to the left or to the right. Historically it has been the foundation more for fascism than communism, especially in the twentieth century; but its appeal to the masses rests precisely on the promise of redressing the grievances of the dispossessed, disenfranchised, ignored, and downtrodden. Unlike Marxist socialism, however, populism makes no fundamental critique of capitalism nor does it advocate worker control of the means of production or a worker-run state. Instead populists use the strength of the state, in the hands of capitalists, as a patronage machine to appease workers and meet the demands of mass movements. At different times both Perón and Vargas voiced their admiration for Italian fascism, and both used the repressive arm of the state to silence their critics; but they also rebuilt labor movements and parties as their base of support. In return for the protection and recognition of the state, the working class offered support. In a brief comparison between Latin America and the fascist regimes of Germany, Italy, and Spain, historian Eric Hobsbawm remarked: "European fascist regimes destroyed labour movements, the Latin American leaders they inspired created them. Whatever the intellectual filiation, historically, we cannot speak of the same kind of movement."[1]

Getúlio Vargas and "New State" Politics

Getúlio Vargas was a 47-year-old rancher who traded on influence and political cunning to win the governorship of Brazil's southernmost state, Rio Grande do Sul, in 1928. Two years later he made a bid for the presidency, losing narrowly to Julio Prestes, in what was considered a fraudulent election. Refusing to accept the results, Vargas, along with many of the *tenentes* from the failed military uprisings of the 1920s, toppled the Republic and installed a new one. The military coup that placed Vargas at the helm of the government ended the First, or Old, Republic (1889–1930), introduced a new phase in Brazilian politics, and marked the decisive entrance of previously silent and marginal groups into the political equation. Getúlio Vargas moved to centralize power in the hands of the federal government, and in so doing angered many governors and state and local powerbrokers. He established new "presidents" in the states, bypassing elected officials everywhere except Minas Gerais, where the elected governor was allowed to continue. Vargas wrapped his authoritarian measures in national, and often nationalistic, terms, reflecting the impact of the world economic depression and the rise of fascism abroad. Eventually Getúlio Vargas nationalized rail and sea transportation and established a number of state-owned firms including Petrobras, the national oil industry, Chembras, the national chemical industry, and others.

Borrowing a page from Franklin Roosevelt's New Deal, Vargas increased the scope, size, and importance of the federal bureaucracy. He gained considerable support from organized labor – after making sure that anyone who opposed him was eliminated. The government initiated construction on some of the long-promised workers' housing in Rio de Janeiro and São Paulo. Opened with much publicity and fanfare, Vargas took credit for finally completing a promise that had been held out to the urban masses since the urban renewal of the early twentieth century. However, official propaganda failed to mention that the new housing was far from adequate to meet the needs of the growing urban population, was doled out as favors to unions for distribution among their most loyal members, and was never extended to the poorest regions of the country. Other improvements such as electrification, a national steel industry, expansion in public health services, more schools and better education also reached only urban dwellers.

Vargas's ideological convictions are hard to pin down. Although he operated in ways that promoted Brazil's national interests, he was quick to suppress any social force that disagreed with him. In 1930 he made overtures to the hero of the *Tenentes* uprising, Luís Carlos Prestes, offering him a position as head of the military, but Prestes refused, opting instead for the Brazilian Communist Party (PCB). Formed less than ten years earlier, the PCB already had a substantial following among urban intellectuals and the labor movement, but a communist-led revolt in November 1935 was immediately and severely repressed. Vargas suspended civil rights, jailed opposition trade unionists, and strengthened police powers. He opportunistically used a rumor of a communist uprising on November 10, 1937 to stage a coup d'état and launch his corporatist *Estado Novo*, or "New State," which lasted for the next seven years. The *Estado Novo* curtailed states' rights, banned strikes and lockouts, and centralized decision making in the hands of the all-powerful executive.

To avert class conflicts, Vargas promised something for both workers and employers, incorporating them into *sindicatos*, or state-regulated interest groups. In this way, the president was able to establish a pattern of leadership that claimed to place national interest above regional or class-based interests. Labor and political historian Barbara Weinstein points out that what Vargas actually did was join the interests of the industrialists with the state and manage them as one. The *Estado Novo* borrowed elements from European fascism current at that time. Unlike Mussolini and Hitler, however, Vargas did not build his base in a new political party, relying instead on the military to back him, until 1945. Moreover, rather than crush the workers' movement, as had occurred in Europe, Vargas organized the Brazilian Labor Party, incorporating only the trade unions and their leaders who had benefited from his policies into his base of support.

The army and members of the industrial elite grew fearful that Vargas was planning to usurp all power into his own hands, and moved to depose him on October 29, 1945. He retreated to his estate and private life in Rio Grande do Sul until 1950 when he returned to politics, ran for President, and was elected by a wide margin. The political and economic scene of the 1950s was not, however, conducive to rebuilding and sustaining either Vargas's own personal popularity or his ultra-nationalist program, with or without working-class support. Congress was divided and much of it opposed to him; inflation was out of hand; and a newly powerful North American business community was strong-arming its way into Brazilian industry and investing on its own terms. Corruption, graft, infighting, and criminal activity characterized nearly all branches of the government. Confronted with a military demand that he resign, Vargas took his own life on August 24, 1954, leaving behind a suicide note blaming "outside powers," clearly referring to US interference in Brazilian affairs. In his death note Vargas attempted to depict his suicide as a necessary step to maintain Brazilian integrity and sovereignty in the face of outside pressures. The real story, as we have seen, was more complicated, especially when the entire record of corruption, political repression, and favoritism that marred the Vargas era is brought into the equation.

Juan Perón and Peronism

The best known of Latin America's populist leaders, and one whose legacy has endured for generations, was undoubtedly Juan Domingo Perón. The phenomenon known as "Peronism" grew out of the failure of repeated attempts by Yrigoyen to establish a middle-class-based political system from 1916 to 1930 – mainly because his UCR had neither the will nor the means to effectively oppose the dominance of the oligarchy. In January 1919, police response to a factory owner's request to break up a metalworkers' strike and demonstration soon escalated into a street melee and subsequent three-day-long battle. Right-wing youths from neighborhoods throughout the city, and even from surrounding towns, converged on the city's Jewish neighborhoods, blaming immigrant Jewish shopkeepers for labor agitation. The police looked on while hundreds of the immigrant poor were indiscriminately attacked and killed. By week's end 1,500 people were reported dead and over 4,000 wounded, earning the week the name *Semana Trágica* (Tragic Week). Despite this blot on his record, and accusations of incompetence, Yrigoyen managed another term in office before he was overthrown in 1930 by a military coup, followed by a number of military regimes interspersed with civilian governments. The importance of this period lies not in the names of these governments, nor even the circumstances that surround each of the coups and returns to elections, but rather in the recognition that by the 1930s Argentina had reached an entirely new stage. Ineffective as a mediator between the oligarchy and the workers, tending generally to side with the former over the latter, the UCR and Yrigoyen's middle-class leadership moved to the back seat. The new military junta demonstrated little inclination to reverse this political process. However, one military officer recognized that the industrial working class was not necessarily an impediment, and could be mobilized to serve as the basis for building a corporatist state that joined the interests of labor with that of at least a large section of the national bourgeoisie to promote a nationalist agenda. That military officer was Juan Domingo Perón who, since his first appearance on the political scene in 1943, exerted a major influence over Argentine political life.

From his position as Secretary of Labor in the government that took power in 1943, Perón built a base of support among trade unionists and the urban poor by calling for increased pay, union recognition, and better working and living conditions. As a result of his clever maneuverings, he won the 1946 presidential elections and remained in power until 1955, when he was ousted in a military coup. Even in exile, Perón cast a long shadow over the next two decades of Argentina's politics. In 1973 he returned from exile in Spain to serve again as president, but died the next year. Perón's tremendous influence stemmed from a number of factors, including the popularity of his first wife, Eva Duarte Perón (1919–52), who through the Peronist-created Social Welfare Agency, and later the Eva Perón Foundation, distributed clothing, money, housing, and other benefits to the working poor. Snubbed by fashionable society ladies, whom she called "*las señoras gordas*" (the fat ladies), Eva Perón personally received literally thousands of people in her marble monument. An attractive young woman, she built a fanatically loyal following by meeting with, listening to, and genuinely helping people who had been all but ignored throughout Argentine history (Figure 9.2).

Perón's – or the Peróns' – success relied on a combination of factors. First, real reforms benefited working people. Wages for industrial workers (not all workers, granted, but for a sizeable, and very visible, core in industry) increased by 53 percent between 1946 and 1949. In addition unions won recognition, collective bargaining rights, protection from capricious dismissal, and regulated hours, working conditions, and vacation and sick time. Benefits and wages were not uniformly high, and at times fell, but improvements on the job combined with a greater respect for working people to boost Perón's popularity. Secondly, Peronism created a worker identity by building a sense of community. The government used public relations tactics designed to win adulation for Perón, including parades, huge demonstrations, sporting events, beauty pageants, and other contests, to create a perception of cohesion between working-class and Peronist goals. Thirdly, Peronism redefined the contours, and the tools, of the class struggle. According to historian Daniel James, Juan Perón effectively redirected workers' previous political loyalties as socialists, communists, and radicals toward allegiance with him personally, his wife Evita, and the Peronist labor party. By means of repression, Perón erased and marginalized the leftist parties and organizations with which the working class and poor had previously identified, substituting a new identity for workers as integral to, even the pride of, a new national, political community. Finally, Peronism sought to build – perhaps more rhetorically than actually – a "New Argentina" in which

Figure 9.2   First Lady Eva Perón, in an elaborate *haute couture* gown, and President Juan Perón at the Teatro Colón, Buenos Aires, ca. 1950.

Argentines could take pride. Perón's nationalization of the British rail system was greeted enthusiastically as a source of national self-respect, despite dubious benefits to the Argentine economy, since the system was not returning much of a profit for the British. The latter, it has been argued, were happy to be rid of it, since it was inefficiently operated and in need of costly repairs. Careful investigation has shown that many of the improvements Peronism initiated were of short duration, lacked sustainability, and owed more to graft than real reform, but the image was quite the opposite. After only a few short years in office, the slogan of the administration was *"Perón cumple!"* ("Perón delivers!").

In general Perón expanded the franchise, thereby dramatically widening his base of support among the poor, workers, and women. People who before 1943 had been locked out of the national decision-making process found themselves at its center. Perón boasted that he had made possible the entrance of "more than 900,000 women" into the paid workforce in all kinds of jobs and professions. "It is our duty," he argued, "to morally and materially dignify their efforts." Perón encouraged full voting rights for women and the expansion of protective legislation. In 1949 he formed a new wing within his own party, the Peronist Feminist Party, under the leadership of Eva Perón, proclaiming that: "The Peronist Feminist Party opens its doors to all women of the people, and especially to the humble women who have been forgotten by the poets and by the politicians." (He also founded a "Men's Party" branch, as well as a branch for "Workers."). Interestingly, in its founding platform the women's branch included a quote from Eva Perón stating that women need their own branch because "just as only workers could wage their own struggle for liberation, so too could only women be the salvation of women." Yet Evita always positioned herself in an adoring relationship with her husband, repeating often that he completed her and that she was only fulfilled through him. The 1951 election was dramatically different from any before or since, and nearly unparalleled in the world: 90 percent of Argentine women voted, compared with 86 percent of men. Not only did women vote heavily for Perón, but, true to Eva's point, they also voted for themselves: seven women were elected to the Senate and 24 to the House of Deputies.

Perón's Fall from Grace

Argentina's economic honeymoon, which had allowed for the expansion of worker benefits and other social expenditures, drew to a close in the early 1950s as the world economy underwent a harsh correction and Argentina's agricultural exports met increasing competition from other countries. In 1951 Perón attempted to restore his standing through the bold move of placing Eva on the ticket as vice-president, but this was vetoed immediately by the military, which had no interest in seeing the Peróns consolidate their power so decisively. The military and their supporters in the oligarchy, who hated both Juan and Eva Perón, were undoubtedly relieved when Eva died of cancer on July 26, 1952. Not only did her death at 33 cut short any plans the couple might have had to extend their power but, along with the economic downturn, it hastened the end of Juan Perón's popularity.

Before the economic doldrums set in completely, however, the country confronted the full impact of Eva Perón's death: "The entire city and the entire country instantly went into the deepest, most heartfelt state of mourning. Cinemas stopped their movies, theaters interrupted their plays, restaurants and bars immediately showed customers to the door, their shutters slamming down over suddenly darkened street fronts. Within a matter of minutes the city was silent and dark."[2] The government suspended all operations for two days and many labor unions, especially those that Eva Perón had most supported, ordered their members to attend the wake and funeral. Thousands of people passed by her well-embalmed body for the two weeks it remained on view to the public. Over a million people crowded the streets to watch the mile-long funeral procession, headed by Perón, government officials, and members of the Peronist Feminist Party. Eva's supporters began a campaign to nominate her for sainthood in the Catholic Church, while her husband drew up plans for a mausoleum three times taller than the Statue of Liberty, where he intended to keep her body on display forever.

Neither of these grandiose projects came to pass. If Perón's popularity had bene-fited from his wife's work, her premature death contributed to his fall from grace. The military launched a coup in 1955, forcing Perón into exile in Paraguay and then Europe. Until his return to Argentina in the 1970s Perón lived in Madrid, where he passed much of his time in the very apolitical job of entertaining himself with María Estela (Isabel) Martínez de Perón (b. 1931), a young nightclub entertainer he met and married in Panama during the early years of his exile. Isabel Perón returned with him to Argentina in the early 1970s and was able to do what Evita could not: run for the vice-presidency and assume the presidency upon her husband's death in 1974.

Politics Engendered

Although Eva Duarte and Isabel Martínez were significant female participants in Latin American political life, they were simply two individuals who came into the national limelight as a result of extraordinary circumstances, and cannot be considered repre-sentative of widespread changes in the role of women in the twentieth century. There were, however, other women whose roles were of more significance, and the era itself witnessed major changes in women's lives. Historian Susan Besse notes that the characteristics of the early twentieth century influenced the form of female participa-tion in society at large and in movements for emancipation. Economic development, industrialization, and urban expansion provided more opportunities for women's work outside the home in factories, transportation, and communication sectors and in the offices of the growing civil and private bureaucracy. Members of avant-garde social movements called into question the role of women in society and heralded the newfound freedom of artistic and cultural expression for and by women pioneered in European capitals and spreading to the cities of the Americas. The rise of radio, movies, and print media, especially magazines and newspapers devoted to the discus-sion of women's goals, aspirations, and lifestyles, connected women with each other and brought to the foreground their role in society.

Although hardly welcomed in conservative or religious circles, suffrage as a basic female right, and women's struggle to achieve it, reverberated through the urban middle and upper classes in many Latin American nations. Argentina hosted the First International Women's Congress in 1910; subsequent conferences were held in

Box 9.1   Bertha Lutz and women's suffrage

In Brazil, Bertha Lutz (1894–1976), the daughter of a Swiss-Brazilian father and an English mother, was the moving force behind the movement to win women the right to vote. An exceptional woman, educated in Brazil and France, Lutz used her training as a lawyer to argue for greater rights for women through the organization she founded in 1922: the Brazilian Federation for Feminine Progress, an affiliate of the International Women's Suffrage Alliance. The signing of the 1932 civil code that granted women the franchise was, in Lutz's view, only the beginning of a long campaign to win equal rights. Elected to the Chamber of Deputies in the 1930s, Lutz was instrumental in pushing for legislation that granted women full social and legal rights, until women and men both lost their political rights when Getúlio Vargas assumed dictatorial powers in 1937.

several Latin American countries through the 1920s. These meetings drew together mostly elite women from professions such as medicine, law, academia, and science, as well as those who used their positions as the wives of powerful men to promote educational, welfare, and social reform, and finally, a small group of social activists associated with socialist and other left-wing organizations (see Box 9.1). The majority of poor and laboring women from cities and the countryside, factory workers, maids, seamstresses, prostitutes, street vendors, shop and office clerks, did not attend – and were probably unaware of – the women's congresses that met over the next few decades. In Latin America, as in Europe and the United States, the campaign for women's suffrage garnered mass media attention; however, most people in Latin America, regardless of gender, were disenfranchised by virtue of their illiteracy, poverty, and race. For example, Ecuador extended the vote to women in 1929, but the race, class, and language restrictions prevented the vast majority in this nation of indigenous people from voting. Women won the right to vote in Brazil and Uruguay in 1932; in Cuba, Bolivia, and El Salvador in the 1930s; in Panama and the Dominican Republic in the years before World War II; and in the rest of Latin America in the decades afterward. Their inability to participate as full citizens by no means placed them in an exceptional position when compared to poor and illiterate men, since most people were barred from the exercise of their rights in societies dominated by men of European extraction.

Despite restrictions on political participation, women in urban areas began to assume a new role in society. Modern styles hit the major cities, and advertisements appeared in newspapers and glossy magazines using women's images to sell products, many of which were directed at a new, exclusively female market. Women who were earning money for the first time, even on a limited basis – working in retail stores, government agencies, and factories – had money to spend on cosmetics, clothes, and entertainment. In major cities such as Buenos Aires, Havana, Mexico City, Lima, São

Paulo, Rio, and other metropolitan areas of Latin America, women came to be seen as consumers, arbiters of culture, and members of the educated society at large. No longer under the strict control of fathers and husbands and now visible in the public sphere, women nonetheless still operated largely under the confinements of home, motherhood, and second-class status in the workplace, or under conditions which Besse calls "restructured patriarchy."[3]

This new trend had its detractors. A powerful right-wing movement feared that newly enfranchised women would bring about the destruction of society. Conservatives in the Catholic Church expressed fears that women were abandoning their roles as mothers and housewives, and, in their view, pushing society to the brink of anarchy. Social change was threatening the traditional order that had ensconced men firmly as heads of household. Some men felt uneasy with the knowledge that women were no longer dependent on them for their livelihood, could now influence the political process with their votes, and could begin to make decisions for themselves. Urban men and women (the innovations rarely reached remote, rural areas) were confronting fundamental changes in one of the most basic institutions of society: the family, and its traditional power relationships. It was not simply the lives of women that were being tranformed, but the entire gender balance of society, or the many ways men and women thought of themselves and sought to live their lives as individuals and as couples.

Revolutionizing Mexico: Lázaro Cárdenas

Whereas both Perón and Vargas drew support from newly enfranchised women, Mexico's revolutionary leaders, with the exception of the communists, clung to patriarchal privilege and refused to consider extending the vote to women – despite the latter's extensive participation in the Revolution and widespread support for social reform. In line with Comintern positions, the Mexican Communist Party (PCM) supported women's suffrage, seeing it as a basic democratic right; the Party also foresaw the important role women could play in the impending struggle against fascism. According to historian Jocelyn Olcott, in 1935 the PCM linked these issues in the slogan: "Ample democratic liberties; women's suffrage; dissolution of the 'Dorados' and 'guardias blancas'" (the latter refer to fascist organizations in Mexico).[4] Fearing that women's votes would represent a conservative bloc in favor of the Church (a not entirely unfounded suspicion), the government withheld the franchise from women until 1953. In other ways a populist like Perón and Vargas, Mexican president Lázaro Cárdenas did not promote women's rights. His six-year term in office (1934–40) is remembered for reforms in labor, education, and social programs, but not women's rights. He was an architect of the artistic and cultural explosion associated with the post-revolution era, bringing to fruition many goals of the Revolution and concretizing the abstract language of the 1917 Constitution into a defined political program. Since his term coincided with the decade in which the advanced capitalist countries were enduring the Great Depression, Cárdenas was able to plot a more independent and self-sufficient course than might have been possible if the interventionist US state had been monitoring political and economic developments in Mexico more closely. Concern about the rise of fascism in Europe also helped keep events in Mexico below the US radar – even when Cárdenas nationalized British- and American-owned oil companies. The formation of *Petróleos Mexicanos* (PEMEX) in 1938 sent shivers down the collective financial spines of European and US businessmen, but Cárdenas appeased corporate and government interests by offering compensation and assurances that there would be no further expropriations of foreign companies.

Cárdenas's 1934 Agrarian Code called for the confiscation of 45 million acres of private land and its redistribution into *ejidos*, a reform more extensive than those of all his predecessors put together. To service the *ejidos* and sustain the livelihood of the peasantry who maintained them, Cárdenas instituted rural schools. The latter were to serve not only as a means of educating rural children, but also of propagating the core values of the revolutionary program: national pride, class-consciousness, and distrust of the Church. When faced with strong opposition from devout Catholics and organized resistance from the hierarchy, Cárdenas relaxed some of the most anti-clerical programs, allowing the Church to play a role in delivering state services, especially education. Cárdenas faced opposition among pro-Catholic, right-wing, and pro-fascist interests in Mexico, but managed to ride out the storm during the final years of his presidency, aided by his support of the Allied forces in the face of the war, which by 1940 was engulfing much of the world. For rural and urban workers who benefited from progressive labor laws, land reforms, and curbs on the authority of *hacendados*, mine owners, and industrialists, Cárdenas embodied the Mexican Revolution and stood as the guardian of its ideals.

Populism in Colombia and Peru

Two other names generally crop up in discussions of charismatic Latin American populists: Víctor Raúl Haya de la Torre (1895–1979) in Peru and Jorge Eliécer Gaitán (1903–48) in Colombia. Neither commanded a fraction of the power nor left a legacy as enduring as Vargas and Perón, nor did they play a role in shaping the contours of a new revolutionary state, like Cárdenas. However, both Gaitán and Haya de la Torre carved out a particular niche in the politics of Colombia and Peru, respectively, and served as models of modern-day political leaders in an era when revolutionary politics, Marxism, and cross-class populism held sway in many Latin American countries.

Jorge Eliécer Gaitán

Because Gaitán's career was cut short when he was assassinated in downtown Bogotá in 1948, there has long been considerable speculation as to what he actually did accomplish, and what he might have accomplished had he risen to the high political office to which he aspired. Born of struggling but respectable middle-class parents, Gaitán worked his way into elite political circles, while always bridging the gap between the middle and lower classes. His particular genius was in connecting his progressive political values with the aspirations of the poor by putting into common language and concrete goals the road to change. Gaitán's writing made him something of a latter-day Thomas Paine, making socialism "common sense"; and he was a charismatic public speaker. Moreover, he was tireless, if idiosyncratic, in his approach. After differing with the leaders of Colombia's Liberal Party – in part because of what he saw as its tepid response to the 1928 banana massacre in Ciénaga – he split off to form his own party. Based on the platform of this party, the *Unión Nacional Izquierdista Revolucionaria* (UNIR, National Leftist Revolution Union) Gaitán built a following that led him to the brink of taking control of the old Liberal Party and ascending to the presidency in 1950.

To the shock of his supporters and adversaries alike, two years before the election Gaitán was killed on the street outside his Bogotá law office. The motive for his death remains a mystery because a mob immediately apprehended and killed his assassin, Juan Roa Sierra. Subsequent to the assassination, rioting broke out in Bogotá with devoted and disappointed followers rampaging through the city in a mass riot that became known as the *Bogotazo*. The exact nature of the crowds' frustrations was not entirely clear, except to indicate that much was expected of Gaitán. He had raised the hopes of the popular classes by attaching his own vision for a more just and prosperous Colombia with the aspirations and goals of a wide swath of his countrymen and -women. Although not a socialist, he used the language of socialism to advocate for a more humane capitalism in which the government intervened to ensure an equitable distribution of wealth, public education, a decent standard of living, and that the benefits of modern society were available to everyone. Unlike Perón and Vargas, Gaitán left a legacy of what might have been. His role in government (where he was not a steady presence, moving in and out of various political offices) is usually discussed in terms of what he advocated, what he intended, and what his policies might have produced in the long term. These imprecise legends, similar to those surrounding Pancho Villa, are surprisingly important aspects of history, as are the myths surrounding what should have, or could have, transpired, but never did.

What happened instead was in many ways incomprehensible: near breakdown of civil society. The *Bogotazo* spread from the capital to other cities and to the countryside; from a few weeks of rioting it turned into 30 years of warfare. Known as *La Violencia*, the battle initially pitted Liberal against Conservative, but later expanded beyond the bounds of mere political rivalry. The term *La Violencia* is indicative. It was the form, the violence, that was remembered, not the grievances, the parties involved, or even the outcome. In brief, riots in Bogotá led to peasant land seizures in rural areas, precipitating in turn severe repression from landowners, who rejected peasant claims and hired thugs to expel them from seized properties. The peasants formed guerrilla armies, which went to war against the *hacendados*' personal armies, turning Colombia's countryside into a battlefield. The *Violence* ended in 1957 when Liberals and Conservatives signed a pact promising to divide political power by sharing some of the key components of governance in a national unity structure. The National Front maintained the peace from 1957 until 1970, but did little to further democracy. By the early 1970s guerrilla warfare had broken out in opposition to the undemocratic government, plummeting Colombia back into a period of violence from which it has never fully emerged. Jorge Gaitán's promise to forge a representative government that would incorporate the majority of Colombians into the decision-making process was never to be. The reassertion of regional rivalries and repressive military solutions to the escalating violence in recent decades, accelerated by the emergence of powerful drug traffickers engaged in refining coca and marketing cocaine, have drowned out the populist vision of the 1940s and 1950s.

Víctor Raúl Haya de la Torre and the APRA

During the pre-colonial and colonial periods Peru was a country rich in resources including silver and gold; an enterprising, hardworking, and dense population; magnificent cities and architecture; and a system of centralized government and towns connected by a vast road network. At the same time, Peru has always been a study in contrasts. Geographically dispersed over an immense area and rugged terrain, the Peruvian people are sharply divided between the rich and powerful and the desperately poor, living in isolated hamlets or crowded urban squalor. A sizeable, educated middle class has infrequently held the reins of government since independence from Spain in 1824. More often, power in Peru has passed back and forth between military and civilian rule, neither of which has managed to improve the lives of the millions of mainly indigenous people who live in grinding poverty.

The career of Peruvian politician Víctor Raúl Haya de la Torre was emblematic of the coalescence of socialist and nationalist ideals played out in the Latin American context. Haya, a student leader in Cuzco who was influenced by Peruvian Marxist Mariátegui, in 1924 founded the Popular Revolutionary Alliance of America, with a program calling for progressive change along the socialist lines that were influential among nationalist and radical political groups throughout Latin America. In subsequent decades Haya's politics followed a more populist, nationalist course, rejecting communism and attempting to forge an APRA-based victory in the electoral arena. Haya himself did not win electoral office until very late in his career – and then only on a populist program that was a mere shadow of earlier Aprista nationalism – but APRA remained a symbol of Latin American attempts to win national autonomy. Moreover, it stood as an ideal for civilian rule in a society that, except for brief intervals, had languished under the shadow of authoritarian and military governments.

Central America

In other places, particularly Central America, nationalist politicians shifted from forging popular unity to mounting armed resistance to US control. Ideologically these movements and their leaders spanned the political spectrum: from populist nationalism, exemplified by Augusto César Sandino in Nicaragua, to embracing communist insurrection, as seen in the program of Salvadoran labor leader Augustín Farabundo Martí. These two Central American revolutionaries, whose lives closely paralleled each other (Farabundo Martí worked with Sandino for a while in Nicaragua despite their political differences, and they both died at the hands of their respective governments at just 39 years of age), set the stage for important insurrectionary movements in the 1970s and 1980s. Finally, Costa Rica's history stands apart from its neighbors in both Central and South America. A country that has democratically elected its leadership every four years for most of the century and abolished its army in the late 1940s, Costa Rica has one of the highest standards of living in the hemisphere. This coffee-producing nation presents an interesting contrast to Colombia, a country similarly based on the growth and export of coffee, and where Liberal and Conservative parties have long competed for power. But while Costa Rica has chosen leaders through the ballot box, Colombia has endured decades of political violence.

El Salvador

El Salvador emerged from the independence era in the early 1820s with a deeply entrenched *latifundio* system in the hands of a small group referred to as the "Fourteen families." This tightly knit oligarchy, interconnected through marriage, acted as a clan that protected its wealth at all costs and shared little power, even with outside investors. Unlike neighboring Guatemala, El Salvador's export economy did not generate a middle-class bureaucracy in the service of foreign corporations or domestic infrastructure until the twentieth century, when it developed a professional and commercial class whose prosperity and livelihood demanded its allegiance to the ruling stratum. The Salvadoran oligarchy stood as a bulwark against reform of any kind, and was quick to act against even the merest whispers of unionization, universal suffrage, or any involvement of the masses in the direction of the government or public life. The Fourteen Families ruled the entire country as if it was their personal fiefdom, and controlled the workings of society to such an extent that even US diplomatic envoys routinely referred to them as the "feudal families." The peasantry and working class endured conditions of extreme poverty, scratching out an existence on tiny plots of land or at minimal wages.

The main struggle for power occurred in 1932, when a budding reform movement coalesced around the leadership of Augustín Farabundo Martí (1893–1932), the Marxist advocate of agrarian reform and universal suffrage. In spite of his admiration for Leon Trotsky, the Bolshevik revolutionary, which he probably picked up during his years in Mexico (after his expulsion from Russia Trotsky lived, and was eventually killed by Stalin's agents, in Mexico), Farabundo Martí transformed El Salvador's Socialist Party into a Moscow-oriented communist party in 1930 and assumed the position of Secretary-General. Two years later, in response to a military coup d'état that overthrew elected president Arturo Araújo and installed General Hernández Martínez as dictator, Salvadoran communists organized a peasant and worker revolt against the government. Scheduled for January 22, 1932, the uprising was discovered before the date, thwarted, and the leadership was apprehended and killed, including Farabundo Martí. The subsequent violent repression, during which the army rounded up an estimated 20,000–30,000 peasants for mass execution – many of whom had no connection to the revolt – is referred to as *La Matanza* (the Massacre). It stands as a moment in

Salvadoran history in which the landed oligarchy no longer even pretended to govern, instead turning over political power to the military, which ruled with an iron fist until the early 1980s. At that time, the insurgency bearing Martí's name, the Farabundo Martí National Liberation Front (FMLN), surfaced to lead a concerted war against the dictatorial government.

Nicaragua

Nicaragua's history and the efforts of Augusto César Sandino (1895–1934) differed from El Salvador in that the opposition movement that emerged in the 1920s was not motivated by communist ideology, nor was it directed solely against a homegrown, domestic oligarchy. Although the US government strongly backed the Salvadoran dictatorship, and continued to do so throughout the 1980s guerrilla movement, there was no direct military intervention, beyond advisors. In Nicaragua, however, except for a few short intervals, US Marines occupied the country for 22 years from 1911 to 1933, while the US government, working at the behest of US interests controlling fruit and coffee production and exports, closely supervised domestic political affairs through an alliance with the Somoza family dynasty that ruled the country from the time the Marines withdrew.

The United States gained a foothold in Nicaragua under the government of José Santos Zelaya (1853–1919), who came to the presidency in 1893 through a military coup. Zelaya was a modernizer who oversaw the construction of roads, port facilities, and railroads, the separation of Church and state, and the initiation of public education. Similar to Porfírio Díaz in Mexico, Zelaya encouraged foreign investment and granted lucrative concessions to US companies doing business in Nicaragua, to the degree that by 1909 they controlled the production of coffee, gold, lumber, and bananas. Concerned that US firms were attempting to exert undue influence on domestic affairs, and hopeful that European investors might render higher profits for the national treasury and the pockets of its powerful and wealthy citizens, the Nicaraguan government invited competitors to bid on a canal across the isthmus. In response, the US government ordered Marines into Nicaragua. Under US pressure, Zelaya resigned in 1910, putting an end to any hope for Nicaragua's autonomous development for more than a half-century. The opposition Conservative Party installed Adolfo Díaz as President, his only qualifications for the job being his employment as a bookkeeper for an American mining company. Diaz's major accomplishment was to accept loans from the New York banking firm of Brown Brothers and Seligman, offering as security a controlling interest in Nicaragua's national bank, state railways, and customs revenues. For more than two decades the US army intermittently occupied Nicaragua, ruling through a series of puppet governments, and exerting considerable influence over the day-to-day workings of society.

Refusing to recognize the legitimacy of a national election until the US army exited the country, Augusto César Sandino, the mestizo son of a moderately prosperous landowner inspired by the nationalist principles of Mexico's revolution, mobilized an army of several thousand volunteers to drive out the American forces. Both as a result of the damage inflicted by Sandino's army and because the economic downturn at home made military exploits abroad unpopular, President Roosevelt withdrew the bulk of the occupation force in February 1932. The US left behind the National Guard it had trained, under the leadership of Anastasio Somoza García (1896–1956), and a government in the hands of a compliant president. Shortly before the withdrawal of the entire military force, the newly installed National Guard commander apprehended Sandino after a meeting with President Juan Bautista Sacasa (1874–1946) and had him executed, a feat of which Somoza boasted in later years. By 1936 Somoza García had consolidated his power and was in control of both the military and civilian wings of the government, ushering in a family dynasty that ruled the country directly and indirectly until 1979, when the triumphant Sandinista National Liberation Front (FSLN, or *Frente Sandinista de Liberación Nacional*) drove the last member of the dynasty, Anastasio Somoza Debayle (1925–1980) into exile in Florida.

Costa Rica

Costa Rica's history differed markedly from that of its Central American neighbors. In the nineteenth century Costa Rica was one of the major coffee-producing and -exporting countries of the Americas. Like other countries in the region, Costa Rica's economy was based on one primary export, coffee, and the ruling elite controlled most of the nation's wealth. As occurred in Guatemala, Minor Keith and the United Fruit Company managed the sale of coffee and other agricultural exports, the combined total of which accounted for virtually all national revenue. Despite a scenario that paralleled the political economy of other nations, privileged Costa Ricans did not rely on the military to maintain power, but worked out a system of passing control of the government back and forth between the Liberal and Conservative parties for most of the late nineteenth and into the twentieth centuries. In 1948 a break in this pattern occurred, and José Figueres assumed leadership of the country with the support of a rebel army. Figueres held the presidency for the next 18 months, as promised, and stepped down. During his time in office Figueres implemented a series of reforms that have remained in place until the present, and helped to ensure a peaceful and prosperous society. Most importantly, he abolished the army, thereby eliminating the incentive for war and the accumulation of arms and military "toys" that have consumed the militaries (and budgets) of most Latin American nations in the twentieth century. He nationalized the banking system, implemented a property tax, limited the presidency to one term, granted women the right to vote, and instituted measures allowing for the democratic transference of power from one politician and one party to another.

Because of a well-managed system of public education, Costa Rica has a 96 percent literacy rate, comparable to the United States, Canada, and Cuba; and a well-run national health service that no doubt contributes to the country's high life expectancy, low infant mortality, and reduced levels of communicable disease. How and why Costa Rica has managed to establish a system that other Latin American countries have not remains something of a mystery. Some of the explanations often proffered are that it has a very homogeneous population; the extent of income inequalities have never been the same as other nations in the hemisphere; and there has been no army for a long period of time. Whatever the reasons, Costa Rica's social welfare system is better than that of any other in the hemisphere except Canada.

The Long Twentieth Century

British historian Eric Hobsbawm refers to the 1930s as the "Great Slump" and notes that the political, and even psychological, cultural, and social, outlook of the world underwent a profound change as a result of the chain of events set in motion by the 1929 Wall Street stock market crash. "The Great Slump confirmed intellectuals, activists and ordinary citizens in the belief that something was fundamentally wrong with the world they lived in."[5] Hobsbawm's insight may be only partially true as regards Latin America, since the great financial shock that undermined the confidence of the major powers in London, New York, Berlin, and Paris reverberated differently in Latin America.

Because the nineteenth-century economies of most nations in the region were based on exporting one, or very few, raw materials (coffee from Brazil, Colombia, and Central America; copper and nitrates from Chile; tin from Bolivia; meat and grains from Argentina), the sudden and severe contraction of demand from the US and Europe, as the Depression deepened, severely damaged the exporting nations at the production end of the commodity chain. Moreover, Latin America's infrastructure, much of it essential for transporting materials to ports and urban markets, had been built with loans and through direct investments from abroad. As Europe and the US demanded servicing of the debt, the debtor nations found they could not pay. Interaction with traditional trading partners in Europe, especially Britain and Germany, halted or underwent change; trade patterns shifted from transatlantic to moving almost entirely north to south and back again. At the height of the Depression, in the mid-1930s, neither goods nor money moved at all. With demand abroad at a standstill and little capital available to stimulate local economies, many nations of Latin America began to turn inward and economic activity slowed to a crawl.

The state of Latin American society at the end of the 1930s and into the 1940s was extraordinarily different from that of the 1890s. Urbanization, immigration, social reforms, and the imprint of charismatic leaders proposing radically new political programs had combined to transform Latin American capitals and major cities. Whereas the countryside in most of the countries remained unchanged, cities were fast approaching the cosmopolitan flavor of their European counterparts. Demographic and economic trends, along with Latin America's assumption of a more central role in international trade, had profoundly affected everyday life. Proscribed roles of gender, race, and class were no longer immutable, just as geographic, national, and ethnic barriers had expanded to bring a wider variety of the new Americans onto the national stage.

Conclusion

The twentieth century was marked by the advent of socialism, an ideology born in Europe but adapted to the reality of poor societies in Asia, Latin America, and Africa with varying degrees of success. Populism proved a more compelling organizing principle in many countries, and the attraction of powerful leaders – Perón, Vargas, Gaitán, Haya de la Torre, and others – retooled the original socialist campaign among the working class and traditional leftist sectors. Many countries witnessed deep-seated political and cultural changes during the first decades of the twentieth century. Mass politics, modern cultural expressions, and movements that demanded broader rights for all members of society cropped up everywhere in Latin America. In the case of Mexico, the demands exploded onto the national scene, originating in the countryside and enveloping the entire country. Finally, no account of the twentieth century in Latin America can ignore the profound importance of the rise to world dominance of the United States, on the one hand, and the repeated outbreak of multifaceted, anti-imperialist, nationalist, and socialist struggles attempting to check US power and secure Latin American self-determination, on the other. While apparent as far back as 1923, with the articulation of the Monroe Doctrine, and reinforced by the 1904 Roosevelt Corollary – as well as frequent acts of "gunboat diplomacy" and other "Big Stick" interventions that marked the implementation of those political doctrines – the full force of US hegemony reached new heights during the second half of the twentieth century, as a product of the Cold War between the US and Soviet Union. The next chapter explores the contours of that struggle.

10 | Post-World War II Struggles for Sovereignty

The war that eventually engulfed much of the world from 1939 until 1945 did not produce the tremendous number of casualties in Latin America as it did in Europe, Asia, and Africa; however, it did not entirely pass the region by either. Economically, Latin America benefited from the worldwide demand for primary goods, especially copper, oil, and agricultural commodities. A new feature of the commodity chain from the producing side was the demand for Mexican laborers to fill jobs in US agriculture left vacant as men entered the army and women took positions in basic industry. Politically, the conflict between right and left playing out on a grand scale in other parts of the world surfaced in far more muted contests between Latin American fascist and communist movements.

World War II

Following the attack on Pearl Harbor in December 1941, the United States placed heavy pressure on Latin American governments to cut off business and trade with the Axis powers. Nevertheless, most attempted to remain neutral; only Central American and Caribbean nations sided with the Allies in 1941, although Mexico followed suit in 1942. Brazil's Getúlio Vargas, who had earlier flirted with fascism, tried to retain his alliance with the US while also maintaining cordial relations with Germany, which was heavily invested in Brazilian industries. But in 1942 the Nazis sunk a Brazilian ship, prompting Vargas to join the Allies. Colombia and Bolivia declared war on the Axis in 1943, but Venezuela, Peru, Chile, Uruguay, Paraguay, and Ecuador waited another two years – when the war was almost over – to follow suit. Argentina, with its German-trained military, large German and Italian populations, and substantial German investments, held out as long as possible. It only entered on the side of the Allies in March 1945, when the Axis defeat in Europe was a certainty and the Japanese surrender less than five months away (Map 10.1). At the same time,

Map 10.1 Latin America in World War II. (Courtesy Cathryn L. Lombardi and John V. Lombardi, *Latin American History: A Teaching Atlas* ca. 1983. By permission of The University of Wisconsin Press.)

Argentina and Cuba, along with the Dominican Republic (the peculiar circumstances of which will be explained later in this chapter), became a major refuge for Jews escaping Nazi-held territories.

Latin American countries' lack of enthusiasm for the war effort may reflect the fact that their economies neither benefited, nor suffered terribly, during the war years. The most pronounced impact was that wartime demand for copper, tin, and oil bolstered the export economies of Chile, Bolivia, Venezuela, and Mexico, while demand for sugar and tropical fruits was a boon to Central American and Caribbean nations. An important shift in commodity exports took place, as the United States replaced Europe as chief consumer. Consumption in Europe was stymied during the war, and then drastically curtailed for decades afterward. In addition to supplying North America's ravenous appetite for minerals, oil, resources, foodstuffs, and manufactures, especially steel from Mexico and Brazil, the war contributed to high levels of employment and the expansion of basic industry in Latin America. In Brazil, the change was dramatic since US investments helped to build a national steel and chemical industry. However, throughout the region disruptions in traditional export markets and trade relations offset many of the gains achieved in specific, war-related export commodities. Mexico, more than any other Latin American nation, supported the US effort by providing strategic resources (copper, zinc, lead, mercury, graphite, and cadmium) and instituting internal price controls to avoid profiteering. Mexico's national income almost tripled between 1940 and 1946, moving from 6.4 billion pesos in 1940 to 18.6 billion in 1945. Per capita income also grew in the same period (from 325 pesos to 838 pesos) although increases were not evenly distributed. Without the ready supply of crucial raw materials from Mexico and other parts of Latin America US defense plants would have encountered great difficulty making the rapid transition from peace to a wartime production schedule.

Temporary Worker Program

The most controversial aspect of US–Mexico cooperation was the Bracero Program. Taking its name from the Spanish word for arm, *brazo*, the program began with an agreement in 1942 between Presidents Franklin Roosevelt (1882–1945) and Manuel Ávila Camacho (1897–1955) to recruit over 300,000 Mexicans as agricultural workers to fill a US labor shortage caused by the combined impact of military conscription and the massive influx of laborers into more highly skilled, and remunerated, work in armament factories. By the time the Bracero Program ended in 1964, an estimated 4.6 million Mexicans had participated. According to the terms, Mexican workers received free transportation to and from the US to work in jobs selected specifically not to displace US workers; they were paid the minimum wage of $0.46 an hour, increased to $0.57 an hour by the end of the war. Ideally, both US and Mexican government inspectors monitored the work camps to assure that laborers were being paid the minimum wage, had good working conditions, and were being provided with sanitary housing and other facilities. During the war years American labor unions closely monitored the situation to ensure that the *braceros* not form a scab labor force, and that US employers would not use them to depress the cost of labor. Employers held to that part of the agreement during the war, but largely abandoned it from 1950 until 1964. The program functioned in over 25 states, including Minnesota and Wisconsin, the Pacific Northwest, and throughout the West, Southwest, and Southeast.

Growers in Texas did not originally ask for *braceros*, mainly because the state had passed a number of highly racist "Caucasian only" labor protections. When in 1944 Texan growers were desperate to fill vacancies in the agricultural sector, the Mexican government refused to send any, citing cases of Texas employers who refused to pay workers what they were owed, racial discrimination, and lax enforcement of the agreed-upon protective measures. Mexico did not relent until 1947, two years after the end of World War II, when it finally allowed *braceros* to work in Texas. Although the terms of the agreement were not enforced everywhere, *braceros* were probably better treated than Mexican agricultural workers at the time. Given the deplorable conditions under which migrant laborers live and work, then as now, the standard set for the *braceros'* working conditions may not have been too high.

Recent scholarship indicates that whatever the intended purpose of the Bracero Program when it was initiated, it evolved into a means to provide cheap agricultural labor in general, not simply to fill a wartime shortage. A study by the Pew Hispanic Center demonstrates that more *bracero* contracts were signed *after* the end of the war than during it. The program ran from 1942 until 1964 – 19 years after the end of World War II and almost a decade after the Korean War (1950–3). The largest number of contracts (450,000) was signed in 1956; that rate was maintained until 1960. Thus several hundred thousand *braceros* entered the US between 1942 and 1946 and then, curiously, arrived in far greater numbers during the 1950s. When, in 1954, the US entered a short, but severe, post-war depression, organized labor called for an end to the program on the basis that owners were using *braceros* for jobs that could go to native-born US workers. Rather than end the program, however, the government launched "Operation Wetback" (its official name, adopted from the derogatory reference to illegal immigrants who arrived in the US after, presumably, swimming across the Rio Grande River). This military and paramilitary operation conducted sweeps through urban neighborhoods where many Mexicans lived and along the US–Mexico border. Over a million workers and their families were deported, many of whom had entered the US legally as *braceros*; others had become US citizens.

When the economy picked up in the late 1950s, agribusiness interests in California, the Southwest, and Florida lobbied the US government to maintain, and even extend, the Bracero Program; as a result over a million laborers signed *bracero* contracts during the early 1960s. The Pew Hispanic Center study tracks the correlation between the decline in *bracero* contracts and the burst in mechanization of US agriculture. By 1962, since machines had replaced a large portion of agricultural work previously done manually, growers required fewer laborers, mainly for harvesting crops. For the *braceros* the most brutal aspect of the plan occurred in the 1950s and 1960s when states, depending on the peculiarities of local demand, began to ship the laborers back to Mexico – with little to no warning, and no thanks at all.

This snapshot of the Bracero Program contains several history lessons. First, most residents of the US are unaware that without the work of Mexican migrants during World War II and the Korean War, the US would not have been able to produce enough food to meet demand on the home front and for the military abroad. In fact, not until 2008 was it revealed that the Mexican government had taken a part of the *braceros*' wages and never paid it to the workers themselves. One can assume that most of the *braceros* were long dead by the time the Mexican government was forced to provide the compensation. Second, US historians have been slow to recognize that the Bracero Program was much more than a temporary, stopgap measure to fill a wartime labor shortage. Instead, it institutionalized through a bilateral agreement a practice in which US business relied on cheap labor from Mexico to depress prevailing wage levels, especially in agriculture, at home. Finally, the main impact of the Bracero Program was to lay the foundation for the exploitation of migrant laborers from south of the border, on a seasonal and as-needed basis, in agricultural fields bordering the western, southwestern, and southeastern states. This practice, which has only accelerated since the 1950s, has served to provide the US consumer with the widest variety of foods, at very low prices, of any major economy in the world. Today, the pattern of reliance on low-cost, transitory, and temporary labor established by the Bracero Program has spread to virtually every form of manual labor in the US, and as a "tradition" stands at the heart of recent debates over the institutionalized "guest-worker" program designed to provide immigrants to fill low-wage jobs.

Post-war Latin America

The most striking change in the post-war era was the global shift in world domination and in the nature of conflict between competing powers. By the 1950s Europe's authority in the Americas, as well as in Africa and Asia, was a fraction of what it had been in 1900. Except for a few colonial outposts held by Great Britain, France, and Holland (including the Bahamas, Barbados, Guyana, Jamaica, Trinidad and Tobago, Antigua, Belize, Dominica, St. Kitts/Nevis, St. Lucia, St. Vincent, and a part of the Virgin Islands), Europe no longer exerted significant influence in the hemisphere. The US had become one of two "superpowers" and by the end of the twentieth century, following the breakup of the Soviet Union in 1991, had emerged as the most powerful military and political force on the planet. With the exception of Puerto Rico and the US Virgin Islands, the United States did not attempt to colonize the hemisphere, as had the Europeans earlier; however, it did not hesitate to flex its military might. The chumminess of the "Good Neighbor Policy," Franklin Delano Roosevelt's Latin American foreign policy during the war years, gave way to an aggressive stance more reminiscent of Teddy Roosevelt's "Big Stick" earlier in the century. When local workers demanded higher wages and better working conditions from US firms operating in a Latin country, for example, or when governments moved to nationalize or tax US-based corporations, Washington did not hesitate to step in to overturn the offending government and replace it with a more compliant regime.

By the mid-twentieth century many Latin Americans had adopted new attitudes toward their own nations and relations with the United States. A stronger nationalist voice was being heard in many countries of the Americas, from newly emergent groups interested in promoting democratic traditions and national sovereignty. The hypocrisy of fighting to end totalitarianism in Europe and Asia while tolerating or even encouraging it at home was not lost on a new generation of Latin Americans. As a result of improved educational levels in the 1950s, the citizenry was not as amenable to the kind of strict authoritarian rule that had existed earlier. Throughout Latin America, increased industrialization, spurred by wartime economies, accelerated demand for a more educated workforce capable of handling everything from technical and managerial tasks to operating more sophisticated machinery. In the post-war decades the number of students in universities grew at astonishing rates. In Mexico the number ballooned from 76,000 in 1960 to 247,000 in 1970 and 1.3 million by 1987; in Brazil, Latin America's most populous nation, university enrollment climbed from 95,000 in 1960 to 430,000 by 1970 and 1.8 million in 1980. Even in places where the overall student population was small, increases were remarkable. Peru's student population grew fifteen-fold, from 16,000 in 1950 to 246,000 in 1980; similarly, Chile's went from 9,000 in 1950 to 120,000 at the beginning of the 1970s.

In a phenomenon that occurred throughout the world, as well as in Latin America, members of the rising middle class, and their newly educated male and female children, were no longer content to languish under the control of a distant elite. Large numbers of women had entered higher education for the first time, and began to make modest inroads into the professions and other employment outside the home. University-educated youths, many the first in their family to complete high school, much less college, expected to join a workforce where education opened doors to better jobs and professions, and to a role in determining the governance and direction of the societies in which they lived. University faculties and administrations also grew, giving rise to a large, progressively minded, and usually left-leaning voice within an organized institutional setting.

In addition, new institutions of higher learning reached locales where youths previously had little access to the world of ideas and technology, or means to obtain a better future than that of their parents. The most elite national universities were located in capital cities, but well-qualified young women and men in more isolated provinces also began to attend universities in the late 1960s. The impact on the nature of the ideological discourse throughout Latin America was nothing short of earth shattering. Privileged oligarchies, military dictatorships, and the landed elite did not fit well with a new generation's conception of a society devoted to the furtherance of a shared public sphere – including libraries, parks, schools, and recreational facilities, as well as publicly owned infrastructure and a government bureaucracy – that existed to serve everyone, rather than only a select few. Finally, a larger mass of educated people translated into a larger proportion of society concerned with inequality, since Latin America's intellectuals had historically been preoccupied with issues of social justice. Referring to Latin America in the 1950s, Jean Franco explains why: "Marxism attracted the intelligentsia because it offered a rational explanation of inequality and

Figure 10.1   Squatter settlements on the outskirts of Buenos Aires. (Nancy Borowick photo)

the goal of liberation from imperialism, both formal and informal."[1] Moreover, injustice was everywhere. If the middle class had grown, prosperity had barely touched the poorest segment of most countries, leaving both the rural and urban poor eking out a subsistence living or crowded into burgeoning makeshift settlements on the outskirts of the cities (Figures 10.1 and 10.2).

Military vs. Civilian Rule

Increased educational levels, along with a greater awareness of the struggle for democracy and against colonialism enveloping many parts of the world – especially Africa – placed many young, informed Latin Americans on a collision course with their own governments. For the United States, however, the watchword of the post-war era vis-à-vis relations with Latin America, and the rest of the world, was *stability*: meaning a stable environment for multinational investment. With the passage of the Military Defense Assistance Act in 1951, the exact nature of what the US government envisioned as the best means of ensuring stability became clear. Initially the Act provided for $38.5 million to the militaries of individual Latin American nations so that they could build up "country missions" for their own internal security. Since no Latin American countries were at war with each other, and since funding every country's military establishment would seem a poor way of preventing conflict among and between them, the purpose was clearly something else. The US wanted Latin American militaries to police their respective civilian populations to ensure domestic

Figure 10.2   The shantytowns inhabited by the poor, mainly recent migrants from the countryside and neighboring countries offer little in the way of schools, parks, and access to public transportation. Residents in this Buenos Aires community have established their own schools, soup kitchens, and cooperative gardens, but children still have little open space to play. (Nancy Borowick photo)

stability. In the years since, a much broader and more comprehensive Military Assistance Act has provided billions of dollars for hardware and training to individual militaries in the hemisphere. Needless to say, the US seldom invaded or strong-armed its way into a Latin America country, nor showered its largess on a country's military, without the express approval – or even invitation – from the military, urban and agricultural elites, and politicians. When under pressure local oligarchies were inclined to run to the American embassy and demand US military protection from uprisings by their own citizenry.

Additionally, in 1946 the US inaugurated a key institution for the formal training of Latin American military officers: the School of the Americas (SOA), dubbed "the School of Assassins" by *Newsweek* magazine. In 2001 it was renamed the Western Hemisphere Institute for Security Cooperation (WHISC). Originally located in the Panama Canal Zone, and moved in 1984 to Fort Benning, Georgia, the SOA has graduated some of the most famous dictators in Latin American history, including General Augusto Pinochet who led the 1973 overthrow of Chile's elected president, Salvador Allende (1908–73); Manuel Noriega (b. 1935), a close associate of the US until his friendship proved to be no longer expedient and he was deposed by the very government that had him, literally, on the payroll; as well as the leaders of notorious death squads, such as El Salvador's Roberto D'Aubisson (1944–92). The particular role of these and other military leaders will be explained later in this and subsequent chapters. A key purpose of the SOA was to create military officers loyal to the US, and to rule out attempts by errant, often junior, military officers who militantly disagreed with the existing government and sought to install more representative leadership, as happened during the 1922 Brazilian *tenentes* revolt, Augusto Sandino's guerrilla war against the US occupation of Nicaragua in the 1930s, and a 1944 junior officer revolt in Guatemala. The founding of the SOA in 1946 was consistent with a US Cold War policy that favored the installation of military governments as a way of maintaining order. From Washington's point of view, the policy was enormously successful. By 1954, pro-US military dictatorships were in power in 13 of 20 Latin American nations.

The Absolute Dictator: Rafael Trujillo

Quite possibly the best example of the absolute dictator, whose loyalty to the United States bordered on the fanatical, was Rafael Trujillo Molina (1891–1961) who ruled the Dominican Republic personally, or through his surrogates, from 1930 until his assassination in 1961. A product of the US military occupation of the island from 1916 to 1924, Trujillo at age 18 joined the National Guard, a local Dominican military force formed during the US Marine occupation army to maintain order.

President Woodrow Wilson had dispatched a Marine force to the Dominican Republic after the 1911 assassination of Ramón Cáceres, a reform politician who had attempted to modernize and reform Dominican society during his time in office (1906–11). Disliked by the local landowning elite and distrusted by US sugar interests, which owned the majority of mills on the island, Cáceres had little opportunity to enact change, and the fighting that broke out after his death dismantled what had been put in place. During the Marine occupation, US companies and soldiers made a number of improvements, including building a system of roads and telegraph lines, improving sanitation and educational facilities, and eradicating disease. When they departed the Marines left behind a military force trained to protect US interests, with a designated commander. Over the next six years the National Guard became the Dominican National Police and finally the National Armed Forces. Trujillo moved in step with each new military permutation; in 1928 he became leader of the Armed Forces, and then self-appointed president of the country in 1930 (see Box 10.1).

The extent of Trujillo's control was legendary. For example, he had the hotel rooms and press offices of international correspondents bugged and employed spies to move among workplaces, government offices, and even on the street to report back any conversations that were anything less than supportive of the regime. During Trujillo's administration there were many improvements to infrastructure, including roads, communication and transportation networks, and a fair amount of construction – but

Box 10.1

Eduardo Galeano wrote a partially tongue-in-cheek summary of the tentacles of Trujillo's reach, which would be humorous if it were not true:

1936 Trujillo City

Trujillo, tireless bane of reds and heretics, was, like Anastasio Somoza, born of a U.S. military occupation. His natural modesty does not prevent him from allowing his name to appear on automobile license plates and his likeness on all postage stamps, nor does he oppose the conferring of the rank of colonel on his three-year-old son Ramfis, as an act of simple justice. His sense of responsibility obliges him to appoint personally all ministers, porters, bishops, and beauty queens. To stimulate the spirit of enterprise, Trujillo grants the salt, tobacco, oil, cement, flour, and match monopolies to Trujillo. In defense of public health, Trujillo closes down businesses that do not sell meat from the Trujillo slaughterhouses or milk from his dairy farms; and for the sake of public security he makes obligatory the purchase of insurance policies sold by Trujillo. Firmly grasping the helm of progress, Trujillo releases the Trujillo enterprises from taxes, while providing his estates with irrigation and roads and his factories with customers. By order of the Trujillo shoe manufacturer, anyone caught barefoot on the streets of town or city goes to jail.

The all-powerful has a voice like a whistle, with which there is no discussion. At supper, he clinks glasses with a governor or deputy who will be off to the cemetery after coffee. When a piece of land interests him, he doesn't buy it; he occupies it. When a woman appeals to him, he doesn't seduce her; he points at her.

Quoted in Galeano, *Century of the Wind*, v. 3, pp. 105–6.

This description captures the essence of Trujillo's rule, and refers to actual events. For example, Galeano's reference to a beauty queen refers to Trujillo's 18-year-old daughter, Angelita, whom he had crowned Queen Angelita Trujillo in December 1955 at an extravagant event (the National Fair of Peace and Brotherhood of the Free World), to which Trujillo invited the world's dignitaries. The Fair cost $50 million (in a country where annual per capita income was $240), and although attendance was mandatory for select Dominicans, almost no foreign dignitary attended.

all the work was done either by the president's own companies or others from which he extracted robust bribes. The improvements, many of which earned him a genuine core of supporters among ordinary Dominicans, were not only personally lucrative but also facilitated oversight of the population. Speed bumps were interspersed along roads to slow down traffic at the hundreds of check points; police and personal servants traveled along the streets to make sure that every house had a picture of the leader on display, lit up and visible from the street. The roads and telegraph lines were also crucial for moving people around. To guarantee an adequate workforce for his many sugar estates and other enterprises, busloads of people and materials were moved in and required to stay until Trujillo allowed them to leave. The rest of the time peasants were tied to the land, requiring a government permit to move from one place to another.

A fitness fanatic and very careful dresser, Trujillo refused to allow anyone to walk barefoot in the capital; shoe stalls were in place on all roads leading into the city so that the poor who had no shoes could rent them when attendance in the capital was required. Smoking in public and automobiles was not allowed, and even on the hottest days men were required to wear jackets and ties in the capital. Not only were there no permits to carry guns, but also it was illegal to walk with a coat over one's arm or wear khaki trousers and shirts of the same color since Trujillo had determined that it was easier to hide a weapon while in such attire. Costly permits were required to hold any festivals or parties, except for gatherings with the immediate family.

After Pearl Harbor the Dominican Republic immediately declared war on the Axis powers, while steadily exporting sugar, cocoa, and coffee at good prices to supply the war effort. Like the Nicaraguan dictator Somoza, whose trajectory and methods were closely parallel, Trujillo could be relied on to back the US in whatever international dispute arose. A notable departure from US policy was the Dominican Republic's acceptance in 1939 of Spanish Republicans forced into exile after the Spanish Civil War and triumph of the fascist government headed by General Francisco Franco. In addition, the Dominican Republic welcomed Jews escaping the Nazi takeover of Europe. On the surface it seems peculiar that Trujillo, who openly admired fascist ideology, was willing to admit its victims, even those, such as the Republicans, with leftist sympathies. In both cases it was apparently the whiteness of the refugees that mattered more to Trujillo – a man who obsessively declared his Spanish heritage and deleted his grandmother's Haitian nationality from every official record – than their ideology. One of the earliest examples of Trujillo's whitening campaign occurred in October 1937 when he ordered the killing of 25,000 Haitians in the border area between the two countries. In a little over a day Dominican soldiers hacked to death thousands of black Haitian men, women, and children migrant laborers who had crossed the border to work on Dominican sugar plantations. After a mild protest from Washington and demands for reparations from Haiti, the Dominican Republic paid $522,000, or $29 for every officially recognized death.

In 1956 Trujillo's agents apprehended a Dominican exile, Jésus de Galindez, a Columbia University professor and outspoken critic of the regime, off the street near his New York apartment. Galindez was smuggled onto an airplane, returned to the Dominican Republic, tortured and killed. The Galindez matter was an embarrassment for the Dwight Eisenhower administration when it was revealed that the plane was piloted by US citizen Gerald Murphy whose relationship with the FBI has always cast a shadow on the extent to which the US government was complicit in Galindez' murder. Two other incidents pushed things over the edge. In June 1959, six months after the triumphant Cuban Revolution, a group of Dominican exiles, with the support of Fidel Castro (b. 1926) and Rómulo Betancourt (1908–81), the reformist president of Venezuela, landed on Dominican shores with the intention of overthrowing Trujillo. Instead, the conspirators and their Dominican allies were arrested, jailed, and/or executed. Furious with Betancourt, Trujillo ordered Dominican agents to place a bomb in the Venezuelan president's car in Caracas, which exploded, injuring Betancourt. In response to Venezuela's outcry, the OAS (Organization of American States) expelled the Dominican Republic. Another case concerned the apprehension and murder of three sisters who were members of the prominent Mirabal family, and whose father was an outspoken critic of Trujillo. The women, all young mothers and critics of the regime, were killed when their car was forced off the road on the way back from visiting their husbands, who were in jail for plotting to overthrow the dictator. Julia Alvarez (b. 1950), one of the Dominican Republic's most prominent authors, chronicled the story in her book *In the Time of the Butterflies*, later made into a movie starring Salma Hayek.

Trujillo's downfall

By 1960 Washington had decided that Trujillo's unfailing loyalty was not enough to excuse his embarrassingly lawless behavior, and took steps to rein him in by levying a special excise tax on Dominican sugar entering the US. To retaliate, Trujillo brazenly dispatched agents to Eastern Europe, presumably with the intent of investigating a new market for sugar, but more likely as an affront to the US. In response the Central Intelligence Agency (CIA) sent arms to opposition groups in the Dominican Republic and, either directly or indirectly, had Trujillo killed in his car on May 30, 1961. Although the CIA did not at the time admit assassinating such a longtime ally and loyal supporter, the release of classified documents have since confirmed the intelligence agency's responsibility.

In the years since Trujillo's downfall, the Dominican Republic has gone through a number of presidents, but no single administration has been able to resolve the profound economic disparities that plague the island. The poorest half of the population receives less than one-fifth of the gross national product, while the richest 10 percent enjoys nearly 40 percent of national income; nearly 20 percent of the population is perpetually unemployed, and over one-quarter live below the poverty line. Statistics on literacy, infant mortality, and life expectancy for men and women are some of the most unfavorable in the hemisphere. Large numbers of Dominicans have migrated to the United States, where they have turned neighborhoods such as Washington Heights in upper Manhattan and Jamaica Plain in Boston into Dominican enclaves. Entire communities on the island live on remittances sent back by relatives in the US, a very few of whom are high-paid baseball players and fashion designers such as Sammy Sosa and Oscar de la Renta. However, overwhelmingly they are minimum-wage-earning workers in service sector and manufacturing jobs, or owners of small businesses, especially *bodegas* (grocery stores).

Americas in Transition: Guatemala and Bolivia

In the years before and immediately following World War II, the US tolerated author-itarian regimes in Nicaragua, Guatemala, Cuba and other countries, as long as those governments maintained a stable environment for investment and trade and supported the US in international policy forums. Nonetheless, many nations attempted to install democratic governments and to transform unequal conditions into ones of relative social and economic equality. Two examples of such attempts were in Guatemala and Bolivia, both of which were successful for a while, but ultimately were derailed by a combination of powerful interests from abroad operating in alliance with domestic con-servative sectors intent on preserving the traditional distribution of wealth and power.

Guatemala

From the time of independence in the mid-nineteenth century until the 1940s, Guatemala was under the rule of military leaders who served the interests of a small group of landed elite and the export market to which they supplied cotton, coffee, bananas, and other fruit. In the post-World War II era, Guatemala received ample foreign investment to support the growth of foreign-owned and -operated manufacturing, includ-ing food processing, pharmaceuticals, and some basic industry. The country's long history of ignoring the needs of its impoverished citizens – above all the indigenous Quiche-Maya population – began to change in 1944 when a group of junior military officers, intent on bringing about greater social equality, overthrew the ruling clique and set the stage for elections. This "October Revolution," as it was called, brought to power a former teacher and moderate reformer, Juan José Arévalo (1904–90). Although orig-inally installed in office by force, Arévalo was subsequently elected to the presidency, from which he presided over the writing of a new constitution that shared many similarities with the Mexican Constitution of 1917. During his five-year term Arévalo initiated a process of constitutional rule by law, outlined a series of economic and social improvements (though most did not get beyond the planning stage), survived 22 attempted military revolts against his government, and managed to oversee the orderly election of his successor, Jacobo Arbenz Guzmán (1913–71). Arbenz, a junior officer who had participated in the 1944 October Revolution before transitioning to civilian life, became in 1950 the first president in Guatemala's history to enter office through the electoral arena.

Despite the election, democratic institutions were exceedingly weak, and power remained concentrated in an elite minority. In addition to a small number of *latifun-dia* in the hands of single families or family-based corporations, much of the land in Guatemala was held by the United Fruit Company (UFCO), whose role in the 1928 Colombian "banana massacre" was discussed in Chapter 8. The company not only owned land; it also controlled freight and shipping rates, owned and operated the telegraph service, and maintained a vast network of company housing for the seasonally employed workforce overseen by a cadre of imported supervisors and estate managers, many from Alabama. Operating under the Jim Crow laws of the US South, United Fruit had imposed on Guatemala, Colombia, and other places a set of policies taken straight from the segregationist handbook, including one that required "all persons of color to give the right of way to whites and remove their hats while talking to them."

Like his predecessor, Arbenz found that he had little latitude to bring about change; however, he embarked on a policy to add economic reforms to the moderate political reforms his predecessor initiated. His plan called for strengthening the Guatemalan private sector by facilitating the growth of nationally owned firms; increasing control over domestic resources and exploiting natural resources, especially oil; and encouraging public works projects contracted to private firms to boost employment. He required foreign firms to pay taxes (including income taxes) and to abstain from intervening in domestic affairs. By far the most daring innovation was an agrarian reform law passed in June 1952. The law called for the expropriation of *uncultivated* plots from large plantations, to be paid for in 25-year government bonds, at a three percent interest rate, based on the land's *reported valuation* in May 1952.

The agrarian reform, modeled on the US Homestead Act of 1862, proposed to distribute 1.5 million acres of uncultivated, expropriated land to 100,000 families – including 1,700 acres belonging to Arbenz and his Salvadoran wife, María Cristina Vilanova. Not surprisingly, this plan met with opposition from the traditional oligarchy and from the UFCO, which owned an estimated 85 percent of Guatemala's land. In addition, the giant company had consistently undervalued its holdings for tax purposes. Therefore, when the Guatemalan government offered to pay at the tax-assessed value of $627,572, UFCO protested, arguing that the land was actually worth over $15 million. Essentially, after having cheated the Guatemalan government for years, United Fruit argued that it was actually owed more than $15 million for assets it had never reported.

Immediately United Fruit raised the alarm among its US stockholders and many sympathizers in the US and Guatemala. The company had many friends in high places, including President Eisenhower's Secretary of State John Foster Dulles (1888–1959), and his younger brother, CIA Director Allen Dulles (1893–1969), both of whom had been partners in a New York law firm whose foremost client was the United Fruit Company. Stephen Kinzer and Stephen Schlesinger's comprehensive account, *Bitter Fruit: The Untold Story of the CIA Coup in Guatemala*, dissects the overlapping web of players connecting the US State Department, the CIA, United Fruit Company, and members of the Guatemalan military who engineered the overthrow of Arbenz. Key operatives, such as E. Howard Hunt, J. C. King, and David Sánchez Morales, played a role in the Guatemalan coup and from there went on to notoriety as CIA operatives and dirty tricksters in the failed 1961 Bay of Pigs invasion of Cuba and the 1972 Watergate break-in of the Democratic Party headquarters in Washington, DC. Despite its role in opposing Arbenz and agrarian reform, there is considerable dispute over how actively United Fruit was involved in engineering the coup. With Washington in the throes of Joseph McCarthy's anti-communist witch hunt, and the CIA eager to flex its muscles on a new "regime change" after a successful intervention in Iran in 1953 to overthrow Mohammad Mossadegh (whose politics were considered too independent for the US), neither the mainstream media nor Congress required much convincing.

In spite of efforts from members of Arbenz's administration to compromise with their US critics, and even the reluctance of some top members of Guatemala's own military to support the coup, the CIA succeeded in forcing President Arbenz to resign in June 1954. After some squabbling among Guatemalan strongmen, General Castillo Armas (1914–57) assumed leadership of the military government that essentially handed rule back to the oligarchy, foreign multinationals, and, until it was indicted on anti-trust charges, the United Fruit Company. The US-backed coup received little support from Latin American governments, with the exception of its two staunchest allies, Dominican dictator Rafael Trujillo and Anastasio Somoza García of Nicaragua.

Guatemala after the coup

In the decades following the downfall of Arbenz, dreams of building a democratic society disappeared. The largest and most populous country of Central America entered one of its darkest phases, characterized by brutal repression of the majority Indian population at the hands of the military, widespread civil and human rights violations, a free hand to corrupt military and civilian police forces, and ultimately a 36-year-long civil war in the 1970s and 1980s that resulted in the deaths of over 100,000 people and displacement of more than a million. Mountainsides were wiped clean of villages, as military and civilian death squads ravaged entire communities, leaving behind horrible evidence of torture, death, and destruction. Decades after the 1954 military coup that unseated President Arbenz, Guatemala's 15 million people have a literacy rate of under 70 percent, life expectancy of less than 69 years, and one of the highest infant mortality rates in the hemisphere. The lack of social progress is presided over by a political apparatus that, despite the 1996 peace accords and return to civilian rule, has never been able to establish a fully functioning civil society. According to the annual review posted on the *Human Rights Watch* website, even under civilian rule Guatemala has made little progress toward functioning under the rule of law. "Guatemala's weak and corrupt law enforcement institutions have proven incapable of containing the powerful organized crime groups that, among other things, are believed responsible for continuing attacks on human rights defenders."[2]

Revolution in Bolivia

Like Guatemala, Bolivia underwent a period of profound hope for social change in the early 1950s, only to flounder, leaving the nation in a state of unrelenting poverty. The modern state of Bolivia was carved from the colonial province of Upper Peru, a mountainous Andean region that was overshadowed in the colonial era by the viceroyalty in Lima. During the wars for independence Bolívar hoped to unite the two territories into a larger, more effective and viable nation, but local loyalties and a weak, fragmented leadership dashed those aspirations. In 1825 Spanish Royalist troops scattered or defected and General Sucre's rebel army liberated the area and established, separate from Peru, a new nation named "Bolivia," after Latin America's most famous liberator. In the wake of independence Bolivia was briefly the focus of contention among the longer-standing and more powerful emerging states of Argentina, Chile, and Peru. Landlocked since losing its access to the sea to Chile in the late nineteenth century War of the Pacific – illustrating Bolivia's difficulty in fending off the incursions of its more powerful neighbors – it has lacked a sea port for the shipment abroad of its valuable resources: silver, tin, natural gas, textiles, and foodstuffs, as well as coca. Its fragmented political structure is best illustrated by the fact that since the nineteenth century Bolivia has had two capitals: La Paz as the seat of government, Sucre as the historical capital and home of the judiciary. The city of Santa Cruz is the industrial and commercial center.

The history of Bolivian mining, encompassing gold and silver in the colonial period (the latter from the famed "mountain of silver" at Potosí), as well as tin, zinc, and iron ore in the twentieth century, has been one in which the indigenous people who comprise roughly 70 percent of the population have toiled for very little reward, instead benefiting distant colonial or imperial powers at the other end of the commodity chain. Bolivia's current population of just 9 million people, sparsely distributed over a formidably arid, mountainous, and mineral-rich terrain, is comprised of the descendants of ancient Aymara, Guaraní, and Quechua people, most of whom speak an indigenous language primarily, and Spanish secondarily, if at all.

Bolivia today is one of the main repositories of natural gas in the Americas, and even the world. Current president Juan Evo Morales Ayma (b. 1959) was elected in 2005 on a socialist platform, promising to retain the greatest share of profit from the sale of goods and resources, especially natural gas, for the benefit of Bolivians. But the current government is not the first to seek to use Bolivia's considerable export revenues for the benefit of the nation. In 1952 a coalition comprising urban professionals (especially teachers and academics), commercial and government workers, and some entrepreneurs, along with miners and rural peasants, succeeded in overthrowing the government of the *latifundistas* and mine owners. Although Bolivian workers, especially miners, had worked under near slave-labor conditions for centuries (formal servitude only ended in some areas in 1945), their grievances fell on deaf ears until the late 1940s and early 1950s.

Under the leadership of Víctor Paz Estenssoro (1907–2001) and his *Movimiento Nacional Revolucionario* (MNR, National Revolutionary Movement), Indian miners and peasants took up arms in 1952 and for the first time in Bolivia's history enacted a radical reform agenda. The MNR's success came about as a result of several factors, primarily a vacuum in military leadership that coincided with the emergence of a viable and activist civilian base. Not only was the political and economic influence of urban-based mestizos increasing in the 1950s, but for a variety of reasons they were willing to align with the largely indigenous working class, a group they had previously shunned. The MNR and Paz Estenssoro managed to pull together an alliance that had proven elusive in the past. Although Paz Estenssoro's reform objectives closely resembled the measures that Arévalo and Arbenz were embarking upon at roughly the same time in Guatemala, Bolivia's revolution fell short more as the result of internal factors than external pressure. The MNR government embarked on an agrarian reform that broke up large estates, creating *minifundio* parcels that could be worked by individual peasant families or small clan and village groups. In addition, the reform intended to deliver credit for the purchase of tools, seed, and other materials, as well as to provide technical assistance to teach farmers how to increase productivity. The latter part of the plan was never delivered and, as a result, over a period of years the newly allotted *minifundio* gradually fell back into the hands of powerful land-owners with access to credit, technical assistance, water for irrigation, and markets for their goods.

In addition, the MNR sought to unify the country by breaking down the barriers that separated the majority indigenous population from Spanish-speaking Creoles, first by dropping the literacy requirement for voting – and thereby instantly incorporating the Indian masses into their base of support – and second by fostering the creation of *sindicatos* (unions) of peasants. Since the peasantry had been occupying the large estates in the wake of the landowners' flight from the land during the first days of the Revolution, the government's move to grant them the right to organize actually sanctioned a fait accompli.

In the end, it appears that Paz Estenssoro's revolutionary council authorized *sindicatos* for the peasantry not so much as a means to support their struggle for better wages and working conditions, but instead as a strategy to keep the *minifundistas* from develop-ing close ties with the powerful and militant mine workers. In later years, when the government failed to grant the demands of the peasants for credit and other resources, the rural workers found themselves isolated from the miners. Many peasants, feeling they had a stake in the status quo and fearful of losing rights to their land, even lined up with subsequent conservative governments against their previous allies in the working class, especially the miners. The loyalty toward the government that the land reform had engendered in a significant fraction of the peasantry was apparent in 1966–7 when Ernesto "Che" Guevara (1928–67), the Argentine-born hero of the Cuban Revolution, attempted to spark an uprising of the peasantry in the southeastern Andean foothills, only to meet with little local cooperation and even betrayal. The few Bolivians who joined Che's abortive cause came from urban areas, while the peasantry steered clear of the outsiders who neither spoke the local language, nor understood the land tenure arrangements that had been negotiated between the government and the peasantry.

Mining and the Voice of Bolivian Activism

The most important change wrought by the 1952 revolution was the nationalization of the principal tin mines, most of which had been in the hands of three companies: Hochschild, Patiño, and Aramayo. According to one contemporary observer, the sale of the companies did not accrue significant benefit to the Bolivian people. The owners only sold off the mines after the tin was depleted; new mine owners eventually took over the mines and other resources, and "as bad luck would have it, new rich people have been created and the [common] people haven't enjoyed any benefits from the nation-alization." After 1952 the mines were operated under Comibol, a state-run management/labor board, which was designed to distribute a fair share of benefits to miners. However, by 1963 the management board was squarely in the hands of the owners, who, a bit too conveniently, claimed to have no more money to share with the workers. Tin prices, like those of copper in Chile, often fluctuated on world markets, rising and falling in sync with large-scale wars and manufacturing booms and busts. After World War II a decline in both tin and copper prices swept across the globe, throwing Bolivia and Chile into a depression as their main source of export revenues shrank in value. By the mid-1950s, as the price of tin on the international market plummeted, the MNR cut back on the share of export earnings earmarked for maintaining its reform agenda. Wages for miners declined, prices rose as Bolivia struggled to meet international payments on loans, and planned social services were all but eliminated. Paz Estenssoro and the MNR moved to the right, bit by bit abandoning the socialist program on which they had come into office.

In the impoverished Bolivian highlands of the mid-twentieth century, Domitila Barrios de Chúngara (b. 1937) became one of the most outstanding champions of the Latin American working class, overcoming barriers of gender and socioeconomic status. From her humble roots and difficult childhood, Domitila grew into an independent and strong-willed woman who went to incredible lengths to fight the injustices suffered by tin miners, their wives, peasants, and all Bolivians she saw as oppressed by the mine owners and authoritarian governments. Although she had only a sixth-grade education, her observations and understanding of the complexities of economics, law, and labor issues far surpassed those of others with more privileged upbringings. She drew the attention of both international and domestic organizations to the plight of poor Bolivians, at one point tersely dismissing the efforts of a government official to intimidate the workers with columns of facts and figures on a blackboard with the remark: "Well, we don't live off of numbers. We live from reality."[3]

The reality was grim. Workers in the tin mines of the Bolivian highlands labored under exploitative and unsafe conditions, and were forced to live in company-owned hous-ing that could be taken away with no notice. The average life expectancy of a tin miner in the mid-1960s was 35 years. Women married to miners had few rights when widowed, abandoned, or charged with the care of children and husbands incapacitated from disease and accidents. Frustrated by this situation, Domitila became the leader of the Housewives' Committee of Siglo XX, formed in 1961 with the aim of joining efforts of men and women in the community to organize against the horrific abuses and poverty suffered by workers and their families. Her involvement in labor movements and a large number of strikes and demonstrations to create jobs for women, improve the conditions of miners, and fight repression brought her into conflict with those in power. Her activism resulted in multiple arrests, during which she suffered greatly for her cause, leading hunger strikes, falling victim to brutality and torture, and even losing an unborn child. Despite setbacks, danger to herself and her family, and constant discouragement, she was able to win modest improvements in the lives of miners and peasants (see Box 10.2).

Box 10.2   *Let Me Speak!* The voice of a Bolivian activist

Domitila's story is chronicled in a testimony compiled with Moema Viezzer, follow-ing her involvement in the International Women's Year Tribunal in Mexico, organized by the United Nations in 1975. Her remarks demonstrate her deter-mination and loyalty to the cause of ending oppression of the working class and her decision to put herself and her family second to the struggle to overcome the misery of others. One particularly striking example of her courage comes from a confrontation she and other labor organizers had with representatives of the repressive General Hugo Banzer (dictator 1971–8, later elected President 1997–2001), after their destruction of Siglo XX's radio transmitters in response to a strike. Domitila bravely stood up to those in power, and eloquently expressed her opinions on the repressive regime:

> We women, like the workers, repudiate this attempt against our culture and our people . . . We won't stand for this treatment. And we demand you immediately return our property, which has cost us so much to get . . . General Banzer has taken office in a country where no one elected him. He came in through the force of arms, he killed a whole lot of people and among them our children and our compañeros. He machine-gunned the university; he repressed and goes on repressing a lot of people. Our resources are being turned over to foreigners, especially to Brazil.
>
> Now I ask you, which measure has been in favor of the working class?

From Domitila Barrios de Chúngara, *Let Me Speak!* (New York: Monthly Review Press, 1978), p. 187

The Revolution in Decline

Throughout the late 1950s, the Bolivian people witnessed systematic erosion in the revolutionary goals that had mobilized the masses earlier in the decade. The Bolivian government moved to restore the mines to their previous owners, even offering to pay them concessions. It invited in new foreign investors, ended labor's participation in Comibol, reduced welfare benefits to disabled and out-of-work miners, and refused to offer miners protection when they went out on strike. Instead, Paz Estenssoro ordered the army to break up strikes, and even to gun down workers on the picket line. By the early 1960s, the military, mine owners, and landed oligarchy had gained in strength, and in May 1964 the military formally returned to power under General René Barrientos (1919–69). While the US denied any direct involvement in the Barrientos coup and subsequent repression, the soldiers and police who restored the oligarchy to power were enthusiastic followers of the US, had been trained on US bases in Central America and the United States (including the School of the Americas), and fought with planes, tanks, and machine guns manufactured in and provided by the United

States. Despite periodic and widespread opposition from students, miners, peasants, and even some reformist nationalists among the armed forces and domestic bourgeoisie, various authoritarian civilian and military governments remained in power from 1964 until the end of the century. In 1980 Colonel García Meza (b. 1932), a dictator known not only for his repressive rule but for bringing Bolivia into international drug-dealing circles, came to power in the aptly named "Cocaine Coup." During García Meza's first year in office, the price of coca leaves jumped from $50 to $15,000 a ton and, coincidentally or not, Bolivia's economy (like others in Latin America) fell into a depression, creating just the desperate economic climate needed to convince many small farmers to turn to coca production. Only somewhat later, however, did the highly lucrative illicit drug trade achieve a firm foothold in Bolivia's economy.

Similarities between Guatemala and Bolivia are instructive. They are both lands with majority, or near majority, indigenous populations, mountainous terrain, poor and isolated Indian communities, reliance on outside investors and markets for trade of a limited number of goods, a long history of exploitation at the hands of local and national *caudillos*, and power structures controlled by white or mestizo elites. Nonetheless, both nations experienced genuine, widespread social movements in the 1950s that attempted to put in place a more equitable social and political order. Both saw dreams of democracy, stability, and prosperity dashed by the combined forces of an entrenched elite and military, backed by the US government and transnational corporations. In both cases the decades from the 1950s onward have witnessed disastrous rates of infant mortality, poverty, illiteracy, death rates far above those of other nations in the region, and widespread discontent. Guatemalans suffered enormous consequences stemming from the unwillingness of the ruling elite to share even a portion of the wealth with the impoverished majority. Their position was secured with assistance from the CIA and US government in the 1950s. Similarly, Bolivia has suffered years of stagnation, but at this writing, the current President Morales' ability to win over the entrenched oligarchy and sectors of the country that control water and natural gas resources to a program that would distribute wealth more equally remains in question.

Conclusion

The outcome of World War II was pivotal to the realignment of power in the second half of the twentieth century. Latin America had played only a marginal role in the war, but it had benefited from selling raw materials and thus emerged with the potential to experience more long-term economic prosperity. By contrast, the introduction of cheap labor from Mexico in the Bracero Program showed US industries the potential for enormous profits by exploiting cheap labor. The temporary worker program ended in 1964, though since that time large numbers of laborers from Latin America have crossed the border illegally to work at below minimum wage levels in agriculture and many other areas of employment. In the 1960s, simultaneous with the end of the Bracero Program, US companies stepped up investments in Latin America, transplanting operations from high-wage Ohio, Michigan, Pennsylvania, and other communities to low-wage Guatemala, Brazil, Chile, and Peru and more.

In the post-war era the protection of US "interests" became increasingly tied to a policy of protecting US corporations against any demands for better wages and working conditions from domestic workers in Latin America. Companies such as United Fruit called on the US government to come to their aid when they found their profits threatened by political and economic reformists in Latin America. The case of Guatemala began to repeat throughout the hemisphere. Simultaneously, the politics of the Cold War left no place for neutrality, and allowed the traditional Latin American elite to dismiss indigenous calls for reform, for labor rights, for better wages and living conditions as "Soviet interference." The polarized political situation provided entrenched elites in many countries with an excuse for their failure to provide for the public good. Liberal reformists, such as Arbenz and Paz Estenssoro, were few, but even their meager attempts to hold multinational corporations accountable met with stiff resistance.

As a result it was not the war but the post-war era and the division between the Soviet Union and the US that had the greatest impact on Latin America. Left to themselves, the republics of the hemisphere may have been able to build on the prosperous trading relations established during the war years to increase revenues and promote modernization. Unfortunately, Latin American nations were not left free of outside interference.

11 | Cuba: Guerrillas Take Power

No event has played a greater role in realigning internal and external alliances, in reformulating national agendas, and even in inspiring change in the hemisphere than has the Cuban Revolution. The events of January 1, 1959 had a dramatic effect on the US political agenda toward Latin America, as well as giving birth to a whole new branch of study in US universities. According to Stanford political science professor Richard Fagen, no one did more than Fidel Castro to promote the study of Latin America in academic and government circles. Ironically, it is to Castro and the Cuban Revolution that generations of US scholars working on Latin America owe their jobs.

Even before the 1959 revolution put Cuba more squarely on the international map, the island was a major contributor to worldwide culture, politics, letters, and economics. For what might seem a tiny producer for the commodity chain, Cuba's output in the years before, and continuing after, the Revolution has been tremendous: major innovations in music, art, dance, literature, and political theory, not to mention rum, cigars, and baseball players. The rumba, cha cha, and mambo all originated in Cuba, as did salsa, the most recognizably Latin dance. Salsa developed out of Cuban rumba in the nineteenth century and, largely as a result of Puerto Rican influence, captured New York and the rest of the world in the late twentieth century. In the nineteenth and twentieth centuries Cuba was a pioneer in orchestra and symphony music, opera and modern dance, while current artists, especially Silvio Rodríguez (b. 1946), are known throughout Latin America. Silvio's protest lyrics intersected with the New Song movement arising in Chile in the 1960s and have gone on to have enormous impact on Latin American protest music in every country. Cuba is, as well, the birthplace of some the continent's major authors, poets, and theorists, including José Martí, Antonio Maceo, Guillermo Cabrera Enfante (1929–2005), Nicolás Guillén (1902–89), Alejo Carpentier (1904–80), Fidel Castro, Reinaldo Arenas (1943–90), artists such as Ana Mendieta (1948–85), Wifredo Lam (1902–82), and José Bédia (b. 1959), and major prima ballerina and choreographer Alicia Alonso (b. 1920). Musicians famous in both the US and in Cuba are too many to name, including singers Benny Moré (1919–63),

Celia Cruz (1925–2003), Israel "Cachao" López (1918–2008), Arturo Sandoval (b. 1949), Pablo Milanés (b. 1943), and more.

Cuba has played a disproportionately significant role in the colonial and post-colonial eras. Its importance is evident in the splendor of Havana's architecture, emblematic of the importance of the city as a colonial-era capital. From the 1930s until the end of the 1950s, however, Havana was a wide open city where, for a price, most anything was available, and the wealthy from throughout the world made it a point to partake. In the heyday of US Prohibition (1919–33), rum-runners and other members of organized crime syndicates established a steady business supplying the speak-easies of the northeastern states with alcohol from Cuba. When Prohibition was repealed in 1933, organized crime was well established in Havana, and able to turn to other forms of lucrative entertainment, including prostitution, gambling, and drug peddling. Through the efforts of a string of military dictators, the most brutal being Gerardo Machado y Morales (1871–1939) whose nickname "The Butcher" conveys his particular governance style, Cuba remained for decades under the watchful gaze of its powerful northern neighbor. Machado was overthrown by the Cuban military in 1933 and forced into exile, eventually in Miami, where six years later he died. Disliked and distrusted on all sides at the time of his death, subsequent Cuban governments have refused to allow his remains to be returned to Cuba for burial.

Similar to the brief democratic experiments in Bolivia and Guatemala, Cuba also entered a reformist phase in 1934 with the founding of the *Auténtico* (Authentic) Party under the leadership of Dr. Ramón Grau (1887–1969), who oversaw the writing of Cuba's first genuinely independent constitution in 1940 and set in place a political reform program designed to lay the foundation for a democratic society. Despite the timidity of Grau's plan, which made no mention of equalizing pervasive income inequalities, it provoked heated opposition. US investors, especially powerful sugar interests, perceived a threat to their power, while the Cuban left argued that the new constitution did not go far enough. The latter came together in the *Ortodoxo* (Orthodox) Party, whose charismatic leader Eddie Chibás (1907–51) was a young man with a strong following among fellow university students and other activists in Havana. Chibás warned that the 1952 election would be stolen by the right, and in an effort to draw attention to widespread corruption in the political process and the lack of justice in Cuban society, he committed suicide in 1951 – on the air during his weekly nationwide radio broadcast. The election was indeed stolen, and Fulgencio Batista (1901–73), a member of the Cuban military, assumed the presidency, a post he held until January 1, 1959 when he fled the country just as Fidel Castro Ruz and his 26th of July Movement rolled into Havana.

"History Will Absolve Me"

Inspired by earlier populist revolutionaries in other parts of Latin America (having been arrested in Colombia in 1948 while attending an anti-imperialist conference organized by Jorge Gaitán), Fidel Castro, a young lawyer from a prosperous planter background, led a small group of revolutionaries in an unsuccessful attack on the Moncada military barracks in the southeastern city of Santiago de Cuba on July 26, 1953. Originally able to flee to the mountains nearby, Castro and his followers (subsequently labeled the "26th of July Movement") were arrested and brought to trial. Fidel Castro's defense at his trial on October 16, 1953 has since become one of the most famous speeches by a Latin American political leader, particularly in the challenge delivered in the final line: "Sentence me. I don't mind. History will absolve me." The young lawyer's trial had been moved to a hospital ward to keep it out of the public's eye, so only a few members of the court, and medical personnel who stopped by to listen in, heard the five-hour-long speech delivered (as has become Castro's style ever since) from a few pages of notes. In it the 27-year-old leader of this small group of youths described the country's social conditions, and laid out the justification for taking up arms against the Batista dictatorship. Between the time of the speech defending the attack on Moncada in 1953, the group's subsequent short prison term and later exile to Mexico, and the return invasion of the island in late 1956, both opposition to Batista and Castro's popularity had spread. The latter had accurately articulated the grievances of many Cubans, and during his three-year absence the "History will absolve me" speech had been distributed and read. Much of the success of the Cuban Revolution can be attributed to widespread dislike of the Batista regime.[1]

Causes for Discontent

Cuba's problems were similar to those of other small countries in the region: sharp income inequalities and lack of political rights. Nonetheless, Cuba was not like Guatemala or Bolivia. Instead it had one of the highest standards of living in Latin America in the 1950s, behind Argentina and Uruguay. Women had been voting since the 1930s, not long after US women won suffrage, and Havana had hosted more than one Pan-American conference promoting women's rights. Cuba's universities were some of the oldest and most prestigious in the Americas, and its capital city of Havana was a major cosmopolitan center that attracted mainstream tourists, intellectuals, and artists, as well as those seeking disreputable entertainment. What made Cuba ripe for revolution was the combination of these factors. Income distribution was grossly uneven, especially between urban and rural areas. Many educated and sophisticated Cubans were forced to endure humiliating treatment at the hands of international visitors and institutions that excluded them. The country was rich, and many Cubans prospered; however, the political structure was ridden with corruption, favoritism, and privileges for foreigners and their companies.

Castro's famous speech captured that combination of grievances, noting that the government served merely to deliver Cuba's wealth abroad; for example, 85 percent of Cuba's small farmers paid rent to foreign-owned corporations, including the infamous United Fruit Company and the West India Company. Most of the land remained uncultivated, and the small number of factories engaged in processing food, tobacco, textiles, lumber, and sugar sent those goods abroad, forcing Cuba to import even many basic foodstuffs. Particularly humiliating was the fact that Cuba did not control fishing rights off its shores, nor possess the ability to use the sea for its own national benefit. As a result, many in the island nation went hungry because the wealth of the sea was strictly in the hands of foreign-owned pleasure boat and fishing companies. The people who toiled to produce Cuba's wealth lacked basic human services; many children died of preventable maladies such as tapeworms, parasites, influenza, and dysentery. Castro called for improvements in education, especially the establishment of schools to train technicians, engineers, and scientists and thus break the nation's dependence on foreign expertise. He noted that in the rural areas illiteracy, isolation, and ignorance undermined national unity and any chance that the majority of Cubans could participate as full citizens.

In addition to the exhaustive list of failings, Castro outlined his own inspiration for launching a political movement. He referred to the North American Revolution against England, to the French Revolution, and to other movements for reform and revolution that had united and inspired people abroad. Indicative of his years of education in Jesuit academies and universities, Castro invoked the Enlightenment thinkers, major philosophical movements, and the right of individuals to seek redress for their grievances. Repeatedly he came back to José Martí, the framers of the liberal Constitution of 1940, and other democratic ideals. There was in the speech no indication that he was influenced by Marxism; indeed, as a student Castro had shunned the communists, although his brother, Raúl Castro Ruz (b. 1931), joined the Communist Party. "History will absolve me" looked to Martí, not Marx or Lenin, for its political inspiration. Its genius, and resultant popularity, rested in the breadth of its perspective: it addressed the grievances of middle-class intellectuals, entrepreneurs, and professionals, along with those of seasonal sugar-cane cutters, illiterate peasants, and urban factory workers. There has been much debate as to whether Castro was hiding his leftist agenda in the early stage of the Revolution or whether he was simply a political novice. Regardless, his opening salvo, contained in his most important speech, offered hope to every honest Cuban patriot in the new society.

The Revolutionary War

Regrouping in Mexico after a general amnesty reduced his prison term to 18 months, Castro and the 26th of July Movement encountered a more sophisticated group of revolutionaries, including Argentine Ernesto "Che" Guevara and exiles from the Spanish Civil War who had received asylum in Mexico after the defeat of the Republican cause in 1939. Armed with both political and military strategy, the group re-entered Cuba in late 1956, and, after a rocky start, eventually launched a concerted struggle that linked guerrilla camps in the mountains with organizations operating in the cities, especially among the trade unions. Frank País (1934–57) mobilized a series of daring demonstrations in Santiago de Cuba and built an organization that linked up the underground network in many cities and towns. Killed on the streets of Santiago before the Revolution's victory, País's skillful work was instrumental in bringing news of the guerrilla movement to urban areas, creating constant disruptions that distracted Batista's army, and apprehending arms and supplies that were then distributed to the guerrilla camps in the mountains and throughout the island.

In early 1957 Herbert Matthews (1900–77) interviewed Fidel Castro in the latter's camp high in the Sierra Maestra mountains for a series of stories that appeared in the *New York Times*. Much of the world became familiar with Castro because of Matthews' sympathetic portrayal of the charismatic leader and his band of idealistic and resourceful young combatants. Combined with the failure of Batista's counter-insurgency methods and the apparent unpopularity of the corrupt regime, the US drew back from supporting the dictatorship. On New Year's morning of 1959 the dictator, his family, and close associates fled the country, along with much of the moneyed Cuban elite, and foreign members of the entertainment, investment, and business communities, as well as many hundreds of foreign tourists. The hasty exodus of the wealthy and the corrupt stood in dramatic contrast with the cheering populace that lined the streets from Santa Clara to Havana to greet the guerrillas' triumphant entry into Havana a week later.

Although the fighting had at times been intense, the revolutionary war was not the proving ground for the new society; that would unfold over the subsequent years. In recognition of the unpopularity of Batista's government and in hopes of maneuvering to bring the new regime under its wing, Washington immediately recognized the new government. But within two years the relationship between the two countries had deteriorated completely. Similar to events in Guatemala and Bolivia earlier in the decade, and in Mexico at the zenith of its revolution, the main areas of contention with the United States developed when the revolutionary government instituted a land reform, including expropriation of estates and US-owned properties. In response to pressure from the sugar trusts, as well as in retaliation against the requirement that US-owned oil refineries in Cuba agree to process all crude oil in the country – whether bought from US companies or not – President Eisenhower broke off diplomatic relations in the last days of his administration. It was, however, under John Kennedy's (1917–63) presidency that the most acute tensions emerged between the two nations, initiated by the bungled invasion on April 17, 1961 at Playa Girón (Bay of Pigs) and culminating a year and a half later during what came to be known as the "Cuban Missile Crisis."

A joint effort between the CIA (many of whom were veterans of the 1954 Guatemalan coup) and anti-Castro Cuban exiles, the Bay of Pigs invasion was from start to finish a poorly conceived operation. It proved embarrassing to the US, only serving to validate Cuba's claim that the tiny island was the victim of latter-day "Big Stick diplomacy" and, most importantly, it forced Cuba to turn to the Soviet Union for protection. Already in the works under Eisenhower, the invasion was founded on the faulty premise that the Cuban populace would rise up to greet the invaders. In fact, quite the opposite occurred and the small island nation rallied to the government's defense – especially when Castro was able to parade captured military officers from Batista's army before the Cuban public. The disastrous 1961 Bay of Pigs invasion was only the most widely known failure among many attempts to bring down the Cuban regime, ranging from other, less high-profile, invasions; botched schemes to assassinate Fidel Castro (including explosive cigars, food poisonings, etc.); sabotage against crops, especially the delicate tobacco plants; to the longstanding embargo that prevents both trade with and travel to Cuba.

None of these efforts succeeded in deposing the Cuban government – and many might argue that they have been counter-productive, serving to bolster Castro's reputation among other Latin American nations and radical youth; isolating and demoralizing some reformers within Cuba; and probably intensifying Castro's popularity among hardliners resistant to broader democracy. Thus the Cuban government has been able to use the David versus Goliath scenario to its advantage, refusing to discuss persistent criticisms in the area of human rights. The blatant aggression of the Bay of Pigs invasion provided an entrée, or perhaps an excuse, for Cuba to turn more decidedly toward the Soviet camp. Castro declared Cuba a Marxist-Leninist state, and the centrist, bourgeois phase of the revolution ended. In October 1962 Cuba's decision to install Soviet nuclear-powered missiles – ostensibly to defend itself from further US attacks – precipitated one of the most intense crises of the Cold War. For 13 days in October the world stood at the brink of nuclear war between the reigning superpowers, as the two sides attempted to defuse the tension without losing face. Ultimately the standoff was ended in an agreement between Soviet Premier Nikita Khrushchev (1894–1971) and President Kennedy; Castro was relegated to the sidelines. The US promised never again to invade Cuba, and to withdraw missiles from Turkey aimed at Moscow, while the Soviets withdrew the missiles from Cuba. Although a key moment in Cuban history, the October 1962 crisis is actually most memorable as the event that solidified the world into the two superpowers' spheres of influence. For years afterward, the US proffered only rhetorical opposition to Soviet repression in Eastern Europe, while the Soviets extended heated condemnation of US policies, but tepid concrete assistance to Latin American struggles for self-determination. The exception was Cuba, which after the early 1960s entered fully into the orbit of the communist bloc, became a key trading partner with the USSR and Eastern Europe, and depended on the Soviets for millions of dollars in economic aid. In return, Cuba became one of the Soviet Union's most reliable allies in the subsequent Cold War battles.

Undeniably, the Revolution's accomplishments since 1959 in terms of social services, if not participatory democracy, are impressive. On a continent where democratic experiments have been short-lived, precariously balanced between military coups and rule by local strongmen, the most undemocratic feature has been grinding poverty, malnutrition, illiteracy, disease, crime, and corruption. In sharp contrast, Cuba has ensured basic health and wellbeing for every citizen. Education through to university level, medical care, complete freedom of choice in abortion and birth control, social security, child care, maternity leave, rent, and many social services are free, or nearly so. Women were mobilized from the earliest days of the Revolution and obtained rights unparalleled in Latin America – or most of the world – such as the 1975 Cuban Family Code, whereby discrimination against women and girls, even within the family structure, was outlawed. During periods of hardship and contraction, such as the early 1990s, when subsidies from the Soviet Union ended, the maintenance of social services often fell back on women as mothers, wives, and caregivers, indicative that Cuba had not fully equalized gender responsibilities. Yet it must be noted that only a few northern

European democracies have even attempted to enforce such strict gender equality. Through the Federation of Cuban Women (FMC), one of the foremost mass organizations established after the Revolution's triumph, the government has been able to closely monitor women's progress and ensure oversight. Women have achieved impressive parity in university education, pay scales, and local government positions; however, they hold only one-quarter of high-level administrative positions in government.

The political gains of women, or lack thereof, were apparent in the speculation over who was to succeed Fidel Castro as head of state, when he became ill in 2006. Of the 12 to 15 names mentioned, which include the inner circles of Cuba's leadership, not one was a woman. The most prominent woman in the government was FMC founder Vilma Espín (1930–2007), a member of the Central Committee of the Communist Party and the party's Political Bureau. Although capable, her appointment could not have been hurt by the fact that she was married to Raúl Castro, Fidel's brother. A chemical engineer with a degree from MIT, Espín left a life of comfort as the daughter of a Bacardi Rum executive to work with Frank País in Santiago in the early days of the guerrilla movement and clearly had independent leadership credentials. Feminist critics in Cuba have argued that she was reluctant to demarcate a path of women's autonomy independent from the prevailing view of the Party. Essentially, it is difficult to say what motivated Espín or any other leader, since one of the main problems of the Cuban system is lack of transparency.

There was one head of state, Fidel Castro, from 1959 until 2006, when his brother Raúl assumed power after the elder Castro suffered a stroke. In February 2008 Fidel Castro surrendered his position and Raúl was elected president the following week. This lack of substantive change in leadership is bound to take a toll, even if apologists for the system argue that the Castros are enormously popular with the majority of Cubans. The media is carefully censored and the ability to print criticisms, to speak openly, and to meet in opposition to the government is limited. Opposition to one-party rule has erupted periodically but the ability of Cubans to obtain refuge in the US has served to mitigate against internal dissent. Ironically, the fanatical wing of the Cuban exile community has little interest in supporting freedom for dissenting views among its own ranks. Attempts by cultural and political groups to normalize relations with Cuba usually meets vociferous, even violent, opposition from hardliners. Dissenting views are often as censored among exiles in Miami as they are in Cuba, sometimes more so.

The Special Period in Peacetime

Like other Latin American countries, Cuba has long depended on the export of a single crop: sugar. When the Soviet Union dissolved in the early 1990s, Cuba overnight lost access to 75 percent of its imports, over 90 percent of its external market, untold millions in financial assistance, and, most importantly, more than 90 percent of the crude oil it had exchanged for sugar at a highly favorable rate. From 1991 until 1996 Cuba's standard of living plummeted, food shortages were widespread, the highly mechanized agricultural system stood paralyzed, and the absence of pharmaceuticals and vaccines threatened the nation's health. Nonetheless, Cuba weathered this era, called the "special period in time of peace," with little discernible fall in health, literacy, and life expectancy statistics. Indicative of the island's income equality, everyone lost about 20 pounds of weight, regardless of occupation, status, or relationship to the center of power and wealth. By century's end, economic growth was returning, based on an aggressive campaign to attract European and Canadian tourism, a turn toward sustainable, pesticide-free, organic farming learned from Australian agronomists, an oil-for-sugar exchange with Venezuela promoted by socialist ally President Hugo Chávez, a healthy influx of investment from European Union nations, especially Spain, and a remarkable level of ingenuity and perseverance on the part of the Cuban people.

Critics of US policy argue that the continued embargo suits only the hard-line anti-Castro faction of South Florida, and has hurt the US by cutting it off from a ready market for capital investment and agricultural goods. Oddly, since 2003 the US has been the main supplier of food to Cuba, sent under a special provision that allows food sales. In addition, members of the US Congress, including a fair number of conservative Republicans from the Midwest agricultural heartland, have traveled to Cuba to promote bilateral trade. Over the last five years Cuba has purchased $1.5 billion in food and related products from the US, including chicken, wheat, corn, rice, and soybeans. Since Cuba pays in cash, many politicians from farm states are anxious to expand the trading relationship, as is Cuba. Yet the economic and social transformation of the 1990s has taken a toll on socialist principles. Attracting tourists has meant pouring money into luxury hotels and foreigners-only resorts, forcing decision makers to devote a larger proportion of Cuban resources to serve foreigners. Prostitution has re-emerged after having all but disappeared after 1959, highly educated professionals have given up jobs in medicine or academia to work in the more lucrative tourist trade, and many critics argue that Cuba is reverting to the bawdy pre-revolution days.

Cuba and the World

Cubans still brave the dangerous 90-mile passage to land on US shores, where, for domestic political reasons, they enjoy special privileges accorded no other refugees: instant citizenship, welfare, and social benefits. Highly prized baseball players such as José Canseco and Liván and Orlando Hernández have defected to sign for multi-million dollar contracts with the Major Leagues.

In 1980 thousands of Cubans left in a series of boatlifts out of the port of Mariel destined for South Florida after the Carter Administration opened access for Cuban-Americans to visit the island. Cuban-Americans flooded the island bringing presents, money, and verbal enticements to their relatives in Cuba. As a result, many of the "Marielitos," as they were called, jumped at the opportunity to join family members already in the US, while others were attracted by the easy refugee policy and promise of a more materially rewarding life. In retaliation for the embarrassing exodus, Castro allowed prisoners and people with mental disabilities to leave, much to the consternation of the US customs agents. The Mariel Boatlift from April to October 1980 proved that Cuba was not an island paradise and that many people wanted to emigrate. Yet if the border were opened for any country of Latin America, or the developing world, and its citizens were allowed to enter the US freely and become instant citizens, many hundreds of thousands would do so. The appeal of a better life in a rich country has always been a powerful magnet. For the time being, the status quo between Cuba and the outside seems to be in place, and will most likely remain that way until significant changes take place in US or Cuban leadership.

As regards its role in the rest of the world, the more the United States sabotaged, opposed, undermined, and isolated the tiny nation, the more other nations openly or begrudgingly admired it. Speaking of Cuba in its heyday during the 1970s, Mexican politician and writer Jorge Castañeda contends: "Cuba's activities abroad made the humiliated isle of the Platt Amendment and the whorehouses of Havana a player on the world stage. It was reviled by Washington, resented by Moscow, but respected, indeed admired and revered, throughout the Third World."[2] The United Nations General Assembly votes overwhelmingly against the United States' commercial embargo of Cuba in a yearly non-bonding resolution. In November 2005, the 182-to-4 tally left the United States joined only by Israel, the Marshall Islands, and Palau, with one abstention, Micronesia. Cuba severed diplomatic ties with Israel in 1973 at the time of the Yom Kippur War, when Cuba's offer of safe haven for Palestinian combatants and support for Palestine left the two nations at odds; however, private tours of Cuban Jews to Israel persist, as do excursions sponsored by Jewish-American organizations. The Israeli flag flies at Havana's José Martí Airport, along with those of other nations. Outside the airport one can see a construction project operated by an Israeli company, and outside the city there is a joint Israeli–Cuban agricultural cooperative. This peculiar relationship parallels the contradictory stance of many US citizens toward Cuba. An estimated 2 million international tourists travel to Cuba yearly, at least 250,000 of whom are US citizens who visit the island in defiance of the embargo; since 1999, governors, senators, and members of Congress from at least 30 states have traveled to Cuba. The largest source of "foreign aid" to Cuba probably comes out of South Florida, in the form of dollars sent clandestinely by Cuban-Americans to their relatives in the homeland. In 2009 President Barack Obama (b. 1961) lifted the Bush-era ban and allowed Cuban-Americans to travel from the US to Cuba. Many political observers assume that one day all travel restrictions will be lifted.

Ernesto "Che" Guevara

The best-known face of the 26th of July Movement was not a Cuban at all, but a young, bearded Argentine: Ernesto "Che" Guevara. His image, made famous in a photograph snapped by Alberto Díaz Gutiérrez, known as Alberto Korda (see Box 11.1), or simply "Korda" (1928–2001), has come to personify the romantic revolutionary icon (Figure 11.1). It graces the walls of college dorms, the stages of rock and roll bands and Broadway musicals, is a ubiquitous presence at political rallies across the globe, crops up in cartoons and television shows, adorns T-shirts, and enjoys a status accorded to few other symbols of popular culture. Art critics have labeled it the "most famous photograph in the world and a symbol of the twentieth century" (Maryland Institute College of Art).

Figure 11.1   Ernesto "Che" Guevara. (Alberto Korda photo)

Che Guevara joined up with Fidel Castro and the other members of the 26th of July Movement in Mexico several years after leaving his native Argentina. Already embracing socialism, and more radical than Castro in his strategy for bringing about revolutionary change, Che had witnessed the overthrow of Jacobo Arbenz in Guatemala in 1954. He developed the idea of the "new man and woman" (originally it was only "the new man") and called for a profound cultural transformation from the individualist Enlightenment-based principles Castro invoked in his "History will absolve me" speech, to those of mutual giving and sharing in a society motivated by moral incentives rather than material rewards. As with Mao Zedong's Cultural Revolution in China, the idealism proved unworkable in Cuba, although it did not result in the widespread starvation or political purges that occurred in China. Cuba abandoned strict moral incentives in all but rhetoric by the late 1960s, at a time that coincided with Guevara's departure from Cuba (a coincidence that has led to

Box 11.1   Alberto Korda and the photo that launched an international icon

On March 5, 1960, at a commemoration for the death of 80–100 people who were killed when a French freighter, *La Coubre*, exploded in Havana harbor (allegedly due to CIA sabotage), a Cuban fashion photographer turned journalist of the Revolution, Alberto Korda, snapped a single photograph of Che Guevara as the young guerrilla joined a line of other leaders of the Revolution flanking Fidel Castro on a platform at the cemetery. Korda's photo, taken with a Leica camera using Kodak Plus-X film, captured a single image of Che staring into the distance, framed by his long hair and wearing a beret studded with a single star. Although Korda kept a small cropped print for himself, he did not publish it, possibly because on the same roll were photos of Jean-Paul Sartre and Simone de Beauvoir, and it was the famous French philosophers in attendance at the service whose images appeared in the news accounts of the event.

The photo of Guevara remained unpublished and in Korda's possession, tacked to the wall of his apartment for the next seven years. At the time of Che Guevara's death in Bolivia on October 9, 1967, an Italian poster publisher, Giangiacomo Feltrinelli, obtained the original landscape-format negative, cropped Che's Cuban compatriots from either side of him, and published it on a poster. Korda's image of the Argentine-born martyr rapidly became a symbol for the emerging world-wide student revolt. In 1968 Irish artist Jim Fitzpatrick produced and distributed a high-contrast print of a drawing that slightly modified the original image, so that Che's eyes are gazing toward the distant horizon, conveying a heroic impression of a man looking upward and toward the future.

Korda never asked for royalties on the photo and only once intervened to prevent its use – in 2000 when Smirnoff Vodka attempted to use it on an advertisement. A lifelong communist, Korda maintained that "as a supporter of the ideals for which Che Guevara died, I am not averse to its reproduction by those who wish to propagate his memory and the cause of social justice throughout the world, but I am categorically against the exploitation of Che's image for the promotion of products such as alcohol, or for any purpose that denigrates the reputation of Che." Korda won an out-of-court settlement of about $50,000, which he donated to the Cuban medical system. Since Korda's death in 2001, there has been no one to object to any use of the Che image, capitalist, socialist, or otherwise. Nonetheless, despite its widespread reproduction on every product imaginable, Che's face yet persists as one of the most famous international revolutionary icons.

widespread speculation, but no real proof, that there was a falling out between the two main figures of the Revolution).

El Che, as he was known, set out to reproduce the guerrilla movements' triumph, first in the African Congo and later in the mountains of Bolivia. Drawing on French philosopher Regis Debray's (b. 1941) guerrilla warfare strategy, which he termed *focoismo*, Che argued that the Latin American hemisphere was ripe for socialist revolution, that the conditions for a socialist insurrection could be accelerated by a small band of armed militants drawn tightly together under disciplined leadership. Instead of opting for the clandestine armed struggle as a last resort, when conditions prohibited an above-ground movement, the *foco* formula envisioned the opposite: the emergence and proliferation of mass organizations *as a result* of armed actions by a covert revolutionary cadre. In this regard Che's view broke decisively with – rather than simply ignoring, as had been the strategy of Cuba's 26th of July Movement – the Moscow-oriented Latin American communist parties and with the conventional wisdom of Marxist-Leninist theory.

Guevara chose the Bolivian Altiplano to test this theory, bringing together a tightly knit group of Cubans, an East German woman with the code name Tania, and a few urban-based Bolivian and Peruvian communists. The plan failed miserably. In 1967 Bolivian rangers, trained and supplied by the US Special Forces, captured, executed, and buried Guevara in an unknown grave, after sending to the press a photo of his tortured and emaciated body. When news of his death reached radicals and social activists in Latin America, and the student movement abroad, Che was elevated to hero status, regardless of the failure of his ill-conceived plan or that the very peasants they hoped to incite betrayed the rag-tag outsiders to the Bolivian army. As noted earlier in this chapter, Che and his followers did not speak the native Quechua language and thus could not communicate their aims, nor did they understand that the peasantry had recently won an important reform during the 1952 Bolivian Revolution. Moreover, it was Bolivia's miners, with whom Che had no contact, who were actually the most revolutionary stratum of the highland proletariat. Nevertheless, youthful groups of revolutionaries throughout Latin America and in the developed and developing world read his works, adopted his strategy, and attempted to reproduce the success of Cuba, rather than the failure of Bolivia, in their own homelands.

What Difference Did the Revolution Make?

Despite the myriad problems Cuba faced, its obvious dependence on the Soviet Union and consequent obedience to the Moscow line, the tiny island offered hope to young radicals in many parts of Latin America (Figure 11.2). Not only had it overthrown an entrenched dictatorship, it had succeeded in the very shadow of the US itself. Moreover, Cuba was willing to provide advice, assistance, safe haven, and refuge, even rest and relaxation, to revolutionaries struggling to bring about social change or to overthrow their own repressive governments. Castañeda, in his admired and vilified book, *Utopia Unarmed: The Latin American Left after the Cold War*, attributes the respect Cuba earned to the vision of Fidel Castro and the genius of his longtime friend and head of

Figure 11.2   Near the Plaza de la Revolución. The billboard marking the 44th anniversary of the Revolution features Fidel Castro and Camilo Cienfuego, heroes of the revolutionary war. Camilo died in battle, Fidel went on to lead the country. The billboard depicts the mass of Cubans as patriotic, hardworking, and peace loving, cheering amidst a sea of flags, machetes, and doves. On the street in front of the billboard, a pre-1959 US automobile in remarkably pristine condition stands as an ironic symbol of revolutionary Cuba's conflicted relationship with the United States. (Martin Benjamin photo)

internal security, Manuel Piñeiro Losada (1934–98). Piñeiro trained the young men, his "*muchachos*," as he called them, who infiltrated abroad and schooled at home a whole generation of revolutionary recruits for the Latin American guerrilla movement. Piñeiro, a contemporary of Fidel's from a prominent Havana family, attended Columbia University, where it was assumed he would study business and make the connections to follow in his father's footsteps as an executive with Bacardi Rum. Rejecting his roots and opting for the revolution, the charismatic, beguiling, and attractive red-bearded Piñeiro is credited with building an impenetrable security structure in Cuba and directing insurgencies throughout the hemisphere in what Castañeda calls "the most heroic chapter in its history." Castañeda, a critic of the guerrilla strategy, an advisor to conservative Mexican president Vicente Fox, and a man who has ruffled many feathers with his argument that Fidelismo was ultimately neither productive nor in the best interest of social change in Latin America, nonetheless admired the project Cuba attempted. Castañeda's conclusions, despite hints of paternalistic sentimentality, are nonetheless worth pondering:

> Piñeiro and the Revolution's attempts to fan the fires of revolt across Latin America began
> as the most heroic chapter in its history. From the earliest guerrilla landings in Venezuela

and the Dominican Republic to Che's sacrifice in Bolivia, not to mention the countless Cubans who fought, or helped others fight, in guerrilla wars extending over three decades, Fidel's vision of a revolution that had to be exported included some of its finest hours: generous, idealistic, unselfish. In the brief moments of victory or success, and during the long years of defeat and retribution, the Cubans stood by their friends, cared for the widows, orphans, and maimed who survived the hemisphere's Thirty Years Wars. They opened their doors to many who had nowhere else to go and gave much of the best of themselves and their experience to bringing change in Latin America. One may disagree with the tactics, or even with the goals, but they pursued both with perseverance and dignity.[3]

So long as Cuba existed, there was no such thing as non-alignment among the Latin American nations. The OAS (Organization of American States) was founded in 1948 with headquarters on the Mall in Washington DC, alongside the Museum of American History and the National Archives. It was not an institution that symbolically or realistically stood for national sovereignty. Cuba was expelled after the revolution and the beginning of disagreements with the US. More importantly, every other state of the Americas was required for the next 30 years to break diplomatic ties with Cuba or risk expulsion as well. To paraphrase the English historian Eric Hobsbawm, as the "iron grille of the Cold War was clamped across the globe" nearly every state in the world was required to join one or the other system of alliances. With the single exception of Mexico, no country in the OAS that wanted to stay on good terms with the US could also be friendly with Cuba throughout the Cold War, while the mere mention of Fidel Castro in the inner circles of a Latin American government was rumored to be enough to bring in the CIA and initiate a covert action against a leader.

Democratic Shortcomings

Despite the many social reforms since the Revolution, the Cuban government has never allowed widespread democratic freedoms, including freedom of the press, of assembly, and the right to mobilize opposition to government policies. While many countries have official, government-sponsored, news agencies, Cuba's media is controlled and censored. This is not to say that alternative views are entirely absent, especially in movies and books, but a capricious level of control prohibits the existence of a culture of freedom. Curbs on freedom of expression have driven many in the artistic, literary, and academic community to abandon Cuba. The most celebrated case was that of Reinaldo Arenas (1943–90), a talented writer, poet, and playwright, who suffered persecution for refusing to submit to self-censorship in what he wrote and to curb his openly homosexual lifestyle. Arenas's 1992 autobiography, *Before Night Falls* (which was later made into a movie after the author's death from AIDS in New York), graphically recounts the physical and mental repression he suffered at the hands of the Cuban authorities. However, Arenas might find Cuba much altered today. Mariela Castro Espín (b. 1962), daughter of Raúl Castro and Vilma Espín, leads the Cuban National Center for Sex Education, an organization devoted to promoting acceptance of Cuba's LGBT (lesbian/gay/bisexual/transgender) community. As a result of the center's work and other initiatives, tolerance for same-sex relationships and the openly gay lifestyle has changed dramatically, to the point that gay-oriented travel guides list Havana as one of the world's gay-friendly cities.

Cuban officials blame the US embargo and the persistence of Cuban exile counter-insurgency campaigns for the lack of freedom, stating that the need to repel invasions from the outside has prevented the government from lifting the surveillance of its own people. Undoubtedly that is partially true; however, it is also clear that Cuba has evolved its own "culture of censorship" over the last near 50 years. On the one hand, censorship has allowed corruption to spread, since open investigation, organized opposition, and freedom of expression are key tools for rooting out favoritism, ineffi-ciency, and graft. On the other hand, US hostility toward the regime has prevented reasonable dialogue on future relations between the two nations. The US has been a powerful enemy, no one can doubt, but Cuban officials have also used that enmity to enforce allegiance and conformity with the prevailing party line, often at a high cost to the intellectual, cultural, and social life of its people.

Conclusion

The 1959 overthrow of Cuba's Fulgencio Batista, one of Washington's closest allies in the region, shocked diplomatic circles on both sides of the Caribbean. Although Trujillo's machinations in the Dominican Republic might have been an occasional thorn in Washington's side, up to that point the US had been able to manage the embarrassing and potentially unfavorable press resulting from its relationship with one or another authoritarian regime. That all changed when Fidel Castro's bearded guerrilla army marched into Havana on January 1, 1959, unleashing a series of revolutionary or reform movements in several countries.

Cuba's successful revolution had a dramatic effect on the rest of the hemisphere. Populations that had waited patiently (or not so patiently) to share in their nations' wealth and witness a leveling of gross inequalities, or whose hopes had been raised by reform governments subsequently overthrown by traditional elites, military or external (mainly US) forces, drew renewed inspiration from the band of young men, and a few women, who toppled an entrenched dictatorship the US had long supported. The Cuban Revolution turned back the dismal cycle in which Latin American nations seemed to be caught, which prominent Mexican novelist and political commentator Carlos Fuentes (b. 1928) calls the ultimate Catch 22:

> We start a democratic process, such as the one that took place in Guatemala in the forties and fifties, such as the one that took place in Chile in the seventies, and it is promptly destroyed, promptly intervened, and promptly corrupted by the same people who create the illusion that Latin Americans are incapable of governing themselves. If there has ever been a Catch 22 in history, it is this one.[4]

12 | Progress and Reaction

By the late twentieth century Latin America had grown immensely; its population increased from 61 million in 1900 to 200 million in 1968. Ten cities, spanning the region from south to north – Buenos Aires, Rio de Janeiro, São Paulo, Recife, Santiago, Lima, Caracas, Bogotá, Mexico City, and Havana – already had more than one million inhabitants, and the region was becoming the most urbanized in the world. Class differences were apparent in cities, where a prosperous middle class was emerging, but the rising tide was not lifting all boats. The majority of laborers earned wages that kept them in persistent poverty; recent migrants from the countryside crowded into shantytowns mushrooming on the cities' outskirts. From the early 1960s until 1990, Latin America was one of the most turbulent regions on the world's political stage. Tensions pitted armed, nationalist movements for self-determination – generally influenced, if not fully guided, by socialist, anti-imperialist ideas – against pro-capitalist, multinational business interests loyal to landowning oligarchies, the military, and commercial elites. A variety of groups, political parties, and social movements embarked on a range of strategies to enact change. Although some movements for political and economic change turned to armed struggle, others sought to bring about reform through the electoral arena.

Modernization and Progress

Mexico, the only country, apart from Cuba, to have undertaken a prolonged social revolution in the twentieth century, fell into bureaucratic complacency that left social inequality intact, even at the cost of violently repressing dissent. The Party of the Mexican Revolution (PRM, *Partido de la Revolución Mexicano*) changed its name in 1946 to the Institutional Revolutionary Party (PRI, *Partido Revolucionario Institucional*), with "institutional" the operative word. Although nominally a member of the Socialist International, the PRI no longer represented the socialist labor movement, intellectuals, and agrarian reformers, except through rhetorical flourishes every six years during presidential campaigns. The PRI had become a party of technocrats and bureaucrats; economists trained at the Harvard Business School and other graduates of North American MBA programs; entrepreneurs, professionals, and members of the expanding middle class. Its goals were prosperity and stability, to be achieved through traditional capitalist channels. In contrast to Cuba, which the US continually berated for lack of a "two-party system" that mimicked its own, Washington was unconcerned that Mexico's PRI made little pretense of sharing power. Like the Liberal Democratic Party of Japan and India's Congress Party, the PRI emerged from the post-World War II era as a monolith that shifted electoral offices back and forth among competing factions of little ideological difference. Although sporadic violence, strikes, and peasant, student and worker protests usually met with severe repression from police and military forces – especially in 1968 – Mexico experienced no repeat of the turbulence that marked the early decades of the twentieth century.

In other areas of Latin America, especially the Southern Cone, tensions between left and right dominated politics during the 1960s and 1970s. The 1964 military coup in Brazil, followed by years of censorship, dismantling of activist forces in trade unions, community organizations, universities, and religious orders, was the opening salvo in a string of dictatorships that enveloped the region for decades. Brazil's military junta drew the blueprint for what came to be known as the "National Security Regime," a particular form of authoritarianism characterized by systematic surveillance of the civilian population, combined with the use of torture and disappearance against sometimes randomly selected suspects, to instill widespread fear and compliance.

At this time the US government, working largely through the CIA, sought to ensure that Latin American allies followed a staunch anti-communist, pro-US business agenda. As a result, even moderate governments with little affection for communism and the Soviet Union, who were merely interested in a neutral stance regarding the two superpowers or who wanted to maintain diplomatic ties with Cuba, became the object of CIA intervention, resulting in a string of military coups stretching from Brazil in 1964 to Chile and Uruguay in 1973, and Argentina in 1976. The CIA maintained a base of operations in Panama and a Southern Command Headquarters in Paraguay, a country that all too well illustrated the results of maintaining a close alliance with the US. Paraguay had barely been rebuilt since the genocidal War of Triple Alliance (1865–70); it languished under the 35-year military dictatorship of Alfredo Stroessner (1912–2006). A staunch ally of the US, Stroessner ruled from 1954 to 1989, during which time he brooked no opposition, under penalty of torture and death, while presiding over a people with one of the lowest income and literacy levels, and highest infant mortality rates, in the hemisphere.

Brazil's Military Coup

The chain of events that led the military to intervene in 1964 against the democratically designated president João Goulart (1919–76) resembled events in Guatemala in the early 1950s. Like Juan Arévalo, Janio Quadros (1917–92) won the presidency in 1961 on the basis of promises to take a neutral stance in foreign policy, increase manufacturing and overall industrial growth, lay the groundwork for a broader participatory democracy, and take up the issue of land reform. Communist-inspired Peasant Leagues under the leadership of Francisco Julião (1915–99) were demanding equitable distribution of land and higher wages for rural workers in a massive campaign that penetrated 13 of Brazil's then 22 states (currently 26). The Peasant Leagues, or *ligas*, pursued a number of strategies, encouraging peasants to seize unoccupied land, and uniting rural workers into trade unions through which they demanded higher wages, better living conditions, and regulated hours. Operating under the slogan "land reform by law or by force," the *ligas* were prepared to take up arms to win demands if peaceful tactics failed.

Agitation in the early 1960s was not limited to land issues, nor were the *ligas* the only activists. Members of the Catholic clergy, supported by activist bishops, urban trade unionists, students, and professionals were increasingly vocal in calling for schooling and medical care for the urban and rural poor, decent wages and improved access to water, roads, public transportation, and other services needed to guarantee a better quality of life for the majority of the country's citizens. Conditions at home, combined with the example of the Cuban Revolution, inspired a generation of young Brazilian activists to replicate the socialist revolution that was claiming to bring equality to Cuba. Reminiscent of the chain of events in Guatemala, Quadros's timid responses to agitation from the left met with heated opposition from conservative landowners, industrialists, and politicians. In a land where powerful rural bosses had exerted unchecked raw force since colonial times (a situation immortalized in the tales of Brazil's foremost novelist, Jorge Amado), attempts to impose even moderate reforms met with outrage. They called on their allies in the military and police to crush rural workers, small landowners, and impoverished peasants who occupied disputed landholdings. In a gamble that backfired, the beleaguered Quadros resigned after only a year in office, speculating that he would be reinstated since the prospect of the more radical vice-president, João Goulart, becoming president would be completely unacceptable to hard-line conservatives. Quadros miscalculated, however, and Goulart, with the backing of a group of powerful politicians, became president in August 1961.

From the very first days rumors of a military takeover swirled around Goulart's presidency, serving as a powerful brake on the few reforms the government hoped to enact. The rural oligarchy's refusal to consider agrarian reform was joined by business interests in Brazil and in the United States who viewed the political situation as unstable, especially when Goulart's closest political ally, Leonel Brizola (1922–2004), the governor of Rio Grande do Sul, nationalized a subsidiary of International Telephone and Telegraph (IT&T). Multinational companies interested in reaping high profits counted on a docile workforce that would tolerate meager wages and abysmal working conditions, on a government that offered favorable tariff agreements, low taxes, and lax enforcement of health and safety laws. In the US, the Lyndon Johnson administration was less than pleased. In an era of intense Cold War rivalry between the US and the communist world, exacerbated by the successful Cuban Revolution and widening conflict in Southeast Asia, the US distrusted any political leader who sought to maintain a middle ground or spoke of even moderate reform. Vice-President Goulart had traveled to China (and was there when Quadros resigned), which angered a US State Department that considered any attempt by Latin American governments to forge a non-aligned foreign policy as contrary to US interests; friendly relations with "Red" China were out of the question. Finally, Goulart's mismanagement of state affairs and hesitancy in dealing with a considerable opposition made his term in office precarious from the start.

In early 1964 the expected began to unfold. On March 31 troops under the command of General Olimpio Mourão Filho (1900–72) marched on the federal capital in Rio de Janeiro, setting the coup into motion. Other branches of the military joined within hours and, under the leadership of General Humberto Castello Branco (1900–67), deposed the legal government. João Goulart flew into exile in Uruguay, where he lived until dying of a heart attack in 1976. Many initially greeted the military intervention enthusiastically, including most of the media, the hierarchy of the Catholic Church, the business and political elite, and even a group of prosperous women who believed that Goulart's policies had caused prices to climb and granted their maids too many rights. On the other hand, some sectors that greeted the coup warmly, in hopes that it would halt rampant inflation and instability, drew back as the full force of the military's repression, especially the arrest and torture of thousands of citizens, unfolded. The US promptly recognized the military regime and set about negotiating a generous military and economic aid package. This warm relationship continued through the string of dictators that ruled Brazil from 1964 until the return of democracy in 1988, despite the regime's widely publicized human rights violations.

The National Security State

For the working class, the rural and urban poor, the landless, homeless, and illiterate, as well as democratic forces, the coup was a severe setback. The 1964 coup d'état ushered in a new type of military regime. Rather than a government based on the politics of personal clientelism and corruption, the new regime adopted a bureaucratic and institutional military rule. In contrast with the single, self-interested rule of Rafael Trujillo in the Dominican Republic, Anastasio Somoza in Nicaragua, or Fulgencio Batista in Cuba, for example, the Brazilian model demonstrated an ideological commitment by the full military bureaucracy to hold power. Beginning in 1964, a coalition of generals sought to transform both state and society, introducing a model of national economic growth secured within a controlled environment that permitted virtually no opposition. The national security state evolved over a number of years. Originally, from 1964 until 1967, Brazil's military junta ruled through a series of exceptional measures without changing the basic structure of the government. At the same time, they began a process of rewriting the national constitution. In 1967 a compliant Congress ratified a new constitution that allowed indirect elections for president; however, only military leaders could be candidates. It granted the president the right to govern through decree, even when the legislature was in session, effectively eliminating congressional disagreement or debate. While on paper laws existed to protect individual rights, they were either not enforced or constantly nullified by decrees to ensure "national security." What began as a "moderate" military dictatorship in 1964, based on purging the system of opponents while keeping some institutions of civil society in operation, turned more repressive in the midst of growing opposition a few years later.

Latin America's Youth Movement

In Brazil, and throughout the world, 1968 was a pivotal year. It began with the "Tet Offensive" – in which the Viet Cong army shocked the world by demonstrating its ability to overpower American forces in Saigon, Vietnam – and continued on as a period marked by student protests in Paris and many universities in the United States and Europe, culminating in a bloody massacre of students before the opening of the Olympic Games in Mexico City. In Brazil students mounted huge demonstrations against the generals, joined by powerful sections of the industrial working class in São Paulo and Rio de Janeiro. Seeing the "communist threat" everywhere, fearing the rise of an opposition movement among workers, intellectuals, and even some of the traditional elites, and equating any call for democracy with subversion, the regime cracked down. Late in 1968 the military began to govern through a series of institutional acts added to the framework of the constitution. Institutional Act 2 allowed for indirect elections, dissolved all existing political parties and created two new ones: the Brazilian Democratic Movement Party (PMDB, *Partido do Movimento Democrático Brasileiro*) as the opposition party (at least on paper), and the National Renovating Alliance (ARENA, *Aliança Renovadora Nacional*) as the pro-government party. For so-called crimes against a broadly interpreted notion of "national security," Institutional Act 5 suspended the legislature, forced three Supreme Court judges into retirement, eliminated many lower court judges, and suspended habeas corpus (the right to challenge detentions and imprisonment).

Mexico

In Mexico, ostensibly a democracy and thus unlike Brazil, students directed their anger at the official party, the PRI. They decried the failure of the 1910 Revolution to right the wrongs of society, and noted that despite the half-century since the Constitution of 1917 a majority of Mexicans and all but a handful of indigenous people lived in poverty. They contended that Mexico's opposition to US imperialism rang hollow, despite its refusal to join the US-mandated 1961 OAS boycott of Cuba. The Mexican left argued that the PRI maintained diplomatic relations with Cuba only so long as none of the nation's social reforms reached Mexico. In hopes of winning peace at home and prestige abroad, Mexico launched a full-scale campaign to host the 1968 Olympics. The effort succeeded, and despite widespread criticism that sponsoring the Olympics would deplete valuable resources needed for social programs, Mexico became the first (and to date only) Latin American country to host the games. At a cost of $200 million, an astronomical figure at the time, Mexico began an ambitious building project in the capital, including hotels, housing for athletes, tourists, and visiting dignitaries, massive stadiums and athletic facilities, and even a new subway system.

Throughout the summer before the games were to open, unrelated intermittent protests based on inter-school rivalries, and a few full-scale riots, broke out in Mexico City high schools. A peaceful demonstration celebrating the July 26 anniversary of the Cuban Revolution turned violent when the *granaderos* (police riot squads) overreacted in an attempt to disperse the participants. By August the demonstrations were constant and had spread to most high schools, as well as the major universities in Mexico City. Tension mounted as the opening date of the Olympics grew near and the demonstrations grew in size; one in the Zócolo, Mexico City's central plaza, called by the student strike committee, drew nearly a million people, making it one of the largest demonstrations in the city's history, and certainly the largest protest since the days of the Revolution. Although centered on student demands, the protests began to attract supporters from broader sectors of society, including the working class and even rural peasants, who added their own grievances to those of the students. The police once again met the protests with extreme violence, bringing in tanks and unleashing the *granaderos*, who fired on the crowds. By the end of the summer, some students had been killed; many had been beaten and jailed.

The Massacre at Tlateloco

During subsequent months the demonstrations began to die back; however, a group of militant students called a demonstration for October 2, 1968 in Tlateloco Plaza in central Mexico City. The rally at first drew only 5,000–6,000 participants, many of them residents of the building who stopped to watch on their way home from work. Also at the plaza were a number of people who were chatting and socializing, children playing games before the evening meal, and a number of passers-by, who were simply in the vicinity. Without warning the police stormed the building and other police, already posted inside, opened fire on demonstrators, onlookers, and children alike. Troops advanced, helicopters circled and dropped flares. In one of the most shocking shows of force in Mexican history, hundreds of people were killed outright, and others died en route to the hospital. Reports that surfaced later revealed that police pulled the wounded from ambulances who were trying to take the victims to hospitals, military vehicles prevented medical personnel from reaching the wounded, and hospital emergency rooms near the plaza were invaded by the military, who dragged bodies back into the street. The government attempted to dismiss the entire event, claiming that fewer than 30 people died (observers put the number at between 300 and 500), that the students initiated the attack, and that the police and *granaderos* actually exercised restraint in the face of wild provocations from the demonstrators. However, the presence of a large contingent of international press in the city to cover the Olympics revealed the true story to the world. Nonetheless, the Olympics went ahead as scheduled and the government moved swiftly to cover up the event, which came to be known as the Massacre at Tlateloco. So long as the PRI remained in power the 1968 incident was seldom mentioned.

The PRI's loss of the presidency in 2000 laid the basis for a full investigation of the Massacre and of the disappearance of hundreds of other dissidents during the 1970s. In 2006, two days before the close election that pitted PAN (National Action Party) candidate Felipe Calderón (b. 1962) against the leftist PRD (Democratic Revolutionary Party) candidate, Andrés Manuel Lopéz Obrador (b. 1953), a judge ordered the arrest of former president Luis Echeverría (84 years old and ailing), for his responsibility in the killing of the students in 1968 and the disappearance and deaths of hundreds more while he was president from 1970 to 1976. The timing of his arrest led PRD supporters to argue that the current PAN president, Vicente Fox, was attempting to win support for Calderón by showing his ability to get tough on past human rights violations, and thus turn attention away from criticisms of his own conservative administration's record of abuse, especially against the indigenous population in Oaxaca and the more remote area of Chiapas.

Throughout Latin America the experience of the Mexican students reverberated against a continuing chain of demonstrations and upheaval. In 1968 the Brazilian dictatorship entered its most repressive phase. The institutions of civil society either disappeared or were restructured; military officers presided over all universities; student groups were closely monitored; and many of the country's leading intellectuals, artists, musicians, and writers went into exile. In other countries, however, the intensity of student protests mirrored those occurring elsewhere throughout the world, and Cuba remained a beacon of inspiration for revolutionary change, despite Castro's embrace of the Soviet Union which was in turn suppressing pro-democracy activists in Czechoslovakia, East Germany, and other areas of Eastern Europe. In Latin America the 1970s opened with the election in Chile of a socialist head of state. Argentina saw the return, and demise, of Juan Perón, Latin America's best-known populist and demagogue, while elsewhere some of the continent's most brutal military regimes held sway. The decade drew to a close with the Sandinistas' victory in Nicaragua, after a decade of fighting. The late 1960s and 1970s saw Latin American nations traveling down vastly divergent paths, few of them peaceful.

The Chilean Road to Socialism

Chile, hemmed in as it is by high Andean peaks along its entire eastern side, is a 4,000-mile-long, string-bean-shaped country. With a population of just 11 million in the late 1960s, Chile had a limited domestic market for its own manufactures and agricultural products. The economy mainly relied on the export of copper from mines owned and controlled by Kennecott and Anaconda, Canadian- and US-based companies. In 1960 the two mines accounted for 11 percent of the country's gross national product, 50 percent of its exports, and 20 percent of government revenue, pumping

$150–200 million a year into the economy. Despite this heavy reliance on commodity exports to support internal growth, on the surface Chile's economic house appeared stable, though closer scrutiny revealed otherwise. A key issue was unemployment and seasonal unemployment, since neither the landholding system nor the copper mines utilized large numbers of laborers. Land was used mainly for raising sheep and cattle, neither of which demanded much care. With a few farm hands, and the addition of more in the busy season, ranchers could tend large herds of livestock, harvest crops, slaughter animals, shear wool, and maintain their operation.

With so much of Chile's economy reliant on copper exports, and the mines controlled by foreign corporations, the economy was vulnerable to demand fluctuations of the international commodity chain. During wartime (including World War II, Korea, and then the Vietnam War) copper prices were high, since it is an essential mineral used in war materiel. In the late 1960s, however, prices fell when the military market was glutted with copper and demand declined. President Eduardo Frei (1911–82) of the dominant Christian Democrat Party, who held office from 1964 to 1970, attempted unsuccessfully to resolve Chile's development problems, including breaking the inflation–stagnation economic cycle resulting from a too-heavy reliance on exports and on the narrow, consumer-driven market. These constant problems, combined with discontent over low wages and massive inequalities in income distribution, laid the groundwork for the success and ultimate victory of a new approach proposed by the *Unidad Popular* (UP, Popular Unity) coalition. With the right and center divided, Salvador Allende, a medical doctor and perennial Socialist Party candidate, squeaked into office with 36 percent of the vote and the narrow approval of Congress, which ultimately had decided the outcome in favor of the UP.

The forces of conservatism (landed oligarchy, multinational and domestic corporate executives, the Catholic Church, rightists in the military and the media) moved into action to stymie implementation of the UP political program. Similarly, the election of a socialist, no matter what his particular program might be, attracted the attention of high-level US government officials, many of whom had been actively working to prevent the rise to power of a reformist ticket since the 1960s. After Allende's election they shifted from surveillance and intelligence gathering to direct action, justified by Henry Kissinger's (b. 1923) cavalier dismissal of the Chilean elections. The US Secretary of State and former National Security Advisor to President Richard Nixon (1913–94) reportedly remarked: "I don't see why we should have to stand by and let a country go communist due to the irresponsibility of its own people."[1]

The UP experience in the early 1970s was a microcosm of the deep-seated dilemmas and divisions facing many Latin American societies. Allende came to power through elections, not through armed struggle along the lines of Castro's Cuba or Guevara's *foco* strategy. As such he was tied to a program of redistributing wealth and mounting social reforms within the confines of a constitutional process, even in the face of intense opposition from an entrenched elite and powerful military at home, and a hostile set of policymakers and corporate managers abroad. Peter Winn's book *Weavers of Revolution* captures the essence of that tug-of-war as it played out on the shop floor of a single domestic textile plant owned by Juan and Amador Yarur. According to Winn:

"Yarur came to symbolize both the demise of the old regime and the new socialist order struggling to be born."[2] In a pattern that mimicked the broader struggle in Chilean society, older, unskilled, socially conservative workers lived in fear of being fired, aware as they were that their minimal education provided them few other options in society. Begrudgingly or not, they had become resigned to their exploitation and grateful for the occasional bonus or Christmas roasting hen that the Yarur management doled out to loyal workers. In the 1960s a younger, better educated, and socialist-inspired workforce launched a union organizing drive, rejected the owners' paternalism, demanded decent wages, rational work rules, employee benefits, and modern working conditions. Yarur thus represented a microcosm of Chile, where a younger, more militant segment of the population was mobilizing for change, both at the ballot box and on the factory floor, and coming up against a traditional society that feared it.

To create chaos in the Chilean economy and undermine President Allende, and with the financial support of the Anaconda and Kennecott copper giants, IT&T and other major multinationals, factory owners in Chile cut back on production. With ample funding from the fiercely anti-communist US labor federation, the AFL-CIO, independent truckers refused to deliver goods to cities, thereby sparking widespread shortages and inflation. At the same time, throughout the country the UP's program was being put into practice by ordinary people who supported Allende, sometimes without any officially sanctioned right to do so. When owners abandoned factories, workers took them over, expropriated the property from under the old owners, and began to work the machines on their own. Peasants occupied land long denied them, and shantytown dwellers moved into vacant lots and set up soup kitchens and rudimentary housing. Caught between a rock and a hard place, the constitutional government was powerless to stop the insurrection from below, while fully aware that the more the poor demanded, the more precarious was Allende's chance of remaining in power. Leadership for an aggressive confrontation with the right came from university students and militant youths in the radical left-wing *Movimiento de la Izquierda Revolucionário* (MIR, Movement of the Revolutionary Left), a group that supported the UP, but claimed that Allende's only security lay in arming the workers and peasants and moving more rapidly with factory and land occupations to stave off the imminent assault from the right. As Allende was maneuvering for gradual change, the MIR was calling for armed struggle in the spirit of Che Guevara.

The Chilean Road to Socialism Dead Ends

On the morning of September 11, 1973 the military, under the leadership of General Augusto Pinochet (1915–2006), an army officer who had managed to neutralize or eliminate military officers loyal to Allende and the Constitution, began the bombardment of the Moneda, Chile's presidential palace. A fleet of US navy warships took up positions off the port at Valparaiso, in a move reminiscent of the gunboat diplomacy the US had exerted earlier in the century, and a group of US military advisors gathered in the coastal town of Viña del Mar with the Chilean military. Despite repeated denials from US government officials, declassified documents have since shown that Nixon and Kissinger, along with public and private intelligence agencies, were apprised of, and even enmeshed in, planning and executing the military takeover. Allende died in the Moneda, most likely taking his own life. His close associates were apprehended and killed, or fled into exile. Military leader General Augusto Pinochet moved swiftly to close Congress and ban all media outlets supportive of Allende or opposed to the military takeover. Universities were purged of opposition; the military ruled through executive order; and Chile entered the dark days of repression, torture, disappearance, and death for thousands of activists who were unable or unwilling to leave. For a while militants remained inside the country, attempting to mount resistance to the junta, but many who tried were rounded up and their organizations crushed and dismantled. An estimated one million people left the country.

The efficacy of the "Chilean Road to Socialism" would be debated in years to come: Did the UP fail because the left pushed too hard, thus precipitating the military coup? Did sabotage from the right leave the UP with no other choice but to mobilize in an attempt to save the social gains Allende had initiated? Was it possible to transform a society through the ballot box, especially in countries of Latin America with deep-rooted militaries and powerful oligarchies? Was it the US, the CIA, and the multinational corporations who overturned Allende's government, or were the contradictions between the agenda of the left and the powerful interests on the right, between rich and poor, and between competing definitions of revolutionary strategy within Chilean society most responsible? Because Chile's economy eventually revived under military rule, some economists contend that the dictatorship brought prosperity to a disorganized economy, while others argue that the massive sell-off of public resources that characterized the Pinochet period actually undermined the nation's economy. Throughout the years of the dictatorship income distribution was highly unequal and suffering and persecution was widespread.

Questions about the Allende government persist on into the twenty-first century, especially because Chile is now in its second socialist administration since the return to democracy in 1990. After years of legal wrangling, including a dramatic house arrest in London and eventual deportation back to Chile to face charges on human rights abuses, kidnapping, and murder, General Pinochet died before going to trial. Other officers have been charged and convicted in what remains a long-running attempt to redress the grievances caused by the lengthy and brutal dictatorship.

Urban Guerrilla Warfare: Uruguay

Overshadowed by the more widely publicized military takeovers in Chile, the events in Uruguay were possibly even more tragic in terms of the chain of events that led to the destruction of a vital democracy. Nearly the smallest country of Latin America, Uruguay for much of the twentieth century was reputedly one of the most prosperous. Similar to Argentina, early genocidal campaigns against the indigenous people left the plains and rolling hills vacant of inhabitants. Uruguay welcomed immigrants, mostly from Italy, some from Spain and other parts of Europe, who settled on the land

and developed the main economic enterprise: agriculture. In 1903 José Batlle y Ordóñez (1856–1929) assumed the presidency after a protracted civil war between conservative and liberal factions. His efforts at unifying the country and establishing a complex social welfare system are credited with raising Uruguay's standard of living on a par with that of industrialized European nations. Its advanced social system, the cosmopolitan capital and major port city of Montevideo, and long-running, stable democracy earned it the nickname "Switzerland of the Americas." With an economy heavily reliant on agricultural exports, especially beef, mutton, hides, and tallow, as well as wheat and other grains, Uruguay prospered during both world wars, particularly World War II. When world food prices dropped after war-ravaged Europe and Asia recovered, Uruguayan exports plummeted, and the nation entered a crisis for which it was quite unprepared. Social services were cut, wages fell for the unionized workforce that had been accustomed to fair compensation for their labor, and social tension mounted. By the 1960s the period of economic and political stability had begun to unravel, and the government faced widespread opposition from the students, workers, and low-income families who were bearing the brunt of economic hardship.

Like their counterparts in other Southern Cone countries, Uruguayan students and radical young professionals spearheaded an underground guerrilla movement that was for many years one of the most daring and successful organizations in Latin America, if not beyond. Named after the Inca revolutionary Túpac Amaru II, who fought against the Spanish colonial army in late eighteenth-century Peru, the "Tupamaros" attracted members of trade unions, peasants from some of the poorest rural areas, and university students. Initially the Tupamaros staged highly creative, and popular, "Robin Hood-type" guerrilla actions, such as robbing banks and invading food warehouses and distributing the cash and food to the poor. They became well known for publishing exposés of graft and corruption among businessmen and politicians, much to the embarrassment of Uruguay's elite. The Tupamaros had both an underground revolutionary organization and an above-ground counterpart organized into the *Frente Amplio* (Broad Front), which was effective in winning support for the clandestine movement among some sectors of the population, but not enough to win electoral office, as the Unidad Popular was able to do at roughly the same time in Chile.

By the late 1960s their tactics escalated to political kidnappings and assassination. Their most spectacular feat was the kidnapping and subsequent assassination of Dan Mitrione, a US Agency for International Development (AID) public safety officer who was known for his role in training police throughout Latin America in surveillance and torture methods. From 1969 through 1971 the Tupamaros successfully kidnapped and held for ransom a powerful bank manager, Pereyra Rebervel, and Geoffrey Jackson, England's ambassador to Uruguay (in one case in exchange for the release of political prisoners and in the other as a guarantee that national elections would proceed on schedule). As the economic crisis deepened, the military and police escalated their war against the insurgents. Soon the civilian government collapsed and the army seized power in 1973, ushering in 11 years of military rule that were among the most repressive in all of Latin America. Montevideo, once a stunning port city of European-style architecture similar to Buenos Aires, fell into disrepair; a huge number of Uruguayans emigrated to Australia, Europe, and other countries of Latin America; and much of Uruguay's prosperous middle-class life ceased to exist.

In 1984, after over a decade of stultifying repression, the dictatorship ended. In the same wave that restored democratic governments in Argentina and Brazil, the military stepped down in Uruguay, and Julio María Sanguinetti became president of a country that the military had all but destroyed. In a general amnesty, Tupamaros held in prison for over a decade were released; they regrouped under the Frente Amplio and began winning elections. The current president, Tabaré Vásquez (b. 1940), a medical doctor who trained in France, traces his roots to the Tupamaros. After serving as mayor of Montevideo in the early 1990s, he ran unsuccessfully for the presidency on the *Frente Amplio* ticket in 1994 and 1999, but was elected in 2004.

Urban Guerrilla Warfare: Argentina

Whereas Uruguay's path to armed conflict represented a dramatic shift away from years of European-style social democracy, Argentina's descent into a chaotic war between the military and police on the one hand, and urban guerrilla organizations on the other, constituted yet another chapter in that nation's twentieth-century struggle between left and right. For the most part, the right held power through a string of military governments. In the 1940s and 1950s the Peronist government, despite its corruption and uneven record of defending the masses, had managed to wring from the traditional oligarchy and industrialists concessions that improved the lives of many working people. From 1970 to 1976 Argentine politics began another tug-of-war and, although there were many players, this round of the struggle pitted the government, supported by military and paramilitary forces, against powerful underground urban guerrilla combatants. What led to this shift?

After he was deposed in 1955, Juan Perón had spent his time in exile as the guest of a series of right-wing governments: Paraguay, Venezuela, the Dominican Republic, and Panama, where he met his third wife, nightclub dancer María Estela (Isabel) Martínez. He eventually settled in Spain. In Argentina, despite years of military rule interspersed with civilian governments supported by the urban middle class, Peronism, with its contradictory strains of social welfare, personalist demagoguery, and corruption, lingered just below the surface of Argentine political life, permeating civil society institutions, especially the trade union federation. For its part, the military was presiding over a nation in economic chaos, resulting from the accumulation of an enormous foreign debt that in turn fed inflation, as the government borrowed more and more money from abroad to make payments and stabilize Argentine society. By the late 1960s the central government was unable, or unwilling, to wring concessions from the oligarchy in order to increase wages, offset rising hunger, or hold onto a modicum of support from middle-class consumers unable to buy essentials, much less luxuries. The government attempted to install wage and price controls by printing money in hopes of staving off the crisis, but this simply contributed to spiraling inflation.

Confronting constant demonstrations and increasing attacks from guerrilla movements, especially the People's Revolutionary Army (ERP) and the leftist, Peronist-inspired Montoneros, the government decided to allow the Peronists to field a candidate in the 1973 presidential elections. Winning with a bare 49 percent of the vote, Peronist candidate Héctor Cámpora (1909–80) assumed office in a caretaker capacity, awaiting Perón's return from exile later that year. On June 30, 1973 a crowd estimated at 3.5 million people came to Buenos Aires' Ezeiza Airport to welcome the 77-year-old Perón home from exile in Spain. This huge congregation included members of militant left- and right-wing Peronist groups, powerful trade unions, organized political parties, and a huge number of unaffiliated citizens who hoped that Perón's return would bring an end to the internal conflict. Instead, marksmen from the terrorist *Alianza Anticomunista Argentina* (Argentine Anticommunist Alliance), better known as the "Triple A," opened fire on the crowd, killing at least 13 and injuring hundreds. The Triple A was a far-right group under the leadership of José López Rega (1916–89), Perón's personal secretary who had accompanied him into exile. This event, known as the Ezeiza Massacre, marked the opening round in a battle between left and right factions of the Peronist movement that terrorized Argentina until the 1976 military coup. With Perón back in the country, Cámpora stepped down, thereby signaling the end of the left's hold on the presidency, and paving the way for Perón to run for president with his third wife as vice-president. He won easily, garnering 62 percent of the vote.

During 1973–4 Perón failed (or refused) to unite and pacify the wings of the Peronist movement, opting instead to allow the military to hunt down and jail any supposed opponents of the regime. He had signaled in an August 1973 speech to the governors of the country his disavowal of support for the Montoneros, for the tactics of discontented youth, and for the strategy of guerrilla warfare. Perón's 1973 speech was the signal that drove the entire guerrilla opposition permanently underground, and members of above-ground mass organizations ceased to operate openly. After a corrupt, ineffectual, and repressive couple of years in office, Perón died and his 43-year-old wife Isabel became head of the fourth civilian government in 14 months. With no governmental experience, and less political sense, Isabelita Perón was a disaster, her presidency nothing short of a catastrophe. From 1974 until the military stepped back into formal power in March 1976, the government was actually in the hands of José López Rega, who served as the president's confidante, astrologer, and henchman. From his position as Minister of Social Welfare, López Rega directed the "Triple A" paramilitary death squads, who worked in tandem with the army, navy, and air force to terrorize the population into submission (see Box 12.1).

In response, guerrilla movements stepped up their opposition. The Montoneros, the largest of the groups, had achieved a high level of notoriety as a result of their daring bank robberies and kidnappings, and were known to have accumulated a very substantial cache of money from multinational corporations who paid protection money to ensure the safety of their executives. Formed in 1964, the Montoneros were a clandestine army with broad influence in the above-ground opposition movement, including trade unionists, university students, and community activists. Although they claimed the mantle of Perón, especially the social welfare programs run by Eva

Box 12.1   The US and Operation Condor

Declassified government documents show that the US was supportive of a plan called "Operation Condor," a secret alliance linking the military dictatorships of Chile, Argentina, Paraguay, Uruguay, and Brazil that coordinated the arrest, detention, disappearance, and torture of dissidents in these countries during the 1970s and 1980s. Under the military dictatorship of Alfredo Stroessner, Paraguay served as the center for this coordination and the conduit between the military regimes and the United States. In a cable from US Ambassador Robert White (Paraguay) to Secretary of State Cyrus Vance, sent October 20, 1978, the ambassador states in part:

> On October 11 I called again on Chief of Staff (Paraguay) Alejandro Fretes Davalos. He read me the Acta or Summary Minutes resulting from the visit of General Orozco, Chief of Intelligence to Asunción . . .

The document is basically an agreement to coordinate all intelligence resources in order to control and eliminate subversion. It speaks of exchange of information, prompt use of communication facilities, monitoring of subversives, and their detention and informal handover from one country to the other. It repeats over and over the need for full cooperation and mutually facilitative acts in the context of a fight to the death against subversion . . .

> Brazil, Argentina, Chile, Bolivia, Paraguay and Uruguay make of [sic] the net, although Uruguay is now almost on the inactive list . . . They keep in touch with one another through U.S. communications installations in the Panama Canal Zone which covers all of Latin America.

From *National Security Archive* (2001: 1). Available online: www.gwu.edu/~nsarchiv/news/

Perón in the 1940s and 1950s, the Montoneros stood apart from conservative trade union leaders, whom they criticized for refusing to oppose the fascist tendencies of López Rega and other right-wing Peronists.

Dictatorship and State Terror

On March 24, 1976, the military, under the leadership of General Jorge Rafael Videla (b. 1925), overthrew Isabel Perón's government and launched a campaign they called the "War Against Subversion."[3] For seven years, from 1976 to 1983, the army embarked on a program no previous government, civilian or military, had attempted: to wipe out all vestiges of Peronism (ignoring ideological distinctions) and

Figure 12.1   The Navy School of Mechanics, or ESMA (*Escuela de Mecánica de la Armada*), Buenos Aires. The largest of the many torture centers spread throughout the city during the dictatorship, the ESMA continued as a school for training cadets while areas of the building served as torture cells, storage lockers for property stolen from prisoners, and a small "hospital" where young women gave birth before their babies were taken from them and given to friends of the military leaders. All but a handful of people taken to the ESMA "disappeared." (Andor Skotnes photo)

its organizations, along with the last remnants of democratic, civil society. Once the military dictators outlawed all representative bodies, silenced the legal opposition, and began arresting anyone they deemed suspicious, the guerrilla forces headed by the ERP and Montoneros were all that was left to continue the struggle, until their defeat around 1978.

The repression of the 1970s and 1980s claimed the lives of more than 30,000 civilians, the vast majority of them never accounted for and simply "disappeared" from society without leaving behind any record of arrest, detention, or charges (Figure 12.1). On December 27, 1978, at the height of the war, the US Embassy officer in charge of human rights, F. Allen "Tex" Harris, wrote in his briefing memo to the US State Department that the "armed services had been forced to 'take care of' 15,000 persons in its anti-subversion campaign." Today that number is known to have been much higher, since the Federal Court of Argentina earlier that same year had compiled a secret document (made public after the dictatorship left power) reporting that 22,000 of the disappeared had been killed.[4] Years after the return to civilian government in 1983, a few conscience-stricken former military officers, such as navy captain Adolfo Scilingo, testified before the National Commission on Disappeared People. Scilingo described how prisoners were drugged, loaded onto military planes, and thrown out, naked and semi-conscious, into the Atlantic Ocean. Residents of towns along the Rio de la Plata have for years discovered human remains washed up on the shore; more recently mass graves have been exhumed in remote areas of the coastline, where either compliant or fearful citizens, along with military regiments, attempted to bury the evidence of the massive number of executions.

Who were the victims of state terror? The sweep of the military was broad and often indiscriminate. In factories and workplaces unionists were sorted out and disappeared. At the Ford Motor plant 25 union delegates were detained and disappeared inside the plant's very own clandestine detention center for days, weeks, or months until they were secretly transferred to the local police precinct transformed into a military center. According to Pedro Troiani, a union delegate for six years in the Ford plant in Pacheco until the 1976 coup, "The company used the disappearances to get rid of unionism at the factory." Similarly, an estimated 20 workers disappeared from the Mercedes-Benz plant, which had also been transformed into a clandestine torture and detention center. At least 46 workers from the offices of the Buenos Aires Provincial Bank were singled out for union organizing activity, apprehended, and never seen again.

According to the Commission's report, *Nunca Más*, published in 1984 (translated into English as *Never Again*, 1986), most of those arrested and disappeared were university and high school students, young professionals and workers. Some had been active in political organizations, but many others were simply taken because their name was in the address book of a detainee. The overwhelming majority of those arrested and disappeared were under the age of 35, as, oddly enough, were the men and women who arrested, tortured, humiliated, and executed them. A disproportionate number were Jews; the military's anti-Semitism was documented in *Prisoner Without a Name, Cell Without a Number*, newspaper editor Jacobo Timmerman's graphic testimony of his arrest and torture, published after an international outcry secured his release. In addition to the more than 30,000 disappeared and presumed dead, over 800,000 people left the country.

Mothers of the Plaza de Mayo

During the darkest period, from 1976 to 1982, the lone voices of public opposition belonged to a few mothers who began to gather in the plaza in front of the presidential palace, called the Casa Rosada (the Rose, or Pink, House). They began marching at first on Sundays and later every Thursday, demanding to know the fate of their disappeared children. Wearing white scarves as a symbol of their children's diapers, and carrying photographs of their young adult sons and daughters, the Mothers of the Plaza de Mayo began to draw international attention to the brutal repression the military had unleashed (Figure 12.2). They exposed the blind eye of most world governments

Figure 12.2   The Mothers of the Plaza de Mayo (wearing white scarves embroidered with the names of their children and carrying a photograph) march every Thursday afternoon in front of the presidential mansion (Casa Rosada) in Buenos Aires, demanding to know the fate of their children and grandchildren who disappeared during the military regime. (Nancy Borowick photo)

in relation to human rights abuses in Argentina, and denounced the warm relationship between the US government and the generals. Recently declassified cables sent from Washington to Buenos Aires reveal that Secretary of State Henry Kissinger, in the days after the March coup, had ordered his subordinates to "encourage" the new regime by providing financial support (see Box 12.2). A month after the coup and amidst reports of widespread human rights abuses in Argentina, Washington approved $50 million in military aid to the junta. At the urging of the US, on March 27, 1976, three days after the coup, the IMF extended the military government $127 million in credit.

The War of the Malvinas/Falkland Islands

Despite repression and forced austerity that reduced wages by 40 percent in a little over a year, the regime was unable to resolve the economic crisis. A record number of bankruptcies occurred in 1982; inflation soared from a destabilizing 300 percent in 1975–6 to 500 percent the same year, and the international debt continued to

Box 12.2   March 26, 1976 – State Department Staff Meeting Transcripts: Secretary of State Henry Kissinger, Chairman, DECLASSIFIED SECRET

Two days after the military coup, Secretary of State Kissinger convened his weekly staff meeting. In this declassified secret transcript of the first conversation on Argentina, Assistant Secretary for Latin America, William Rogers, informs Kissinger that for the Argentine generals' government to succeed, they will make "a considerable effort to involve the United States – particularly in the financial field." Kissinger responds, "Yes, but that is in our interest."

Rogers advises that "we ought not at this moment rush out and embrace this new regime" because he expects significant repression to follow the coup. "I think also we've got to expect a fair amount of repression, probably a good deal of blood, in Argentina before too long. I think they're going to have to come down very hard not only on the terrorists but on the dissidents of trade unions and their parties." In response, Kissinger makes his preferences clear: "Whatever chance they have, they will need a little encouragement . . . because I do want to encourage them. I don't want to give the sense that they're harassed by the United States."

Other documents reveal that in September 1976 several Argentine military officers traveled to Washington where they met with Secretary Kissinger and other US officials. They returned to Argentina "euphoric" over the approval their tactics had received from the US, especially from Kissinger, who reported that he realized there would be "a lot of blood."

Source: National Security Archive. Available online: www.gwu.edu/~nsarchiv/news/

skyrocket. The economic crisis added to general disquiet at home, and mounting criticism from abroad over human rights abuses and highly publicized cases of disappearances. News that the children of pregnant detainees were being sold for international adoption or turned over to military families after their mothers were killed was especially damaging to the military regime.

In an attempt to win popular support, the military launched in April 1982 a drive to take back the Malvinas, or Falkland, Islands from the British, who had taken them from the Spanish in 1833. Argentina's claim that the islands should have reverted to them along with the rest of the territory when the country achieved independence from Spain had languished in international courts for years. General Leopoldo Galtieri (1926–2003), the military officer who launched the attack on the sparsely inhabited islands over 500 miles off the coast of Argentina, never thought Great Britain would defend their possession; in the language of modern invasions, he though it would be a "cake walk." Britain did, however, send a small, but extremely well equipped force, including nuclear-powered submarines, and dislodged the Argentine invaders in a matter of weeks. In addition the Argentines miscalculated badly when they assumed the US would side with them against the English, although such an assumption was not without basis. President Reagan (1911–2004) had warmly received General Galtieri at the White House when he visited Washington in 1981; the Argentine army was clandestinely training an army of "Contras" to dislodge the victorious Sandinistas from the government of Nicaragua; and the US ambassador to the United Nations, Jean Kirkpatrick, argued publicly, and unsuccessfully, in favor of allying with the Argentines against England. The fiasco of the Malvinas spelled the death knell of the military regime. The nationalist fervor that gripped the nation in April 1982, when the Argentine army strutted its seizure of the islands from its former neocolonial power, had evaporated by June, when the starving army returned to Buenos Aires in humiliating defeat. General Galtieri resigned as head of the junta and his successor promised elections.

In 1983 the Radical Party candidate Raúl Alfonsín Foulkes (1927–2009) won the presidency and began the process of rebuilding the devastated economy and political structures. Alfonsín successfully prosecuted and imprisoned many of the previous military rulers and their collaborators, but was not able to turn around the economy or stem hyperinflation. In 1989 conservative Peronist candidate Carlos Saúl Menem (b. 1930) was elected president. He promptly pardoned many top military officers convicted of human rights violations and adopted a subservient stance toward the neoliberal policies of the IMF and World Bank in hopes of rehabilitating the economy, including a disastrous scheme of pegging the value of the peso directly to the dollar. Not only was Menem personally dishonest, but graft and corruption permeated every branch of his administration. His governments and those that immediately followed oversaw the further demise of Argentina's once rich and stable democracy, until such point that the nation was teetering on the edge of bankruptcy by December 2002.

The movements in pursuit of a socialist alternative in the Southern Cone drew together members of an ethnically homogenous population whose divisions existed along lines of class, urban vs. rural, region and gender. In the Andean countries, on the other hand, popular uprisings have often foundered on ethnic and racial divisions that have persisted from as far back as the colonial era. There have been, however, times when leaders from both sides of the cultural divide have attempted to find common ground to change society.

Movements for Revolutionary Change: Peru

Peru's history with guerrilla struggle dates back to the 1960s, with the emergence of Cuban-inspired Marxist groups similar to those that appeared in other parts of Latin America. Years of intermittent military government, along with the failed experiment of Haya de la Torre's left populism, led progressive reformers to believe that the only way to achieve even a modicum of equality was by embracing a revolutionary Marxist program. In the years after Haya's demise, Trotskyist agronomist Hugo Blanco (b. 1934) attempted to organize a land reform movement in the country around the highland city of Cuzco. Although the program never got off the ground, Hugo Blanco succeeded in leading strikes and land seizures that put the issue of agrarian reform before the government in the 1960s. Failure to win reform through legitimate channels produced the same outcome in Peru as it had in neighboring countries: an insurgent guerrilla movement, uniting intellectuals and some on the left who had been involved in the ongoing struggle for social change. As in Uruguay, Argentina, and Chile, recruits to the new guerrilla movement had grown discontented with the go-slow approach of existing leftist organizations, especially the Peruvian Communist Party.

The most prominent of the 1960s groups was the Army of National Liberation (ELN, *Ejercito de Liberación Nacional*), which attempted to organize the rural peasantry into strategic hamlets capable of attacking the seat of government. By 1970 the ELN had all but disbanded, most of its leadership was in jail, and the remaining militants were unable to convince the moribund Communist Party of the need to adopt a more activist program. While many activists looked to the Cuban model, in hopes of bringing the same transformation to their own country, a small fraction of the Peruvian left was looking further east, to China and its Cultural Revolution (1966–76), as a model for revolutionary change, eventually spawning the most doctrinaire Maoist organizations in the hemisphere.

Sendero Luminoso, The Shining Path

Under the leadership of Abimael Guzmán Reynoso (b. 1934), a philosophy professor at the University of San Cristóbal of Huamanga University in Ayacucho, a city in the central Andean region, a faction of the Communist Party of Peru formed itself into a highly disciplined guerrilla organization that came to be known as *Sendero Luminoso*, or Shining Path. The name derived from a quote from the founder of Peru's Communist Party José Carlos Mariátegui ("Marxism-Leninism will open the shining path to revolution") that appeared on the masthead of the group's newspaper in 1964. The name "Shining Path" was used by outsiders to distinguish the organization from other (pro-Moscow, or pro-Cuba/Guevarist) Peruvian communist parties. In the late 1960s Shining Path emerged as a powerful political force among intellectuals, running for electoral positions at Huamanga, in particular, as well as other universities, and distinguishing itself by its serious application of Marxist ideas to the local university struggle. Eventually the party's rigid sectarianism caused it to fall out of favor among intellectuals, and it left the university milieu to organize among impoverished peasants.

In a society with high poverty rates and disastrously low educational levels, abysmal health care and very weak infrastructure to connect urban and rural areas, Peru's indigenous people were by far the most deprived, isolated, and forgotten members of society. These descendants of the ancient Aymara, Quechua, and other indigenous groups scattered along the Amazon River basin in the far northeast were concentrated in remote villages far from the institutions of European custom and culture. Indicative of the scale of the indigenous presence in the population is the fact that Quechua is one of Peru's two official languages, along with Spanish, and there are many areas of the country where Spanish is seldom spoken. Illiterate and non-conversant in Spanish, Indians who left the countryside in search of work in urban areas found few opportunities and ended up crowded in shantytowns on the outskirts of Lima, Cuzco, Arequipa, Callao, and other cities. It was, however, in the countryside, not urban areas, that Shining Path developed its strongest following.

Shining Path launched its first military operation in May 1980, on the eve of Peru's first national elections in 17 years. The timing of this event illustrates the group's unique politics and differentiates its strategy from those of other guerrilla forces in the hemisphere. Rather than resorting to clandestine actions after legitimate above-ground movement had been suppressed, as was the case in Argentina and Uruguay, Shining Path sought to use the clandestine arena to destroy, or in their words to "expose," the hypocrisy of bourgeois elections. The opening salvo in May 1980 was followed by more than a decade of guerrilla warfare that targeted the police, military, and government officials, as well as large numbers of social reformers, political activists, and managers of state-controlled agricultural collectives. Arguing that even trade unionists, community activists, and human rights workers were supporters of the status quo, Shining Path cadres sought to destroy all vestiges of Peru's European heritage and to replace it with a "pure" rural, communal indigenous society. Throughout the 1980s Shining Path expanded the territory under its control and increased the number of militants in its organization, particularly in the highlands and around Ayacucho. It gained some support from peasants, by publically beating and killing widely disliked figures such as cattle rustlers, tax collectors, and wealthy local merchants. While peasants may have supported the guerrillas' goals, only a small minority ever adopted the strict Maoist dogma emanating from the tiny cadre of leaders clustered around Abimael Guzmán.

At first the national government viewed Shining Path as an aberration, unable to believe that a university professor preaching a Maoist doctrine among non-Spanish-speaking indigenous peasants in remote rural areas would achieve much success. Once the government registered the threat, it launched a brutal and unforgiving attack on the villagers, without bothering to separate Shining Path followers from those who remained neutral or even opposed the guerrillas' tactics. As the military swept through Ayacucho and other regions where Shining Path was known to have sympathizers, arbitrarily arresting, torturing, and raping whomever they encountered, the effect on the peasantry was nothing short of disastrous. Whole villages were wiped out, and many rural dwellers found themselves victims of both *senderista* attacks and military reprisals.

By the mid-1980s Shining Path had moved from the countryside to the cities, stepping up assaults on key infrastructure, industries, and residential neighborhoods in Lima. Beginning in 1983 and continuing over the next decade, the *senderistas* increasingly controlled wide swaths of territory on the outskirts of Lima, stretching into the central and southern regions of the country. From bases in the countryside they attacked urban areas, cut power to whole quarters of Lima, bombed APRA party headquarters, detonated explosives in shopping centers, and set off a huge car bomb in the wealthy neighborhood of Miraflores, which killed over 20 people and injured many more. In addition to targeting government institutions and the wealthy, Shining Path also sought to eliminate those it considered to be competitors for the loyalty of the masses – particularly other leftists, progressives, and human rights activists. It came into conflict with the Túpac Amaru Revolutionary Movement (MRTA), another armed guerrilla organization, and some smaller leftist parties and peasant self-defense groups. In 1991 a Shining Path cadre killed three foreign missionaries (one Italian and two Polish) who were working among the poor in Ancash. In an especially gruesome finale, the guerrillas then exploded the priests' bodies in the center of town. In February 1992, they assassinated María Elena Moyano, a much admired community activist in one of Lima's largest shantytowns. Simultaneously, Shining Path was abandoning whatever socialist, reformist doctrine it had originally espoused and turning into a cultish terrorist organization, grouped around its bizarre and increasingly self-absorbed leader, Abimael Guzmán (called "Comrade Gonzalo").

Women and Shining Path

One of the unique features of the Shining Path guerrilla organization was the high percentage of women cadres. Journalist Robin Kirk conducted an extensive study of the "*senderistas*" and reported that according to Peruvian police intelligence records, of the 19-member Central Committee, eight were women. Compared to other political organizations, clandestine or above-ground, this was a remarkably high number. Women were frequently commanders of army units, carried out attacks on villages, were known to lob dynamite sticks hidden in their shawls at police stations or other targets, and were often designated to carry out the final, execution-style, assassination of Shining Path's captives. According to Kirk, not only was the first guerrilla to fall in battle a woman, but women were in leadership in the military and communication wings of the party. Peruvians, the majority of whom were appalled by the *senderistas*' brutal tactics, were even more at a loss to explain the particularly violent actions of, mainly, indigenous women.

Women may have been drawn to the Shining Path because it provided a sense of purpose and promised to create a better life for them and their children. Moreover, when *senderistas* took control of an area they immediately prohibited drinking, imposed a strict code of discipline for sexual relations between men and women, closed brothels, and outlawed infidelity, gambling, and other vices that were seen to interfere with party discipline and pose security risks. The appeal of a group was considerable when it banned the main scourges indigenous women endured from their husbands and boyfriends – alcoholism, infidelity, and abuse. Possibly women who had faced a lifetime of violence may have welcomed the chance to learn to fight, shoot a gun, and otherwise defend themselves. The party also actively recruited women to its ranks, and, like most revolutionary organizations, argued that women's liberation would come about as a result of their active participation in the struggle. On the other hand, while Abimael Guzmán promoted women's emancipation and wrote frequently of its importance in party dogma, he maintained paternalistic, even patriarchal, control over the women with whom he had contact, to the extent that they were expected to worship "Comrade Gonzalo" and satisfy his sexual demands. In spite of this, the large number of women and girls involved in Shining Path was unprecedented for Latin American guerrilla movements at the time. While many women were involved in the Central American revolutions of the 1980s, even in Nicaragua and El Salvador the number of women leaders never matched those in Shining Path.

Owing to its widely publicized abuse of the population and increasingly brutal military tactics, Shining Path became known far more for its atrocities than its ability to redress the grievances the poor. Caught between two powerful forces – the military and the guerrillas – most Peruvians were hard pressed to decide which was worse. The organization's reprehensible tactics were met with reprisals from local townspeople; men and women organized into anti-Shining Path militias, sometimes retaliating with the same brutal tactics as the guerrillas. Based on a tip from neighbors, the police began monitoring an apartment in Lima, which eventually led to the capture of the Shining Path leadership, including Guzmán himself. By the late 1990s Shining Path militants were in jail, on trial, or had retreated from their activist program and splintered into competing factions, rendering the organization impotent. While the possibility of a resurgence of Shining Path activity cannot be discounted, Peru's attention shifted to the extra-legal activities of its military and government.

Repression and Fujimori

Controversy still swirls around Alberto Fujimori (b. 1938), the man who headed Peru during most of the turbulent era when guerrilla activity was at its height. The debate over Fujimori's leadership revolves around whether the government's tactics were as bad as, or worse than, the tactics of the Shining Path. As far back as the early 1990s, Fujimori promised economic reforms but delivered mainly austerity and indiscriminate repression as a way of quelling the violence that gripped society. A member of Peru's small Asian community, comprised of Chinese and Japanese immigrants, Fujimori was a middle-class entrepreneur who rose in politics through business connections rather than through the military or political parties – the traditional road to national political prominence. As the first Japanese-American to win the highest office in any nation of the Americas, North or South, Fujimori initially was trusted (possibly due to stereotypes of Japanese businessmen as efficient managers) to be the kind of leader who would work diligently to attract foreign investment, create jobs, and otherwise stimulate the economy. This did not prove to be the case. Although elected to three terms, he was ousted from office in November 2000 in the face of widespread corruption charges that extended to his top ministers as well. Offered asylum in Japan, where his family had maintained citizenship rights after emigrating to Peru, Fujimori moved to Tokyo. Despite his continued popularity among many sectors of the population who approved of the draconian measures he enacted to curb the violence, his bid to return to political prominence collapsed when he was detained in Chile and subsequently extradited to Peru for trial. After several delays, the Peruvian Supreme Court in early 2008 found the former president guilty as charged and sentenced him to prison.

Despite the failure of his appeals, Fujimori's fate remains in question because of his continuing popularity among nearly a third of the electorate, and the unpopularity of his successors. Alejandro Toledo (b. 1946) held office from 2001 to 2006, but failed to turn around the economy and to put a stop to endemic corruption. Many Peruvians were particularly disappointed with Toledo's downfall because his rags-to-riches personal story held out hope for a new beginning. Born into an impoverished family with 15 brothers and sisters, Toledo rose to earn a PhD in economics from Stanford University before becoming president. After a hotly contested race in 2006, Alan García (b. 1949), a former APRA president, won office with promises of a new beginning and return to stable governance, despite charges of ineptitude and corruption during his earlier administration.

Conclusion

The focus of this chapter has been primarily political. The struggle to improve education and health care, to provide a social safety net for the chronically unemployed, the disabled, ill, and needy members of society, was taken up in the political arena. Members of different Latin American countries proffered solutions, with greater and lesser degrees of sincerity and practicality, but none succeeded. In the 1980s most of the region was under the boot of repressive military dictatorships or authoritarian regimes. The forces in control of the government answered moderate and radical demands with the same repressive measures, despite the resilient opposition of many sectors of Latin American society. From Mexico to Argentina, the era of student protest, urban guerrilla warfare, and socialism-through-the-ballot-box had burst forth only to be brutally stifled.

By the late twentieth century nationalism had proven the most enduring of the many ideological currents rocking Latin America. But this was the case not because of its cultural and political cohesion among disparate Latin American nations; rather because nationalism reflected widespread wariness, hostility, and suspicion of the United States. Even right-wing governments whose very subsistence depended on foreign aid found it convenient to play the nationalist card when their popularity sagged. The Argentine misadventure at the Falkland/Malvinas Islands in 1982 was a case in point, and a lesson on how easily such schemes could backfire.

For its part, from the end of World War II until the fall of Eastern European communism in 1990, the US justified its interference in Latin American internal affairs as necessary for stopping the spread of communism. Washington readily labeled modest attempts at self-determination, such as Guatemala in 1954, Brazil in 1964, or Chile in 1973, as communist takeovers that threatened the national security interests of the hemisphere. From the Monroe Doctrine of the early nineteenth century to the Roosevelt Corollary a century later, the US defined Latin America's interests as essentially one with US corporations. Falling under the weight of internal opposition as much as external interference, mild reform, violent revolution, and social democracy failed in Mexico, in huge Brazil, in cosmopolitan Argentina and Uruguay, and in neighboring

Chile. Peru fell into a brutal and distorted revolutionary conflict with little clear difference between the side seeking social change and the one enforcing the status quo. Nevertheless, in a few tiny countries of Central America rural and urban youth once again embraced the Guevarist strategy in a new attempt to wrest power from the traditional oligarchy. The next chapter looks at the success and failure of those insurgencies.

13 | Revolution and Its Alternatives

Late twentieth-century Latin Americans debated who constituted the nation and who were the rightful owners of the continent's national identity. Were the people of this vast continent moving toward a compatible mixture of race and ethnicity, or remaining mired in irreconcilable differences between Europeans, Indians, Africans, and their mixed descendants? More importantly, how could the social inequality stemming from regional, class, and ethnic difference disappear? The left embraced Marxist socialism, some form of revolutionary anti-imperialism, or state intervention to alleviate inequality, while the right argued for neoliberalism, free markets, and privatization, sometimes to enrich the entrenched elite, but in many cases as the only way to clean up corrupt bureaucracies.

A battle over religion was also raging. This current pitted liberation theology and Christian community activism on the left against fundamentalist Protestant evangelicalism on the right. These ideological impulses – Marxism versus neoliberalism, liberation theology versus evangelical Protestantism – were not, however, clearly demarcated. Not all evangelicals sided with the political right, and although liberation theologians leaned left, not all embraced Marxism. Even interpretations of Marxism varied; some of the left-wing guerrilla organizations were more dogmatic in their acceptance of socialist and communist ideology than others.

Previous chapters have demonstrated that as long as the United States was locked in conflict with the Soviet Union, and Cuba remained a Soviet ally just 90 miles away, US governments of both liberal and conservative persuasion were willing to overlook human rights violations in return for strict loyalty to the US agenda. The best guarantee of such allegiance had always been military dictatorships maintained by generous military aid, training, and arms supplies from the United States. From the 1960s through the early 1990s Central America (with the notable exception of Costa Rica) became the battleground for this fierce ideological war, the result of which was to push already impoverished peoples – primarily in Nicaragua, El Salvador, and Guatemala – toward even greater misery and devastation. Particularly in Nicaragua and El Salvador, leading activists in the Catholic Church spoke out against these trends, inserting a new activist religiosity into politics.

A Changing Catholic Church

The Central American wars formed the backdrop for a profound shift in priorities in Latin America's Catholic Church. Beginning in the 1960s and peaking during the 1980s, a large number of working clergy turned away from the Church's traditional alignments with the powerful elites, ignored threats from the Vatican (and often their own hierarchy) to avoid radical movements, and instead took up the struggle for equality and rights for the poor. Catholic activism in support of social change profoundly influenced guerrilla movements in Nicaragua, El Salvador, and Guatemala, introducing a moral and spiritual justification that had not been part of previous guerrilla uprisings, especially in Cuba. Throughout Latin America and the Caribbean, a wing of the Church surfaced as a powerful ideological force in the struggle to end authoritarian regimes.

This new theology, referred to as the "Theology of Liberation," had its strongest expression in Brazil, Nicaragua, and El Salvador. Throughout history individual priests and nuns have chosen to minister to the poor and call attention to injustice. Outstanding examples include Father Bartolomé de las Casas's condemnation of Indian slavery in the sixteenth century and the insurrections led by Fathers Hidalgo and Morelos in nineteenth-century Mexico in defense of indigenous people, among others. But for the most part, the Catholic Church hierarchy had not sided with the poor. Indeed, on a number of occasions the Church had strongly opposed social reforms instituted by secular authorities – from *caudillos* of the nineteenth century to authoritarian presidents and military dictators of the twentieth. The Catholic Church played almost no role in opposing the slavery of Africans, a practice that endured for several centuries in Brazil and other parts of Latin America. In impoverished Indian and mestizo parishes priests charged for services such as weddings, baptisms, and funerals no matter the financial burden placed on grieving families. The Church historically opposed rights for women, intervening repeatedly to prevent women from obtaining reproductive rights as well as the rights to divorce, vote, and have freedom from abusive fathers and husbands. Instead, the Catholic Church concentrated its efforts on the administration of orphanages, hospitals, schools, and an extensive network of charities that serviced the needy. At the same time, the Church's wealth was apparent everywhere. Grandiose and elaborately decorated cathedrals, often built by conscripted Indian and slave labor, towered over the center of even the smallest town. Priests and bishops lived well, dined with the aristocracy, and routinely considered themselves a part of the elite of the towns and cities of the empire, and later of the region's independent republics.

Transformation in the Latin American Church stemmed from the liberal climate encouraged by the Second Vatican Council, convened in 1962 under Pope John XXIII (1881–1963). Beginning as a reform movement at the center of the Church in Rome, and instigated in no small part because the Church was in desperate need of modernizing both its theory and its practice to hold onto its following, Vatican II swept away many feudal customs and outdated ideas. It transformed the distant and impersonal Latin Mass, eliminated the more mystical saints, and generally attempted to pull Church doctrine more into line with modern social conditions and problems. Because Pope John XXIII led the modernizing process, calling the first ecumenical council in over 400 years, and guiding the Church in a new direction that included the needs of the poor and oppressed, Vatican II carried enormous weight.

Although Vatican II did not embrace the socialist principles that came to be associated with liberation theology – and John XXIII excommunicated Fidel Castro for his embrace of Marxism – it did call into question the Church's traditional alliance with elites and oppressive governments. Moreover, the ecumenical movement within the Church provided an opening for the "working clergy," those who had daily contact with the poor and saw first-hand their conditions, to push the hierarchy to adopt a more activist, reformist position. This group argued that the Church needed to divorce itself from its alliance with the rich and the powerful and to commit itself instead to the struggle for social justice and to the task of raising the awareness of the masses and making them understand that they need not endure abuse in order to win salvation. Activist priests, nuns, and lay people were determined to unite as Christians and use the power of the Church to change oppressive economic and political systems.

Years earlier, the Colombian priest Camilo Torres (1929–66), convinced that guerrilla movements were the only way to stop oppressive governments, joined the communist-led guerrilla National Liberation Army of Colombia. Arguing that he was still a Catholic and therefore could not be a communist, nor could he accept atheism, Father Torres nonetheless joined the guerrillas because they were the only group that was fighting effectively against hunger, illiteracy, and poverty. He believed in revolutionary change, going so far as to say, "the Revolution is not only permitted but is obligatory for all Christians who see in it the most effective way of making possible a greater *love for all men*" (emphasis in original).[1] Father Torres's association with the guerrilla movement was a radical break from his upbringing. He was from a very aristocratic, landowning family, and had joined the priesthood and developed a reputation as a scholar and teacher before he began to move to the left. He died in February 1966 in a battle with the Colombian military, having participated in a movement that did not succeed in producing enduring change. Camilo Torres was nonetheless an inspirational figure, remembered as a poet and an idealist, and something of a path breaker for the role he played in proposing a radical alternative for Catholic activists.

Marxism and Catholic Humanism

Father Torres was the forerunner of a new breed of religious activists that was cropping up in the midst of social struggles throughout the world, including South Africa, the Philippines, and the United States. It was in Latin America, however, that Marxist socialist ideology mixed with radical grass-roots Catholic theory and practice to produce a powerful new ideology. In Latin America, Jesuits tended to be at the forefront of the movement for social justice. As early as 1962 they published a newspaper *Mensaje* (the Message) in Santiago, Chile, warning that the people were tired of waiting for social change and calling for a swift and thorough overhaul of the system. *Mensaje*, while stopping short of directly advocating a socialist program, nonetheless praised Marxists for their efforts in attempting to create social equality.

The term "liberation theology" is thought to have developed in 1964 at a meeting of Latin American theologians held in Petrópolis, near Rio de Janeiro, Brazil, at which Peruvian theologian Gustavo Gutiérrez (b. 1928) defined religious ideology, or theology, as a reflection on practice rather than as an interpretation of revealed truth and scripture. The term "liberation theology" appeared in various teachings, but became the label for the new movement when Gutierrez's book, *A Theology of Liberation: History, Politics, Salvation*, was published in multiple languages in 1971. Soon an outpouring of writings appeared from other theologians, among them Brazil's Leonardo Boff (b. 1938), Ignacio Ellacuría (1930–89) in El Salvador, and Ernesto Cardenal (b. 1925) in Nicaragua, interpreting and extending the meaning of the new doctrine.

At the Second General Conference of Latin American Episcopacy (CELAM, Consejo Episcopal Latino Americano) in Medellín, Colombia in 1968, religious activists urged the bishops to accept the doctrine of "preferential option for the poor" as a strategy for liberating the masses. Although the doctrine did not reject work among members of any social class, the emphasis on defending the poor as the direction for pastoral work was a clear departure from past church practices, and also broke from the fundamental classless theology on which Catholicism was based. Liberation theologians pushed practice as a way of recognizing theory, organizing the faithful into Christian Base Communities (CEBs). These grass-roots organizations brought the poor together to study scripture as a guide to enacting social change. Thus Christ's teachings, along with socialist tracts, might form the basis for a lesson in a CEB, which in turn would organize community members to demand land, water rights, better wages, an end to abuse, or to address other grievances affecting participants.

Liberation theologians never accepted socialist doctrine in its entirety, nor did they reject it, as did the Vatican. One of the most important prelates in Latin America, Archbishop Hélder Câmara (1909–99) of Recife, issued a statement in 1968 signed by 25 bishops from throughout the developing world, declaring that socialism and Christianity were not incompatible doctrines, calling on the Church to speak out against the oppression of the poor, and rejecting the systems of "feudalism, capitalism and imperialism." This statement inspired many of the most left-wing among the liberation theologians to identify with socialism. In a pastoral letter in July 1970, Bishop Sergio Méndez Arceo (1907–92) of Cuernavaca, Mexico stated, "I believe that a socialist system best conforms to Christian principles of true brotherhood, justice, and peace." Méndez Arceo became known as the "Red Bishop." Despite the Vatican's general hostility toward the leftward push in the Latin American Church, Pope Paul VI (1897–1978) tried to strike a conciliatory tone in his speech at the opening session of the Medellín Bishops' Conference by denouncing the "international imperialism of money." The final statement affirmed the commitment of the Church to the task of liberating the people of Latin America from neocolonialism and "institutionalized violence," a stance that left the door open to cooperation with leftist movements pushing for a radical social agenda. In April 1972 over 400 people, including 200 priests, came together in the first convention of Christians for Socialism in Santiago, Chile. Drawing on the teachings of the Jesuit theologian Thomas Aquinas, they argued that violent revolution may be necessary to overthrow tyrants. Archbishop Oscar Romero (1917–80), who became the movement's leading martyr after his assassination in El Salvador by right-wing death squads, stated in one of his last sermons: "When all peaceful means have been exhausted, the Church considers insurrection moral and justified."[2]

The Opposition

Many people from all levels of the Church viewed this trend of Christian socialism and religious-based political activism with everything from skepticism to outright hostility. In 1978 a new pope, John Paul II (1920–2005), a Polish cardinal possibly less sympathetic to the leftist clergy, began to alter the Vatican's approach to the Latin American Church. While outwardly accepting many of the ideas of the liberation theologians, he disciplined, demoted, and censored activist priests. For example, at the Third CELAM meeting in Puebla, Mexico in 1978 he stated that the Church condemns the "situation of inhuman poverty in which millions of Latin Americans live, with starvation wages, unemployment and underemployment, malnutrition, infant mortality, lack of adequate housing, health problems, and labor unrest." He told a gathering of 40,000 Indians in Oaxaca that "you have a right to be respected and not deprived of the little you have, often by methods that amount to plunder," a clear slap at the Mexican government. At the same time, he publicly reprimanded Father Ernesto Cardenal, a Trappist monk, prominent advocate of liberation theology, and a member of the Sandinista government in Nicaragua, on a visit there in 1980, and called the radical priest Father Leonardo Boff from Brazil to a hearing at the Vatican and stripped him of his authority. Boff subsequently left the priesthood. The Vatican's most outspoken critic of liberation theology was Cardinal Joseph Ratzinger (now Pope Benedict XVI; b. 1927), who saw radical priests as defying the power of Rome and rejecting the hierarchy on which the Church depended. As a cardinal, Ratzinger dismissed the "option for the poor" as exclusionary and contrary to the mission of religion to address the needs of everyone: "All human beings are poor. All people need spiritual sustenance; some need material sustenance also"[3] (1986).

The Somozas versus Sandino: the Next Generation

From the 1960s through the early 1990s, the struggle between left and right played out fiercely in Nicaragua. On the one side was a leftist liberation movement that included Cuban-backed Marxists, Catholic priests and religious workers influenced by liberation theology, nationalist, middle-class advocates for change, and large numbers of impoverished workers and peasants desperate for an end to their misery. On the other was a longstanding, entrenched dictatorship, powerful military, conservative Catholic hierarchy, and tiny oligarchy strongly backed by the US. The conflicts that ravaged Nicaragua were the final chapter in the struggle for sovereignty Augusto César Sandino had begun decades earlier (see Chapter 9).

Following Sandino's assassination in 1934 and subsequent consolidation of the Somoza family dynasty, the potential for Nicaraguan sovereignty and improved conditions for its people all but disappeared. While Nicaragua had no major export products that garnered a high price on the international market – relying as it did on coffee, sugar, cotton, and timber – the needs of its population of just 2.7 million could have been met on the basis of this revenue. However, the Somoza family was stealing the nation's income and natural wealth out from under the people. By 1936 Anastásio Somoza García had consolidated his power, organized around his own personal military group called the Blue Shirts. An admirer of Mussolini and Hitler, Somoza employed his paramilitary shock troops to break up demonstrations and strikes, and to threaten, apprehend, jail, rough up, or kill anyone who persisted in opposing his methods. Somoza García remained in the presidency until 1956, when a young poet assassinated him. He was succeeded by his son, Luís Somoza Debayle, and eventually by his grandson, Anastásio Somoza Debayle, who held power until he was ousted in 1979. Except for a few years when caretaker presidents held office, Somozas directly controlled the presidency and the National Guard for over 40 years.

By 1970 the Somoza family controlled about 25 percent of agriculture and a large proportion of industry, leaving their wealth estimated at $500 million in a country where annual per-capita income was just $256. This level of extreme control had always generated an opposition, but it grew more vocal in the 1960s. Middle-class entrepreneurs, professionals, and small landholders, and even a scattering of large landowners, resented the petty regulations and constant shakedowns in the form of bribes and "gifts" to the family to obtain standard services. The working class chafed under repressive labor policies, and the majority of poor and landless peasants, well over 50 percent of the population, grew increasingly desperate as they faced year after year of hunger, disease, and poverty. In addition, Catholic priests and nuns, who in the past had sided with the elite, began to raise criticisms of the degradation endured by the country's majority.

The Sandinista Opposition

In 1961 three university students and political activists, Carlos Fonseca (1936–76), Silvio Mayorga (1936–67), and Tomás Borge (b. 1930), formed the Sandinista National Liberation Front (FSLN, *Frente Sandinista de Liberación Nacional*), named for Augusto Sandino, the hero of the anti-US campaign of the 1930s. The FSLN, also known as the Sandinistas or simply the *Frente*, attracted support from trade unions, community groups, peasants, women, youth and religious organizations, and eventually formed a guerrilla wing centered in mountainous areas outside the major cities of Managua, Masaya, and

León. The FSLN was in the foreground of popular consciousness inside and outside the country. As the guerrilla movement's stature rose, Somoza's declined, leading some observers to wonder if the old dictator had outlasted his staying power.

The first event was a massive earthquake in December 1972 that killed 10,000 people, destroyed the entire center of the capital of Managua, reduced to rubble most homes, businesses, and hospitals, and left thousands without water, electricity, housing, or medical care. In response to the catastrophe, more than 25 countries sent millions of dollars in aid, although by early 1973 international relief agencies reported that much of the aid was not reaching the victims. As with other high-profile disasters, celebrities jumped in to raise money for the relief effort, including the Rolling Stones who raised $350,000 at a benefit concert in London in early 1973. The Stones rarely performed benefits, but this time they did so at the request of lead singer Mick Jagger's then wife and native of Nicaragua, Bianca Morena Jagger (b. 1950). Major League baseball player, Roberto Clemente (1934–72), a native of Puerto Rico, became intensely involved in raising money and assistance for the earthquake victims, but died when the small plane in which he was transporting goods crashed.

The earthquake and the international relief effort it spawned served to focus attention on Nicaragua, and thus on the corrupt practices of the Somoza government. International criticism of the regime mounted as it became clear that Somoza had funneled relief money into his own pockets, using it to buy up land around the capital and then selling it at a profit to proprietors looking to restart their businesses. Pedro Joaquín Chamorro (1924–78), an outspoken critic of the regime from one the country's oldest families and editor of La Prensa, Nicaragua's leading newspaper, published a series of articles revealing a scheme by which Somoza was profiting from selling abroad blood plasma intended for earthquake victims. La Prensa's exposé of Somoza's bold-faced graft was particularly effective because the newspaper and its editor were highly respected at home and abroad. Criticism turned to outrage when in January 1978 gunmen killed Chamorro at point-blank range as he was traveling through the ruins of Managua. Since no one doubted Somoza's role in the popular editor's assassination, the event provoked a widespread outcry in Nicaragua. Many people argued that if a man of such high social standing could be killed, then no critic was safe from Somoza's henchmen. Nora Astorga (1948–88), a young lawyer who in her twenties worked initially clandestinely and later as a part of the guerrilla command, commented on the impact of Chamorro's death:

> I finally understood that armed struggle was the only solution, that a rifle cannot be met with a flower, that we were in the streets, but if that force didn't get organized we wouldn't achieve much . . . For me, it was the moment of conviction: either I took up arms and made a total commitment or I wasn't going to change anything.[4]

Meanwhile the Sandinistas had demonstrated enormous success in mobilizing international support for their campaign to oust Somoza and were enjoying widespread approval within the country. In December 1974 the Frente stormed a Christmas party at the house of one of Managua's leading politicians where hundreds of the wealthiest people in the country, including Somoza himself, the US ambassador to Nicaragua, and other friends of the regime were in attendance. Surrounding the party, the guerrillas took 40 guests hostage, who they traded for a $5 million ransom, the release of 15 political prisoners, and safe passage to Havana. Although Somoza and the US ambassador had already left the party, the guerrillas' ability to penetrate the mansion's tight security system – and the later revelation that it was actually the daughter of the host, a clandestine *Frente* sympathizer, who had provided access – caused many in high circles to doubt Somoza's chances of defeating the guerrillas.

In August 1978, eight months after Chamorro's assassination, the world's attention was again drawn to a spectacular Sandinista action. On a sunny morning in August, 25 guerrillas surrounded and invaded the National Palace under the command of a brilliant military strategist, Edén Pastora (b. 1937), known as *Comandante Cero* (Commander Zero, his code name for the operation). Disguised as National Guardsmen, they killed the real Guards, seized most members of the Chamber of Deputies as it was in session (including Somoza's half-brother), and held them and some 2,000 public employees for ransom. Before the hostages were released, the *Frente* had obtained the freedom and safe passage to Panama for 59 of their comrades and a ransom in the millions of dollars. Just as the year before the death of Pedro Chamorro had signaled that no one was safe from Somoza's assassins, the August seizure of the National Palace revealed that the Sandinistas were able to penetrate the inner reaches of the government, that they had widespread support in Nicaragua, and that a neighboring country, Panama, was willing to provide refuge. In fact, most Latin American governments were concluding that Somoza was in his final days.

As the Sandinista armies, a number of them under the command of female officers, encircled the capital of Managua in late June 1979 (Figure 13.1), US President Jimmy Carter made a final appeal to the OAS to send a peacekeeping force to Managua to negotiate power away from the FSLN and force them to include business and political elements friendly to Somoza in the new government. Much to the embarrassment of the US envoy, the OAS unanimously refused to cooperate; the US failed even to win the support of staunch allies such as the dictators of the Dominican Republic, Honduras, Chile, and Argentina. Finally, when a National Guardsman was caught on camera shooting a correspondent for *Time* magazine, the Carter Administration withdrew its support. Somewhat contemptuously, Nicaraguans pointed out that Somoza's National Guard had killed thousands of their fellow citizens with bullets supplied by the US government, but it took just one photograph of the Guard killing a US citizen for decades of military and political support to come to a halt. On July 16 Somoza received asylum in Stroessner's Paraguay, where he lived until his assassination in 1980 at the hands of a faction of the Argentine guerrilla movement. The bulk of Somoza's National Guard retreated to neighboring Honduras, after first bombing much of the country. The FSLN and its allies entered Managua on July 18, 1979, and were greeted with a gigantic celebration.

When the euphoria receded, the triumphant guerrillas faced the Herculean task of rebuilding a country devastated by a war that had killed 50,000 people (2 percent of the population), and wreaked destruction estimated at $1.3 billion, including large

Figure 13.1   Sandinista soldiers at a barricade outside Matagalpa, Nicaragua, during the last days of the fighting. The victorious army entered the capital of Managua on July 19, 1979. (Susan Meiselas/Magnum Photos)

sections of the ruined capital city that had never recovered from the earthquake nearly five years earlier. When they entered the offices of the president, the new leaders discovered that Somoza had looted the national treasury of $1.6 billion, most of which he deposited in US banks. Nicaragua never managed to retrieve the bulk of the stolen treasury from uncooperative US banks, despite Somoza's frequent presence in Miami.

Sandinistas in Power

The Sandinistas quickly announced a nine-member coalition government, comprised of Marxist FSLN leaders, including Tomás Borge, the only founding member of the *Frente* to have survived the war, two bankers, two Catholic priests who had lived for years in the US, and Violeta Chamorro (b. 1929), widow of the slain newspaper editor. Daniel Ortega Saavedra (b. 1945), the leader of the Sandinista political wing, headed the government, while his brother Humberto (b. 1942) commanded the armed forces. Moving cautiously, and hopeful of obtaining support from the US and Western European democracies, the revolutionary government eschewed some of the more drastic steps that had characterized the early days of the Cuban Revolution. It outlawed capital punishment and instituted a program to "rehabilitate" any members of the Nicaraguan military who wished to remain in the country, so long as they were loyal to the new government.

The ruling coalition introduced a mixed public–private capitalist economy, maintaining 60 percent of all holdings in private hands; began a process of land reform that sought to distribute 80 percent of the land to small farmers; and left 75 percent of manufacturing under private ownership. The new rules also included payment of minimum wages, regulated working hours, safety practices, maternity leave, child care, and pensions. These measures immediately generated opposition from both landowners and manufacturers, who claimed that it was impossible to manage their business without the freedom to impose their own conditions. Over the next few years, workers and owners entered into a long series of disputes over what constituted acceptable living and working conditions. In defiance of the government, some firms closed and owners took their capital with them to the United States or elsewhere; others scaled back production in hopes of waiting out the government and/or sabotaged production. By 1983 Nicaragua was experiencing an 11.7 percent decline in the output of private industry, and 44 firms had abandoned the country. When domestic and international firms shut down, arguing that paying a living wage cut into their profits, the US government and media accused the Sandinistas of unfairly limiting the freedom of corporate and business interests. When firms and landowners left their property behind, the Nicaraguan government took them over and ran them either as agricultural cooperatives or state-owned businesses, generating further accusations from domestic conservatives and external critics.

By 1980 more than 50,000 workers had been added to the state sector, accounting for 20 percent of coffee production, 15 percent of cotton, and 15 percent of livestock. During 1979–80 the state moved immediately to stimulate small enterprise: private farmers accounted for 87.2 percent of production of maize, 79.1 percent of beans, 73 percent of livestock, 30 percent of cotton, and 18 percent of coffee. Despite accusations that Nicaragua was massively collectivizing and driving out individual entrepreneurs, the majority of land ownership and production remained in private hands. Nonetheless, a small country like Nicaragua, which had for its entire modern existence been oriented toward exporting primary goods, is always vulnerable to variations in international prices and demand and natural disasters that affect supply. Shortly after the triumph of the revolution, Nicaragua was faced with a fall in global sugar prices, followed by floods in 1982 and drought later that year that destroyed or limited agricultural output, especially coffee. The major threat to economic stability, however, was the war on Nicaragua by CIA-funded counter-insurgents, made up primarily of former National Guard officers (see Box 13.1). This force, known as the "Contras," was never strong enough to win, a fact that the CIA always admitted; however, it wreaked havoc on the economic and political life of Nicaragua from the early 1980s until the election of 1990.

Despite its many problems, after just a few years the revolution had begun to show significant gains. A 1983 United Nations survey of conditions in Nicaragua showed real improvement, including a 40 percent increase in individual food consumption, 50 percent reduction in urban rents, doubling of school enrollment, and a 28.7 percent reduction in infant mortality rates. That same year Nicaragua was awarded UNESCO's

Box 13.1   The new face of Sandinismo: Nora Astorga

During the many years of war against Somoza, a number of women rose to prominent positions in the FSLN leadership. One of the most daring was Nora Astorga.
A lawyer, politician, judge, and later Nicaragua's Ambassador to the United Nations
(1986–8), Astorga was the poster child for the empowerment of women
involved in guerrilla struggles. Born to a prosperous, conservative, religious
family in Managua, Astorga shocked her parents when she refused to support
Anastasio Somoza in 1967. Although she was sent to study in the United States
in hopes of changing her mind politically, the visit seems to have had the opposite effect. She returned to Nicaragua and became a lawyer in a government
ministry, providing information to the Sandinistas. Astorga gained national,
even international, prominence as a pivotal figure in the assassination of General
Pérez Vega, deputy commander of the National Guard, one of Somoza's closest
military advisors, and a man widely known for his brutal tactics. On March 8,
1978, (International Women's Day) Astorga finally agreed to Pérez Vega's
persistent entreaties for a sexual liaison. In a prearranged trap, she invited him
to her house where three Sandinista commanders seized him from her bedroom.
While the plan had been to hold the general for ransom, he put up such a
struggle that he was murdered. No longer safe as an above-ground operative,
Astorga left that day to join the Sandinista command in the mountains.

After the victory, Nora Astorga served as Vice Minister of Justice presiding over
the trials of former National Guardsmen. President Ronald Reagan rejected her
1984 appointment as Nicaragua's Ambassador to the US because of her role in
Pérez Vega's death (the general had been a CIA informant). So Astorga became
ambassador to the UN, where she was instrumental in gaining support for a World
Court decision that declared US support of the Contras illegal. Nora Astorga died
of cancer in 1988. Asked if she regretted her role in Pérez Vega's death, she replied,
"It was not murder. He was too much of a monster . . . He really was a monster.
I understood his death as part of the liberation struggle."

From "Nora Astorga In Her Own Words," *Revista Envío* (Digital), No. 82, April 1988.

top prize for its literacy campaign. Prior to 1979 half of all adults were illiterate; the
number dropped to 12 percent by 1983. These improvements came about in several
ways. In the first place, copying the successful literacy program initiated in Cuba after
the 1959 revolution, Nicaragua called for educated volunteers from urban areas to travel
to remote villages throughout the country to teach basic literacy. Not only were peasants and workers anxious to learn, they studied hard, displayed enormous motivation,
and learned quickly. Maintaining high literacy levels was harder, since the state needed
to establish schools and supply paid teachers everywhere in Nicaragua, a task that
required investment and expertise beyond the parameters of the first literacy movement.

Second, Nicaragua benefited from an outpouring of material aid, volunteers, and expertise from individuals in Europe, Japan, and the United States. Members of the large Nicaraguan exile community in the US held fundraisers for organizations back home; some returned to bring money and goods to relatives or to work in construction and education projects. Volunteers from foreign-based human rights, progressive and religious organizations, as well as doctors, nurses, and college students traveled to Nicaragua to show solidarity with the attempts to improve the health, education, and general welfare of the people. Typical was a nurse from a small town in upstate New York who recruited volunteers from her local health maintenance organization to contribute medicines and spend their vacation time in rural villages of the highlands, helping to coordinate vaccination programs. In addition, the Netherlands, Scandinavian countries, and Canada entered into formal agreements with the new government, providing loans and other financial assistance, as well as teams of medical personnel, agronomists, educators, and engineers.

The largest amount of assistance on a state-to-state level came from Cuba. Naturally delighted at the victory of another guerrilla force in Latin America, especially one with some leaders that embraced Marxism and anti-imperialism, Cuba was anxious to solidify its ties with Nicaragua as a way of breaking out of its own isolation. Throughout the decades of fighting, the Cuban government had provided political advice, military training, material aid, exile, and a place for guerrillas to take an occasional break from the war. Defining Nicaragua's relations with Cuba, however, was an extremely sensitive matter for the Sandinistas, who knew that close association with Cuba – even accepting medical aid – would antagonize the US and serve as justification for opposing the new government. Because the standard complaint of the US toward Cuba was that Fidel Castro did not stand for election, the Sandinistas were careful to hold elections. In 1984 Daniel Ortega won the presidency with 60 percent of the vote, a slightly higher margin than Ronald Reagan's (1911–2004) victory over Walter Mondale (b. 1928) the same year.

United States and the Sandinistas

Relations with the US were strained from the very beginning. Following the Sandinista victory, during the remaining six months of the Carter Administration, the US maintained an embassy; maintained cordial relations, including trade; and offered a loan of $75 million – exclusively for the private sector. When the Reagan Administration entered office in January 1980, however, it adopted a hostile tone toward Nicaragua – including placing a freeze on the $15 million left on the loan, but not breaking off relations. However, the Reagan White House immediately set about undermining the government by arming and training a group of soldiers (mostly from Somoza's National Guard) on bases in Honduras, from which they launched a "secret war" to overthrow the Sandinistas. The blatant illegality of the move, as well as widespread disagreement with the policy among the American population, eventually led Congress to cut off all funding for the Contras.

Since Congress had cut off money for military aid to the Contras, a particularly important project of President Ronald Reagan, the Office of National Security devised a secret plan to sell weapons to Iran, a country with which the US had no diplomatic relations, as a way of obtaining the release of a group of American hostages. Originally the transactions passed through Israel, but later they were negotiated directly between the US administration and Iran. Under the direction of Marine Lieutenant Colonel Oliver North (b. 1943), the weapons were marked up anywhere from 15 to 40 percent, thereby rendering a healthy profit that could be funneled to the Contras and more than compensated for the funds the Democratic-controlled Congress had ended. For its part, Iran was willing to pay any price for arms to carry out its six-year-long war with Iraq, a war in which the US, ironically, was supplying President Saddam Hussein's (1937–2006) Iraqi military.

By 1986 the operation, called the Iran–Contra affair or sometimes Irangate, was fully exposed and laid out before the American public in a series of televised Congressional hearings in which Oliver North; his boss, Admiral John Poindexter (b. 1936); Reagan's National Security Advisor, Secretary of Defense Casper Weinberger (1917–2006); CIA Director William Casey (1913–87); Undersecretary of State for Latin American Affairs, Elliott Abrams (b. 1948); and other officials of the Reagan White House detailed, denied, protested, and parried their role in the remarkable scheme in response to the committee's questions. Eventually the office of Special Prosecutor Lawrence Walsh brought the principals in the case to trial, but the convictions of Oliver North and John Poindexter were overturned on appeal on technical grounds, and Casper Weinberger and others were pardoned by President George H. W. Bush (b. 1924), who had been vice-president under Reagan. CIA Director Casey died of a brain tumor, and several others of those convicted, such as Elliott Abrams (whose role in the affair was that he flew to London using a fake name and passport to solicit a $10 million contribution for the Contras from the Sultan of Brunei) were pardoned. Abrams was subsequently appointed deputy national security advisor for the Near East in the administration of George Bush (b. 1946).

For years President Reagan denied any knowledge of the Iran–Contra affair, leaving him open to accusations of negligence, but not necessarily wrongdoing. Eventually, on March 4, 1987 in a televised press conference the President admitted his knowledge of the scheme, stated that his previous assertion that the US did not trade arms for hostages was inaccurate, and said that Vice-President Bush (a former director of the CIA) knew of the plan. Reagan's personal popularity with the electorate undermined the Democratic opposition's political will to punish any wrongdoing.

Effects of the Contra War

The Contras were never successful in overturning the Nicaraguan government, but they did succeed in disrupting society, destroying infrastructure, bleeding the life out of the revolution, and exhausting the population to the extent that Daniel Ortega lost the presidency in February 1990. The United States donated over $300 million to opposition candidate Violeta Chamorro, an early member of the Sandinista directorate who later parted ways with the leadership and went on to win the election. Initially observers inside and outside Nicaragua were astounded at the Sandinistas' defeat, but in the weeks after the elections the underlying motives became clearer. First, voters believed that Chamorro's election was the country's only way to end the Contra war. Second, internal strife exacerbated divisions among the leadership, leading to accusations that the Ortegas were enriching themselves while the majority of Nicaraguans lived in deprivation. The fact that many Sandinistas had come from prosperous families and could move back into sumptuous homes angered many and sowed dissension.

Gioconda Belli (b. 1948), in her account of the struggle, *The Country Under My Skin*, places the blame for many of the Sandinistas' failures on the Ortegas and other members of the inner leadership whose arrogance, sexism, and self-importance separated them from the day-to-day life of ordinary people. Ultimately, many who had hoped for change saw only defeat, arguing that the only way out was to reach a compromise with the Contras and attempt to salvage what was left of the reforms. Even with widespread international support, including victories at the World Court and United Nations that found the US culpable of carrying out illegal acts of aggression against the tiny country, many Nicaraguans felt they could never effectively fight off the anti-Sandinista forces within the country. For many people, the prospect of peace was a powerful incentive and, they argued, electing Violeta Chamorro president did not mean a return to the Somoza regime.

Under her presidency the war against the Contras ended immediately, and Chamorro was able to negotiate for foreign aid and loans from the IMF and Inter-American Development Bank. Consistent with the neoliberal economic policy that triumphed in the post-Cold War years, bankers advocated a development strategy based on privatization of resources and massive cuts to social services. Real wages, never adequate in the past, fell and unemployment rose to the point that the CIA World Factbook lists the distribution of income in Nicaragua as one of the most unequal on the planet. Absolute poverty, malnutrition, preventable disease, and illiteracy have increased in the last decade, while the country's meager resources have been devoted to servicing the debt. Adding to these woes, in October 1998 Hurricane Mitch, one of the deadliest hurricanes in Atlantic history, caused massive death and destruction, exacerbating the longstanding state of disrepair in Nicaragua's infrastructure after previous natural catastrophes and the Contra war.

A key Reagan Administration rationale for funding the Contras rested on its claim that the Sandinistas were assisting rebels in El Salvador, the Farabundo Martí National Liberation Front (FMLN), who were trying to overthrow a corrupt military dictatorship. Although Nicaragua consistently denied the claim and the US never proved it, the assertion worked well enough with the US Congress to allow the White House to pursue its semi-legal, and even illegal, war. Later the Sandinistas admitted that they did aid the FMLN initially, asserting that it was their right to assist a neighboring country and that the overthrow of the Salvadoran dictatorship was necessary for their own revolution to survive.

Central America in Turmoil: El Salvador and Guatemala

Like Nicaragua, El Salvador is a very small country that has long suffered from gross income inequalities. It was ruled by a tiny elite and thrust into the very center of international policymaking because of the guerrilla war that raged from the 1970s until 1992. With a population of almost seven million people in a space about the size of Massachusetts, El Salvador is the most densely populated nation of the region. The poor own less than two percent of the land, and the most productive acreage is in the hands of the country's so-called "Fourteen Families," the economic and political elite. Like Nicaragua, El Salvador's treasury depends heavily on a small number of agricultural exports, especially coffee, sugar, beans, and corn, as well as processed foods and textiles.

While El Salvador and Nicaragua were both essentially police states, they differed in key ways, and should also be seen in contrast to neighboring Guatemala. The Somoza dynasty operated essentially as a stand-in for the United States, like Rafael Trujillo in the Dominican Republic and Fulgencio Batista in Cuba. These military men were not part of the elite, nor had they risen to power as a result of their relationship with wealthy landowners, many of whom scorned them as crude upstarts. Rather, they achieved their positions based on their subservience to the United States military, each having been personally selected for his position by a US envoy. The prescient comment of Franklin Roosevelt in reference to Anastásio Somoza sums up the relationship: "He may be a son of a bitch, but he's our son of a bitch."

In both El Salvador and Guatemala, however, the ruling elite had evolved as a force in their own right, not as a stand-in for the US. As a result, the local oligarchy had generated their own loyal armies and ruled with the interests of their class at the forefront, although they were quick to call on the US (as Guatemala's elite did in 1954) if they proved unable to manage their affairs alone. El Salvador's Fourteen Families had retained control, without much assistance or concern from the US, for most of the twentieth century. They had put down the peasant uprising of 1932 without outside assistance, while the ominous memory of Farabundo Martí's popularity galvanized them. Guatemala had far more involvement with the US than El Salvador, but, with the exception of the short experiments with democracy under Arévalo and Arbenz in the 1940s and 1950s, Guatemala's oligarchy was in charge of its own military affairs. And just as the Salvadoran elite remembered in horror the uprising of 1932, so too the Guatemalan counterparts had memories of the late 1940s and early 1950s. These attempts at change gave purpose to and unified the respective governments. Finally, unlike pre-1979 Nicaragua, the ruling classes of Guatemala and El Salvador probably experienced less disaffection or disloyalty from the members of younger generations, many of whom coalesced around far-right goals and objectives. There were, of course, some significant cracks in the elite alliance and some individuals broke with the rightists and even joined the left opposition.

Politics of Repression in El Salvador

For most of the 1970s Salvadoran democratic forces attempted to influence the military government, but were largely unsuccessful. In 1972, in the face of 60 percent inflation and 30 percent unemployment, a coalition of opposition parties formed to run against the oligarchy's official candidate. A number of parties, spanning the ideological spectrum from moderate-right Christian Democrats to more moderate-left, to the Communist left, came together in a united front, the *Unión Nacional Opósitora* (UNO, Union of National Opposition). The coalition ran a candidate in the national elections, a centrist businessman named José Napoleon Duarte (1925–90). Duarte won the election by some 72,000 votes, but the electoral commission overturned the results and, despite a complete lack of evidence, declared the conservative candidate, Colonel Arturo Armando Molina (b. 1927), the victor by 100,000 votes. To prevent Duarte from contesting the results, the military had him arrested, tortured, and exiled to Venezuela, where he remained until his return to El Salvador in the late 1970s. Molina's government was known for its friendliness to the interests of foreign investors, export companies, landowners, and anyone who supported his repressive rule. Reminiscent of Mexico's disastrous decision to host the Olympics in 1968 in hopes of defusing domestic discontent, Colonel Molina managed to host the Miss Universe pageant in 1975, a feat that cost $30 million. As in Mexico, there were outcries over the costliness of the event, given El Salvador's pressing social and economic problems. Also similar to Mexico, the military fired on protestors, killing 37 in the days leading up to the pageant.

Inequality grew during the 1970s. In 1960 about 12 percent of the peasantry, which forms the overwhelming majority of the nation's population, had no land. This figure had grown to 80 percent by the mid-1970s. In response to their misery, and having been left with few alternatives, peasants and urban workers – with considerable aid from the increasingly radical Catholic clergy – began in the 1970s to organize and protest their condition. On February 15, 1977 the police and military opened fire on a peaceful protest in San Salvador, killing 200 people as they scrambled to shelter inside the cathedral on the central plaza. Captured on film by the international press covering the event, the scene was shown on the nightly news throughout the world and raised doubts in the US about the nature of the Salvadoran government and questions about the millions of dollars in military and humanitarian aid being sent to prop it up.

The event was pivotal in the life of El Salvador's leading Catholic cleric, Archbishop Óscar Romero. The Archbishop had been an outspoken critic of the Salvadoran military, having been convinced by the murders of priests trying to assist the poor that the government was doing nothing to curb the brutality of the military and paramilitary death squads. In 1980 he angered high authorities in the government, in the Catholic Church in Rome, and in Washington by calling for an end to US military aid to his country, arguing that so long as the state received assistance it would continue to murder innocent civilians. When he called on individual soldiers in El Salvador to disobey their superior officer death threats turned to reality. On March 24, 1980 he was assassinated while saying evening mass. Since the order to kill such a prominent figure in Salvadoran society would have had to be cleared at the very top of the military chain of command, it has been assumed that it came come from the head of the far right ARENA party (Alianza Republicana Nacionalista or National Republican Alliance), Roberto D'Aubuisson. Robert White, US Ambassador to El Salvador during the Carter Administration, called D'Aubuisson a "pathological killer," citing his consistent involvement with the death squads.

In November 1980 one of the few members of the Fourteen Families who formed part of the opposition, Enrique Alvarez (1930–80), was murdered when he and others returned from exile, after a pledge that they could participate in elections. The following month, four US religious workers, including three nuns who had been ministering to the poor, were raped and murdered by the paramilitaries. By the mid-1980s support for the Salvadoran government and military, estimated at over $200 million, was highly unpopular among US citizens. Not only the expense, but the reports of human rights abuses, news footage of atrocities committed in broad daylight, and the deaths of Catholic workers and priests, as well as two USAID technicians who were shot execution-style while sitting in a downtown hotel café. During one 12-month period in 1980–1, death squads reportedly killed 30,000 civilians, the rough equivalent of killing more than 2 million people in the United States.

Death squad violence, growing malnutrition and misery from failed land policies, the battle between the government and opposition forces, and extremely high rates of unemployment spurred more than 500,000 Salvadorans to migrate to the US. Most entered illegally, settling in Los Angeles and other California cities. The Los Angeles County Department of Public Health reported in 1984 that the Salvadoran and Guatemalan populations arriving in the Los Angeles area displayed "the common characteristics of malnutrition and disease encountered in other refugee populations, but also never-before seen signs of a terrorized people" (*LA Times*). When US immigration authorities turned away Salvadoran asylum seekers, local authorities stepped in to provide refuge. Over 400 cities throughout the US were convinced by religious denominations and peace activists to declare themselves "sanctuaries"; local authorities stepped in to protect Central American (mostly Salvadoran and Guatemalan) refugees from arrest and deportation.

The Opposition

In 1981 a new Salvadoran opposition united along a broad set of principles into a *Frente*, or popular front coalition. Like the Sandinistas, they adopted the name of the martyr from the 1930s, Farabundo Martí, and organized under the banner of the FMLN (*Frente Farabundo Martí de Liberación Nacional*), with an above-ground wing, the *Frente Democratico Revolucionario* (FDR, Democratic Revolutionary Front) based in Costa Rica. The FMLN struggled against enormous odds for over a decade, fighting throughout the country, gaining control of provinces outside the capital, and engaging in cat-and-mouse guerrilla tactics with a very well-equipped Salvadoran army. Despite the latter's abundant supply of money, arms, and expert advice from Washington, and the common knowledge that the guerrillas fought with weapons, uniforms, and materiel captured from fallen soldiers, neither side was able to reach a decisive victory. The military had virtually no support from the citizenry, except when terrorized or forced to aid them; the guerrillas had more support, but lacked sufficient arms to launch a full-scale assault on the capital. Many civilians had cause to fear getting involved, since recriminations by the military for aiding the insurgents were severe.

The difficulty of fighting an extremely brutal military government, combined with the political idealism of the liberation movement's intense struggle for unity, meant that the movement itself fell prone to the very violence and intransigence it was resisting. In 1975 one of El Salvador's leading writers, Roque Dalton (1935–75), became a member of the People's Revolutionary Army (ERP, *Ejército Revolucionario del Pueblo*) over the opposition of other leading Salvadoran revolutionaries who thought he better served the cause with his politically charged poetry. In 1975 he was accused of being a double agent for the CIA and executed. The charges were never proved and the murder stands as one of the bleakest moments in the history of El Salvador. Roque Dalton is today on a postage stamp. Less than ten years later, Mélida Anaya Montes, a leading figure in another organization that formed a part of the FMLN was assassinated in a heated struggle for leadership. Her death then led to the suicide of the group's founding leader, Salvador Cayetano Cárpio. Although every movement for social change engenders intense rivalries, the FMLN has a particularly bloody and combative history. The futility of these killings is horrendous, mitigated and comprehensible only in the violent context in which they occurred.

The war in El Salvador was widely reported in the international press, and several TV and feature movies appeared in the US and abroad detailing the events there. Director Oliver Stone's film, *Salvador*, is based on the real life story of a ne'er-do-well Los Angeles drug dealer, Richard Boyle, who co-wrote the script with Stone. Boyle and his sidekick Doc travel to El Salvador looking for women, drugs, and fun only to be shocked at the carnage they encounter. The movie was (and still is) an especially astute portrayal of the tremendous, and often devastating, effect of US foreign policy on people in a distant and tiny country, unbeknownst to, and often of little concern to, most Americans.

In spite of the negative publicity, Washington remained firmly in support of various Salvadoran administrations, both civilian and military, claiming that to pull out would mean turning power over to the far right. Nonetheless, efforts to find a more moderate group or political leader proved elusive. Religious, human rights and relief workers attempted in vain to convince the US Congress to end all aid, pointing out that anything that entered El Salvador was funneled immediately to the military, police, and various corrupt government agencies that were carrying out, or facilitating, the killing.

The Fighting Ends

After 12 years of fighting, the war was ended through a negotiated settlement that paved the way for elections. In 1992 the FMLN disarmed; in 1994 they emerged as the second largest political force in the national assembly. When the peace treaty in

El Salvador was signed in 1992, the US had spent $4 billion propping up the Salvadoran government and 75,000 people – the majority civilians – were dead. If the US public was confused about where their money went and what had happened in El Salvador, the United Nations was not. In March 1993 the body issued a report stating that the responsibility for the killings of thousands of Salvadoran civilians in the civil war must be assigned to senior military figures in the army, strongly backed by the United States.

Since the early 1990s, El Salvador has become a prime location for clothing, sporting goods, and other "sweatshop" manufacturers. One of the poorest countries of the world, El Salvador relies heavily today on remittances from immigrants, mainly in the US since the 1980s. The money Salvadorans send to relatives back home amounts to 17 percent of the nation's GDP. Despite the end of the civil war, El Salvador has not overcome the hardship, misery, and poverty that fueled the rebellion in the first place. Ecological devastation has been particularly acute as a result of the wars and agricultural practices that relegate the most productive land to Salvador's Fourteen Families, keeping the majority landless. Given the country's small size and heavy population density, the resultant crowding has led to overuse and widespread soil exhaustion. In the twenty-first century the former guerrillas remain an important group on the Salvadoran political landscape with a plurality in both national and local political offices. In March 2009 FMLN candidate Mauricio Funes won the presidential elections. Nonetheless, years of fighting have strained the already contentious coalition, which, combined with economic woes, serves to undermine the government's effectiveness.

Guatemala: The Bloodiest War

Events in Guatemala in many ways paralleled those in El Salvador, except that the country's military government carried out such extreme human rights violations that even the US distanced itself from this close ally. The liberation movement of the 1970s and 1980s coalesced around various groups, including organizations seeking indigenous rights, trade unions and communities affiliated with the Catholic Church, human rights and pro-democracy advocates. Similar to El Salvador, but unlike Nicaragua, no single military dictator controlled Guatemala; rather a series of repressive regimes ruled from the time of the CIA-sponsored coup that ousted Arbenz in 1954. The largest of the Central American republics, with a population of slightly more than 12 million, Guatemala relied on a servile Maya labor force to produce the coffee, cotton, and fruits that served as the main agricultural exports. Guatemala City became the site of a considerable amount of foreign investment in the automotive, beverage, textile, and pharmaceutical industries, which were attracted by the plentiful supply of cheap labor in a country where trade unions were either outlawed or severely circumscribed.

For a period of time the US Congress refused to supply Guatemala with aid, but observers have maintained that support entered through third parties, especially Israelis, who were enlisted to carry out training and supply arms to the Guatemalan government in

Box 13.2   Rigoberta Menchú and the controversial story of a Guatemalan woman

Rigoberta Menchu told her story to Elizabeth Burgos Debray, an anthropologist who published the account of the murderous rampage of the Guatemalan military against the indigenous people over several decades. In her introduction to *I, Rigoberta Menchu*, she states: "My story is the story of all poor Guatemalans. My personal experience is the reality of a whole people." With the publication of Rigoberta Menchu's *testimonio* in 1983, the 23-year-old Guatemalan Quiche-Maya woman became a leader and the voice for the indigenous people of her country. Because of the power and the moving content of her story, Menchu became a celebrity; her book was widely read, and in 1992 she received the Nobel Peace Prize. Rigoberta Menchu became the international champion of indigenous women's rights.

Along with her fame came criticism. US anthropologist David Stoll wrote in his book *Rigoberta Menchu and the Story of All Poor Guatemalans* that Menchu purposely distorted her story, included events she never witnessed but stated that she had, and grossly exaggerated other moments. Stoll based his argument on interviews with people in Guatemala who had witnessed the events Menchu described. For example, he reports that Menchu's detailed account of the gruesome death of her brother at the hands of the military never occurred, and that her description of a conflict between her father and the government over land titles was instead a property dispute with in-laws. Ultimately, Stoll claims that the book is a leftist apology for the guerrilla movement that was shaped by Menchu's own political agenda and ideology.

During the ensuing controversy, some writers have sided with David Stoll, arguing that the testimony is marred by exaggerations and untruths and thus not a believable account – although no one disputes the brutal murder and displacement of thousands of Quiche-Maya people. Others, including many anthropologists with extensive experience in the region, have come to Rigoberta Menchu's defense. Their view is that the overall message is what is most important; even if some of the events described are inexact, or even false, the truth is that thousands of people died within her community, and, as she says on the book's first page, her testimony reflects the experience of Guatemala's indigenous people.

return for US generosity toward Israel. In a well-known book, Rigoberta Menchu, a Maya peace activist who was awarded the 1992 Nobel Peace Prize, publicized the extent of the genocidal policies toward indigenous people (see Box 13.2).

The CIA World Factbook obliquely refers to the enormous suffering that characterized Guatemala's history during the years following the 1954 military coup until the late 1990s, stating: "During the second half of the twentieth century, it experienced a variety of military and civilian governments, as well as a 36-year guerrilla war. In 1996, the government signed a peace agreement formally ending the conflict, which had left more than 100,000 people dead and had created some 1 million refugees." (CIA World Factbook). President Bill Clinton traveled to Guatemala in March 1999 to address a meeting of leaders from many sectors of Guatemalan society, including indigenous leaders, women, government officials, and representatives of the truth commission, and spoke far more directly. In one of the more remarkable moves by a US president, Clinton "on the third day of his Central America trip, apologized for US support of Right-wing governments in Guatemala that killed tens of thousands of rebels and Mayan Indians in that nation's 36-year civil war." After delivering his apology, the President called for "reconciliation" throughout Central America.[5]

The Evangelical Alternative

With the defeat of the liberation movements in Nicaragua and El Salvador, Latin Americans, especially in Central American countries that had been wracked by civil war, began to turn away from Christian radicalism and liberation theology. Instead, a part of the world that for over 500 years had been considered synonymous with Catholicism was fast becoming a Protestant stronghold. Moreover, it was precisely in the areas where liberation theology had blossomed that Evangelical and Pentecostal Christianity also flourished. Pentecostalism is a form of Protestantism that relies on baptism, speaking in tongues, demonstrative acceptance of the Holy Spirit, and emotional ritual. At the beginning of the 1980s, when liberation theology was at its peak, there were an estimated 18.6 million Evangelicals in Latin America; a little over a decade later there were approximately 60 million and a reported 8,000 Latin American converts daily, according to the Latin American Catholic Bishops Conference. By 2005 Guatemala was already close to losing its Catholic majority, with more Protestants than any other Spanish-speaking country. In Brazil and Nicaragua, Protestants and members of African and indigenous religions outnumber Catholics; elsewhere in Latin America one in five people now identify themselves as Protestants.

Why has this form of Protestant Christianity grown so rapidly in Latin America? First, it might be argued that the emotionally charged Protestantism that has taken hold in Latin America has built on the strength of liberation theology, whose popularity had preceded it. The Christian Base Communities that were the foundation of liberation theology brought people together around the pursuit of social justice and linked in a common cause. Achieving these goals, however, was more difficult, especially as massive social inequalities refused to disappear and poverty remained intractable. Obtaining democratic rights proved to be a more daunting task than uniting in prayer – and was certainly more dangerous. Secondly, if traditional Catholicism was hierarchical and distant, liberation theology, with its reliance on socialist realism, was highly rational. The emphasis on demanding rights and defeating poverty in the world today, rather than waiting for salvation in the next life, was ultimately discouraging, since in the free market, neoliberal world of the 1990s, poverty only increased. Constant entreaties from religious workers for people to dedicate their lives to economic improvements that never materialized grew demoralizing. Thirdly, Evangelicals, especially the raucous Pentecostals, emphasize emotion in the form of communal worship, giving congregants an experience with the divine through spiritual ecstasy. Pentecostalism filled a gap and satisfied people's spiritual cravings. By contrast liberation theologians disparaged such things as processions, prayers to patron saints, the fanatical veneration of Mary, and other popular forms of piety as "non-transformative," displeasing many of the devout who thrived on the uplift from such rituals.

Finally, Pentecostalism in Latin America, as everywhere, has relied on aggressive use of the media. Worshippers come together in huge arenas; televised religious services boast celebrity evangelists who claim to channel God's power to heal the disabled, cure the sick, bring peace and happiness to the afflicted. Televised services allow congregants to feel a part of a huge mass of people, while watching or listening in their own living rooms or at local storefront churches. Preachers travel to remote villages of rural Latin America to hold revivals similar to the nineteenth-century tent meetings of the "Second Great Awakening" and other eras of intense spiritual revivalism in the US and elsewhere. Hence, the "organized togetherness" of the CEBs laid the foundation for the emergence of Protestant meeting halls. Evangelicals and Pentecostals took root on the edges, and then occupied the center, of communities that came together in hopes of transforming society, and in the end it seemed easier to transform oneself than a brutally hostile society; to find individual ecstasy than obtain social equality.

Further facilitating the growth of Pentecostal churches is the issue of inclusiveness. The majority of Pentecostal ministers in much of Latin America are indigenous, while women comprise over two-thirds of congregations and hold positions of leadership. In contrast, traditional Catholicism has nothing but the most secondary role for women, and liberation theology was not able to extend the boundaries much further. Most members of Pentecostal churches are poor and uneducated; however, many from the middle and upper classes have begun to attend, providing an even more appealing phenomenon. Protestant church services bring together disparate classes, races, and ethnicities, and, unlike the Catholic Church in Latin America, ministers too are often from the lower class; some are women, others people of color. Relying mainly on trained male priests, the Catholic Church cannot compete.

Relations between the Evangelicals and Latin American political parties have not followed a consistent pattern. In both Guatemala and Colombia Evangelical political parties have been formed, and Guatemala had a Pentecostal leader in 1982, General Efrain Ríos Montt (b. 1926). Ríos Montt was a military dictator and thus his political power did not represent a mass base for electing a Pentecostal, although in general Evangelicals and Pentecostals tended to be hostile toward guerrilla forces. Amnesty International estimated that over 10,000 indigenous Guatemalans and peasant farmers were killed from March to July 1982, and that 100,000 rural villagers were forced to flee their homes during Ríos Montt's rule. He was such a brutal dictator that some Evangelicals concluded that nothing was to be gained by mixing religion and politics. Tying a political party, or a leader's identity, to his religious affiliation might do more to undermine the spread of Protestantism than increase it.

In the early days of the evangelical movement in Latin America, some observers saw the embrace of Protestantism and rejection of Catholic radicalism as a conservative victory. This, however, is not necessarily the case. At the very time that Protestantism has spread and liberation theology declined, many countries have elected leftist and socialist presidents, or have a majority of leftists in their representative assemblies. What this has meant in terms of Protestant votes is therefore inconclusive.

Colombia: The Longest War

The wars in Central America largely captured the most media attention in the latter decades of the twentieth century; however, it is the ongoing conflict in Colombia that has resulted in the most casualties, has been the most costly, and has presented the most intractable outcome. In 1953 *La Violencia* had reached a temporary halt with the formation of the National Front, through an agreement between the dominant Liberal and Conservative parties. However, the violence could not really be stopped because so many of the competing groups and factions were left outside the ruling coalition. Thus internecine warfare, in an even more uncontrolled manner, commenced anew. Since 1953, Colombia's history has continued to be marked by guerrilla warfare, brutal military repression, and numerous attempts by workers, trade unionists, and community and civic organizations to forge a civil society. The United States government's campaign over the last few decades to halt coca production has become another source of violence, pitting guerrilla groups against extremely well-armed military and paramilitary forces, with innocent civilians caught in between.

Observers have argued that the thousands of lives lost during military counterinsurgency campaigns might have been avoided if both guerrillas and *narcotraficantes* (drug traffickers) had been left to cultivate their respective crops in designated areas. The guerrillas grow coca to sell on the market, while ostensibly prohibiting its use in the areas they control. *Narcotraficantes* follow much the same course, since excessive consumption of cocaine both cuts into profits and results in a debilitated workforce. The main interference in this arrangement has come from the national government, whose income over the past 20 years has become increasingly dependent on foreign aid. As the chief drug supplier to the US market, Colombia has been on the receiving end of large amounts of capital and military hardware, intended to curb the flow of drugs to markets in the US and Europe. Beginning in the 1990s, President Andrés Pastrana (b. 1954) proposed during a trip to Washington that coca and opium poppy production could only be curbed if his country received massive economic development aid, including loans and grants to small farmers so that they could end coca production and raise legitimate crops. President Bill Clinton responded by offering to expand trade, beef up funding for oversight of human rights, and press hard for extensive peace negotiations with the Revolutionary Armed Forces of Colombia (*Fuerzas Armadas Revolucinaria de Colombia*, FARC), the communist-inspired guerrilla movement that has been at war with the government since the 1960s. In the end, the US handed over $560 million in military assistance alone to fight the guerrillas, who were more often than not conflated with the *narcotraficantes*, forming the foundation for what came to be known as "Plan Colombia: A Plan for Peace, Prosperity and the Strengthening of the State." Plan Colombia quickly morphed into a $600 million scheme to fund military operations against insurgents. Even before September 11, 2001 Colombia ranked third, behind Israel and Egypt, as the largest recipient of US military assistance. Despite the costly Plan, now a part of Homeland Security, there is no indication that the flow of drugs into the US has lessened. The Plan offers no strategy for curbing money-laundering operations in the US, the Caribbean, and Colombia, nor does it include measures to stop a fairly steady demand for illegal drugs in the US, Canada, and Europe.

Plan Colombia, and the enormous outlays in military funding it entails, has undermined and distorted Colombia's national priorities. With very little money for social services and few job opportunities besides the huge government bureaucracy, some textile, coffee, and other industries – and of course growing, processing, and selling coca – the situation of the average Colombian has become extremely precarious. During the last decade thousands of Colombians, many of them highly skilled and well educated, left the country to swell the ranks of immigrant communities in Florida, New York, and California. The exact number of Colombians who have migrated to the United States is not known for sure, but the US census bureau estimated that 150,000 were living in the country illegally in 2000. In her book *From Ellis Island to JFK: New York's Two Great Waves of Immigration*, anthropologist Nancy Foner describes the peopling of vast sections of the borough of Queens in New York City by successive waves of Colombians, a pattern that has been duplicated in other major North American cities.

The War on Drugs in Latin America

Despite the large quantities of cocaine that enter North America each year, the US military typically has limited its intervention to high-profile campaigns to apprehend known Latin American drug dealers, such as the arrest of Manuel Noriega in Panama in 1989 and the 1993 death of Pablo Escobar in Medellín, Colombia.

Manuel Noriega

The most surprising drug lord interdiction was the arrest of General Manuel Noriega (b. 1936) following the invasion of Panama in December 1989. What started as an indictment on drug trafficking and money laundering by the district attorney's office in South Florida turned into a major military action involving thousands of US troops, carried out under the lofty code name "Operation Just Cause." The consummate opportunist, Noriega had at one point facilitated arms shipments from Cuba to the Sandinistas in neighboring Nicaragua while working as a paid informant for the CIA. Noriega was one of the US intelligence service's longest-standing operatives in Latin America. He first began providing information to the US in the late 1950s when studying at a military academy in Peru. By the mid-1960s he was a full-fledged informant. For his work in helping Panamanian president Omar Torrijos rig an election against a popular opponent, Noriega was promoted from transit police chief to commander of the Panamanian Defense Force. According to his many letters of commendation from the CIA, Noriega was one of the best intelligence informants in the hemisphere, maintaining files on every major figure up and down the continent, including one on the sexual activities of his boss, Torrijos.

As early as the 1970s it was clear that Noriega was heavily involved with drug trafficking. According to the records of the US Senate Intelligence Committee, an official with the Drug Enforcement Agency (DEA) reported to John E. Ingersoll, Director of the Bureau of Narcotics and Dangerous Drugs, in 1972 that Noriega's drug dealing was so extensive that the agency considered having him assassinated, but then decided against it. In 1976, when George H. W. Bush was director of the CIA, electronic eavesdropping equipment showed that Noriega was spying on Cuba for the CIA while also providing his Cuban intelligence associates with a list of every telephone number US intelligence agents were monitoring. Even after Washington learned of Noriega's work as a double agent, he continued on the CIA payroll. Furthermore, the Carter Administration played down Noriega's drug connections and dubious role in espionage as part of its effort to win ratification of the Panama Canal treaty.

Following the death of Omar Torrijos (1929–81) under mysterious circumstances in an airplane crash, Noriega became president of Panama, and an even closer ally of the US. So long as Noriega was supporting the Reagan Administration war against the Sandinistas, his drug-dealing activities were overlooked. As the Iran–Contra files revealed, the Panamanian president earned around $10 million for his aid to Oliver North, who played the pivotal role in setting up clandestine operations in support of the Contra war against the Nicaraguan government. Documents reveal that Noriega even offered – and North accepted but was then overruled by his boss, National Security Advisor John Poindexter – to have the entire Sandinista leadership assassinated. According to the Senate Investigation Committee on the Iran–Contra affair in 1988, CIA Director William Casey met repeatedly with Noriega but refused to warn the latter to end his drug dealing because Casey considered the Panamanian too valuable an ally in the war against the Sandinistas.

That changed in December 1989 when various government agencies, including the DEA, determined that Noriega had outlived his usefulness. With the Canal treaty set to expire in 1999 and the canal's maintenance turned over to Panama, the US wanted a more reliable president and a restructured Panamanian Defense Force on the ground. President George H. W. Bush sent several thousand troops into Panama, in a military action that cost the lives of 23 US soldiers and as many as 3,000 Panamanians. After several days of standoff against Noriega, who took refuge in the Papal Nunciature (the Vatican Embassy), he was eventually forced out after days of psychological "torture," including bombarding the compound with loud heavy metal rock music, especially Van Halen's "Panama" and tapes of the Howard Stern radio show. After his surrender, Noriega was brought to trial in Florida, where he was charged with multiple counts of drug trafficking and money laundering, and sentenced to 40 years in prison.

There are several important features to this sorry tale, not least of which is that drug interdiction in Latin America is very much tied up with politics. So long as the relationship of necessity, not admiration, served its purpose, dictators such as Noriega basked in the glow of Washington's largesse. When the usefulness of these disreputable sycophants ran out, for whatever reason, their status was transformed from best friend to worst enemy; their crimes were exposed, and they were assassinated or jailed. Affidavits proved that General Noriega earned a salary of $110,000 a year when George H. W. Bush was director of the CIA, but a few years later, under the Bush presidency, he was apprehended, tried, and jailed for crimes that had been apparent to everyone for years. The real losers were the ordinary citizens of Panama. Forced to endure the brutality of a drug-running dictator when he was protected by the US, they then found their country invaded, their houses bombed, and thousands killed when the dictator fell out of favor. Finally, Noriega was little more than a stand-in for the cocaine operations centered further south, in Colombia.

Pablo Escobar: The cocaine "Robin Hood"

The most notorious drug baron of the 1980s was Pablo Escobar (1949–93), a controversial head of the Medellín cartel who was listed in the 1989 *Forbes* magazine as the seventh richest man in the world, taking in an estimated $30 billion annually. Reputedly one of the most brutal and daring of the Colombian *narcotraficantes*, with a network of refining, buying, and selling cocaine that stretched from Bolivia and Peru, through Colombia and from there to entrepôts abroad, Escobar controlled 80 percent of the cocaine market by the end of the 1980s. Despite his notoriety, Escobar was something of a hero to the poor of Medellín, where his protection from capture was based on the willingness of the local populace to warn him of any encroaching enemies. He built football stadiums in poor neighborhoods, organized sports teams, gave away food, built houses, and personally distributed money. He was especially popular with the local Catholic clergy because he financed the construction of many churches throughout the city. While Escobar cultivated his Robin Hood image among the people of Medellín, he was making enemies among rival drug cartels and the Colombian government. In 1993 a special force of US Navy Seals (at that time called Delta Force) and a crack Colombian military unit invaded the drug baron's compound, killed Escobar, and destroyed his cartel. Nevertheless, the drug trade did not end with Escobar's death, nor did it seriously interrupt the flow of narcotics abroad since there were other drug barons waiting to step into the void. As then Colombian President Andrés Pastrana said in 2000 on the television program *60 Minutes*, "even if we win in Colombia, there will always be another country to supply the US with drugs, as long as the demand for them remains."[6]

Currently that country is Mexico. Major drug-running operations (originating in Colombia for the most part) have moved into Mexico full force, turning the Texas–Mexico border into a place of constant violent drug wars. Journalist Alma Guillermoprieto reported in a *New Yorker* article in late 2008 that sources in Mexico claim that more than 40 years after a string of "drug-war initiatives – as much as thirty percent of Mexico's arable land is suspected of being under cultivation for clandestine crops, drug violence in Sinaloa has taken a quantitatively different turn, and the Sinaloa traffickers have generated entire dynasties of criminals who are at war in nearly every one of Mexico's thirty-one states, as well as Mexico City."[7] In 2009 President Barack Obama acknowledged that as the world's number one consumer of illegal drugs, primary source of illegal weapons, and main locale for drug money laundering, the US shares responsibility for Mexico's drug wars.

Conclusion

The conflicts in Central America in the 1970s and 1980s were like a stage play of the last gasp of the Cold War. As tiny, impoverished nations tried to assert their own national identity, which was in some cases influenced by Marxist socialism and communism, and at other times by progressive Catholicism, and pro-capitalist nationalist ideologies, their progress crashed head-on into the brick wall of US national interests. These were, as defined by the White House, entirely opposite from the goals of the Central American liberation movements. A decade later it would not have mattered so much and these conflicts might have been resolved in a far less brutal and violent way, but it is very hard to say for sure.

An intransigent ruling class in El Salvador, Guatemala, and Nicaragua left very little space for experimentation with alternative forms of national liberation. Colombia and Mexico have presented their own circumstances, including an ongoing civil war among factions of the FARC and the *narcotraficantes* in Colombia, and massive US monetary assistance and seemingly futile drug interdiction efforts in both countries. Finally, the decades of conflict brought to the foreground divisions that have been in existence since the early days of the European invasion 500 years before: entrenched racism that prevented indigenous people from full participation in civil society; a Catholic hierarchy and working clergy at odds with each other over what the true mission of the Church should be; and a long list of disagreements over the role of women, the reasons the poor are poor, and the responsibility of the state to alleviate poverty. In every case discussed in this chapter the revolutionary leadership was young, their idealism led to mistakes, but, unfortunately, they were allowed no leeway to make mistakes and correct them. The process of sovereign state building shipwrecked on the rocks of the Cold War. In the next, and final, chapter, we take up the changing social and political conditions in Latin America since the end of the competition between the two superpowers and examine the new lines of demarcation and contention.

14 | The Americas in the Twenty-first Century

The twenty-first century promised to be a new chapter in Latin America. Neoliberalism, a program calling for maximum wage controls, dismantling of state-owned industries, and promotion of free trade, became the watchword of Latin America. In 1990 the defeat of the Sandinistas in the Nicaraguan elections, occurring simultaneously with the demise of Soviet and Eastern European communism and the stalemate in the war in El Salvador that led to a negotiated settlement, signaled a profound alteration in the old Cold War antagonisms. By century's end, the United States stood alone, no longer contending with the Soviet Union and Eastern Europe as one of two superpowers. Not only did Cuba lose over 75 percent of its financial and trade support and enter a "special period" of extreme austerity and deprivation, but it was no longer a safe haven for Latin American revolutionaries.

Although the Soviet Union had provided very little direct aid to Latin America's revolutionary struggles (apart from aid and arms funneled through Cuba), it had served as a competing voice at the UN and other world arenas, a tactic that had generally stayed the hand of direct US military aggression around the world. Whereas the left had not greeted Soviet aggression abroad with great approval, it had more often remained silent. Only a few egregious examples elicited disapproval, such as the invasion of Prague in 1968, mid-1970s support for Ethiopia against the Eritrean People's Liberation Front in Africa, and, most decidedly, the military occupation of Afghanistan, a debacle that bore an eerie similarity to US interventions in Latin America and Southeast Asia in the 1960s and 1970s. However, the rapid demise of Soviet communism shocked many leftists. When the USSR collapsed, many socialists were appalled to learn the degree of exploitation, corruption, environmental destruction, and inequality the Soviet system had tolerated internally.

The Washington Consensus

In the final decades of the twentieth century Washington and its surrogate agencies in the World Bank, IMF, the Inter-American Development Bank, and a host of similar financial powerhouses were free to exert enormous influence on the future course of Latin American nations. As if to drive home the point, the dramatic change in the balance of power was apparent in the term used interchangeably with "neoliberalism" in Latin America: the "Washington Consensus." As the revolutionary phase in Central America ended, so too did the military dictatorships that had held sway from one end of the continent to the other. The national security states in Argentina, Chile, Uruguay, Brazil, and Peru crumbled and left-leaning populist republics took their place. The political and economic prospects facing many Latin American nations at the start of the new millennium were in stark contrast to the strife of the 1970s, when almost every country, except for Colombia, Mexico, and Venezuela, was under military rule – and the three exceptions were hardly beacons of democracy. The current group of left-populist and moderate socialist governments that have come to power through the ballot box have accommodated to free-market demands, eschewed the Cuban model, and developed particular and varied relationships with international creditors. Above all, Latin America's future is tied closely to that of other countries in the hemisphere, since after 500 years the Americas are increasingly interdependent politically, economically, and culturally.

Mexico, the country most closely linked to the United States, may find itself in the most daunting position, as the economic downturn in the capital of finance deepens. Politically Mexico is stable, but lacks the reform-oriented government found in other parts of Latin America. In the late 1980s a center-left coalition, the Democratic National Front (FND), formed a reformist current in the PRI (*Partido Revolucionario Institutional*) to challenge the standard political practice of the outgoing faction appointing the incoming candidate – tantamount to choosing the next president. The FND backed Cuauhtémoc Cárdenas (b. 1934), son of former President Lázaro Cárdenas (president 1934–40), but the young Cárdenas had the candidacy stolen from him in 1988 when the traditional faction backed Carlos Salinas de Gortari (b. 1948), who went on to win the election. The center-left forces then broke off to form the Party of the Democratic Revolution (PRD, *Partido Revolucionario Democratico*), and under Cárdenas's leadership ran against the PRI in elections throughout the country, with considerable success on the local level. However, in 2000 it was a challenger from the right, Vicente Fox (b. 1942) of the National Action Party (PAN) that finally unseated the PRI. When the PAN won again in 2006, after a torturously prolonged and disputed election in which Felipe Calderón (b. 1962) ultimately was declared the victor, the PRI was reduced to a shadow of its former self. Since the 2006 election, the PAN has emerged as Mexico's strongest party, controlling most seats in Congress as well as the executive. Later in this chapter we examine current political trends in Mexico in more detail.

Brazil and the Workers' Alternative

Brazil's current political and economic successes and failures play out on a scale unequaled in the rest of the Latin America. With its large population, industrial base, varied climate and terrain, and extreme income inequalities, Brazil faces one of the largest challenges in the hemisphere. Under the left-leaning Workers' Party (PT, *Partido dos Trabalhadores*), neoliberalism has been, rhetorically at least, on the defensive. Luíz Inácio "Lula" da Silva had promised a dramatic change in social priorities – health care, educational reform, a living wage, help for the poor – when he was elected in 2002 and re-elected in 2006, but progress has been slow. If Lula's personal history is inspirational, his presidency has been pragmatic.

Lula emerged as a key trade union leader in the industrial belt around São Paulo in the late 1970s. The trade union movement developed into a formidable force opposed to the military government and spearheaded the return to democracy and presidential elections in 1989. At the head of the Workers' Party ticket, Lula ran in 1989 and lost to the corrupt Fernando Collor de Mello, a photogenic former karate champion and member of a wealthy family in the small, far-north state of Alagoas. With the help of Roberto Marinho, the conservative head of Brazil's huge *O Globo* media empire, Collor's laissez-faire economic program defeated Lula's left-leaning social democratic platform. Collor's "economic shock plan," in step with the mandates of international capital, called for selling off state-controlled enterprises to the private sector (mainly to those enjoying political or personal connections to the president) and instigating a stringent austerity program to arrest inflation. Despite monitoring by international lenders, the economy span out of control, matched only by the corruption scandal that soon enveloped the Collor administration. Much to the disappointment of Brazil's electorate, the first democratically elected presidency in nearly 30 years began to unravel after only two years in office, ending in Collor's impeachment and resignation in December 1992.

The demise of the Collor administration bore all the markings of a *telenovela*, beginning with his brother Pedro Collor's public exposure of Fernando's cocaine habit and moving on to revelations of an embezzlement/kickback scheme that funneled money into a host of private bank accounts benefiting family members, cabinet ministers, and political allies. The newly uncensored press reveled in stories of First Lady Rosane Collor's plastic surgery, $20,000-a-month clothing allowance, and Parisian shopping sprees, as well as photos of elaborate house renovations – all at tax payers' expense. Nonetheless, Brazilians could be proud that their newly revived justice system worked, in some ways more efficiently than that of the United States. Collor received no presidential pardon – unlike Richard Nixon in 1974 – and no immunity from prosecution.

Vice-President Itamar Franco served out the rest of Collor's term. He appointed Fernando Henrique Cardoso (b. 1931), a former Marxist sociology professor from the University of São Paulo, to serve in the cabinet as Finance Minister. Ushering in a new currency, the *real*, and launching an austerity program, Cardoso's term as head of finance, and subsequent two terms as president, are seen as Brazil's insertion into the Washington Consensus model. Leaving behind his leftist roots, Cardoso carved out a center-right position by aligning his own Brazilian Social Democratic Party (PSDB, *Partido da Social Democracia Brasileira*) with the more rightist Liberal Front Party (PFL, *Partido do Frente Liberal*), in opposition to Lula's Workers' Party. While the government followed the dictates of international lenders and policymakers, progressive groups organized around cultural and social issues, and the trade unions kept up a steady drumbeat of demand for economic improvements. The years from 1994 until 2002 were characterized by lively debate, innovation, intense cultural and political activism, and no small measure of conflict. Some have seen it as the apex of the ideological and political influence of the Workers' Party, and a time when activist groups such as the Landless Workers Movement (MST, *Movimento dos Trabalhadores Rurais sem Terra*), those involved in grass-roots organizing for racial and gender equality, environmental reforms, social and political rights for workers, the poor, and the disenfranchised, were at their zenith. The intense political mobilization, while the PT was building its base and vying for power, made the last decade of the twentieth century one of Brazil's most exciting and hopeful.

The Workers' Party in Power

After running unsuccessfully for president in 1994 and 1998, Lula won in 2002 on a program that, critics claimed, departed from the PT social agenda, considerably softening the working class's longstanding denunciation of Cardoso's neoliberal economic policies. Instead of a confrontation with the IMF and World Bank, Brazil under Lula has restructured its payments, staved off creditors, and attempted, haltingly, to reduce widespread and endemic poverty, crime, and hunger. In stark contrast to the years in which he climbed to fame denouncing first the subservience of the military governments, and then Cardoso, to international creditors, Lula reversed his stance and accepted the core of the neoliberal agenda: debt repayment based on "fiscal responsibility" and austerity, coupled with scaled-back anti-poverty programs, a freeze on wages, and postponement of environmental protections.

Hammered by charges of political corruption in the innermost circle of the PT, a much-weakened Lula won re-election in a run-off in 2006. The analysis of that victory reveals the fundamental contradictions facing anyone attempting to enact change in a country as vast and as plagued by centuries of inequality and corruption as Brazil. Lula won in 20 out of 27 states, carrying virtually all of the poorest districts of the North, and losing or splitting in most of the prosperous South. In fact, the smaller and the poorer the district, the better Lula did. Part of his support was based on his core supporters' loyalty to the poor boy from an impoverished background who rose through the ranks of the working class. Another part was dismissal of the validity of corruption charges (or resignation to the belief that politics is always corrupt). But a major share of his victory rested on the electorate's fear of the alternative. If Lula, as many claimed, had failed to resist vigorously the neoliberal agenda, Geraldo Alckmin, the businessman who ran against him, promised to embrace the Washington Consensus and turn back some of the PT's major successes: an increase in the minimum wage, monetary payments to over 11 million families through the *Bolsa Familia* Program, over 200,000 scholarships to private universities for low-income students, reduced taxes on food and other essentials, and an increase in family incomes, sometimes by as much as 40 percent. It was not the workers' paradise the PT had promised, but it was better than the alternative.

Brazil is a country faced with enormous challenges on a vast scale. Centuries of poor land use and failure to implement the agrarian reforms required to sustain small producers in the countryside have resulted in a continual exodus from rural to urban areas. Brazil now boasts some of the largest cities in the world: São Paulo's metropolitan region has 20 million inhabitants, including large sections that are essentially ungovernable. A country of nearly 200 million people, 20 percent of whom are illiterate, with an infant mortality rate more than twice that of the US and widespread unemployment, Brazil's potential as an industrial and agricultural giant has been consistently undermined by poverty and its consequences, especially drug use, crime, and massive official corruption. While Brazil could out-produce every other nation in Latin America and has enormous resources in land, minerals, a recently discovered oil reserve, and a huge workforce, future economic health depends on years of prolonged growth, as well as leaders who can and will steadfastly root out corruption and distribute the benefits to the population at large. With 175 million acres of arable land, even without clearing the Amazon rainforest, Brazil hopes to double its share of exports, primarily to China, but also to India and other areas. Although the United States out-produces Brazil in soybeans, the latter has recently emerged as the largest exporter, sending 11 million tons of beans to China alone.

The rising demand for food exports – mainly soybeans, which are one of Brazil's key export commodities and one for which there is insatiable demand in China – is encountering competition for land use from sugarcane destined for ethanol production. Brazilian producers are severely handicapped by the nation's primitive system of roads, railroads, and infrastructure necessary for moving goods from the interior of the country to ports. Shipping costs are four times those in the US. Clearly the many years of neglect under military governments – especially in relation to infrastructure, and developing a cadre of managers and technical and service sector employees – has hindered Brazil's ability to accrue the revenue it should from international sales. The financial crisis in late 2008 has affected the ease with which Brazil has been able to maintain strong export markets. Depending on the extent to which the crisis will affect credit supplies (and credit is essential for agricultural production), Brazil may face shortfalls in supplying its external market, or in finding buyers for crops already in the ground. Either scenario could have a disastrous ripple effect in other sectors of Brazil's developing economy.

Bolivia: Twenty-first-century *Indigenismo*

As left-leaning populist governments have become more the rule than the exception, a different sort of struggle has emerged among and between them. For example, President Evo Morales of Bolivia has faced conflict with neighboring Brazil and Argentina, both headed by leftist governments sympathetic to Bolivia's progressive agenda. However, because a large share of Bolivia's natural gas reserves were in the hands of Brazil's state-owned company Petrobrás, Morales' nationalization plans came into direct conflict with Brazil. Similarly, Argentina feared increased prices for Bolivian natural gas, since Morales hinted that increased revenues from gas sales are needed to implement the domestic reform platform on which he was elected. Higher prices would anger Argentine consumers, the main market for Bolivia's natural gas, and thus possibly undermine the popularity of President Cristina Kirchner (b. 1953), herself one of Morales' prime backers. To the west, President Morales seems interested in improving relations with Chile. He attended the inauguration of Michelle Bachelet, and she was present at Morales' inaugural, signaling a thaw in the chilly diplomatic relations that have divided their nations for more than a century, since Chile cut off Bolivia's access to the sea after the latter's defeat in the War of the Pacific. These socialist governments will need to settle their longstanding disputes and reach accords that they can sell to their respective constituencies.

Like Brazil and other South American countries, Bolivia has begun forging international agreements with partners outside the hemisphere. In September 2006 Jindal Steel and Power of India contracted with the Bolivian government to mine one of the world's largest veins of untapped iron deposits. Meanwhile, the Australian Republic Gold Company invested $26 million in the Amayapampa mine in the high Andes, beginning production in 2008. Investment from South Asian and Australian firms invokes less suspicion and hostility than that of the US or powerful neighboring countries with a history of dominating the landlocked Andean country, but the fact remains that Bolivia is still reliant on infusions of external capital. This is of particular importance given that Morales faces domestic discontent. Although 64 percent of the population lives below the poverty line, Bolivia is nonetheless unevenly poor. Natural gas reserves and the best agricultural land is concentrated in the more prosperous eastern region, presenting the government with the task of holding onto the loyalty of all regions, while maintaining an equitable balance of resources across the country. Tension came to a head in a battle over adopting a new constitution in December 2007. The resource-rich Santa Cruz area in the east refused to accept new constitutional protections for indigenous groups, languages, and election procedures. More importantly, the more prosperous eastern regions objected to the use of gas and oil revenues to finance improvements in the standard of living for the most impoverished areas where indigenous people predominate. Resolving the disputes and decisions facing Morales – and other leftist and progressive leaders – will require untangling longstanding tensions among like-minded Latin American nations, forging cooperative agreements to take the place of traditional dependency on foreign investment, and building national unity across deeply divided racial, ethnic, and regional lines.

Venezuela and Hugo Chávez

Looming over the continent, and liable to play an active role in whatever course Latin American nations pursue, is the figure of Venezuelan president Hugo Chávez (b. 1954) and, more importantly, the oil he controls – the fifth-largest oil reserve in the world and one of the most important sources of heavy crude. Chávez, a former army paratrooper, came to power in 1998 in a country which, unlike others in the hemisphere, had enjoyed an unbroken period of representative government since 1958, despite the domination of two, largely corrupt, political parties. Very little of the nation's wealth from oil revenues had benefited the bulk of Venezuelans: witness the fact that from 1970 to 1998 per capita income fell by 35 percent, one of the sharpest, prolonged declines in the world. Promising "revolutionary" social policies and realization of nineteenth-century liberator Simon Bolívar's dream of independent democratic republics throughout South America, Chávez launched his "Bolivarian Revolution" aimed at spreading the nation's wealth to the majority of poor residents. A career military officer, Chávez was a founder of the left-wing Fifth Republic Movement, a group of army officers and cadets who came together after two failed military coups – one in February and another in November 1992 – against then President Carlos Andrés Pérez (b. 1922). Jailed for conspiracy and amnestied after two years in prison, Chávez emerged with even greater strength to back his campaign for political office and complete the transition from army officer to civilian politician. Winning the presidency in 1998 on a platform that promised relief for the millions of Venezuela's poor, Chávez has managed in the years since to survive a recall, a failed coup, and spates of dramatic declines in popularity (Figure 14.1).

Chávez's brash, sometimes uncouth, style combined with his unabashed admiration for Fidel Castro and the political system in place in Cuba, on the one hand, and his

Figure 14.1   US Navy Commander Officer Robert S. Kerno (left) points out the sights to Venezuelan President Hugo Chávez during a tour of the USS *Yorktown* in Curaçao Harbor, Netherlands Antilles in 2002. The ship was a part of *Unitas* (Unity), the largest multinational naval exercise conducted by the US. Caribbean, Central, and South American naval forces gathered with the focus on building a hemispheric coalition for mutual defense and cooperation. This photo was shot a month before the abortive coup against Chávez, which the US supported. Despite periodic tension between leaders of the US and Venezuela, the two countries maintain commercial and diplomatic ties. (Martin Maddock, USN, photo)

repeated denunciation of the Washington Consensus, on the other, have garnered him both begrudging admiration and outright hostility from many of his neighbors. Supported by Bolivia's Morales, Argentina's Kirchners (Nestor (b. 1950) and Cristina), Ecuador's Rafael Correa (b. 1963), and, more tepidly, by Lula in Brazil, Chávez has been able to keep the open hostility of the USA at bay, and even dramatically roll back attempts to oust him from power.

The changed state of Latin America's relationship with Washington, despite the strength of the neoliberal agenda, was no more evident than in April 2002. On April 11, conservative forces drew on support from a wing of the military discontented with Chávez to launch a coup d'état. Chávez was detained at a military base outside Caracas, while the rebellious military, in consultation with powerful figures in the Venezuela elite and media conglomerates, installed Pedro Carmona (b. 1941) as Venezuela's interim president. A former president of *Fedecamaras* – an organization representing the heads of the country's banking, agricultural, commercial, and oil interests, a kind of Venezuelan Chamber of Commerce – Carmona represents the business community that had vehemently opposed Chávez's social reforms. Carmona immediately annulled the reform agenda, disbanded the National Assembly and the judiciary, and declared marshal law. Despite the blatantly undemocratic nature of the coup and removal of an elected president from office in a neighboring country, the Bush Administration immediately recognized the new government, a tactic that subsequently proved embarrassing. In a stark departure from the Cold War era, the twenty-first century found the US standing alone – not only unable to strong-arm support for its position from the rest of Latin America's leaders, but the object of chastisement and ridicule in the media and among political parties throughout the region, and a scolding from the OAS. Meanwhile, the poorest strata of society poured into the streets of Caracas and other cities, demonstrating their support for Chávez and their unwillingness to accept Carmona as president. In the wake of widespread demonstrations and looting of shops in wealthy shopping districts, and facing a popular uprising supported by a majority of the armed forces, the elite and the media it controlled retreated. Chávez's military supporters stormed the presidential palace and spirited him back into office on April 13, signaling an end to the two-day regime change. After failing to oust Chávez at the ballot box, or through a series of management-led general strikes of better-paid petroleum workers and members of the labor aristocracy, or the military coup, the Venezuelan elite accepted temporary defeat, but maintain a concerted opposition stance.

The Bolivarian Mission

The Venezuelan leader's "Bolivarian Revolution" has hinged on some successful forays into combating disease, illiteracy, poverty, and the generally inadequate level of social services facing the majority of Venezuelans. This campaign, labeled "the Bolivarian Mission," has scored some remarkable improvements in health care, accomplished with the generous assistance of Cuban medical teams. Since 2000 Venezuela has agreed to supply 40 million barrels of oil yearly to energy-deprived Cuba in exchange for teams of doctors, nurses, and medical technicians, who have established neighborhood clinics throughout the country, emulating the practice that proved so effective in the provision of quality health care to remote areas of Cuba. Re-elected in 2000 and 2006, Chávez's popularity rests squarely with the lower classes who have benefited from these health initiatives and similar policies. Venezuela is undoubtedly a country with widespread inequalities and poverty; however, poverty rates fell from 42 to 34 percent from 2000 to 2006, still leaving over 30 percent of the population in this oil-rich nation below the poverty line.

Although many of Venezuela's poor would like to see better results, especially given oil revenues, the masses have continued to back their president at the polls. In December 2007 the Venezuelan leader narrowly lost an attempt to revise the Constitution to allow him to run for office indefinitely, but also to cut the working week, legalize same-sex unions, and increase social spending. Despite accusations that Chávez has attempted to perpetuate his rule indefinitely, the constitutional reform was grounded in the electoral process and as such would not have differed dramatically from other countries, such as the UK where Margaret Thatcher (b. 1925) was Prime Minister for 11 years. In fact, one key distinguishing factor in Venezuela is that Chávez has won repeated elections, despite US attempts to discredit him as an authoritarian demagogue. As historian Greg Grandin notes, "I can think of no other instance where similar attempts to reorder political and social relations have been ratified at the ballot on an ongoing basis."[1] Moreover, the fairness of Venezuela's elections, including an unsuccessful recall in 2004 and the constitutional reform of 2007, have been certified by the Organization of American States, the Carter Center, and the European Union. The media continues uncensored, and most of it relentlessly attacks Chávez, even supporting his overthrow in the failed 2002 military coup, although he nationalized one of the networks in 2006, a step that has made some supporters uneasy. Indications that Chávez's popularity may be waning surfaced in the November 2008 regional elections. While parties friendly to Chávez yet maintain the upper hand in congressional representation, Chávez's party lost out to opponents in many areas of the country.

Chávez and "the Pink Tide"

President Chávez has maintained a highly controversial foreign policy: allegedly siding with the leftist guerrillas in Colombia; claiming for Venezuela a wide swath of tiny neighboring Guyana; and repeatedly disparaging the conservative candidates in elections in Peru and Mexico. Illustrative of the divisiveness his image invokes was the response to his performance at the United Nations General Assembly in late 2006, where in a speech viewed by much of the world, he compared George W. Bush to the devil. Newspapers and other media outlets in the US referred to him as a buffoon at best, while the media in Argentina and Bolivia laughed out loud and cheered him on; Ecuador's Rafael Correa remarked that the comparison was unfair to the devil. No one, however, doubts the influence he can wield using Venezuela's oil supply, and record high oil prices, as clout (see Box 14.1). For example, in 2005 Venezuela underwrote Argentina's loans

Box 14.1   Got milk for oil?

One of the most innovative initiatives of the Bolivarian Revolution is its pursuit of agreements with various Latin American and Caribbean countries to exchange oil for doctors and medical personnel (Cuba); milk and software technology (Uruguay); and cattle and medical equipment (Argentina). In addition oil was sold at preferred prices (or given outright as charity) to the Dominican Republic, Haiti – and even the South Bronx, one of the poorest boroughs of New York City, populated heavily by Latin Americans. In addition to the delivery of cheap oil to the Bronx, parts of Massachusetts and other poor areas, Chávez offered to send relief to victims of Hurricane Katrina in lower Louisiana and Mississippi. The offer, refused by the US government, mimicked Cuba's offer of medical personnel in the immediate aftermath of the hurricane. More importantly, on March 28, 2006 Chávez sent a message to the Bush Administration offering to drop oil to $50 a barrel, down from its then level of $75 a barrel, which would have knocked about a dollar off every gallon at the pump. The White House quickly rejected the offer, denouncing it as so much grandstanding on the part of Venezuela's president. With oil at $40 a barrel at the end of 2008, Chávez has seen his influence curtailed.

from other sources to the tune of $2.4 billion, allowing the Kirchner government to pay off the IMF, and it has bought over $300 million in bonds from Ecuador.

Complicating Social Ties

Hugo Chávez's Bolivarian Revolutionary agenda has not appealed to voters everywhere. In two key elections moderate-to-conservative candidates defeated left populists Hugo Chávez had backed. In the first case, Ollanta Moisés Humala Tasso (b. 1963) ran for the president of Peru in 2006 on a platform calling for social reforms and nationalization of mineral resources. A former lieutenant colonel in the Peruvian army, Humala, like Chávez, had arisen through the ranks of the armed forces, and his past was thus clouded by accusations of human rights violations during the "dirty war" against the Shining Path and other guerrilla movements during the turbulent 1990s. Running for office under a coalition that included the Union for Peru (*Unión por el Perú*) and the Peruvian Nationalist Party (*Partido Nacionalista Peruana*), Humala emerged from the crowded field after the first round, only to meet defeat in the second round to former president Alan García (b. 1949), leader of the Aprista Party (APRA), who had served as president from 1985 to 1990. Voters seemed willing to overlook García's earlier humiliating drubbing in the wake of a series of economic disasters, ineffectual attempts to quell the guerrilla uprising, corruption, and failed social programs. Several commentators argued that Humala might have lost some votes because of suspicions over his human rights record from his military days. Others contend that Alan García benefitted from the backlash set off by Chávez's enthusiastic endorsement of Humala, which many Peruvians interpreted as unwelcome meddling in their own internal affairs.

A second case, marred by even greater acrimony, was the presidential election in Mexico during the fall of 2006. Felipe de Jesus Calderón (b. 1962) of the PAN was elected in a contest so close it is impossible to say whether he really won the election or not. Calderón took office on December 1, 2006 when the national election commission declared him the winner. The opposition PRD screamed fraud, but either because they had tired of the controversy or because the majority really believed Calderón the winner, little was left but the bombast over the outcome. Similar to Peru, Chávez's outspoken support for the PRD candidate rubbed some Mexicans the wrong way, quite possibly throwing a crucial number of votes to Calderón in this extremely tight race.

As luck would have it, the rise of Hugo Chávez coincided with the Bush Administration's general neglect of Latin America. With US concerns focused squarely on the Middle East, wars with Iraq and Afghanistan, and festering problems in Korea, Latin America was mostly left to its own devices, a situation that actually might have allowed for greater autonomy. By the time that George W. Bush launched a mini-tour of South America in March 2007, stopping off in Brazil, Uruguay, Colombia, and Guatemala, many diplomats viewed his foreign policy initiative as too little too late. Commenting on the trip, the Council on Hemispheric Affairs summed up North–South relations tersely: "The general distaste for the Bush administration within Latin America is now a profound fact of life." Met throughout Latin America by demonstrations and media hostility toward the US, Bush attempted to assuage his critics by signing trade agreements with Uruguay, entering into a joint ethanol deal with Brazil, and lending final approval to loan and aid agreements. No matter what Bush had on offer, Hugo Chávez had been there first with proposals the US could not, or did not, match, resulting in a continued unfavorable view of the US among its Latin American neighbors. While Argentina, Bolivia, Ecuador, and Venezuela have aligned more closely with Chávez, and Mexico, Colombia, and Peru with generally more favorable ties with Washington, Brazil, Chile, and Uruguay have attempted to remain aloof from close associations with either camp.

Chile's Transition to Democracy

After the defeat of General Pinochet in 1990 and the return to democracy, Chile's socialist coalition government, *Concertación de Partidos por la Democracia* (Coalition of Parties for Democracy), known as the *Concertación*, has embraced a model that critics on the left have seen as more at peace with neoliberalism and privatization than aimed at reducing socioeconomic inequalities. The picture is more complicated. Under Pinochet, Chile was a poster child for neoliberalism, its economic policy a page out of conservative economist Milton Friedman's (1912–2006) *Capitalism and Freedom*. Although Pinochet has been gone for over a decade, the *Concertación* has not been able to dismantle the extensive privatization that took place under the junta. Defenders of

Figure 14.2   Isabel Reveco, a forensic anthropologist, shows Chilean Judge Juan Guzman the remains of persons presumed "disappeared" during the Pinochet regime, ca. 2000. (Patrick Zachmann/Magnum Photos)

the post-Pinochet governments argue that the state is committed to ending poverty, malnutrition, and illiteracy, but it has been difficult to win over many conservatives in Congress to such an agenda. Nonetheless, private investment has been massive, Chile's copper mines are in the hands of foreign companies, and public works have not addressed the needs of poorer people, for example, building superhighways for auto-mobiles at the expense of expanding public transportation; erecting luxury, high-rise apartments rather than housing for the thousands who remain in desperately poor slums; and facilitating the emergence of private schools and universities thereby draining funds from the public education system.

Chile's growth, as much as eight percent for several years and hovering around five to six percent in 2005, has been based on energetic marketing of agricultural products and wine. Chile now has extensive bilateral trade agreements with the US, China, the European Union, MERCOSUR, South Korea, Japan, and Mexico and is adding more all the time. The agreements provide large markets for many varieties of fruits and vege-tables that ripen when the northern hemisphere is in winter. Record-high copper prices have helped to strengthen the peso and provide high-paying jobs for a small sector of the workforce, but unemployment remains a chronic problem in much of the country. Over the more than two decades of socialist governments education, health care, environmental policies, and social services have improved markedly; however, pressing problems, such as inadequate housing, low wages, inequality, and rural malnutrition, have received less attention.

Chile's most distinguishing feature in 2007 was its president, Michelle Bachelet (b. 1951), who assumed office in 2006, a year when female heads of government doubled across the globe. Bachelet's assumption of political office was seen as paradoxical in a country that is by most standards strongly Catholic and culturally conservative. It bears remembering that right-wing women were at the forefront of the movement that brought down Salvador Allende's socialist coalition in 1973, and many elite women were (and still are) mainstays of the pro-Catholic, conservative opposition to any form of class, social, or gender equality.

Nonetheless, Bachelet's presidency has signaled a tremendous change. A socialist, atheist, unmarried mother of three children from different fathers, a former political prisoner who was tortured in Villa Grimaldi, one of Chile's most famous detention centers, and who was exiled in East Germany, Bachelet is a decidedly new kind of leader (Figure 14.2). Her very election reflects greater tolerance of a more radical, feminist agenda on the part of the electorate, or at least a willingness to consider a more radical cultural makeup. She has introduced several key changes, including sex education in schools; free access to contraception for all girls and women 14 years and older, with or without parental consent; appointment of many women to government posts; and other measures that have sparked the ire of the Catholic hierarchy and the moderate political majority. As a physician, Bachelet is very interested in promoting women's health, and as a feminist politician she is demonstrating a willingness to break through the barriers that have prevented women from achieving meaningful employment at all levels of society. As she proclaimed in her first annual address to the Chilean congress: "I am here as a woman, representing the defeat of the exclusion to which we were subjected for so long."[2] Nonetheless, Chile was one of only three countries in Latin America in 2008 that did not allow abortions, even in the case of rape or when the mother's life was in danger.

New Social Movements

Michelle Bachelet's words can be interpreted more broadly, to include all of those in Latin America who have been excluded. Bachelet and Argentina's Cristina Kirchner have won office because a vital feminist movement has been organizing to break down traditional gender barriers that excluded women from positions of authority. Evo Morales in Bolivia and Lula in Brazil rose through the ranks of the trade union movement and broad political coalitions that promoted a progressive agenda: MÁS (*Movimiento al Socialismo*) in Bolivia and the PT in Brazil. In fact, the most promising change on the political scene today is the rise of activists and social action groups, many of them transnational, throughout Latin America. In country after country dictatorships were brought down and reform-minded leaders won office because of the grass-roots work of countless mass organizations. These "new social movements" have spearheaded a multipronged approach to widening democratic rights throughout Latin America.

With the aid of radical church groups, progressive and leftist political parties, and the joint efforts of domestic and international agencies, a new agenda is in motion calling for laws to distribute land, promote gender equality, protect the environment, win rights for workers, redress centuries of abuse toward indigenous people and people of color, and further the cause of social justice.

The most controversial move of Chávez's Bolivarian Revolution was state-supported land redistribution, including forceful land occupations by peasants armed with machetes and firearms, backed by military units. Although the government claims that peasants who were paid very low wages on big estates in the past have a right to occupy idle land, the previous owners, unsurprisingly, do not agree. More than 160 peasants and eight landowners have been killed in clashes, usually between squatters and hired gunmen working for the landowners, and sometimes escalating into retaliatory attacks against the owners. The peasants have enjoyed the backing of the Chávez Administration, as a part of the latter's efforts to increase Venezuela's self-sufficiency in food production. Toward that end the government has installed thousands of state-financed cooperatives on properties previously owned by cattle ranchers, and, according to the government, little used. The new cooperatives boast towns with modest three-bedroom houses, schools, libraries, internet service, meeting halls, and other amenities, centered around a town plaza adorned with a bust of Simón Bolívar. In both the cooperatives and in small farming communities, the government claims to be putting to use land that was left fallow or underutilized. Individual landowners and the associations have hired gunmen to protect their property from land invasions, a situation that has put the owners in direct conflict with military units working under Chávez's mandate to distribute land to the peasants or to protect squatters who have moved onto unused land.

Land seizures in Venezuela, as well as Brazil, have brought to the foreground conflicts that have been a part of Latin American politics throughout history. The largest social movement in Latin America currently is the Landless Workers' Movement (MST, *Movimento dos Trabalhadores Rurais Sem Terra*), numbering 1.5 million members in 23 states of Brazil. The appearance of a movement to reclaim land is not surprising in a country where just over one percent of landowners control nearly half (47 percent) of land suitable for cultivation. The MST began under the dictatorship in the late 1970s, when rural laborers began to take advantage of the *abertura*, or democratic opening, that came into effect shortly before military rule ended in 1984. The first land seizures occurred in the southern states of Rio Grande do Sul and Paraná. The press began to label the squatters as the people "*sem-terra*" (the landless ones) and, after some initial resistance, they eventually adopted an originally pejorative term for themselves. The first meeting of Landless Rural Workers took place in 1983 in Cascavel, Paraná, and the following year the MST officially organized itself at the national level. Since 1985, the MST has peacefully occupied unused land, won land titles for more than 350,000 families in 2,000 settlements, and protects 180,000 encamped families currently awaiting government recognition. As a result of MST agitation and lobbying, the 1988 Brazilian Constitution legalized the rights of squatters, stating that unproductive land should be used for a "larger social function."

One of the most contentious points in the MST program is differences between those who seek to increase production through the use of pesticides and herbicides, and cooperatives that rely on Bionatur seeds and chemical-free farming. Disagreements over environmental concerns among the landless intersects with the "culture of liberation" adopted by some communities, but not others. The Ministry of the Environment, with additional support from private benefactors in Brazil and abroad, supports a program of environmental education in some communities. However, although the MST website and many of its strongest backers point to the communities' environmental mission, this is not always the case. Splits in regard to the need to preserve the natural environment and human health, uphold gender equality, fight for equality, promote indigenous rights, and ensure sustainability run through the MST. Some are convinced that the socialist-oriented priests and radical organizers who founded the MST and promoted it as a tool for forging a culture of liberation are more in favor of the radical agenda than the farmers who simply joined to make a living. What unites the MST is the view that families have a right to a sustainable life, and that the role of the government is to protect those who fight to provide for themselves by occupying and cultivating unused land.

Movements for Racial and Gender Equality

While the return to democracy in the 1980s and 1990s in many Latin American countries was greeted with enthusiasm by the broad progressive coalitions that had worked for years to end brutal dictatorships and authoritarian rule, it is not easy to calculate the extent of racial discrimination and movements to overcome it in Latin America as a whole. The reason for this has to do with the complicated methods of counting, defining, and categorizing people of color in the many different countries and regions of Latin America. As a key historian of African-descendant people in Latin America, George Reid Andrews, points out, over 70 percent of blacks live in one country: Brazil. However, in many countries – Colombia, Cuba, Venezuela, the Caribbean islands, Panama and other parts of Central America – there are very many people of mixed-race, or (Reid Andrews' term) "browns." Anti-discrimination movements have been complicated affairs. Many people of mixed-race background, who might be identified as "black," have shunned black movements because they have seen themselves as mulatto, or even white, depending on their occupation, education, and social class. In Brazil in the 1930s, mainly middle-class, urban blacks embraced a movement for racial equality, the Negro Front (*Frente Negra Brasileira*, FNB), and achieved minor success in pointing out the fallacy of Brazil's so-called racial democracy. Getulio Vargas banned the FNB in 1937, along with all other political parties, but his purpose in this case was undoubtedly to distinguish any movement by Afro-descendants to build an autonomous movement.

Andrews argues that middle-class blacks have been more interested in culturally defined political organizations in Brazil and elsewhere in Latin America, since the level of discrimination among educated, urban, middle-class blacks has been the most overt and has prevented them from taking higher positions in both the private and public bureaucracy. Discrimination against blacks for industrial, service, and manual labor working-class jobs is less of an issue. Rather than forming separate political organizations, black workers have fought for equality and social justice in trade unions, land and housing occupations, or in the many social movements apparent throughout the continent. Movements for indigenous rights have had similar histories; however, the cultural distinction is more pronounced. In Guatemala, Bolivia, Ecuador, Peru, and Mexico, countries with large indigenous populations, discrimination and isolation have been most keenly felt among non-Spanish-speaking, culturally non-European communities. Bolivia's current crisis, where the eastern provinces are seeking to separate from Evo Morales' government, has everything to do with racial prejudice. Morales' organization MÁS has the loyalty of the indigenous majority, calling for recognition of native languages, educational and governance practices, and an affirmative action program to provide jobs. The white and mestizo Bolivians in the wealthier Santa Cruz area refuse to accept this. Similar to the black–white conflicts of Brazil, Indians have seen greater gains as members of trade unions – miners, coca growers, factory laborers – than in efforts to maintain autonomy.

The musicologist Robin Moore argues that black culture in Latin America has been "nationalized" or diffused through the broader society. African-derived music, dance, even religion, is widely accepted, especially in Brazil, Cuba, much of Colombia, and the Caribbean in general, but acceptance of black culture has not meant the end to racial discrimination. To a lesser extent the Andean music, especially pan pipes, flutes and other instruments, textiles, weavings, dance have been mainstreamed in Peru, Bolivia, and elsewhere, at least as commodities for tourism. Indigenous culture is not mainstream, but the impact of *indigenismo* is quite profound, extending, by pure weight of numbers of people and spread of their produce, culture, and community cohesion, to every corner of Latin America. For example, the influence of indigenous aesthetics can be found throughout the San Telmo street markets in Buenos Aires, along with a growing number of handicrafts. Argentina has not had a strong presence of Indian people for a couple hundred years, but many people from Bolivia, Paraguay, parts of Chile and remote areas of Argentina are now migrating to the outskirts of the city, bringing with them their indigenous crafts from which to make a living in the Buenos Aires marketplaces. Neoliberal programs resulting in the privatization of communal lands, agro-industrial encroachment into regions Indian people have farmed for centuries, loss of water rights, and an inability to maintain their communities in the face of a globalized economy, has forced indigenous people off their land and into shantytowns mushrooming on the outskirts of cities. Whether they will unite into single-issue, indigenous rights organizations, or join with other people of color, industrial or landless workers, will be the story of the twenty-first century.

Women and Politics

While women have played an important role in trade unions, religious organizations, communities, and human rights organizations, the specific agenda of rights for women did not always make it into the new democratic agenda. Surprisingly, despite the key role played by women in the guerrilla movements in El Salvador and Nicaragua, demands for reproductive rights, equality in jobs, and resources for children were relegated to the backburner. Giocondo Belli's memoir, *The Country Under My Skin*, pointed to a history of male dominance and sexual exploitation of *guerrilleras* that undermined the full acceptance of women as equals in the post-revolutionary era. In the neoliberal environment that took hold after the electoral defeat of the Sandinista government in 1990, the left agenda was reshaped to accommodate conservatives and appease their harshest critics. The "new" Daniel Ortega who re-took the presidency in late 2006 was tamed in every way, but, feminists have argued, his disregard of women's rights is not simply a result of conciliating the right; instead it represents his newfound fundamentalist Christianity. The only woman who had served as a *commandante* during the struggle, Mónica Baltodano, attributes Ortega's excessive subservience to the bankers, the Church, and the conservative US agenda on reproductive rights to his own political insecurity. Elected with a hair's breadth margin, a share of which was won by promising favors, Ortega has been unwilling to push for radical reforms.

In another case, Uruguay's left-liberal president, Tabaré Vásquez, has vacillated on attempts to decriminalize abortion. Women's rights in Uruguay have been at the center of political tensions between left and right for much of the twentieth century. Generally heralded as one of the places where women gained political rights earlier than other countries – the right to sue for divorce in 1913 and the right to vote in 1932 – Uruguay has been debating reproductive rights longer than most other countries, with the exception of Cuba, Guyana, and Puerto Rico (which functions under US constitutional law). The 2005 victory of the Broad Front (*Frente Amplio*) was expected to accelerate the passage of reproductive rights legislation for women, a proposal backed by many party members and supported by 63 percent of the population in recent polls. Despite this widespread support, Tabaré Vásquez has excluded reproductive rights, prohibition of workplace and gender-based discrimination, and domestic violence from his planned reforms in areas such as labor law, social services, and education. Some critics argue that the current government's lack of interest in addressing women's oppression stems from the strong influence of the Catholic Church, and the Frente Amplio's reluctance to court disfavor. Others contend that Vásquez is an old-style leftist and as such sees women's oppression as ancillary to the main capital–labor/owner–worker contradiction. Gender inequality, however, does not easily disappear. In the 1990s Cuba has witnessed a resurgence of prostitution, racial exploitation of black women, and other signs of gender and racial discrimination that were supposedly wiped out in the 30 years of socialism.

Notably it is in Mexico where the most far-reaching reproductive rights legislation has been passed. Despite the outspoken opposition of the Catholic Church and Felipe Calderón's conservative government, Mexico City has passed one of the most pro-choice abortion rights laws in the Americas. The law, upheld in the courts in a challenge from anti-abortion forces in August 2008, grants full reproductive rights to any woman or girl, without parental or spousal consent. This law, placing reproductive choice in the hands of the woman alone, stands on a par with Cuba, European countries, and a few states in the US known for liberal reproductive laws.

Women and political office

Despite criticisms of the go-slow attitude that has enveloped some of the left and center-left governments, women in Latin America have moved into government positions at an unprecedented rate, regardless of political affiliation. At the beginning of 2007 the United Nations reported that worldwide more women were members of parliamentary bodies than ever before: a total of 35 out of 262 (13 percent). A number of Latin American nations have adopted affirmative action-type quotas for the number of female candidates mandated to run for office on any given party ticket. In Venezuela, 30 percent of candidates on a party's slate must be women; Chile has a 50–50 gender-parity cabinet; Bolivia now requires that 30 percent of all candidates for local and national elections be women. Even with these measures in place, the pace of achieving gender equality has been slow. Most Venezuelan women, for example, do not know of the rule, and in recent elections even when women were informed of it they voted for men instead of women to fill party slots. Such data has to be scrutinized however, since some anti-Chávez women of the elite class running for office argued that the Bolivarian reforms were raising the wages of domestic help. In Bolivia, the 30 percent has thus far been appropriated by elite, even right-wing, women, and indigenous and rural women have yet to embrace gender parity as an important issue. That these measures designed to increase women's political participation have been less than fully successful does not negate the progress that has been made thus far.

The beginning of the twenty-first century did find Latin America's political profile, both politically and in terms of gender and race much changed from where it stood a mere 50 years earlier (Figure 14.3). The people of Latin America have frequently joined together in movements large and small to win greater freedom and to expand democratic rights. In this regard they have not differed from their North American neighbors, who have similarly forged movements for racial, gender, LGBT, and social equality. Moreover, as we enter the new millennium, it is more and more apparent that these previously divided lands are increasingly overlapping, sometimes creating a new cultural fusion, often giving rise to tensions and antagonism.

The Latin Americanization of the United States

At the dawn of the twenty-first century, the number of people of Latin American origin residing in the United States had reached more than 41.3 million, comprising nearly 15 percent of the population. Of that number 60 percent were from Mexico, with the next largest groups from Central America, the Caribbean, and the rest of Latin America. It is further estimated that the US is now home to 3.5 million Luso-Americans, or people who claim ancestry from a Portuguese-speaking country, of which nearly 1 million are from Brazil (Figure 14.4 shows the origins of *all* immigrants to the US in 2007). Demographers have been tracking the rapid increase in what is variously called the "Hispanic" or "Latino(a)" population for decades, but the spread of migrants from Latin America to many parts of the US broke into the consciousness of the "average American" in the spring of 2006. From March through May of that year well over a million people

Figure 14.3 Then Senator, later President, Cristina Fernández de Kirchner of Argentina and Chilean President Michelle Bachelet greeted well-wishers when Bachelet visited Buenos Aires on March 2006. (Photo from the Office of the President of Argentina)

took to the streets in hundreds of cities and towns throughout the United States in some of the largest demonstrations in recent history. They were protesting the passage of HR 4437, a proposed reform of immigration laws sponsored by Wisconsin Congressman James Sensenbrenner. The bill had passed the Republican-controlled House of Representatives the previous December by a margin of 203 to 164 and was sent on to the

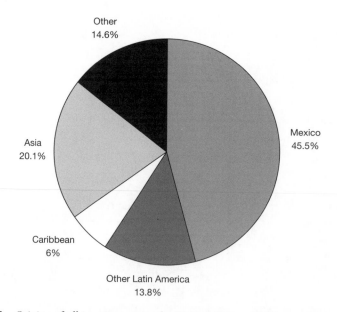

Figure 14.4   Origins of all immigrants to the United States, 2007.

Senate, with the presumption that after some tinkering a compromise bill that preserved the sentiment of the House version would make its way into law. That did not happen.

Controversy broke out immediately, since the bill dramatically escalated the penalties for entering and residing in the US illegally, including classifying as felons all illegal aliens, along with anyone who knowingly helped them enter or remain in the country. Since an estimated 12 million immigrants, mainly from Latin America and the Caribbean, reside without documents throughout the country, this aspect of the law alarmed a broad spectrum of people, including anyone faced with helping recently arrived relatives or friends in distress. Many members of the social service professions, who are required legally and ethically to assist those in need of medical care, counseling, schooling, or advice, regardless of their citizenship status, protested that the law forced them to police their clientele in a manner inconsistent with ethical and professional guidelines.

Several remarkable features characterized the response to the bill, highlighting the changes in twenty-first century America. First, and most obviously, the protests were massive. Their size and geographic diversity shook the Washington establishment, both Republican and Democrat, in a way few other events emanating from the Latino community had. The largest national turnout occurred on April 10, 2006 in 102 cities across the country, including crowds of 50,000–100,000 people in midwestern and southern states previously unassociated with large immigrant populations. Moreover, 1,000 protesters in Tijuana blocked for a full day the busiest international border crossing in the world in support of rights for the migrants who daily move back and forth from Mexico to the US. Nearly all of the protests were peaceful and attracted favorable media attention, although there was forceful criticism from conservative radio talk-show hosts, political commentators, right-wing groups such as the Minutemen, and even from moderate, non-immigrant citizens regarding what they saw as "anti-American" symbolism at some of the protests, especially Mexican flags. Additional rallies in several cities on May Day drew large crowds and support from many quarters.

The second important feature of the response to HR 4437 was the way that it highlighted the existence of Spanish-language media not only in promoting the protests, but, more fundamentally, as a cultural force with a widespread impact on a growing segment of the US population. The new media, encompassing Spanish-language radio and television stations, blogs, and internet sites, was reaching and mobilizing millions of Americans, indicative of a profound shift in the nation's cultural landscape.

The two most important Spanish-language media outlets, Univision and Telemundo, proved to be enormously successful in reaching millions of Latinos, while at the same time unveiling to the non-Latino population a new force on the US political scene. Univision, the largest Spanish-language television network and the fifth largest overall (behind Fox, ABC, NBC, and CBS), began in 1961 in San Antonio, Texas as a subsidiary of the Mexican Telesistema Mexicano network. Now headquartered in Los Angeles with major production facilities in Miami, Univision broadcasts full local news and programming, both its own and from international networks, through over 50 stations in 24 states, as well as on cable, throughout the country. Second in size is Telemundo, founded in Hialeah, Florida in 1984. Newer, and with a smaller market share, Telemundo is nonetheless huge as media outlets go, broadcasting through 55 stations in 20 states to an audience only slightly smaller than that of Univision.

A third distinguishing feature of the protests was the extent to which they galvanized support from a new audience: second- and third-generation Latino youth. The internet, including thousands of personal blogs and chat rooms, proved very important for reaching this younger cohort of English-speaking Latinos who identified with the cause of immigrant rights, even though they spoke little or no Spanish, Portuguese, or French. Through websites such as MySpace and Facebook, the generation of Latin Americans born in the United States, and/or fully integrated into the same youth culture as their non-Latino counterparts were drawn into the protests against HR 4437. More significantly, a new community of young people who might have been previously uninvolved, even uninterested, in the cultural identity of their parents and grandparents, now found reason to embrace their "Latinidad." The protests served as a catalyst for the assertion of an identity forged from the values of earlier generations of Latin American immigrants, combined with the accoutrements of a powerful US youth culture.

Immigration and Free Trade

As the number of legal and illegal immigrants residing in the US increased throughout the twentieth century and their presence was felt in regions of the country heretofore unaccustomed to welcoming recent immigrants – for example the Midwest and parts of the South – politicians, civic leaders, educators, trade unionists, and ordinary citizens became more and more uneasy with the changes occurring on the national scene.

Whereas some of the hostility toward undocumented workers came from tradition-ally conservative sectors, others who nominally supported the expansion of rights, such as African Americans, found themselves in competition with lower-wage Latinos in a declining labor market. Polls have shown around 40 percent of the estimated 100 million people living in Mexico report that they would come to the United States if they had the opportunity and the money. At $2,500 for the cost of a "coyote" to smuggle them across the border, many Mexicans, as well as migrants from Central America, save for years to make the dangerous trip, in which between 400 and 600 die yearly attempting the crossing. The trip seems even more treacherous when one considers that 75 percent of Mexican immigrants remain no longer than three years in the US.

Ironically, one of the main accusations lobbed at illegal immigrants is their use of resources in the US and thus the burden placed on the tax payer. According to Douglas S. Massey, who monitors immigration's effects on his online journal, *Immigration Daily*, "illegal immigrants are less likely than natives to use public services. While 66 percent of Mexican immigrants report the withholding of Social Security taxes from their paychecks and 62 percent say that employers withhold income taxes, only 10 percent say they have ever sent a child to U.S. public schools, 7 percent indicate they have received Supplemental Security Income, and 5 percent or less report ever using food stamps, welfare, or unemployment compensation."[3]

In the debates surrounding the 1993 passage of the North American Free Trade Agreement (NAFTA), proponents, especially the Clinton Administration, argued that the effects of the treaty would dramatically reduce the number of migrants seeking to enter the US. According to President Bill Clinton (b. 1946): "There will be less illegal immigration because more Mexicans will be able to support their children by staying home," while Carlos Salinas de Gortari (b. 1948), Mexico's president, proclaimed that in the post-NAFTA era Americans would get low-cost Mexican tomatoes instead of tomato-pickers. An expansion of the earlier Canada–US Free Trade Agreement of 1988, NAFTA eliminates tariff duties on products traded among the United States, Canada, and Mexico and provides for the gradual phasing out of other tariffs over a 15-year period. Targeted goods include motor vehicles and automotive parts, computers, textiles, and agriculture products; protection of intellectual property rights (patents, copyrights, and trademarks) is also sought. Some terms of the agreement, such as those covering agriculture products and industrial goods, were negotiated bilaterally, but the thrust of the accord was trilateral, with all provisions to be applied equally among the three participants. The most contentious areas of the accord, relating to worker and environmental protections, have been left to supplemental agreements, called "side agreements," which have been signed and implemented irregularly since 1994.

Rather than broaden Mexico's prosperity and create jobs, the effect seems to have been the opposite. Since taking effect on January 1, 1994 NAFTA has mainly benefited Mexico's wealthy landholders and industrialists; an estimated two million Mexican farmers have been driven off the land because the corn and grain grown in small plots could not compete with the better-quality and cheaper, highly subsidized and mechanized, agriculture products flooding the Mexican market from the US and Canada. To illustrate, in 2000 corn producers in the US, just one group of farmers, received $10.1 billion in subsidies from Washington. That amount was ten times the Mexican government's entire annual agricultural budget for all farm output in the country. Desperate Mexicans have left the countryside and poured into the cities where few job prospects exist, forcing many to then join the ranks of migrants crossing into the US to find work.

Opponents Confront Free Trade

The signing of the NAFTA agreement gave rise to the only major guerrilla-styled insurgency of the late twentieth century. The movement burst on the scene on New Year's Day, 1994 in Chiapas, Mexico, calling for the repeal of NAFTA on the day it was scheduled to take effect. Led by a council of 24 Maya Indian *comandantes*, or commanders, and one non-Indian sub-commander (the enigmatic Subcomandante Marcos – see Box 14.2), hundreds of masked men, women, and children carrying firearms, sticks fashioned as guns, machetes, and an array of crude armaments, wearing traditional Indian clothing or makeshift military uniforms, marched through the state capital of San Cristóbal de las Casas. In the tradition of the Sandinistas and El Salvador's FMLN, the Chiapas insurgents took the name of a famous revolutionary from early in the century, Emiliano Zapata. By invoking the memory of Zapata – the Indian leader from Morelos who led an army in the 1910 Mexican Revolution – the newly formed *Ejército Zapatista de Liberación Nacional* (EZLN, Zapatista Army of National Liberation) signaled its intent to fight for the rights of indigenous people, in a nation that had left revolution behind in all but slogans and imagery. The fighting was sporadic; 154 people died in the 1994 uprising, mostly Mayan peasants, and conflict has broken out again from time to time since.

Before Mexico's 2006 national elections, the Zapatista movement focused attention on the inequities of free trade (Figure 14.6). Still in existence, the Zapatistas have not been able to overturn NAFTA, nor to alter the neoliberal policies embraced by the Mexican government. In 1996 President Vicente Fox conceded to the guerrillas some autonomy for their region, although the accords are said to be weakly enforced. The Zapatistas, along with regional, community, labor, and peasant forces, continue to agitate for a more equitable distribution of wealth and power.

The Free Trade Area of the Americas (FTAA) is another US initiative designed to create a single trade zone. The FTAA has been on the table since 1994, but only reached public attention in 2001 during the Summit of the Americas in Quebec City, Canada. Heated demonstrations, similar to those in Seattle, Genoa, and Washington, DC when those cities hosted the meetings of the World Trade Organization (WTO), erupted in Quebec. A later summit in Mar del Plata, Argentina, in 2005 elicited a similar round of condemnation, this time under the leadership of Hugo Chávez, who has called for a union of Latin American and Caribbean nations that excludes the United States. To date Chávez has only won a few countries to his proposed Bolivarian Alternative for the Americas (*Alternativa Bolivariana para las Américas*, ALBA), including Ecuador, Bolivia, Nicaragua, and Cuba, but the notion has not been outright rejected by others.

Box 14.2   Subcomandante Marcos

Despite its indigenous leadership, the most internationally recognized Zapatista is a white, educated man known as Subcomandante Marcos (Figure 14.5), who is thought to be Rafael Sebastián Guillén Vicente, a former university philosophy professor with a graduate degree from the prestigious National Autonomous University of Mexico (UNAM). Conversant in English, Italian, and French, as well as Spanish and the indigenous languages of Chiapas, Subcomandante Marcos is attractive to an international audience. He is very media savvy, and has cut a dashing figure both within Mexico and abroad, helping to promote the group's image. He has appeared on *60 Minutes* and other US news shows, been the object of hundreds of marriage proposals from women writing to Mexican newspapers, and even set out on a motorcycle tour of Latin America, reminiscent of Che Guevara's travels immortalized in the book and film *The Motorcycle Diaries*. Marcos is a smart politician entirely capable of using the media to bring attention to the plight of Mexican peasants.

Figure 14.5   Zapatista Subcomandante Marcos and Comandante Tacho de la Realidad, Chiapas, Mexico, 1999.

Figure 14.6 "Chiles Rellenos Contra Hot Dogs." In this comedic drawing, Mexican artist Francisco Verástegui uses a battle between two iconic national dishes as a stand-in for the broader tension between US and Mexican commerce and culture.

It remains to be seen whether FTAA or ALBA will succeed, since without economic powerhouses Brazil and Argentina no trade agreement will be meaningful or effective. The sharp economic downturn beginning in September 2008 derailed nearly all financial and trade agreements in the hemisphere, for hour long, remains to be seen.

Immigration and Neoliberalism

Immigrants to the US from Latin America have left their homes and communities to forge a better life in a distant land for precisely the same reasons earlier waves of immigrants left Ireland, Italy, and other areas of Europe, pouring into crowded tenements and sweatshops in rapidly expanding cities in both North and South America. Facing starvation, political repression, and economic stagnation at home, millions of people from Europe and Asia in the nineteenth and twentieth centuries pulled up stakes, often with great reluctance, to make a living in the Americas. In the late twentieth century, Latin Americans abandoned lands torn apart by war or, more often, due to the less dramatic, but equally crushing, impact of day-to-day poverty to migrate to the United States. A slogan once splayed across a building in London's heavily populated Asian and West Indian East End – "We came here because you went there" – captures the essence of the mass migration from former colonies, and subsequent neo-colonies, to Britain. The slogan applies equally well to the accelerated emigration of Latin Americans as a consequence of US intervention in Central America in 1980s and 1990s neoliberal policies. Serious observers and a few politicians have begun to probe the reasons so many immigrants from Latin America are desperate enough to work long hours in dirty, unpleasant, boring, and dangerous jobs for less than the minimum wage. As the economic crisis at the end of 2008 deepened, the number of illegal immigrants crossing the border slowed precipitously. For the first time in decades, border police estimated that more migrants seemed to be crossing back into Mexico than entering the US. Consequently, remittances declined, a fact that will only increase the misery of the poor in Mexico, Central America, and the Caribbean.

Nevertheless, in September 2006 the US House of Representatives, followed by the Senate, voted by very wide margins to authorize the construction of a 700-mile long fence separating parts of California, Arizona, New Mexico, and Texas from Mexico. The complex of rolls of barbed wire, concrete barriers, surveillance cameras, and guard posts resembles the Berlin Wall that from 1961 to 1989 divided the German city between the Soviet-allied East and the NATO-allied West. Designed to impede embarrassing political defections and to stop the flow of skilled laborers and professionals from abandoning East Germany for more lucrative careers in the West, the Wall became a symbol of repression. A steady stream of individuals embarked on highly creative, daring, and often deadly, crossings during the Wall's 28-year existence. The twenty-first century fence separating the US and Mexico has generated similar controversy. Supporters argue that it will reduce crime and drug smuggling, but Democratic Representative Sheila Jackson Lee of Texas said it would create "the largest gated community in the Western hemisphere." Since the border extends for 2,000 miles, dividing off a mere 700 miles seems to be little more than a challenge to desperate migrants to search out other ways to cross the barren desert landscape or, as in Berlin, to die trying.

The border wall seeks to stop Mexicans from entering illegally, but every year thousands of illegal immigrants from the Dominican Republic, Brazil, Colombia, Haiti, and many other countries that do not share a border with the US enter by overstaying tourist visas. As long as demand for low-wage labor remains high in the US, and so long as working conditions, educational opportunities, public services, and standards of living in Latin America continue to lag, people will risk entering illegally. The Washington Heights neighborhood in upper Manhattan is home to an estimated three-quarters of a million Dominicans who work in stores, bars, restaurants, and as manual laborers in sweatshops and factories, earning the minimum wage or less. Immigrants living in Washington Heights, the Jamaica Plain area of Boston, whole sections of Queens and Brooklyn, south Chicago, much of Florida, the West and the Southwest send back remittances that sustain families in Colombia, Mexico, El Salvador, the Dominican Republic, and other Latin countries. Without this steady flow of cash from the US, the domestic economies of more than one Latin American nation would enter severe crisis.

Finally, obsessive concerns with preventing the flow of illegal immigrants from Latin America into the US cannot stop the ethnic transformation already underway. The US Census Bureau projects that by 2050 the nation's demographic makeup will be: "European" white, 50 percent, or less; Hispanic 24 percent; black 15 percent; Asian 13 percent. Moreover, the Bureau speculates that not only will the US no longer have a white majority, but that current racial and ethnic census categories will no longer be *in* use because they will no longer be *of* use. In the coming decades the process of ethnic and racial mixture will be so widespread that previous categorizations will make about as much sense as trying to differentiate today between the European nationalities that now blend in a sea of mixed "white" rural, suburban, and metropolitan neighborhoods.

Sharing the Environment and the Cost of Stewardship

If anything, the nations of Latin America are more joined together now than at any time in the modern history of the hemisphere. From movies and music to baseball, food, and labor, the cultural and language divide is shrinking and we are increasingly on the way to becoming a shared "American" culture. But future relations between North and South America hinge on something far more fundamental – the very air we breathe, the water we drink, and our ability to cooperate as stewards of our shared environment. This most crucial of all issues also poses the greatest challenge.

Latin America is home to half of the world's tropical forests and nearly half of the plant and animal diversity of the planet; thus the impact of global warming on the continent significantly affects the world at large. Scientists contend that preservation of the Amazon rainforest is crucial to our very survival. Containing 20 percent of the world's fresh water and generating a rainforest where 16 percent of the planet's species – plant, animal, and human – reside, the destruction of one of the world's most valuable natural resources places us all in jeopardy. The issue has become increasingly urgent, since it is estimated that a portion of the rainforest the size of the state of New Jersey is destroyed each year. In addition, recent calculations have identified Brazil as the fourth largest contributor of greenhouse gas emissions, due primarily to deforestation. Forests are receding elsewhere as well. Between 1990 and 2005, over 20 percent of Ecuador's forest coverage was destroyed as a result of oil operations. One of the most devastating effects of the current drug interdiction program has been the destruction of plant species, pollution of groundwater, and human health hazards resulting from spraying the Colombian, Peruvian, and Bolivian countrysides with a highly toxic herbicide, *Fusarium oxysporum*. Despite a study conducted in Florida that showed the herbicide was a significant threat to the environment and killed all crops indiscriminately, the US Congress appropriated funds for aerial spraying.

Latin America has four of the world's largest 25 rivers, and three of the largest lakes. Ironically, in an area of the world with the highest per capita supply of water, the majority of people are without water for drinking or sanitation. Intensified global warming has exacerbated this situation. The American Geophysical Union predicts that most glaciers in the lower Andes will be gone in a decade, and total glacial runoff will dry up within the next 20 years. The consequences for residents of Peru, the country with the most glaciers, and Bolivia, a close second, are dire, since they rely on fresh water supplies from glaciers for daily use. Not only are water shortages growing severe, but melting glaciers have sparked other catastrophes, such as flooding and mudslides. There are several reasons why an area of the world with the largest share of the planet's water is facing drought. One is poor infrastructure. Mexico City, a parched and dangerously water-starved city, loses 90 percent of its water because of leaky pipes, a phenomenon repeated throughout Latin America. Another reason is the privatization of the water supplies. IMF-imposed structural adjustment agreements have mandated the sale of public utilities to private corporations as conditions for obtaining debt relief. Bolivia's water was sold to the Bechtel Corporation, which then raised the cost of water by 200 percent. The protests were so intense in 2000 that the government was forced to rescind the contract, but the huge corporation turned around and filed suit against Bolivia for $25 million in lost profits.

Global warming affects food production and increases the spread of dangerous tropical diseases such as malaria and dengue fever, both of which surfaced in Brazil in 2008. Another impact of global warming that is already apparent is the increase in hurricanes as a result of warmer oceans. The islands of the Caribbean and countries on the Central American isthmus stand in the direct path of every hurricane and tropical storm, and have increasingly borne the brunt of massive destruction and large-scale loss of human life from major storm events as the frequency of such storms has increased over the past decade.

If sustainable development is an issue that affects everyone on the planet, should the costs be shared? Several Latin American countries have proposed the novel solution of requesting compensation for refusing to develop resources that would prove ultimately to harm the environment. For example, Ecuador has extensive oil supplies that it has not developed, and cannot afford to drill and refine on its own. But a past agreement with Texaco had disastrous consequences. During the 25 years that Texaco operated in Ecuador, the oil company spilled 17 million gallons of crude oil into that nation's waterways, which it has refused to clean up. Hesitant to enter into another such agreement and risk the consequences, Ecuador has proposed a new plan. Instead of inviting one of the major oil companies to exploit this resource, or relying on Venezuela to refine the oil, President Rafael Correa has asked the international community to compensate Ecuador if it refrains from opening new oil fields in the Ecuadorian Amazon. As Correa explains it: "Ecuador doesn't ask for charity, but does ask that the international community share in the sacrifice and compensate us with at least half of what our country would receive, in recognition of the environmental benefits that would be generated by keeping this oil underground."[4] It is estimated that Ecuador is sitting on anywhere from 900 million to a billion barrels of crude oil in the Yasuni National Park. Would the international community, presumably through a UN agency, be willing to pay to prevent an irreplaceable resource – Ecuador's rainforest – from being destroyed by oil exploitation? Brazil has proposed a similar strategy that would provide financial compensation for "avoided deforestation," a plan whereby individual farmers and indigenous peoples are given payment for the "environmental service" of not harming the rainforest.

The plans generated in Ecuador and Brazil lob a direct challenge to the world at large. A version of this proposal was adopted at the December 2007 United Nations Conference on Climate Change in Bali, Indonesia. The 180 nations in attendance agreed in principle to adopt measures to compensate developing nations for refraining from exploiting their natural resources, especially cutting down rainforests. Rather than condemn the developing world for destroying resources that are essential to the health of the planet, the richer, more developed nations, who consume energy at rates hundreds of times greater than the poorer countries, have been called on to pay to preserve valuable resources, and thereby the planet. Needless to say, the bill's proponents recognize that this challenge to "put your money where your mouth is" will only come about through strict enforcement.

The future of the Americas will hinge on how well the people and governments of the hemisphere can cooperate. Despite the many conflicts and differences that have inflicted far too much damage on the people and land over the last hundreds of years, there is much to celebrate. Latin America is a beautiful and rich terrain, the people resourceful and strong, the possibilities limitless. As the writer Gabriel García Márquez reminds us, in comparison with many other parts of the world, especially Europe, Latin America is still young:

> Venerable Europe would perhaps be more perceptive if it tried to see us in its own past. If only it recalled that London took three hundred years to build its first city wall, and three hundred years more to acquire a bishop; that Rome labored in a gloom of uncertainty for twenty centuries, until an Etruscan King anchored it in history; and that the peaceful Swiss of today, who feast us with their mild cheeses and apathetic watches, bloodied Europe as soldiers of fortune as late as the Sixteenth Century.[5]

Latin America too has ancient pre-Columbian civilizations, but as a continent connected with the rest of the world, it is in its infancy. If current trends continue, in fact, the people of the entire hemisphere, North and South, will form a single cultural entity. What remains to be seen is if economic and political unity will follow. Rather than a relationship based on exploitation, destruction of the land in service of short-term gain, and exhaustion of a finite supply of natural resources, the future could be built on collaboration and respect for people and the natural environment. It could celebrate the strength of *mestizaje* – the mixture of races, the fusing of cultural legacies, the realization that all people, men and women, all races, and all ethnic strains, have created a remarkably rich history. If we are careful, both North and South America will go on for ages, but the challenge lies squarely in the hands of those of us who live and work in this hemisphere, and care deeply about its future. We cannot know precisely what lies ahead, especially as the world economic indicators point to possible long-term stagnation, but we must be aware that the consequences of failing to build a sustainable and cooperative future are unthinkable.

Notes

Preface

1 Eduardo Galeano, *Memory of Fire: 1 Genesis*, trans. Cedric Belfrage (New York: Pantheon Books, 1985), p. xv.

1 Introduction to the Land and Its People

1 Eric Hobsbawm, *Interesting Times: A Twentieth-Century Life* (New York: The New Press, 2005), p. 383.

2 Latin America in 1790

1 Creole refers to people born in the "New World." Creoles were of Caucasian, European background, although the term was sometimes used for others, such as to distinguish slaves born in America from slaves born in Africa.
2 Beginning in Columbus's time the term "Indian" was used to describe the original inhabitants of the Americas. While many terms have emerged since that more accurately and sensitively describe these populations, the word "Indian" has widespread usage among people of both indigenous and non-indigenous identity. In this text "Indian" is used interchangeably with "indigenous," to refer to the native populations of the Americas.
3 Quoted in Kirkpatrick Sale, *Christopher Columbus and the Conquest of Paradise* (New York: Penguin Publishers, 1991), p. 285.
4 Stuart F. Voss, *Latin America in the Middle Period, 1750–1929* (Lanham, MD: Rowman & Littlefield, 2001), p. 52.
5 Sonya Lipsett-Rivera, "Gender from 1750 to World War I: Latin America and the Caribbean," in T. Meade and M. Wiesner-Hanks (eds.), *A Companion to Gender History* (Oxford: Blackwell Publishers, 2006), p. 481.

6   Catherine Davies, "Colonial Dependence and Sexual Difference: Reading for Gender in the Writings of Simón Bolívar (1783–1830)," *Feminist Review* 79 (2005), p. 15.

7   Octavio Paz, "Sons of La Malinche," *Labyrinth of Solitude*, trans. Lysander Kemp (New York: Grove Atlantic Press, 1994), p. 88.

8   Guillermo Gomez-Peña, "The Two Guadalupes," in Ana Castillo (ed.), *Goddess of the Americas: Writings on the Virgin of Guadalupe.* New York: Riverhead Books, 1996, p. 180.

3   Competing Notions of Freedom

1   C. L. R. James, *The Black Jacobins: Toussaint L'Ouverture and the San Domingo Revolution* (New York: Knopf Publishing Co., 1989), p. 33.

2   Robert E. Conrad, *Children of God's Fire: A Documentary History of Black Slavery in Brazil* (Princeton: Princeton University Press, 1983), p. 121.

3   Thomas Eubank (1856), quoted in Conrad, *Children of God's Fire*, p. 122.

4   Conrad, *Children of God's Fire*, p. 129.

5   *Jornal do Comercio*, Rio de Janeiro, December 10, 1827. Quoted in Conrad, *Children of God's Fire*, p. 133.

6   James, *The Black Jacobins*, p. 35.

7   Ibid., pp. 13–14.

8   Conrad, *Children of God's Fire*, p. 183.

9   Ibid., p. 153.

10   James, *The Black Jacobins*, p. 114.

11   Stuart Voss, *Latin America in the Middle Period* (Wilmington, Del.: Scholarly Resources, Inc.), p. XX.

12   Ada Ferrer, *Insurgent Cuba: Race, Nation, and Revolution, 1868–1898* (Chapel Hill: University of North Carolina Press, 1999), p. 2.

13   Samuel Cotton, *A Journey into Contemporary Slavery in Africa* (New York: Harlem River Press, 1998).

4   Fragmented Nationalisms

1   Frances Calderón de la Barca, "Letter the Forty-Eighth" (July–Dec. 1841), *Life in Mexico* (Berkeley: University of California Press, 1982), p. 474.

2   Ibid., "Letter the Twenty-Second" (Jan.–June 1840), p. 224.

3   Peter Bakewell, *A History of Latin America*, 2nd edition (Oxford: Blackwell Publishing, 2004), p. 411.

4   John Parish Robertson and William Parish, *Four Years in Paraguay* (Philadelphia: E. L. Carey and A. Hart, 1838).

5   Carole Pateman, *The Disorder of Women: Democracy, Feminism, and Political Theory* (Palo Alto, CA: Stanford University Press, 1990), p. XX.

6   Deirdre Keenan, "Race, Gender, and Other Differences in Feminist Theory," in T. Meade and M. Wiesner-Hanks (eds.), *A Companion to Gender History* (Oxford: Blackwell Publishing, 2006), p. 112.

7   Arlene Diaz, *Female Citizens, Patriarchs, and the Law in Venezuela, 1786–1904* (Omaha: University of Nebraska, 2004), p. 5.

8 Elizabeth Dore, *Myths of Modernity: Peonage and Patriarchy in Nicaragua* (Durham, NC: Duke University Press, 2006).
9 Göran Therborn, *Between Sex and Power: Family in the World, 1900–2000* (New York, Routledge, 2005).

5 Latin America's Place in the Commodity Chain

1 George Canning, *Speeches of the Right Honourable George Canning* (Philadelphia: Key and Biddle, 1835).
2 Arcadia Bandini Brennan, *Arcadian Memories of California*. University of California Libraries, Bancroft Collection, mss. 5206:1,2 (1885), pp. 2–10.
3 Carl Schurz, "Platform of the American Anti-lmperialist League," *Speeches, Correspondence and Political Papers of Carl Schurz* (New York: G. P. Putnam's Sons, 1913).

6 Immigration, and Urban and Rural Life

1 Eric Hobsbawm, *The Age of Extremes* (New York: Random House, Inc., 1994), p. 15.
2 Alured Gray Bell, *The Beautiful Rio de Janeiro* (London: William Heinemann, 1914), p. 20.
3 Charles Darwin, *The Descent of Man and Selection in Relation to Sex* (London: John Murray, 1871), pp. 168–9.

7 Revolution from Countryside to City: Mexico

1 John Womack, Jr., *Zapata and the Mexican Revolution* (New York: Random House, 1968), p. ix.
2 John Tutino, *From Insurrection to Revolution in Mexico: Social Bases of Agrarian Violence, 1750–1940* (Princeton: Princeton University Press, 1986), p. 358.
3 Quoted in June Hahner, *Women in Latin American History, Their Lives and Views* (Berkeley: University of California Press, 1980), p. 159.
4 Womack, *Zapata and the Mexican Revolution*, p. 7.
5 John Reed, *Insurgent Mexico* (New York: International Publishers, Inc., 1988), p. 22.
6 Ibid., p. 211.
7 Hahner, *Women in Latin American History*, p. 162.
8 Ibid., p. 165.

8 The Left and the Socialist Alternative

1 John W. F. Dulles, *Anarchists and Communists in Brazil, 1900–1935* (Austin: University of Texas Press, 1973), p. 53.
2 Gene H. Bell-Villada, *García Márquez, The Man and His Work* (Chapel Hill: University of North Carolina Press, 1988), p. 44.
3 Mary Kay Vaughan, "Introduction," in Jocelyn Olcott, Mary Kay Vaughan, and Gabriela Cano (eds.), *Sex in Revolution: Gender, Politics, and Power in Modern Mexico* (Durham, NC: Duke University Press, 2006), p. 27.

4   José Carlos Mariátegui, "World Crisis and the Peruvian Proletariat," speech delivered to the "Gonzales Prada" People's University, at the Peruvian Student Federation Hall, Lima (June 15, 1923). Available online.

9   Populism and the Struggle for Change

1   Eric Hobsbawm, *The Age of Extremes* (New York: Random House, Inc., 1994), p. 135.
2   Nicholas Fraser and Marysa Navarro, *Eva Peron* (New York: W. W. Norton, 1981), p. 170.
3   Susan K. Besse, *Restructuring Patriarchy: The Modernization of Gender Inequality in Brazil, 1914–1940* (Chapel Hill: University of North Carolina Press, 1996).
4   Jocelyn Olcott, *Revolutionary Women in Post-revolutionary Mexico* (Durham, NC: Duke University Press, 2005).
5   Hobsbawm, *Age of Extremes*, p. 102.

10   Post-World War II Struggles for Sovereignty

1   Jean Franco, *The Decline and Fall of the Lettered City: Latin America in the Cold War* (Cambridge, MA: Harvard University Press, 2002), p. 59.
2   *Human Rights Watch, Universal Periodic Review of Guatemala* (May 4, 2008), http://www.hrw.org/en/americas/guatemala
3   Domitila Barrios de Chúngara, *Let Me Speak!: Testimony of Domitila, a Woman of the Bolivian Mines* (New York: Monthly Review Press, 1978), p. 187.

11   Cuba: Guerrillas Take Power

1   Fidel Castro, *History Will Absolve Me* (New York: L. Stuart, 1961).
2   Jorge G. Castañeda, *Utopia Unarmed: The Latin American Left after the Cold War* (New York: Vintage Books, 1993), p. 55.
3   Ibid.
4   *Americas in Transition*, a movie directed by Obie Benz; Ed Asner narrator (1981).

12   Progress and Reaction

1   These words are widely attributed to Henry Kissinger. In his memoirs, Kissinger boldly justifies US efforts to undermine Chile's democratic process. See Kissinger, *The White House Years* (Boston: Little, Brown and Company, 1979), ch. 17.
2   Peter Winn, *Weavers of Revolution: The Yarur Workers and Chile's Road to Socialism* (New York: Oxford University Press, 1986), p. 6.
3   The period from 1976 to 1983 often has been referred to as "the Dirty War." Numerous scholars, both inside Argentina and outside it, dispute this term. There was no "war" since the repression came from one source: the military. Many civilians who were apprehended were not military combatants, not involved in the guerrilla organizations, and had no means of defending themselves. Also, the idea of "dirty" implied blame on both sides, as though

the military resorted to unseemly, or dirty, tactics in a battle that was in other ways equal. Scholars of the period note that the repression and disappearances were in no way legitimate. I want to thank Argentine colleagues Cecilia Belej and Alejandra Vassallo from the University of Buenos Aires Women and Gender Studies Program for clarifying this point.

4   US Department of State Argentina Declassification Project, 2002. Copy collected by Carlos Osorio in 2006.

13   Revolution and Its Alternatives

1   John Alvarez García and Christian Restrepo Calle (eds.), *Camilo Torres, His Life and His Message*, trans. Virginia M. O'Grady (Springfield, IL: Templegate Publishers, 1968), p. 73.
2   Oscar A. Romero, *A Martyr's Message of Hope: Six Homilies* (Kansas City, MO: Celebration Books, 1981).
3   Edward A. Lynch, "The Retreat of Liberation Theology," *The Catholic Resource Network*, Manassas, VA. (An online Catholic resource).
4   "Nora Astorga In Her Own Words," *Revista Envío (Digital)*, Number 82, April 1988: http://www.envio.org.ni/articulo/3134.
5   *New York Times* (March 11, 1999), p. 1.
6   Quoted in Seth Fallon's article, "Fanning the Flames: U.S. Aid to Colombia is Fueling a Murderous, Bloody War," *Daily Nebraskan* (June 29, 2000).
7   Alma Guillermoprieto, "Days of the Dead: The New Narcocultura," *The New Yorker* (November 21, 2008), p. 2.

14   The Americas in the Twenty-first Century

1   Greg Grandin, *Latin American Studies Association Forum* (Winter 2007), p. 15.
2   NACLA Report on the Americas, vol. 40, no. 2 (March/April, 2007).
3   Douglas S. Massey, *Immigration Daily*, online source: http://idexer.com/
4   Rafael Correa, *Environmental News Service: International Daily News Wire*, online source: http://www.ens-newswire.com/
5   Gabriel García Márquez, "The Solitude of Latin America (Nobel Lecture, December 8, 1982)." Cited in Gabriel *García Márquez and the Powers of Fiction*, ed. Julio Ortega, p. 89.

Glossary

abertura opening; a politically democratic respite under dictatorial or authoritarian rule

affranchis free people of color in colonial Saint-Domingue/Haiti (French)

Afro-descendente Portuguese term for person of African descent; Afro-descendant

Afro-descendiente Spanish-language term for Afro-descendant

alcabala sales tax, imposed by the Spanish Crown

altiplano high plain plateau of the Andean Mountain range

arpillera embroidery or textile designs on burlap, created by female political prisoners in Chile and later spread to many areas of the Americas

bandeirantes Brazilian frontiersmen, from the term "bandeira" meaning flag; they were usually of mixed Indian and white ethnicity

berimbau single-stringed instrument developed by slaves in Brazil, probably brought from Africa

blocos de sujo groups of Carnival revelers; literally meaning "groups of dirty ones"

bodega small convenience store; in New York refers to a Dominican family-run shop

Bolsa Familia monthly stipend introduced by Lula to support poor Brazilian families

bomba Cuban dance and music

botequim a local Brazilian pub or bar

cabildo local city council in colonial Spanish America; called *câmara* in Portuguese America

caboclo Brazilian term for mixed-race Indian and white

cacique indigenous chief or local ruler

cadeira curtained sedan chair in which slaves carried white masters in Brazil

Californio people from or living in Old California

candomblé African-derived religion in Brazil that sees god and spirit in nature

carioca term derived from indigenous language for resident of Rio de Janeiro

Casa de Contratación Board of Trade, established by the Spanish Crown as a regulatory body in the Americas

casa grande   big house on estate, where the patron, master, or slave holder resides

casta   person of multiple mixed-race heritage

caudillismo   epoch of strongmen, patronage rule

caudillo   strongman, local boss, generally in Spanish America

científico   an intellectual "scientist" who supported eugenics and Social Darwinism

cimarrón   Spanish for fugitive slave, maroon

cocalero   coca leaf farmer

colonel   Portuguese term for the local strongman (*caudillo* counterpart)

compadrazgo   system of godparenting, widespread in Latin America as a way of solidifying dependence of lower classes on elites

comuneros   common people of Bogotá who led a rebellion against the colonial sales tax

Consulado   Spanish merchant guild in Seville, with counterparts in the colonies

corregidor   royal administrator in colonial Spanish America with power over Indians

Cortes   Spanish or Portuguese court, headed by monarch, and made up of representatives of the various kingdoms of the realm

Creole (criollo/a)   person of Iberian nationality born in the Americas

curandera   practitioner of herbal medicine, usually an indigenous or Afro-descendant woman

Cuzqueño   pertaining to the Peruvian city of Cuzco; a major art form of Indian artists developed in the late colonial period

donatario   owner of a large land tract conceded to him by official in colonial Brazil

ejido   land owned and worked by an indigenous community (Mexico)

encomendero   Spanish recipient of an *encomienda*

encomienda   Spanish system of allotting Indians to Spanish colonizers for collection of labor and tribute; also the allotment; literally translated as "entrustment"

engenho   sugar mill, or a sugar plantation with a mill (Brazil)

enlightened despotism   the absolute rule of a monarch during the 17th and 18th centuries; enlightened despot rules supposedly with the public good in mind

Enlightenment   a Western philosophical movement that championed the primacy of reason over superstition and religious dogma, the rights of the common people over hereditary aristocratic privilege, the rule of law over feudal authoritarianism

escola de samba   samba school (Brazil)

estancia   large landed estate (Argentina, Chile, Uruguay)

estanciero   owner of an *estancia*

fado   Portuguese folk music

favela   Brazilian shantytown

fazenda   large landed estate or plantation (Brazil)

fazendeiro   Brazilian planter

fueros   the privileged exemptions that allowed the clergy and military to avoid prosecution in Mexico

gaucho   a cowboy from the *pampas*, or plains; also used in Uruguay and southern Brazil

gente de razón   Spanish-speaking people of mixed race who were accepted as white gentry in Old California

granaderos   crack police unit; rapid response team against disturbances (Mexico)

grands blancs   "big whites" in Saint-Domingue who owned most land and slaves

guerrillero(a)   guerrilla war fighter

hacendado   owner of a *hacienda*

hacienda   ranch or large landed estate (Mexico)

hidalgo   a Spanish gentleman or nobleman

Iberia   the European peninsula comprised of Spain and Portugal; "Iberians" refers to the inhabitants of the peninsula

Inconfidência de Alfaiates   Conspiracy of the Tailors; a 1798 revolt in Brazil against the colonial government

indigenismo   cultural and political movement that asserts Indian identity

jefe   chief or man in charge; can be another word for strongman or *caudillo*

junta   term in Latin America for a leadership body; can be of any political tendency, but in the late 20th century referred to an authoritarian military group

Junta da Fazenda   Portuguese Board of Trade, administrative center of empire

latifundia   term in Latin America for system of large landholdings

latifundista   Latin American powerful landowner

liberalism   body of ideas referring to economic, political, and civil rights for the individual, such as private property, freedom of speech, free markets and trade; rose to importance in Europe and the Americas the 18th and 19th centuries

matronas   ladies

mestizaje   race mixture, miscegenation

mestizo   person of European (Spanish usually) and indigenous descent

milreis   Brazilian unit of money in the early 20th century

minifundio   term in Latin America for system of small landholdings, dependent and subservient to the *latifundia*

minifundista   Latin American small landowner, sometimes tenant farmer

mulatto   person of mixed white and African descent

neoliberalism   a late 20th-century revised "liberalism" that seeks to transfer economic wealth from the hands of the state to the private sector; also called the "Washington Consensus" because the key mechanisms for imposing fiscal discipline are the US-based International Monetary Fund (IMF), the World Bank, and other financial institutions

novela   Brazilian term for *telenovela*, or nighttime soap operas

obrajes   sweatshops

pampas   interior grasslands, or plains, of Argentina

patrón   the patriarch in charge of large estates; master

peninsulares   refers to people of the Iberian peninsula living in colonial Latin America who generally enjoyed positions of wealth and privilege

petits blancs   "lesser whites" in Saint-Domingue who worked as overseers, tradesmen, and in a subservient relationship to the big whites

plena   Caribbean folk music

porteño   resident of Buenos Aires; literally "person of the port"

pueblo   a small town; the people (the masses)

pulque   strong, inexpensive alcoholic drink made from the maguey cactus plant in Mexico and Mesoamerica

Quetzalcoatl   ancient Aztec god who mythically was to return to Mexico bringing peace

quilombo   community of runaway slaves in Brazil

real   current Brazilian unit of money

republiquetas   small political divisions, established after Independence in parts of Latin America, under the authority of local bosses and landowners

rurales   local troops that guard and terrorize rural areas

Santería   religion of the Caribbean that combines African and Christian rituals

sem terra   in Brazil a landless person; originally a derogatory term, "without land," that was subsequently embraced by the landless peasants to define their movement

senhores de engenho   most important Brazilian sugar planters, who also had mills

senzala   slave quarters (Brazil)

sindicato   trade union

telenovela   serialized nighttime television drama, "soap opera"

tenente   lieutenant, junior officer in Brazil

tropicalismo   music and cultural movement in Brazilian music associated with Caetano Veloso, Gilberto Gil, Antonio Carlos Jobim, and other 1960s/1970s musicians

visíta: a visit; politically the visit of a colonial official or clergy to check up on the colony and hear the colonists' grievances

visitador: colonial officer, of Church or state, who hears complaints

Washington Consensus   *see* neoliberalism

Zapatista   a member of the EZLN insurgent group in Chiapas, Mexico. Originally it was a person who fought with the army of Emiliano Zapata in the 1910 Revolution.

Further Reading

General Histories, and Regional and Thematic Surveys

Adelman, Jeremy. *Essays in Argentine Labor History*. New York: Palgrave Macmillan, 1992.

Anderson, Benedict. *Imagined Communities: Reflections on the Origin and Spread of Nationalism*, revised edition. London: Verso, 2006.

Appelbaum, Nancy P., Anne S. Macpherson, and Karin Alejandra Rosemblatt, eds. *Race and Nation in Modern Latin America*. Chapel Hill: University of North Carolina Press, 2003.

Balderston, Daniel, and Donna J. Guy, eds. *Sex and Sexuality in Latin America*. New York: New York University Press, 1997.

Beezley, William H., and Linda Curcio-Nagy, eds. *Latin American Popular Culture: An Introduction*. Wilmington, DE: Scholarly Resources, 2000.

Bergquist, Charles. *Labor in Latin America*. Stanford, CA: Stanford University Press, 1986.

Buffington, Robert, and Lila Caimari, eds. *Keen's Latin American Civilization: History and Society, 1492 to the Present*. Boulder, CO: Westview Press, 2009.

Burns, E. Bradford. *Latin American Cinema: Film and History*. Los Angeles: UCLA Latin American Center, 1975.

Burns, E. Bradford. *The Poverty of Progress: Latin America in the Nineteenth Century*. Berkeley: University of California Press, 1980.

Bushnell, David. *The Making of Modern Colombia: A Nation in Spite of Itself*. Berkeley: University of California Press, 1993.

Chasteen, John Charles. *Born in Blood and Fire: A Concise History of Latin America*, 2nd edition. New York: W. W. Norton & Co., 2006.

Chomsky, Aviva, and Aldo Lauria-Santiago, eds. *Identity and Struggle at the Margins of the Nation-State: The Laboring Peoples of Central America and the Hispanic Caribbean*. Durham, NC: Duke University Press, 1998.

Conniff, Michael L., and Thomas J. Davis, eds. *Africans in the Americas: A History of the Black Diaspora*. New York: St. Martin's Press, 1994.

Eakin, Marshall C. *The History of Latin America: Collision of Cultures*. New York: Palgrave Macmillan, 2007.

Fowler-Salamini, Heather, and Mary Kay Vaughan, eds. *Women of the Mexican Countryside, 1850–1990: Creating Spaces, Shaping Transitions.* Tucson: University of Arizona Press, 1994.

French, John D., and Daniel James. *The Gendered Worlds of Latin American Women Workers.* Durham, NC: Duke University Press, 1997.

French, William E., and Katherine E. Bliss, eds. *Gender, Sexuality, and Power in Latin America Since Independence.* New York: Rowman & Littlefield Pub., Inc., 2007.

Galeano, Eduardo. *Open Veins of Latin America: Five Centuries of the Pillage of a Continent.* New York: Monthly Review Press, 1997.

Gilbert, Alan. *The Latin American City.* New York: Monthly Review Press, 1998.

Guillermoprieto, Alma. *Looking for History: Dispatches from Latin America.* New York: Vintage, 2002.

Gunder Frank, Andre. *Capitalism and Underdevelopment in Latin America: Their History in Chile and Brazil.* New York: Monthly Review Press, 1967.

Gutierrez, Gustavo. *A Theology of Liberation: History, Politics and Salvation.* Maryknoll, NY: Orbis Books, 1988.

Halperin Donghi, Tulio. *The Contemporary History of Latin America.* Durham, NC: Duke University Press, 1993.

Htun, Mala. *Sex and the State: Abortion, Divorce, and the Family under Latin American Dictatorships and Democracies.* Cambridge: Cambridge University Press, 2003.

Jaquette, Jane S., ed. *The Women's Movement in Latin America: Participation and Democracy,* 2nd edition. Boulder, CO: Westview Press, 1994.

Johnson, Lyman L., and Sonya Lipsett-Rivera, eds. *The Faces of Honor: Sex, Shame, and Violence in Colonial Latin America.* Albuquerque: University of New Mexico, 1998.

Joseph, Gilbert M., Catherine LeGrand, and Ricardo D. Salvatore, eds. *Close Encounters Empire: Writing the Cultural History of U.S.–Latin American Relations.* Durham, NC: Duke University Press, 1998.

Keen, Benjamin, and Keith Haynes. *A History of Latin America: Vol. 1, Ancient America to 1910* and *Vol. II, Independence to the Present,* 7th edition. New York: Houghton Mifflin Company, 2004.

LaFeber, Walter. *Inevitable Revolutions: The United States and Central America.* New York: W. W. Norton, 1993.

Lavrin, Asunción. *Women, Feminism, and Social Change in Argentina, Chile and Uruguay, 1890–1940.* Lincoln: University of Nebraska Press, 1995.

Martin, Cheryl E., and Mark Wasserman. *Latin America and Its People: Volume 2, 1800 to the Present.* New York: Pearson Longman, 2005.

McCormick, Thomas J. *America's Half-Century: United States Foreign Policy in the Cold War and After.* Baltimore, MD: Johns Hopkins University Press, 1995.

Miller, Francesca. *Latin American Women and the Search for Social Justice.* Hanover: University Press of New England, 1991.

Navarro, Marysa, and Virginia Sánchez Korrol. *Women in Latin America and the Caribbean: Restoring Women to History.* Bloomington: Indiana University Press, 1999.

Oxhorn, Philip, and Graciela Ducatenzeiler, eds. *What Kind of Democracy? What Kind of Market? Latin America in the Age of Neoliberalism.* University Park: Pennsylvania State University Press, 1998.

Rogozinski, Jan. *A Brief History of the Caribbean: From the Arawak and Carib to the Present.* New York: A Plume Book, 2000.

Roseberry, William, Lowell Gudmundson, and Mario Samper Kutschback, eds. *Coffee, Society, and Power in Latin America.* Baltimore, MD: Johns Hopkins University Press, 1995.

Rowe, Williams, and Vivian Schelling. *Memory and Modernity: Popular Culture in Latin America.* New York: Verso, 1991.

Salvatore, Ricardo D., Carlos Aguirre, and Gilbert M. Joseph, eds. *Crime and Punishment in Latin America: Law and Society since Late Colonial Times.* Durham, NC: Duke University Press, 2001.

Shukla, Sandhya, and Heidi Tinsman, eds. *Imagining Our Americas: Toward a Transnational Frame.* Durham, NC: Duke University Press, 2007.

Sommer, Doris. *Foundational Fictions: The National Romances of Latin America.* Berkeley: University of California Press, 1991.

Stern, Steve J., ed. *Resistance, Rebellion and Consciousness in the Andean Peasant World, 18th to 20th Centuries.* Madison: University of Wisconsin Press, 1987.

Thornton, John M. *Africa and Africans in the Making of the Atlantic World, 1400–1800.* 2nd edition. New York: Cambridge University Press, 1998.

Weber, David J. *The Spanish Frontier in North America.* New Haven, CT: Yale University Press, 1992.

1 Introduction to the Land and Its People

Agosin, Marjorie. *Tapestries of Hope, Threads of Love: The Arpillera Movement in Chile, 1974–1994.* Albuquerque: University of New Mexico Press, 1996.

Allende, Isabel. *The House of the Spirits,* translated by Magda Bogin. New York: Bantam, 1986.

Amado, Jorge. *Gabriela, Clove, and Cinnamon,* translated by James L. Taylor and William Grossman. New York: Avon, 1988.

Assis, Joaquim Maria Machadao de. *Dom Casmurro,* translated by John Gledson. New York: Oxford University Press, 1997.

Azevedo, Aluiso. *Mulatto.* Austin: University of Texas Press, 1993.

Burns, E. Bradford. *Latin American Cinema: Film and History.* Los Angeles: UCLA Latin American Center, 1975.

Burton, Julianne. *Cinema and Social Change in Latin America: Conversations with Filmmakers.* Austin: University of Texas Press, 1986.

Dunn, Christopher. *Brutality Garden: Tropicalia and the Emergence of a Brazilian Counterculture.* Chapel Hill: University of North Carolina Press, 2001.

Franco, Jean. *An Introduction to Spanish-American Literature.* London: Cambridge University Press, 1969.

Fuentes, Carlos. *The Death of Artemio Cruz,* translated by Alfred Mac Adam. New York: Farrar, Straus and Giroux, 1991.

Furtado, Celso. *Economic Development of Latin America: Historical Background and Contemporary Problems.* London: Cambridge University Press, 1970.

García Márquez, Gabriel. *One Hundred Years of Solitude,* translated by Gregory Rabassa. New York: Avon, 1971.

2 Latin America in 1790

Arrom, Silvia. *The Women of Mexico City, 1790–1857.* Stanford, CA: Stanford University Press, 1985.

Deans-Smith, Susan. *Bureaucrats, Planters and Workers: The Making of Tobacco Monopoly in Bourbon Mexico.* Austin: University of Texas Press, 1992.

Gutierrez, Ramon A. *When Jesus Came, the Corn Mothers Went Away. Marriage, Sexuality, and Power in New Mexico, 1500–1846.* Stanford, CA: Stanford University Press, 1991.

Jacobsen, Nils. *Mirages of Transition: The Peruvian Altiplano, 1780–1930*. Albuquerque: University of New Mexico Press, 1993.

Maxwell, Kenneth. *Conflicts and Conspiracies: Brazil*. Cambridge: Cambridge University Press, 1973.

Maxwell, Kenneth. *Pombal, Paradox of the Enlightenment*. Cambridge: Cambridge University Press, 1995.

Nazzari, Muriel. *Disappearance of the Dowry: Women, Families and Social Change in São Paulo, Brazil, 1600–1900*. Stanford, CA: Sanford University Press, 1991.

Ramirez, Susan. *The World Upside Down: Cross-Cultural Contact and Conflict in Sixteenth-Century Peru*. Stanford, CA: Stanford University Press, 1996.

Seed, Patricia. *To Love, Honor and Obey in Colonial Mexico. Conflicts over Marriage Choice, 1574–1821*. Stanford, CA: Stanford University Press, 1988.

Socolow, Susan M. *The Merchants of Buenos Aires, 1778–1810. Family and Commerce*. Cambridge: Cambridge University Press, 1978.

Stein, Stanley, and Barbara H. Stein. *The Colonial Heritage of Latin America: Essays on Economic Dependence in Perspective*. New York: Oxford University Press, 1970.

Stern, Steve J. *The Secret History of Gender: Women, Men and Power in Late Colonial Mexico*. Chapel Hill: University of North Carolina Press, 1995.

Tandeter, Enrique. *Coercion and Market: Silver Mining in Colonial Potosi, 1692–1826*. Albuquerque: University of New Mexico Press, 1993.

Taylor, William B. "The Virgin of Guadalupe in New Spain: an Inquiry into the Social History of Marian Devotion," *American Ethnologist*, February 14, 1987, pp. 9–33.

3   Competing Notions of Freedom

Blanchard, Peter. *Slavery and Abolition in Early Republican Peru*. Wilmington, DE: SR Books, 1992.

Burns, E. Bradford. *The Poverty of Progress: Latin America in the Nineteenth Century*. Berkeley: University of California Press, 1980.

Conrad, Robert Edgar. *The Destruction of Brazilian Slavery, 1850–1888*. Berkeley: University of California Press, 1973.

Conrad, Robert Edgar, ed. *Children of God's Fire: A Documentary History of Black Slavery in Brazil*. University Park: Pennsylvania State University Press, 1994.

Costa, Emilia Viotti. *The Brazilian Empire: Myths and Histories*. Chicago: University of Chicago, 1985.

De Queiros Mattós, Katia M. *To Be a Slave in Brazil, 1550–1888*, translated by Arthur Goldhammer. New Brunswick: Rutgers University Press, 1986.

Dubois, Laurent. *Avengers of the New World: The Story of the Haitian Revolution*. Cambridge, MA: Harvard University Press, 2005.

Equiano, Olaudah. *The Interesting Narrative and Other Writings*, edited by Voncent Carretta. New York: Penguin, 1995.

Freyre, Gilberto. *The Masters and the Slaves: A Study in the Development of Brazilian Civilization*, translated by Samuel Putnam. Berkeley: University of California Press, 1986.

Graham, Sandra Lauderdale. *House and Street: Domestic World of Servants and Masters in 19th Century Rio de Janeiro*. Austin: University of Texas, 1992.

James, C. L. R. *The Black Jacobins: Toussaint L'Ouverture and the San Domingo Revolution*. New York: Random House, 1963.

Johnson, John J. *Simon Bolívar and Spanish American Independence, 1783–1830*. Princeton, NJ: Van Nostrand Co., 1968.

Karasch, Mary C. *Slave Life in Rio de Janeiro*. Princeton, NJ: Princeton University Press 1987.

Moreno Fraginals, Manuel. *The Sugarmill: The Socioeconomic Complex of Sugar in Cuba, 1760–1860*, translated by Cedric Belfrage. New York, Monthly Review Press, 1976.

Morse, Richard M., ed. *The Bandeirantes: The Historical Role of the Brazilian Pathfinder*. New York: Alfred A. Knopf, 1965.

Phelan, John L. *The People and the King: The Comunero Revolution in Colombia, 1781*. Madison: University of Wisconsin Press, 1978.

Radding, Cynthia. *Wandering Peoples: Colonialism, Ethnic Spaces, and Ecological Frontiers in Northwestern Mexico*. Durham, NC: Duke University, 1997.

Schwartz, Stuart B. *Sugar Plantations in the Formation of Brazilian Society, Bahia, 1550–1835*. Cambridge: Cambridge University Press, 1985.

Schwartz, Stuart B. *Slaves, Peasants, and Rebels: Reconsidering Brazilian Slavery*. Urbana and Chicago: University of Illinois Press, 1992.

Scott, Rebecca J. *Slave Emancipation in Cuba: The Transition to Free Labor, 1860–1899*. Princeton, NJ: Princeton University Press, 1985.

Tenenbaum, Barbara A. *The Politics of Penury: Debts and Taxes in Mexico, 1821–1856*. Albuquerque: University of New Mexico Press, 1986.

Van Young, Eric. *The Other Rebellion: Popular Violence, Ideology, and the Mexican Struggle for Independence*. Stanford, CA: Stanford University Press, 2001.

4 Fragmented Nationalisms

Borges, Dain. *The Family in Bahia, Brazil, 1870–1945*. Stanford, CA: Stanford University Press, 1992.

Butler, Kim D. *Freedoms Given, Freedoms Won: Afro-Brazilians in Post-Abolition São Paulo and Salvador*. New Brunswick: Rutgers University Press, 1998.

Chambers, Sarah C. *From Subjects to Citizens: Honor, Gender, and Politics in Arequipa, Peru, 1780–1854*. University Park: Pennsylvania State University Press, 1999.

Hunenfeldt, Christine. *Liberalism in the Bedroom: Quarrelling Spouses in Nineteenth-century Lima*. University Park: Pennsylvania State University Press, 2000.

Lewin, Linda. *Politics and Parentela in Paraiba: A Case Study of Family-based Oligarchy in Brazil*. Princeton, NJ: Princeton University Press, 1987.

Mallon, Florencia E. *Peasant and Nation: The Making of Postcolonial Mexico and Peru*. Berkeley: University of California Press, 1995.

Martin, Cheryl English. *Rural Society in Morelos*. Albuquerque: University of New Mexico Press 1985.

Mayo, Carlos A. "Landed but not Powerful: The Colonial *Estancieros* of Buenos Aires (1750–1810)," *Hispanic American Historical Review*, vol. 71, no. 4 (1991), pp. 761–79.

Sarmiento, Domingo F. *Facundo: Civilization and Barbarism*, translated by Kathleen Ross. Berkeley: University of California Press, 2004.

Stein, Stanley J. *Vassouras: A Brazilian Coffee Country, 1850–1900*. Cambridge, MA: Harvard University Press, 1970.

5 Latin America's Place in the Commodity Chain

Albert, Bill. *South America and the First World War: The Impact of the War on Brazil, Argentina, Peru, and Chile*. New York: Cambridge University Press, 1988.

Gootenberg, Paul. *Between Silver and Guano: Commercial Policy and the State in Post-independent Peru*. Princeton, NJ: Princeton University Press, 1989.

Gootenberg, Paul. *Imagining Development: Economic Ideas in Peru's "Fictitious Prosperity" of Guano*. Berkeley: University of California Press, 1993.

Helg, Aline. *Our Rightful Share: The Afro-Cuban Struggle for Equality, 1886–1912*. ChapelHill: University of North Carolina Press, 1995.

Hurtado, Alberto. *Intimate Frontiers: Sex, Gender, and Culture in Old California*. Albuquerque: University of New Mexico Press, 1999.

Jimenez, Michael F. "Traveling Far in Grandfather's Car: The Life Cycle of Central Colombian Coffee Estates. The Case of Viota, Cundinamarca *(1900–30),*" *The Hispanic American Historical Review*, vol. 69, no. 2 (May 1989), pp. 185–219.

Mintz, Sidney W. *Sweetness and Power. The Place of Sugar in Modern History*. New York: Viking, 1985.

Salvucci, Richard J. *Textiles and Capitalism in Mexico: An Economic History of the Obrajes, 1539–1840*. Princeton, NJ: Princeton University Press, 1987.

Sowell, David. *The Early Colombian Labor Movement: Artisans and Politics in Bogota, 1832–1919*. Philadelphia: Temple University Press, 1992.

Striffler, Steve. *In the Shadows of State and Capital: The United Fruit Company, Popular Struggle and Agrarian Restructuring in Ecuador, 1900–1995*. Durham, NC: Duke University Press, 2002.

Suarez, Findlay, Eileen J. *Imposing Dependency: The Politics of Sexuality and Race in Puerto Rico, 1870–1920*. Durham, NC: Duke University Press, 1999.

Topik, Steven, Carlos Marichal, and Zephyr Frank, eds. *From Silver to Cocaine: Latin American Commodity Chains and the Building of the World Economy, 1500–2000*. Durham, NC: Duke University Press, 2006.

Wasserman, Mark. *Capitalists, Caciques and Revolution: The Native Elite and Foreign Enterprise in Chihuahua Mexico, 1854–1911*. Chapel Hill: University of North Carolina Press, 1984.

Weber, David J. *The Mexican Frontier, 1821–1846: The American Southwest under Mexico*. Albuquerque: University of New Mexico Press, 1982.

Weinstein, Barbara. *The Amazon Rubber Boom, 1850–1920*. Stanford, CA: Stanford University Press, 1983.

6   Immigration, and Urban and Rural Life

Andrews, George Reid. *The Afro-Argentines of Buenos Aires, 1800–1900*. Madison: University of Wisconsin Press, 1980.

Bocketti, Gregg P. "Italian Immigrants, Brazilian Football, and the Dilemma of National Identity," *Journal of Latin American Studies* 40 (2008): 275–302.

Da Cunha, Euclides. *Rebellion in the Backlands*, translated by Samuel Putman. Chicago: University of Chicago Press, 1944.

De Abreu Esteves, Martha. *Meninas perdidas: Os Populares e o cotidiano no amor no Rio de Janeiro da Belle Epoque*. Rio de Janeiro: Paz e Terra, 1989.

Dean, Warren. *Industrialization of São Paulo 1880–1945*. Austin: University of Texas, 1969.

Dias, Maria Odila Silva. *Power and Everyday Life: The Lives of Working Women in Nineteenth-century Brazil*. New Brunswick: Rutgers University Press, 1995.

Guardino, Peter F. *Peasants, Politics, and the Formation of Mexico's National State: Guerrero, 1800–1857*. Stanford, CA: Stanford University Press, 1996.

Guy, Donna J. *Sex and Danger in Buenos Aires: Prostitution, Family, and Nation in Argentina*. Lincoln: University of Nebraska Press, 1991.

Guy, Donna J. *White Slavery and Mothers Alive and Dead: The Troubled Meeting of Sex, Gender, Public Health, and Progress in Latin America*. Lincoln: University of Nebraska Press, 2000.

Hahner, June. *Poverty and Politics: The Urban Poor in Brazil, 1870–1920*. Albuquerque: University of New Mexico Press, 1986.

Hahner, June E. *Emancipating the Female Sex: The Struggle for Women's Rights in Brazil, 1850–1940*. Durham, NC: Duke University Press, 1990.

Holloway, Thomas. *Immigrants on the Land: Coffee and Society in Sao Paulo, 1886–1934*. Chapel Hill: University of North Carolina Press, 1980.

Holloway, Thomas. *Policing Rio de Janeiro: Repression and Resistance in a 19th-century City*. Stanford, CA: Stanford University Press, 1993.

Mayo, Carlos A. *Estancia y sociedad en la pampa*. Madrid: Revista de Indias, 1996.

McGowan, Chris, and Ricardo Pessanha. *The Brazilian Sound: Samba, Bossa Nova, and the Popular Music of Brazil*. New York: Billboard Books, 1991.

Meade, Teresa A. *"Civilizing" Rio: Reform and Resistance in a Brazilian City, 1889–1930*. University Park: Pennsylvania State University Press, 1997.

Needell, Jeffery D. *A Tropical Belle Epoque: Elite Culture and Society in Turn-of-the-Century Rio de Janeiro*. New York: Cambridge University Press, 1987.

Peard, Julyan. *Race, Place, and Medicine: The Idea of the Tropics in Nineteenth-century Brazilian Medicine*. Durham, NC: Duke University Press, 1999.

Rodney, Walter. *A History of the Guyanese Working People, 1881–1905*. Baltimore, MD: The Johns Hopkins University Press, 1981.

Stepan, Nancy Leys. *"The Hour of Eugenics": Race, Gender and Nation in Latin America*. Ithaca, NY: Cornell University Press, 1991.

Vianna, Hermano. *The Mystery of Samba: Popular Music and National Identity in Brazil*. Chapel Hill: University of North Carolina Press, 1999.

Wade, Peter. *Music, Race, and Nation: Musica Tropical in Colombia*. Chicago: University of Chicago Press, 2000.

Zulawski, Ann. *Unequal Cures: Public Health and Political Change in Bolivia, 1900–1950*. Durham, NC: Duke University Press, 2007.

7 Revolution from Countryside to City: Mexico

Alonso, Ana Maria. *Thread of Blood: Colonialism, Revolution, and Gender on Mexico's Northern Frontier*. Tucson: University of Arizona Press, 1995.

Bliss, Katherine Elaine. *Compromised Positions: Prostitution, Public Health, and Gender Politics in Revolutionary Mexico City*. University Park: Pennsylvania State University Press, 2001.

Blum, Anne S. "Cleaning the Revolutionary Household: Domestic Servants and Public Welfare in Mexico City, 1900–1935," *Journal of Women's History*, vol. 15, no. 4 (2004), pp. 67–90.

Gonzales, Michael J. *The Mexican Revolution, 1910–1940*. Albuquerque: University of New Mexico Press, 2002.

Katz, Friedrich, ed. *Riot, Rebellion, and Revolution: Rural Social Conflict in Mexico*. Princeton, NJ: Princeton University Press, 1988.

Katz, Friedrich. *The Life & Times of Pancho Villa*. Chicago: University of Chicago Press, 1998.

Knight, Alan. *The Mexican Revolution*, 2 volumes. Cambridge: Cambridge University Press, 1986.

Macias, Ana. *Against All Odds: The Feminist Movement in Mexico to 1940*. Westport, CT: Greenwood Press, 1982.

Meyer, Jean A. *The Cristero Rebellion: The Mexican People between Church and State, 1926–1929*, translated by Richard Southern. New York: Cambridge University Press, 1976.

Paz, Octavio. *The Labyrinth of Solitude: Life and Thought in Mexico*, translated by Lysander Kemp. New York: Grove Press, 1961.

Salas, Elizabeth. *Soldaderas in the Mexican Military: Myth and History*. Austin: University of Texas Press, 1990.

Schell, Patience A. *Church and State Education in Revolutionary Mexico City*. Tucson: University of Arizona Press, 2003.

Soto, Shirlene. *Emergence of the Modern Mexican Woman: Her Participation in Revolution and Struggle for Equality, 1910–1940*. Denver, CO: Arden Press, 1990.

8   The Left and the Socialist Alternative

De Shazo, Peter. *Urban Workers and Labor Unions in Chile, 1902–1927*. Madison: University of Wisconsin Press, 1983.

Farnsworth-Alvear, Ann. *Dulcinea in the Factory: Myths Morals, Men and Women in Colombia's Industrial Experiment, 1905–1960*. Durham, NC: Duke University Press, 2000.

Hutchison, Elizabeth Quay. *Labors Appropriate to Their Sex: Gender, Labor, and Politics in Urban Chile, 1900–1930*. Durham, NC: Duke University Press, 2001.

LeGrand, Catherine. *Frontier Expansion and Peasant Protest in Colombia, 1850–1936*. Albuquerque: University of New Mexico Press, 1986.

Liss, S. B. *Marxist Thought in Latin America*. Berkeley: University of California Press, 1984.

Machado de Assis. *Dom Casmurro*. Oxford: Oxford University Press, 1997.

Mariátegui, Jose Carlos. *Seven Interpretive Essays on Peruvian Reality*, translated by Marjoy Urquidi. Austin: University of Texas Press, 1971.

Putman, Lara. *The Company They Kept: Migrants and the Politics of Gender in Caribbean Costa Rica, 1870–1960*. Chapel Hill: University of North Carolina Press, 2002.

Rubenstein, Anne. *Bad Language, Naked Ladies, and Other Threats to the Nation: A Political History of Comic Books in Mexico*. Durham, NC: Duke University Press, 1998.

Ruggiero, Kristen. "Honor, Maternity, and the Disciplining of Women: Infanticide in Late-Nineteenth-Century Buenos Aires," *Hispanic American Historical Review*, vol. 72, no. 3 (1992).

Stern, Steve J., ed. *Resistance, Rebellion and Consciousness in the Andean Peasant World, 18th to 20th Centuries*. Madison: University of Wisconsin Press, 1987.

Stoner, K. Lynn. *From the House to the Streets: The Cuban Women's Movement for Legal Reform, 1898–1940*. Durham, NC: Duke University Press, 2002.

Wade, Peter. *Blackness and Race Mixture: The Dynamics of Racial Identity in Colombia*. Baltimore, MD: Johns Hopkins University Press, 1995.

9   Populism and the Struggle for Change

Adelman, Jeremy. *Frontier Development: Land, Labour, and Capital on the Wheatlands of Argentina and Canada, 1890–1914*. New York: Oxford University Press, 1994.

Beattie, Peter M. *The Tribute of Blood: Army, Honor, Race, and Nation in Brazil, 1864–1945*. Durham, NC: Duke University Press, 2001.

Becker, Marc. *Indians and Leftists in the Making of Ecuador's Modern Indigenous Movements*. Durham, NC: Duke University Press, 2008.

Euraque, Dario A. *Reinterpreting the Banana Republic: Region and State in Honduras, 1870–1972*. Chapel Hill: University of North Carolina, 1996.

Fischer, Brodwyn M. *A Poverty of Rights: Citizenship and Inequality in Twentieth-Century Rio de Janeiro*. Stanford, CA: Stanford University Press, 2008.

French, John D. *The Brazilian Workers ABC: Class Conflict and Alliances in Modern São Paulo*. Chapel Hill: University of North Carolina Press, 1992.

Friedman, Elisabeth J. *Unfinished Transitions: Women and Gendered Development of Democracy in Venezuela, 1936–1996*. University Park: Pennsylvania State University Press, 2000.

Gould, Jeffery L. *To Die in This Way: Nicaraguan Indians and the Myth of the Mestizaje, 1880–1960*. Durham, NC: Duke University Press, 1998.

Hale, Charles R. *Resistance and Contradiction: Miskitu Indians and the Nicaraguan State, 1894–1987*. Stanford, CA: Stanford University Press, 1994.

Hamilton, Nora. *The Limits of State Autonomy: Post-Revolutionary Mexico*. Princeton, NJ: Princeton University Press, 1982.

Hanchard, Michael George. *Orpheus and Power: The Movimento Negro of Rio de Janeiro and São Paulo, Brazil, 1945–1988*. Princeton, NJ: Princeton University Press, 1994.

Hart, John M. *Anarchism and the Mexican Working Class, 1860–1931*. Austin: University of Texas Press, 1987.

Horowitz, Joel. *Argentine Unions, the State and the Rise of Peron, 1930–1945*. Berkeley: Institute of International Studies, University of California, Berkeley, 1990.

James, Daniel. *Resistance and Integration: Peronism and the Argentine Working Class, 1946–1976*. Cambridge: Cambridge University Press, 1993.

James, Daniel. *Doña Maria's Story: Life History, Memory, and Political Identity*. Durham, NC: Duke University Press, 2000.

Joseph, Gilbert M. and Daniel Nugent, eds. *Everyday Forms of State Formation: Revolution and the Negotiation of Rule in Modern Mexico*. Durham, NC: Duke University Press, 1994.

Klaren, Peter F. *Modernization, Dislocation and Aprismo. Origins of the Peruvian Aprista Party, 1870–1932*. Austin: Published for the Institute of Latin American Studies by the University of Texas Press, 1973.

Klubock, Thomas Miller. *Contested Communities: Class, Gender, and Politics in Chile's El Teniente Copper Mine, 1904–1948*. Durham, NC: Duke University Press, 1998.

Langley, L. D. *The Banana Wars: An Inner History of American Empire, 1900–1934*. Lexington: University Press of Kentucky, 1983.

Mallon, Florencia E. *The Defense of Community in Peru's Central Highlands: Peasants' Struggle and Capitalist Transformation, 1860–1940*. Princeton, NJ: Princeton University Press, 1983.

Matos Rodriguez, Felix V. *Women and Urban Change in San Juan, Puerto Rico, 1820–1868*. Gainesville: University Press of Florida, 1999.

Podalsky, Laura. *Specular City: Transforming Culture, Consumption, and Space in Buenos Aires, 1955–1973*. Philadelphia: Temple University Press, 2004.

Weinstein, Barbara. *For Social Peace in Brazil: Industrialists and the Remaking of the Working Class in São Paulo, 1920–1964*. Chapel Hill: University of North Carolina Press, 1996.

Welch, Cliff. *The Seed Was Planted: The Sao Paulo Roots of Brazil's Rural Labor Movement, 1924–1964*. University Park: Pennsylvania State University Press, 1999.

Wells, Alan. *Yucatán's Gilded Age: Haciendas, Henequen, and International Harvester, 1860–1915.* Albuquerque: University of New Mexico Press, 1985.

Wolfe, Joel. *Working Women, Working Men: São Paulo and the Rise of Brazil's Industrial Working Class, 1900–1955.* Durham, NC: Duke University Press, 1993.

Yashar, Deborah J. *Demanding Democracy: Reform and Reaction in Costa Rica and Guatemala, 1870s–1950s.* Stanford, CA: Stanford University Press, 1997.

Zolov, Eric. *Refried Elvis: The Rise of the Mexican Counterculture.* Berkeley: University of California Press, 1999.

10   Post-World War II Struggles for Sovereignty

Carmack, Robert M. *Rebels of Highland Guatemala: The Quichē-Mayas of Momostenango.* Norman: University of Oklahoma Press, 1995.

Gleijeses, Piero. *Shattered Hope: The Guatemalan Revolution and the United States, 1944–1954.* Princeton, NJ: Princeton University Press, 1991.

Gould, Jeffery L. *To Lead as Equals: Rural Protest and Political Consciousness in Chinadega, Nicaragua, 1912–1979.* Chapel Hill: University of North Carolina Press, 1990.

Jonas, Suzanne. *The Battle for Guatemala: Rebels, Death Squads, and U.S. Power.* Boulder, CO: Westview Press, 1991.

Klein, Herbert S. *Bolivia: The Evolution of a Multi-Ethnic Society,* 2nd edition. New York: Oxford University Press, 1992.

Larson, Brook. *Colonialism and Agrarian Transformation in Bolivia: Cochabamba, 1550–1900.* Princeton, NJ: Princeton University Press, 1988.

Levenson-Estrada, Deborah. *Trade Unionists Against Terror: Guatemala City 1954–1985.* Chapel Hill: University of North Carolina Press, 1994.

Piccato, Pablo. *City of Suspects: Crime in Mexico City, 1900–1931.* Durham, NC: Duke University Press, 2001.

Vaughan, Mary Kay. *Cultural Politics in Revolution: Teachers, Peasants and Schools in Mexico, 1930–1940.* Tucson: University of Arizona Press, 1997.

Wood, Bryce. *The Dismantling of the Good Neighbor Policy.* Austin: University of Texas Press, 1985.

11 Cuba: Guerrillas Take Power

De la Fuente, Alejandro. *A Nation for All: Race Inequality, and Politics in Twentieth-century Cuba.* Chapel Hill: University of North Carolina Press, 2001.

Eckstein, Susan. *Back from the Future: Cuba Under Castro.* Princeton, NJ: Princeton University Press, 1994.

Halebsky, Sandor, and J. M. Kirk, eds. *Cuba: Twenty-five Years of Revolution, 1959–1984.* Westport, CT: Praeger, 1985.

Karol, K. S. *Guerrillas in Power: The Course of the Cuban Revolution.* New York: Hill & Wang, 1970.

Kornbluh, Peter, ed. *Bay of Pigs Declassified: The Secret CIA Report on the Invasion of Cuba.* New York: The New Press, 1998.

Lewis, Oscar, Ruth Lewis, and Susan M. Rigdon. *Living the Revolution: An Oral History of Contemporary Cuba,* 3 volumes. Urbana: University of Illinois Press, 1977.

Lumsden, Ian. *Machos, Maricones, and Gays: Cuba and Homosexuality.* Philadelphia: Temple University Press, 1996.

O'Connor, J. R. *The Origins of Socialism in Cuba.* Ithaca, NY: Cornell University Press, 1970.

Perez, Jr., Louis A. *Lords of the Mountain: Social Banditry and Peasant Protest in Cuba, 1878–1918.* Pittsburgh, PA: University of Pittsburgh Press, 1989.

Perez, Louis A. *Cuba: Between Reform and Revolution.* New York: Oxford University Press, 2006.

Perez-Stable, Marifeli. *The Cuban Revolution: Origins, Course, and Legacy,* 2nd edition. New York: Oxford University Press, 2003.

Rosendahl, Mona. *Inside the Revolution: Everyday Life in Socialist Cuba.* Ithaca, NY: Cornell University Press, 1997.

Smith, Louis M. *Sex and Revolution: Women in Socialist Cuba.* New York: Oxford University Press, 1996.

Whitney, Robert. *State and Revolution in Cuba: Mass Mobilization and Political Change, 1920–1940.* Chapel Hill: University of North Carolina Press, 2001.

12   Progress and Reaction

Green, James Naylor. *Beyond Carnival: Male Homosexuality in Twentieth-century Brazil.* Chicago, IL: University of Chicago Press, 1999.

Jesus, Carolina Maria de. *Children of the Dark: The Diary of Carolina Maria de Jesus,* translated by David St. Clair. New York: Signet, 2003.

Joseph, Gilbert M., Anner Rubenstein, Eric Zolov, and Elena Poniatowskia, eds. *Fragments of a Golden Age: The Politics of Culture in Mexico Since 1940.* Durham, NC: Duke University Press, 2001.

Maybury-Lewis, Biorn. *The Politics of the Possible: The Brazilian Rural Workers' Trade Union Movement, 1964–1985.* Philadelphia: Temple University Press, 1994.

Menzel, Sewall H. *Fire in the Andes: U.S. Foreign Policy and Cocaine Politics in Bolivia and Peru.* Lanham, MD: University Press of America, 1996.

Nash, June. *We Eat the Mines and the Mines Eat Us: Dependency and Exploitation in Bolivian Tin Mines.* New York: Columbia University Press, 1993.

Petras, James, and F. I. Leiva, with Henry Veltmeyer. *Democracy and Poverty in Chile: The Limits to Electoral Politics.* Boulder, CO: Westview Press, 1994.

Power, Margaret. *Right-wing Women in Chile: Feminine Power and the Struggle against Allende, 1964–1973.* University Park: Pennsylvania State University Press, 2002.

Rosemblatt, Karin Aljandra. *Gendered Compromises: Political Cultures and the State in Chile, 1920–1950.* Chapel Hill: University of North Carolina Press, 2000.

Skidmore, Thomas L. *The Politics of Military Rule in Brazil, 1964–85.* New York, 1988.

Stokes, Susan C. *Cultures in Conflict: Social Movements and the State in Peru.* Berkeley: University of California Press, 1995.

Timerman, Jacobo. *Prisoner Without a Name, Cell Without a Number.* Madison: University of Wisconsin Press, 2002.

Weschler, Lawrence. *A Miracle, a Universe: Settling Accounts with Torturers.* New York: Penguin, 1990.

Wilentz, Amy. *The Rainy Season: Haiti Since Duvalier.* New York: Simon and Schuster, 1990.

13 Revolution and Its Alternatives

Ehlers, Tracy Bachrach. *Silent Looms: Women and Production in a Guatemalan Town*. Boulder, CO: Westview Press, 1990.

Ellner, Steve. *Organized Labor in Venezuela, 1958–1991: Behavior and Concerns in a Democratic Setting*. Wilmington, DE: SR Books, 1993.

Enriques, Laura J. *Agrarian Reform and Class Consciousness in Nicaragua*. Gainesville: University Press of Florida, 1997.

Falla, Ricardo. *Massacres in the Jungle: Ixcán, Guatemala, 1975–1982*. Boulder, CO: Westview Press, 1994.

Garst, Rachel, and Tom Barry. *Feeding the Crisis: U.S. Food Aid and Farm Policy in Central America*. Lincoln: University of Nebraska Press, 1990.

Gleijeses, Piero. *Conflicting Missions: Havana, Washington, and Africa, 1959–1976*. Chapel Hill: University of North Carolina Press, 2002.

LaFeber, Walter. *Inevitable Revolutions: The United States and Central America*. New York: W. W. Norton, 1993.

Lancaster, Roger N. *Thanks to God and the Revolution: Popular Religion and Class Consciousness in the New Nicaragua*. New York: Columbia University Press, 1988.

Lancaster, Roger N. *Life Is Hard: Machismo, Danger, and the Intimacy of Power in Nicaragua*. Berkeley: University of California Press, 2003.

Montegomery, T. S. *Revolution in EL Salvador, Origins and Evolution*, 2nd edition. Boulder, CO: Westview Press, 1982.

Murillo, Lewis E. *The Noriega Mess: The Drugs, the Canal, and Why America Invaded*. Berkeley: Video-Books, 1995.

Paley, Julia. *Marketing Democracy: Power and Social Movements in Post-Dictatorship Chile*. Berkley: University of California Press, 2001.

Randall, Margaret. *Sandino's Daughters Revisited: Feminism in Nicaragua*. New Brunswick: Rutgers University Press, 1994.

Scheper-Hughes, Nancy. *Death Without Weeping: The Violence of Everyday Life in Brazil*. Berkeley: University of California Press, 1992.

Scott, P. D., and Jonathan Marshall. *Cocaine Politics: Drugs, Armies, and the CIA in Central America*. Berkeley: University of California Press, 1998.

Tiano, Susan. *Patriarchy on the Line: Labor, Gender, and Ideology in the Mexican Maquila Industry*. Philadelphia: Temple University Press, 1994.

Trouillot, Michael-Rolph. *Haiti: State Against Nation: The Origin and Legacy of Duvalierism*. New York: Monthly Review Press, 1990.

Tula, Maria Teresa. *Hear My Testimony: María Teresa Tula, Human Rights Activist of El Salvador*. Boston, MA: South End Press, 1994.

Vilas, Carlos M. *Sandinista Revolution: National Liberation and Social Transformation in Central America*. New York: Monthly Review Press; Berkeley: Center for the Study of the Americas, 1986.

14 The Americas in the Twenty-first Century

Collins, Joesph. *Chile's Free Market Miracle: A Second Look*. Oakland, CA: Food First, 1995.

Dean, Warren. *With Broadax and Firebrand: The Destruction of the Brazilian Atlantic Forest*. Berkeley: University of California Press, 1997.

Dupuy, Alex. *Haiti in the New World Order: The Limits of the Democratic Revolution.* Boulder, CO: Westview Press, 1997.

Friedman, Milton. *Capitalism and Freedom,* 2nd edition. Chicago, IL: University of Chicago Press, 1982.

Guillermoprieto, Alma. *Samba.* New York: Vintage, 1991.

Gutmann, Matthew C. *The Meanings of Macho: Being a Man in Mexico City.* Berkeley: University of California Press, 1996.

Hillstrom, Kevin, and Laurie Collier Hillstrom, eds. *Latin America and the Caribbean (World's Environments Series): A Continental Overview of Environmental Issues.* New York: ABC-CLIO, Incorporated, 2003.

Keck, Margaret E. *The Workers' Party and Democratization in Brazil.* New Haven, CT: Yale University Press, 1992.

Simms, Andrew, Hannah Reid, and Juan Mayr Maldonado. *Up in Smoke? Latin America and the Caribbean: The Threat From Climate Change to the Environment and Human Development.* London: Oxfam Publishing, 2006.

Index